UNITED UNIVERSITY PROFESSIONS

UNITED
UNIVERSITY
PROFESSIONS

PIONEERING IN HIGHER EDUCATION UNIONISM

Nuala McGann Drescher,
William E. Scheuerman, and Ivan D. Steen

SUNY PRESS

Cover photograph taken by Karen Mattison.

Published by State University of New York Press, Albany

© 2019 State University of New York

For information, contact State University of New York Press, Albany, NY
www.sunypress.edu

Library of Congress Cataloging-in-Publication Data

Names: Drescher, Nuala McGann, author. | Scheuerman, William, author. |
  Steen, Ivan D., [date], author.
Title: United University Professions : pioneering in higher education unionism /
  Nuala McGann Drescher, William E. Scheuerman, and Ivan D. Steen.
Description: Albany : State University of New York Press, [2019] | Includes
  bibliographical references and index.
Identifiers: LCCN 2018033283 | ISBN 9781438474670 (hardcover : alk. paper) |
  ISBN 9781438474687 (pbk. : alk. paper) | ISBN 9781438474694 (ebook)
Subjects: LCSH: United University Professions (Association : N.Y.)—History. |
  Universities and colleges—Employees—Labor unions—New York (State)—History. |
  College teachers' unions—New York (State)—History.
Classification: LCC LB2335.865.U6 D74 2019 | DDC 331.88113781209747—dc23
LC record available at https://lccn.loc.gov/2018033283

10 9 8 7 6 5 4 3 2 1

Contents

Contents

Acknowledgments

This book would not have been possible without the encouragement and help of many individuals. UUP's president Fred Kowal directed his staff to assist in any way possible, and that's exactly what they did. Special thanks go to our old friend and colleague Maureen Karius, who answered tough questions and provided gaggles of legalistic information in her own quiet and efficient manner. Karen Mattison opened the vault of the communication's department to give us access to back issues of *The Voice*; Tina George and Doreen Bango assisted whenever called upon. And Lynn Alderman made us feel welcome and comfortable as she coordinated the staff's efforts to provide us with the material we needed. A special thanks to Lynn for having boxes of files shipped to the UUP office in Albany from the union's warehouse in Rochester, New York. In the spirit of academic and union solidarity and collegiality, our friends and colleagues of the SUNY Senate cooperated with this endeavor every step of the way. We thank you. Senate staffer Carol Donato deserves special recognition for making material from the senate's archives available and generally assisting us in every way imaginable. Finally, our colleagues at the University at Albany Library's M. E. Grenander Department of Special Collections and Archives deserve special recognition. Words cannot adequately describe the assistance Brian Keough, Jodi Boyle, and the entire staff provided. With incredible efficiency they helped us in so many ways, and always with smiles on their faces. We also express our appreciation for the assistance of the staffs of the New York State Archives and Records Administration and Cornell University Library's Kheel Center. Thanks also to those, including Rowena Blackman-Stroud, Tina Kaplan, Peter Martineau, Ray Peterson, Jo Schaffer, and Louise Scheuerman who read early drafts of selected chapters. Finally, thanks must go to Michael Rinella and the good people at SUNY Press for the patience and support. Needless to say, the authors appreciate all the help and support many people provided, but this work is the sole responsibility of the authors, who are responsible for its shortcomings. Thank you.

Introduction

This is a book about the United University Professions (UUP), the nation's largest higher-education union, its history, its many challenges, and its many accomplishments. Its members work at four doctorate-granting university centers; four medical schools, three of which have hospitals; fifteen liberal arts institutions; four technical colleges (formerly the two-year agricultural and technical colleges); and five specialized colleges. On its inception in 1973, UUP became a one-of-a-kind statewide organization that many observers viewed as a grand experiment in higher-education collective bargaining. Given the wide spectrum of different types of institutions represented by UUP, it follows that the union is also the most professionally diverse. Across SUNY, UUP represents faculty and professional staff, originally called "nonteaching professionals," as well as librarians, who were labeled as "academic" without enjoying the advantages and prerogatives of their regular academic colleagues. Its members range from Nobel Prize–winning scientists, neurosurgeons, National Book Award winners, and philosophers to trout farmers, glass blowers, shepherds, and almost everything in between. As a statewide union, UUP has to negotiate a single contract acceptable to its extraordinarily diverse professional membership.

UUP not only represents a professionally disparate membership, its members are also spread across the state of New York. Geographically, SUNY's institutions range from Plattsburgh near the Canadian border south to the Brooklyn Health Science Center in southern New York City, and from Fredonia near the Pennsylvania border in western New York to Stony Brook on eastern Long Island. The costs of living, particularly housing costs, vary greatly in different parts of the state. This further complicates UUP's ability to serve its members effectively. In addition to dealing with professional diversity in a single contract, the union's agreement with the state must also address geographical differences in living costs.

The decision by New York's Public Employment Relations Board (PERB) to establish UUP as a statewide bargaining unit may have anointed UUP as the largest higher-education union in the country, but it also presented the emerging union with an array of challenges. The first of these were obstacles that arose from the historical and political struggles that eventually culminated in the formation of the State University of New York itself. As chapter 1 describes, New York's private institutions of higher learning dominated the state's higher-education community throughout much of the state's history. As early as the eighteenth century, New York's politicians gave financial succor to the private schools, a generosity that accelerated throughout the nineteenth century and continues even to this day. Not surprisingly, the privates enjoyed their privilege and used their political clout to maintain and protect it. Consequently, New York became the last state in the union to form a state university. When the state finally responded to increasing public pressures to establish SUNY, it tightly wrapped the new university in a straitjacket of limitations designed by the private sector. The new university was underfunded and underenrolled. The scope of programs it offered was limited, and most of its faculty lacked doctoral degrees. Despite the legislature's vision-ary mission statement, the new university was not established to compete with private institutions. It was designed to play a subordinate or ancillary role.

SUNY's subordinate role changed during the Rockefeller years. Committed to building a first-rate public university, Nelson Rockefeller convinced New York's legislators to pour hundreds of millions into SUNY. Under Rockefeller's leadership the university expanded rapidly. In anticipation of the growing enrollments of the baby-boomer generation, Rockefeller directed SUNY to acquire or construct new campuses. Taxpayer dollars modernized and expanded existing campus facilities, including the construction of new student dormitories at campuses across the state. The university's growth, of course, was not limited to the expansion of its brick-and-mortar facilities. SUNY also invested additional dollars in an effort to upgrade a second-rate faculty. The university paid higher salaries, encouraged research, and recruited hundreds of new, more highly trained faculty. Teaching remained a top priority, but research and publishing assumed a larger role in the university's culture.

The influx of a new and better-educated faculty led to significant cultural conflicts on SUNY's campuses. A key source of conflict was the new faculty's general rejection of the top-down, noncollegial management style that previously characterized the university. What they wanted was a relationship with adminis-trators already enjoyed by many other faculties at established colleges and uni-versities. This new generation of faculty believed that the intellectual interaction between faculty and students was the central purpose of higher education and that the primary role of university and campus administrators was to support that purpose. Unlike many of their pre-Rockefeller colleagues, the new faculty sought a culture of collegiality, a community of scholars. For the most part, this conflict stayed beneath the surface as long as there were plenty of public dollars for salary raises, research, and all the other accoutrements needed for a vibrant academic career. But when the flood of public dollars began to dry up, the con-flict surfaced, and many faculty wanted more control of their professional lives.

The flood of public dollars turned into a trickle just as a national wave of public worker strikes led to the legal right of public employees to form unions. As discussed in chapter 2, in response to significant labor unrest, including illegal strikes in the public sector, in 1967 New York State passed the Taylor Law, legislation that gave public employees in the state the right to form unions. During those heady days of public-sector organizing, public workers joined unions in droves. But that wasn't the case in academe. At SUNY, many academics opposed unions. They feared that unions would destroy the quest for excellence and promote the rise of mediocrity. They also felt that collective bargaining threatened the basic foundations of the academy, including faculty governance, academic freedom, and tenure. Consequently, an internal battle surfaced between those who sought to protect the intellectual crafts they practiced through the formation of a union and those who opposed collective bargaining at the university. Eventually supporters of collective bargaining prevailed. SUNY faculty opted for unionization, but opposition to it remained strong. Finally, after a series of internal battles and false starts, SUNY faculty and professional staff formed the United University Professions.

Not surprisingly, the new union was initially fraught with internal conflicts and schisms. In addition to a large number of faculty and staff who openly opposed collective bargaining, significant distrust of the union existed among many of its constituency groups. The so-called "nonteaching professionals," who at the time constituted about one-third of the bargaining unit, feared the faculty would ignore their interests. Librarians, who constituted a miniscule proportion of the new bargaining unit, felt the same way. At the health science centers, problems existed between basic scientists and medical doctors, between academic personnel and clinical professionals, between the medical schools with their own hospitals and the one without a hospital. Interns and residents had special needs that faculty and staff often ignored. Clinical practice governance and the distribution of clinical earnings were a major source of turmoil and conflict within the union. Part-time employees represented still another faction, as they often viewed their full-time cohorts as enemies rather than colleagues. These structural and occupational conflicts were matched by a major philosophical debate on the nature of unions, a debate that gave birth to political parties within UUP. On the one hand, some wanted the union to participate in the larger arenas of reform and social change. On the other, a numerically greater group envisioned the union as primarily a tool for collective bargaining. They supported the kind of "pure and simple" unionism espoused by Samuel Gompers that focuses on serving the needs of their members.

As the following chapters record, the early history of UUP is the story of efforts to transcend the problems created by these basic differences among the union's occupationally diverse membership and by the ongoing struggle to create an institution that adequately and fairly represented the economic and professional interests of all constituent groups without violating the fundamental culture of the academy. Even after faculty and professional staff voted to form a union, the initial cadre of SUNY employees who enthusiastically backed collective bargaining was small and faced hostility, distrust, and apathy. The new union had to find ways to convince skeptical colleagues to accept and perhaps even participate in the collective bargaining process. The many conflicts arising from the broad professional and ideological diversity of its members shaped the contracts negotiated by UUP, many of which contained innovative and unique provisions.

Although the primary purpose of the United University Professions is collective bargaining, from its earliest days its activities went far beyond the bargaining table. Most obviously, the legal and moral obligations of collective bargaining require a cadre of trained experts to assist in negotiations and enforce the union's agreement with the state. As the following chapters illuminate, contract enforcement involves a host of services to the membership. UUP's affiliation with the large and powerful New York State United Teachers (NYSUT) provided the new higher-education union with the highly trained staff necessary to fulfill these functions. As NYSUT employees, these field staff remained independent of the union's internal politics; they were legal technicians. Affiliation with NYSUT also entailed an association with the giant national teachers union, the American Federation of Teachers (AFT). These affiliations gave UUP much material support and boosted its prestige with SUNY managers and within the labor movement. But since a portion of the dues paid by UUP's members went to each of the two affiliates, at different times in UUP's history the new union's leaders questioned the wisdom of such affiliations. Over the years different factions within UUP debated and even fought over the issue of the cost of these affiliations and whether UUP received sufficient service in return for the dues it paid. This book also chronicles the nature of the relationship between UUP and its state and national affiliates.

In addition to negotiating a contract and providing key services to its members, UUP played an active role in the state's political arena from the time of its formation. Since the New York State legislature ultimately approves and pays for the collective bargaining agreement, UUP had to make its presence felt in the halls of the legislature and on the second floor of the state capitol building where the governor presides. Over the years, as New York faced various fiscal crises that threatened to weaken or at times even destroy SUNY, the union increased its political activities. With the backing of NYSUT, UUP gradually became a major player in New York politics. As UUP grew and matured, its political clout became at least as important as what it achieved at the bargaining table to protect and better its members' interests.

The gains often came slowly, and they never came easily, but UUP's progress was steady and consistent. By the end of the Scheuerman administration in

2007, UUP had reached the zenith of its power and influence. The union had become a unified 35,000-member leviathan that served its members effectively at the bargaining table and in the political arena. That's not all UUP accomplished. The history of UUP demonstrates the important role that unions can play in preserving faculty governance and academic freedom. When SUNY's "activist trustees" attacked academic freedom and undercut shared governance, the SUNY Faculty Senate turned to the union for help, and the two organizations successfully beat back the attacks. UUP eventually became the national voice of academic freedom, playing an active role in refuting the unfounded accusations made by the righteous-sounding Academic Bill of Rights. The same may be said of UUP's role when tenure—the bedrock of academic freedom—came under attack. The SUNY/UUP experience clearly indicates that unions not only can and do support the culture of academe, but at times play an instrumental role in preserving the culture so essential to the pursuit of truth and knowledge.

UUP emerged at a time in American history when public-sector workers had gained the right to organize and were joining unions in large numbers. During those heady days of unionization the labor movement was strong, a political and social force to be reckoned with nationally and even internationally. At the time of its formation in 1973, almost one in three workers belonged to unions. But even in liberal New York State, where the existence of unions is accepted as a fact and even today more than two-thirds of all public-sector workers are unionized, governors have frequently scapegoated public-sector unions by blaming them for state budgetary deficits.[1] During the late 1970s and into the '90s, for instance, Governors Hugh Carey and Mario Cuomo were less than hospitable to SUNY and its union. Budget cuts to SUNY, faculty layoffs, and contracts that sought significant givebacks almost became routine practices during the Carey and Mario Cuomo years. But UUP met the challenges it faced during these harsh fiscal times. In fact, the union grew stronger in its quest to protect its members and the university. The election of the fiscally conservative governor George Pataki in 1995 signaled a new war on public spending and on all of the state's public institutions. The new governor sought record-breaking budget cuts to SUNY. Campus closings and massive retrenchments became a reality. At the bargaining table, the Pataki administration attempted to undermine the practice of tenure. But UUP prevailed, and these attacks again only made the union stronger, more unified, and more effective.

The pages that follow chronicle the growth and development of the nation's largest higher-education union. Over the years UUP has consistently responded effectively to the myriad attacks on its members and the professions they practice. But, as the old Bob Dylan song so clearly puts it, "the times they are a-changing," and as far as unions are concerned, not for the better. Organized labor is under the gun. Long gone are the days when a US president would march over to AFL-CIO headquarters to meet with top union leaders. A hostile legal system, corporate warfare, globalization, internecine fighting within the labor movement, and a growing reliance on robotics and other forms of automation have crippled unions in the private sector.[2] Today with only 6.5 percent of private workers in unions, organized labor is slowly but steadily sinking into political and economic irrelevance. Nevertheless, while private-sector unionism is in a precipitous downfall, the public sector is still thriving. The rate of unionization in the public sector today is 34.4 percent, some five times higher than that of workers in the private sector.[3] This helps explain the recent political attacks on public employee unions at both the state and federal levels.

The war against public unions may have begun in 1981with President Reagan's firing of about 11,000 striking members of the Professional Air Traffic Controllers Organization (PATCO), but it certainly intensified with the election of right-wing Republican governors. The new breed of Tea Party governors worships the myth of a magical free market that would certainly bring prosperity to all if only big government would get out of the way. Despite studies showing that public-sector workers generally earn less than their counterparts in the private sector,[4] these Tea Party governors demonize public-sector workers, who, they claim, are better off than most taxpayers. Unionized public employees, they insist, are overpaid and have costly "Cadillac" health plans, extravagant pensions, and job security that other workers lack. The cost of these luxuries, they claim, is passed on to ordinary citizens, who are drowning in high taxes. Therefore, they conclude, it's in the public interest to take these privileges away from public-sector workers.[5]

Ironically, these right-wing opponents of big government are quick to use the power of government to crush public-sector unions. Beginning in Indiana in 2005, when Governor Mitch Daniels issued an executive order barring collective bargaining for public-sector workers, through the much publicized anti-labor exploits of Wisconsin's Scott Walker and the more recent (2017) efforts of Illinois's Bruce Rauner to create "union-free zones," some sixteen states have unleashed aggressive attacks on public-sector unions. These assaults include lay-offs, stripping away the right to collective bargaining, cutting back workers' health insurance, reducing pension benefits, and prohibiting the collection of "fair-share" payments by nonunion members, even though they benefit from the union's collective bargaining accomplishments.[6]

Worse yet for public unions, early in 2018 the United States Supreme Court, at the behest of today's robber barons,[7] took aim at what's left of organized labor by ruling against unions in *Janus v. American Federation of State, County, and Municipal Employees, Council 31*. The *Janus* case, a follow-up to the Court's 2016 4-4 deadlock in *Friedrichs v. California Teachers Association*, challenged the legitimacy of "fair-share" payments, a primary source of union revenues. Fair share is frequently confused with union dues, but it is very different. Federal and state labor laws guarantee that no one must join a union or pay union dues, even though unions are legally obligated to provide the same services, negotiated salary increases, benefits, and other protections to *all* bargaining-unit members. In return, many state and federal laws allow for agreements between unions and employers that make nonmembers pay a fee to cover the costs of the benefits they receive. This fee is not union dues; it's called "fair-share" or "agency" fee. States with "right-to-work" laws prohibit unions and employers from making fair-share agreements. But fair-share agreements prevail in those states with the bulk of union membership. The court's backing of *Janus* prohibits fair share; in the words of the executive director of Americans for Prosperity–Michigan, a Koch-brothers-backed right-wing think tank, it will "take the unions out at the knees." According to one estimate, public-sector unions could lose about one-third of their annual dues revenue, which is estimated to range somewhere between four and eight billion dollars.[8]

When the Court heard the *Friedrichs* case in 2016, the Obama administration issued an amicus brief in support of fair-share agreements. That's not the case with the anti-union Trump administration. President Trump's rhetoric backing working people excludes the millions of workers who belong to unions. In December 2017, the Trump administration submitted a brief in support of *Janus*, in other words, in favor of removing fair-share payments.[9] But that is just a start. President Trump has taken a series of other actions hostile to collective bargaining. He appointed anti-union members to the National Labor Relations Board (NLRB), who quickly reversed a series of union protections, including one that kept employers from manipulating bargaining units to ensure fair union certification elections. His education department also is attempting to impose a collective bargaining agreement on members of the American Federation of Government Employees that they previously rejected.[10] These actions make it clear: the president of the United States is using the vast power of his office to break the labor movement.

New York State remains a pro-union stronghold. That is good for UUP. But, as this history of UUP makes clear, even in liberal New York State unions can take nothing for granted. From its humble beginnings through its development into a mature and powerful organization, the United University Professions has successfully fought some extraordinarily tough battles to protect and enhance its members' interests, the interests of the university, and the entire SUNY community. As the following pages document, UUP's history to this point is, on the whole, one of success. Now the nation's largest higher-education union is facing new attacks that threaten its very existence. Yet, if the past is indeed prologue, there is reason to approach the future with confidence. After all, UUP is a democratic organization that belongs to and is controlled by the members it represents. It is ultimately up to the membership to mold and shape the union into the kind of institution it wants. As the pages below indicate, UUP's members have met past challenges with vigor, solidarity, and intelligence. However difficult future challenges may be, UUP's members have proven time and time again that their union is more than capable of protecting and enhancing the intellectual and practical crafts they practice.

Chapter 1

The State University of New York
Prior to Unionization

Beginning with the founding of Harvard College in 1636, for over 200 years American higher education was predominantly the preserve of privileged white men, both as students and as faculty. Yes, there were some exceptions, such as the female seminaries that began appearing in the mid-1700s to prepare genteel women as teachers, followed in the 1800s by a number of public normal schools. But the widespread access to public college education we know today has its roots in the Morrill Act of 1862. When Abraham Lincoln signed it into law, many states took advantage of its generous provisions to establish land-grant state universities. We can thank the Morrill Act for such public institutions as Ohio State University, Purdue University, and scores of other equally great institutions. New York State's politicians used the Morrill Act in a very different way. Rather than create a state university, they established a great new private institution, Cornell University. Shocking as this may seem to some contemporary readers, in New York State the use of public funds to establish a private university was in keeping with long-standing public policy. Understanding this historical bias in favor of private institutions is essential to understanding the origins and development of higher-education unionism at the State University of New York (SUNY).

Prior to the formation of the United States and continuing to this day, the story of higher education in New York State, which predates SUNY by more than 150 years, is a tale of public support for private institutions. Not surprisingly, the privates wanted to keep it that way. For decades they used their political clout to squelch any attempts to create a state university. Responding to the rising postwar demand for public higher education, in 1948 New York State became the last state in the nation to create a public university. Nonetheless, the politically powerful private colleges convinced the state legislature to make sure the new university would only supplement rather than compete with them. Consequently, SUNY was not established to be a nationally esteemed scholarly

1

community. From the start, the new university was not committed to hiring a first-rate faculty and did not embrace the important practices of shared governance. Instead, SUNY's campuses were largely staffed with faculty who lacked doctoral degrees and administered with a paternalistic top-down managerial style. It is not surprising that SUNY unionized fairly early in its history, and when it formed a union—the United University Professions—it immediately became the largest organized university system in the country.

SUNY remained a parochial second-rate institution for the first decade and more of its existence. This began to change during the expansionary years of the Rockefeller administration. Galvanized by the passing of New York's Education Act in 1961, and guided by a governor who wanted a first-rate public university, the university eventually reached a rough parity with the privates. Nevertheless, the old historical issues remained. Resentment toward SUNY's top-down management style made an increasingly better credentialed faculty recognize the United University Professions (UUP) as its collective bargaining agent in 1973.

This chapter traces the historical rise of the private colleges and universities in New York State, the role the state played in promoting their interests, and how their dominance helped shape the terrain on which SUNY and UUP were created and evolved. It also examines the massive changes at SUNY during the Rockefeller years, the university's rapid growth and bureaucratization, and the emergence of a new generation of faculty who ultimately embraced unionization as the vehicle to gain control of their professional lives.

State Policy Promotes the Privates

It was not by chance that New York was the last state to create its own state public university. It was also not accidental that during its first decade SUNY was a small, politically weak institution with low enrollment. Governor Rockefeller's Heald Commission Report described SUNY's condition in blunt language in 1960, when it characterized the university as "limping and apologetic."[1] This is not the book to provide a detailed history of public support of private colleges in New York State. Much has already been said and written about that subject.[2] But some background is essential to understand the role private institutions played in shaping SUNY and setting the stage for the emergence of UUP.

On the eve of the establishment of SUNY in 1948, New York's public higher-education system consisted of a handful of small state-run teachers' colleges and a number of well-established, politically powerful private institutions, both secular and sectarian.[3] The private institutions were the backbone of higher education in New York State and enjoyed a long tradition of benefiting from public largesse. The precedent for public aid to private colleges was set as early as 1754, when a royal charter established King's College, which later became

Columbia University. The relationship between public government and private colleges became closer in 1784, when the New York State legislature established the Board of Regents during its first session and charged it with regulating and managing Columbia, which by then had already become the alma mater of many of the legislature's members. The regents were expected to protect Columbia for the "affluent youth of the state."[4]

Despite the close relationship with the regents, the trustees of the newly renamed university did not like the idea of the Board of Regents running its affairs, so three years later the legislature changed the charge of the regents. In 1787 Columbia was given back its autonomy and the regents were granted much broader powers regarding higher education. The legislature now charged the regents with regulating *all* higher education in the state through granting charters and setting academic standards.[5]

Columbia may have regained its autonomy, but the regents' financial commitment to the university remained strong. Almost immediately they provided the university with loans and special appropriations of land and money. In so doing, they made it clear that in New York State private higher education was a public responsibility.[6] The Board of Regents, acting under its revised charge, continued to provide public funds to private colleges and universities. They chartered Union College (1795), and in 1814 gave Union the generous sum of $200,000.[7] In the pre–Civil War period, regular subsidies went to other institutions besides Columbia and Union; New York University, Hobart College, and the Albany Medical College all received public funds.

The legislature's acceptance of private higher education as a public responsibility was buttressed by the regents' laissez-faire approach to regulation. However, when it came to regulating how private institutions of higher learning spent their money, including public dollars, the regents refused to interfere.[8] The regents justified this hands-off approach through their interpretation of the US Supreme Court's decision in the 1818 case of *Dartmouth College v. Woodward*. In that famous contract-clause case, the court ruled that state-supported colleges remained private institutions. Therefore, their charters were contracts beyond the reach of the state. The regents interpreted this ruling to mean they could not tell private institutions how to spend their dollars. Whether the dollars were public or private, it did not matter.[9]

In 1862, when the United States Congress passed the Morrill Land Grant Act, states across the nation took advantage of the law by creating their own public state universities. New York was a notable exception. Instead of creating a public university system, New York used the federal money to establish a major new private institution, Cornell University. In establishing Cornell, the legislature was generous to a fault, pouring all of New York's proceeds from the act—about one tenth of the total national revenue—into the new institution. The legislature justified using Morrill funds to create Cornell by requiring Cornell to provide a tuition-free education to one student from each of the state's assembly districts. Given this proviso, the regents happily chartered the new institution.[10]

The decision not to create a public university system with funds from the Morrill Act was one of many actions state policymakers took to protect the privates. Another came in 1904 when the legislature passed the Unification Act, a law establishing the New York State Department of Education (SED) with the Regents as a division. This department created policies that further undercut the role and effectiveness of New York's already weak normal schools.

In 1904 Governor Odell appointed Andrew S. Draper, the former superintendent of public instruction, as commissioner of education. Draper had a distinguished record as an innovator in the K–12 sector, but when it came to higher education, he had a strong predilection toward the privates. In fact, in his role as superintendent, in 1889 he supported teacher training at private institutions rather than expanding the state's normal schools. Indeed, restricting the role of the state's normal schools was at the core of his vision of the state's system of higher education. He insisted that normal schools should have the narrow function of training teachers and articulated his belief that they should not offer a wide range of academic subjects. Restricting the curricula at normal schools, he argued, would reduce competition between these state-run institutions and the private sector.

Draper's vision became a reality during his tenure as commissioner of education. Under his stewardship, normal schools were only allowed to admit students who wished to become teachers, leading him to proudly announce the elimination of most subject-matter courses. Normal schools now became narrow teacher-training institutions focusing primarily on teaching methods. These reforms had the effect of preventing many deserving low-income students from gaining a general academic education while also reducing the academic quality of the normal schools, an issue that would surface later when SUNY was finally formed.

Draper also worked closely with the private sector, taking the initiative in 1906 to help establish the Association of Colleges and Universities of the State of New York (ACUSNY), a collective lobbying body consisting mainly of the privates. With Draper's encouragement, the private sector began to cooperate more closely to develop a stronger relationship with the regents. The Education Department in conjunction with ACUSNY used its political clout in support of tuition scholarships to the private schools as an alternative to a public university. The new organization soon began to reap rewards. In 1913 Governor Sulzer signed a bill advocated by the Education Department and the ACUSNY that provided 3,000 state scholarships at $100 a year for four years. At the bill signing Sulzer characterized the scholarships as "practically the equivalent of the maintenance of a state university."[11] The close cooperation between the regents, the Department of Education, and ACUSNY had profound positive benefits for private institutions of higher learning, leading one scholar to comment "the interests of the private colleges and the state became so intertwined as to make them indistinguishable."[12]

Scholarships to attend private institutions remained the alternative to forming a state university for the next forty-five years even though private colleges were finding it increasingly difficult to meet the growing demand for higher education. Driven by the Depression and high unemployment rates, high school attendance increased by almost 50 percent between 1926 and 1933, and the demand for higher education skyrocketed.[13] Studies at the time found that thousands of qualified New Yorkers from modest economic backgrounds simply could not afford the tuition at the state's private colleges. With the exception of the municipal colleges in New York City, these students had no place in the state to go. The federal government addressed this important nationwide issue by funding a series of higher-education institutions, some sixteen in New York, designed to provide jobs for unemployed college faculty and to give unemployed high school graduates an opportunity to take first-year college courses. Even here, the interests of the private sector took precedence. To ensure that the federal institutions would not compete with the state's privates, no enrollments were permitted until the privates completed their student registrations.[14] The federal experiment did not last too long. By the summer of 1937 all these federal institutions were closed.

The regents' response to increased enrollment pressures was predictable. Instead of supporting the formation of a state university system, a 1935 regents study recommended that higher-education policy in the state focus on increasing aid to and working more closely with the privates. Toward this end, the report called for doubling the number of undergraduate scholarships to 6,000 and increasing the annual stipend to $300 a year. It also recommended the establishment of 100 graduate fellowships at $400 each. The report made no mention of the increased enrollment projections of up to 15,000 more students.[15]

This scenario repeated itself yet again with the release of a Regents report in 1943 regarding a postwar plan for education in New York State. The report made clear the primacy the regents placed on the privates by proudly declaring that preserving "the strength and integrity of these private colleges . . . has long been the policy of the Board of Regents."[16] In 1944 and 1945 Governor Dewey followed suit by signing bills establishing 2,400 War Service Scholarships with an annual stipend of $350. In short, protecting and enhancing the interests of the privates at the expense of public higher education was a fundamental policy the regents planned to pursue in the future, and the state's leading politicians, particularly Republicans upstate where the bulk of private colleges were located, fiercely supported this policy.

By the time World War II ended, the state's public higher-education institutions, all controlled by the Board of Regents, consisted of eleven state

teachers colleges, seven professional colleges under contract with private institutions, six two-year schools of applied arts, and six agricultural and technical
colleges. Additionally, in New York City there were four municipal colleges. The
postwar period put new pressures on policymakers to create a state university.
The most obvious was the passing of the GI Bill and the increasing demand
by returning soldiers for access to affordable higher-education institutions in
the state. Some estimates had as many as 100,000 returning GIs prepared to
seek higher education in New York, a number far beyond what the privates
could meet.[17] Sidestepping opposition from the privates, the state had already
created special temporary colleges to meet the skyrocketing enrollments, but
this was not enough. It was clear that New York's municipal colleges and state
teachers colleges just couldn't meet the new demand. The situation was further
exacerbated by a shortage of medical schools and by the practice of ethnic
discrimination by private institutions.

Many of the privates had admission quotas for Jewish and minority students on both the undergraduate and graduate levels. This was particularly true
regarding admission to medical schools.[18] In fact, antisemitism was often blatant.
Indeed, one president of Columbia, after bowing to pressures to admit bright
children of immigrants, mainly working-class Jewish students, complained that
many of the new students just did not conform to the type of "boy" who came
to Columbia. In fact, he went on, they were more like the students who attended
the City College of New York.[19] As bright and academically qualified as they
were, these new students just did not conform to the "gentlemanly" standards of
the upper crust. Admitting such students to Columbia and many other privates
ran against the grain of their privileged sensibilities. Ethnic discrimination by
the privates became less tolerated after the war. Unveiling of the horrors of the
Holocaust illuminated the immorality and ugliness of discriminatory admission
practices. Public attention on the issue in the state grew thanks to litigation by
the American Jewish Congress against New York's Tax Commission for giving tax
breaks to Columbia, even though the college violated the law with its ethnically
discriminatory admission policies. The public consciousness raised by this case
fueled the demand for a public state university.

In 1946 President Truman brought the federal government into the picture.
In response to the growing national demand for higher education, Truman created a higher-education commission charged with analyzing the state of higher
education in the country, including enrollment projections, and making recommendations to address the issues. Following over a year of extensive deliberations, in the fall of 1947 Truman's commission, Higher Education for American
Democracy, released its report. The report's recommendations were broad and
wide-ranging. It called for the expansion of public higher education and the need
for greater access for minorities and the economically disadvantaged, changes in
higher-education curricula to promote the values of democracy, the extension

of two-year free public colleges, and federal scholarships and grants to students. Significantly, it also projected the doubling of college attendance by 1960.[20]

Truman's involvement was crucially important to higher-education policymakers in New York. Since New York's Governor Dewey was about to face Truman in the next presidential campaign, Dewey had to demonstrate his support for significantly expanding public higher education in New York State. As Dewey's biographer Richard Norton Smith observed, "Dewey read election returns as well as anyone."[21] In February of 1946 Dewey called for the legislature to create a Temporary Commission to Study the Need for a State University.[22]

Predictably, an alliance among the private colleges, the State Education Department, the regents, and Republicans upstate where the bulk of the privates were located, opposed Dewey's proposal. The coalition feared that the creation of a low-cost public university would place the privates at a disadvantage and force some to close.[23] In contrast, downstate Democrats and various minority groups—victims of the private's discriminatory admission policies—supported the creation of a state university. An astute politician, Dewey put representatives from both factions on the new Temporary Commission.[24] The privates continued to resist the establishment of a public university, but should they fail to stop its creation, they aimed to make sure the new university would not pose a real threat to their existence. Consequently, they used their clout to support a university with a decentralized series of campuses without the flagship campus model of the midwestern public universities. They also wanted the new institution placed under the aegis of their historical ally, the Board of Regents.

The commission's recommendations set the parameters for the new university. For instance, the commission made sure that SUNY would not compete with private colleges and universities, declaring that "the function of state supported post high school education should be to supplement, not supplant, privately supported colleges and universities."[25] This serious restriction on SUNY's role was complemented by another agreement in which, according to scholars, Governor Dewey promised the privates "that no new liberal arts colleges would be established for the next ten years."[26] Finally, in the name of geographical diversity, the new university would not have a flagship campus. The report paved the way for legislation establishing SUNY, legislation that extracted these political compromises favorable to the private sector by severely limiting SUNY's prospects for the future.

The Battle for a State University

In April 1948 Governor Dewey signed the bill creating the State University of New York. New York finally had its own state university system, consisting of thirty-two institutions, including the teachers colleges. SUNY emerged as a decentralized institution without a flagship campus and with significant limits on its role and future growth. In the prescient and perhaps gleeful words of Cornell University's president, "This is a State University that will have presumably no football team that can expect to make the Rose Bowl."[27] SUNY's future looked unpromising. Yet the enabling legislation for SUNY did not give the privates everything they wanted, thereby setting the stage for future growth and triggering another political battle that threatened the university's very existence. To the dismay of the privates, the law creating SUNY gave general administrative responsibilities to a board of trustees appointed by the governor, not to the regents. The regents responded by garnering support for legislation, the Condon-Barrett bill, stripping the trustees of their administrative responsibilities and shifting them instead to the regents, who would serve as guardians to ensure the new university's subservience to the privates. The battle unfolded in the legislature in 1949, when the governor prevailed and Condon-Barrett was soundly defeated.

However limited, SUNY had established its independence from the regents and was now in a position to grow. But growth did not come quickly or easily. In fact, at its conception, SUNY's state-operated campuses had a total of only 22,450 undergraduate and graduate students, both full- and part-time. In the 1949–50 school year it awarded 3,514 bachelor's degrees and some 385 master degrees. By the 1958–59 academic year, some ten years after its creation, SUNY's enrollments had grown by fewer than 15,000 students. With a state population of over twelve million, the university granted only 7,849 bachelor's degrees and 1,230 master's degrees.[28] The numbers suggest that SUNY was a university in name only, given that about 75 percent of all New York undergraduates were enrolled at private institutions and large numbers of college-aged students went to out-of-state colleges. It also did not help SUNY that its trustees still viewed the university's role as limited, "to supplement the efforts of private colleges and universities."[29] Toward this goal, the decentralized university had teachers colleges that still could not offer liberal arts programs, university-wide growth was restricted, most of the faculty lacked doctoral degrees, there was virtually no faculty governance, and management had the uncontested right to define and control basic work conditions, including curricula, workload, salary, and all personnel decisions. Moreover, the university's physical facilities were in a "deplorable state."[30]

In 1957 a consultant's report on the status and potential of research at SUNY lamented the many unfavorable conditions faculty faced: many had excessive teaching loads, often as many as five or six courses each semester; committee assignments were excessive; sabbatical leaves were scarce. Additionally, the report cited another problem facing researchers: the small number of graduate students available to be research and teaching assistants. The report recommended the centralization of SUNY similar to the structure of the large midwestern public universities. This did not happen. The trustees, fearing that the creation of a centralized research institution would present an unacceptable political threat to the privates, rejected the recommendation, thereby ensuring that SUNY would remain exactly what Rockefeller's Heald Commission would later call, a "limping and apologetic enterprise."[31] The regents' opposition to the report and controversy over its release led to the dismissal of SUNY's second president, Frank Carlson, in December of 1957.

The privates did not idly sit by watching SUNY become a growing threat to their existence. In fact, the decision of both the regents and SUNY's trustees was influenced by political efforts of the privates, who formed a centralized lobbying organization on the eve of the consultant's report's release. To represent their interest in the context of a public state university, the privates created the Commission of Independent Colleges and Universities (CICU) as their lobbying arm in 1956. Over the years CICU grew in numbers and influence. It currently represents more than 100 private institutions of higher education in New York State.

The Soviets' launching of Sputnik and the rising tide of baby boomers boosted enrollment projections far beyond the capabilities of the privates, creating significant pressures for a larger and stronger SUNY. In 1957 the public, in an extraordinary display of support for the still-stunted university, voted to approve a $250 million bond issue to address SUNY's deplorable physical infrastructure. But the university was without a president and the bond issue could not be implemented until after the 1958 gubernatorial election, when a new governor would appoint Carlson's successor. In short, the university was at a standstill. It remained under the thumb of the privates and much-needed improvements did not come. But the election of Nelson Rockefeller as governor changed all that. Under Rockefeller's leadership, SUNY rapidly grew, eventually becoming the largest public university system in the United States.

Upon winning the election, Rockefeller pledged to implement the $250 million bond issue, and, as Judith Glazier observed, by the time he left office he had committed ten times that amount, some $2.5 billion, to construction at SUNY.[32] In his inaugural address Rockefeller spoke of the need for the future "expansion of our state institutions of higher education," and almost immediately appointed a commission to review higher education in the state.[33] Headed by Henry Heald, president of the Ford Foundation, the Heald Commission projected the doubling of SUNY's enrollments between 1959 and 1970, with another 50 percent increase coming by 1980, bringing SUNY's enrollments to more than 1.2 million. Since the private sector was incapable of handling this massive influx of students, the public system would have to grow to accommodate enrollment approaching 60 percent of all in-state college students. The commission's report recommended three higher-education goals: (1) higher education should be available to students of various talents and from all income groups, (2) New York's system of higher education should have strong public and private sectors, and (3) academic excellence is an essential objective for all educational institutions.[34]

The governor moved forcefully on the commission's recommendations by engineering the passage of the Higher Education Act of 1961, which provided the legal framework for SUNY's emergence as a giant public university. The law removed SUNY from the State Education Department, giving it more independence. It also established a scholar incentive program, and doubled the number of Regents Scholarships, a program beneficial to both the public and the private institutions.[35] During this same period the trustees, acting on the basis of a Division of Budget Office study of salaries, submitted a three-year plan to raise faculty salaries—a plan whose implementation, the trustees later confessed, was not appreciated by the faculty, partially because of the degree of management discretion given to local campus administrators.[36]

A year later new legislation opened the way for pouring tens of millions of dollars into SUNY's physical facilities. This promised financing, along with the specter of exploding public-sector enrollments, greatly concerned the privates. To address their concerns, the governor, working in conjunction with the regents, appointed a committee in 1967 to determine how the state could help maintain the health of the privates without infringing on their autonomy. The committee, chaired by McGeorge Bundy, recommended a system of direct unrestricted assistance to the privates, which was approved by the state legislature. Beginning in 1969–70 the state would give $400 to private institutions for each baccalaureate and master's degree and $450 for each doctoral degree. That year New York's taxpayers poured $25.5 million into the coffers of New York's independent colleges and universities. In addition to tamping down the privates' resistance to an expanded SUNY, Bundy Aid, as it was called, kept many of the fiscally pressed private institutions alive and established a new "live and let live" attitude between the public and private sectors. Bundy Aid established an uneasy but lasting peace between the two sectors, but political jostling between the publics and privates would continue, especially when elected officials put together a state budget during tough fiscal times.

With all the political pieces in place, SUNY was on the launching pad, prepared to take off. The university reached for the stratosphere with the appointment of Samuel Gould as its fourth president. Gould and Rockefeller wanted a first-rate university, an esteemed, quality institution that would meet the criteria of the Heald Commission report. During President Gould's tenure (in 1967 SUNY changed the title of SUNY's president to "chancellor") from 1964 to 1970, SUNY realized the commission's goals. In 1960, for instance, several years prior to Gould's appointment, SUNY enrolled 48,000 students. By 1968 the number of students had jumped to 139,000, and by 1970 SUNY had an enrollment topping 300,000.[37] Characterized by some as Rockefeller's "Edifice Complex,"[38] new construction tripled the size of the physical plant by 1970. But enrollment numbers and the tons of concrete, steel, and other building materials expended over this period fail to tell the entire story.

In 1964 when Gould took office, SUNY had a poor academic reputation. With a small and largely undistinguished faculty, the university had far to go to reach the goal of academic excellence. With the exception of the medical schools, most faculty members lacked doctoral degrees, a standard by which higher educational institutions are rated. The dearth of faculty with doctoral degrees was true at the PhD-granting university centers as well as the former teachers' colleges and agricultural and technical schools. At SUNY Albany, for instance, only 52 percent of the faculty held doctorates for the 1965–66 academic year, the lowest rate among the four university centers. The four-year colleges were significantly worse, with Fredonia having the highest proportion at 45 percent and Oswego at the bottom with just 27 percent. The agricultural and technical colleges were even worse. Cobleskill held the top position with 17 percent while only 2 percent of Canton faculty held doctoral degrees.[39]

A growing university needs more faculty to keep pace with increasing enrollments, and SUNY certainly was growing. As enrollments increased, the university sought to hire thousands of new faculty. A Faculty Senate report projected the creation of nearly 6,500 new faculty positions between the 1966–67 and 1972–73 academic years. Thanks to legislation that took effect on July 1, 1964, the president of the university, as opposed to the state legislature, was granted the power to determine salaries of professional positions.[40] With the backing of Governor Rockefeller, he advocated for higher salaries, including better starting salaries and significant pay increases for existing faculty. He also provided additional incentives in support of faculty research, including reduced teaching loads, especially at the university centers. Gould also called for faculty involvement in the collegial process through a stronger system of faculty governance.[41] In other words, the new president's willingness to work with faculty led to improved salaries and enhanced research at the still-nascent but now expanding university.

The collegial manner in which Gould began his tenure was a distinct change from the previous culture of limited governance and faculty deference to campus and university managers that characterized the university's culture to this point in its history. The previous style of top-down leadership had contributed to a sense of alienation among many faculty, who felt excluded from the decision-making process. Until Gould's appointment, statewide faculty governance played an insignificant role in SUNY's culture. It is important to note that it took five years before SUNY even created a Faculty Senate, in 1953. Subordinate to the Policies of the Board of Trustees, the Senate was an in-house organization whose existence depended on the university that created and funded it. It had no policymaking power but could give advice and counsel to the president on issues deemed relevant to the Policies of the Board of Trustees. SUNY's president could heed or disregard the advice of the Senate at his discretion. The president also had the power to cut funding if the Senate tried to pursue policies deemed detrimental to the university.

A good example of the top-down style in place prior to Gould's appointment is President Carlson's response to faculty questions regarding a very bad budget for SUNY for the 1955–56 year. When asked by a Faculty Senate member how "the urgent need for better salaries can be achieved," Carlson expressed his strong opinion "that faculty members, local groups, and the like, should not resort to lobbying." Carlson said this despite the fact that SUNY's salaries were not competitive, some of the best faculty were leaving for other universities, and, at this juncture, the legislature was responsible for salary increases. The president's prohibition against lobbying the legislature further highlighted the faculty's lack of any real input into the salary process.[42] At a subsequent Faculty Senate meeting Carlson also made his position on salary increases clear. Salary increments need not go to all, he said. They "should be granted on the basis of merit and not provided automatically every year."[43]

Paternalistic rule existed on the campuses too. SUNY's chief counsel, John Crary, Jr., reported that the practice of granting sabbatical leaves to faculty contingent on their finding their own replacements ran against the Board of Trustees Policies. This practice not only mirrored management's lack of understanding of academic culture, it reflected poorly on the university's professionalism and reputation at the time.[44] Prior to Gould, campus presidents usually hired top-level administrators with little or no formal input from faculty, and faculty were not involved to any degree in hiring campus presidents. Gould later addressed these practices by urging campus presidents and local college councils to consult with faculty on hiring, although the president still had the final word.[45] The university's style was changing, but managers still made the final decisions.

Paternalism also manifested itself in nasty and capricious behavior. Many faculty members grumbled about the arbitrary and often authoritarian rule by their campus presidents and fretted about their lack of recourse in such cases. Brockport faculty complained of the heavy-handedness of President Brown, especially with regard to promotion and salary decisions.[46] Faculty at Buffalo State recalled how campus managers watched over them as if they were children.[47] Cortland faculty said they felt like high school teachers.[48] Canton faculty member Joseph Lamandola made the often-cited claim that the college's president at the time, Albert France, treated faculty paternalistically, telling them, in Lamandola's words, "you do what I tell you, I will take care of you. If you do it, you're a good boy."[49] Eugene Link of New Paltz expressed the view of most faculty when it came to raises, and in fact just about everything else, when he observed, "You took what the administrators said and kept quiet."[50] From campus to campus the complaints were almost all the same. Not all faculty members felt this way. Tensions existed on most campuses between the old teacher-college faculty, who were more accepting of their restricted role in controlling their professional lives, and the new faculty, most of whom were trained in the 1960s and believed they should have a real say in decisions shaping their professional lives.[51]

Whatever the merits of the complaints, the fact remains, SUNY managers called the shots and sometimes did so very heavy-handedly, particularly prior to the appointment of Gould. In 1963, for instance, the university provost announced at a Faculty Senate meeting that new salary increases were unlikely, and, he added, the university was contemplating saving money by deferring a previously scheduled April 1 salary increment until July. But, he assured the Senate, faculty need not worry, the state would assume 3 percent of employees' retirement compensation, allowing for an increase in take-home pay.[52] All this was delivered as a *fait accompli*. Faculty had no effective say in their fiscal fate, the status of their pensions, or the benefits they received. When a faculty member questioned the provost about the prospects for increasing the strength of local faculty organizations, she was reminded rather bluntly, "at no time has the faculty any legal right to overrule the chief administrative officer."[53]

Gould Takes on Salaries and Other Terms and Conditions of Employment

Gould's remarks and attempts to establish collegiality with and among faculty was a change in style, not substance. Under his leadership the faculty played a larger and more active role in many important areas, including salaries. The Faculty Assembly's Personnel Committee, for instance, established a subcommittee on the economic status of the faculty and charged it with developing salary goals over a five-year period. The committee did just that, and Gould listened to its recommendations.[54] But the bottom line remained the same: the chancellor had the ultimate power and authority to set salaries. As a practical matter, implementation of salary increases led the chancellor to delegate this power to campus presidents, although he still had the final say. Procedures based on the peer-evaluation process were established on the campuses to give the faculty a role, but the faculty remained an "advisory and consultative" body, not a policymaking organization. The Board of Trustees governed the university, and the chancellor implemented trustee policies. These facts are made clear in the legislation creating SUNY and further expanded in Article 1 of the Policies of the Board of Trustees: "Nothing in these policies contained shall be construed to restrain the power of the Board of Trustees."[55] It is no wonder that Faculty Senate minutes often record a top-level administrative officer reminding the faculty that repeated requests for changes such as a single salary scale were "unattainable and undesirable."[56]

As the university sought parity with faculty salaries at major universities across the country, the Faculty Senate continued to make recommendations to the president. Gould, with the backing of the governor and state legislature, delivered the goods. Average faculty salaries rose by 6.2 percent for the 1965–66 academic year and another 11 percent the following year. These raises included across-the-board increases to all faculty. Management also implemented discretionary increases, despite some faculty resistance, which took the shape of resolutions and petitions in opposition. The discretionary increases were usually at least 50 percent and often more of the total salary package, giving managers great discretion and, some say, an important tool to increase their control over the faculty.[57]

For the 1967–68 year Gould and SUNY's trustees requested an additional $6,150,000 for salary improvement. The plan was to provide up to six continued increments annually at the discretion of college chief administrative officers. Reporting faculty salaries by average wage increase obscures the impact of discretionary increases on the total salary package. During 1965–66, for instance, when the average raise for returning faculty increased by 6.2 percent, all faculty received raises of 3 percent, but another 5 percent of the total salary package was distributed on the basis of merit. On the surface, it appears that everyone received a raise of about 6.2 percent, but that is not what happened. Some received just 3 percent; others much, much more. In fact, on one campus a faculty member reported that merit increases ranged from 1 to 30 percent.[58]

Here is a simple example often used by former secretary of labor Robert Reich to illustrate the shortcomings of the concept of average raise increase. Reich, who is not quite five feet tall, would ask his audience to imagine him in a room with either Wilt Chamberlin or Shaquille O'Neal, famous basketball players who are both over seven feet tall. In Reich's example, the average person in the room is over six feet tall. His point is obvious: emphasizing average heights obscures the huge size differences between the basketball players and Reich. That's why including discretionary salary monies when calculating average salary increases misrepresents what most faculty received in their paychecks. But salary differences are not necessarily bad. Should productive scholars not reap larger rewards than their less-productive counterparts? This, after all, is the argument behind discretionary pay increases. It is also the underlying reason many faculty members accept and even applaud the availability of discretionary salary increases. The crucial questions are, of course, how is meritorious work determined, and who ultimately decides who receives merit pay? Answers to these questions trigger differences among the faculty. Almost all campuses had a peer process in place that gave faculty advisory input in the discretionary salary process. The process adopted in the discretionary process generally mirrors that for promotions, the major difference being that salary increases apply to a greater number of faculty annually while fewer faculty seek promotions every year. The process usually begins at the top. Guidelines issued by the university chancellor's office serve as criteria for determining eligibility for raises and the amount of the raise. In most cases, departmental committees review the applications of departmental members, compare the applications to the criteria, and make recommendations to a divisional committee. The divisional committee reviews and analyzes the applications and submits recommendations to the appropriate dean, who does the same and passes on the names of the chosen faculty to the campus president for final action. If the president decides, for whatever reason, that a candidate is unworthy and removes the candidate from the list, that is the end of the process for the rejected individual. There is no recourse, even if that person had the unanimous support of peer faculty. The president also has the authority to add new names to the list—in other words, to give a discretionary raise to faculty deemed not deserving by their peers. Moreover, again mirroring the promotions process, campus presidents need not explain their decisions to the faculty, thus leading more than one faculty critic to complain that such decisions are "made under a cloak of secrecy."[59]

The so-called "cloak of secrecy" was just one criticism of discretionary salary increases. The refusal of most campus presidents to make faculty salaries public made matters worse. According to a Faculty Senate bulletin, as late as 1967, only ten campuses made salaries available to the faculty and to the public. Faculty often complained about this lack of transparency, which made it necessary to go to the state comptroller's records to discover what a colleague earned.[60] This secretiveness reinforced the notion that something was unfair about the distribution of discretionary raises.

Other critics of the process claimed that merit rewards had little to do with academic performance. Allegations abounded that campus management frequently gave raises to their favorites, even if the chosen few were not among the most productive on campus. More than one faculty member echoed the sentiments of a Brockport professor who claimed that the college president "was primarily rewarding friends, his personal friends and cronies and that he wasn't being fair in the distribution of raises and promotions."[61] A Faculty Senate Bulletin story cited several cases of this alleged favoritism, including the case of a department chairperson who on becoming an acting dean granted discretionary increases to members of his department ranging from 14 to 25 percent.[62]

Further controversy surfaced alleging that campus presidents withheld discretionary dollars from faculty critical of their administrations. In other words, college administrators used merit raises as a tool to keep faculty members in line. Faculty who were bypassed for discretionary salary increases were likely to gripe, but whatever the merits of their complaints (and they were sometimes difficult to prove), the bottom line remains that faculty had little or no formal control over their salaries. This is not to say that faculty were totally powerless when they requested discretionary raises. They had the moral force of the arguments supporting their requests and there was a limit to how much a campus president could abuse faculty opinion. But the president's decision was binding, and this lack of faculty control triggered great resentment. Some faculty resented what they perceived as the arbitrary and capricious nature of the merit and promotions processes, but the state's fiscal crunch was still a few years off, and as long as the big raises kept coming, most faculty enjoyed the benefits of New York State's commitment to build a first-rate public university. Governor Rockefeller shared that commitment, and he was more than willing to provide the necessary fiscal resources to achieve it. Cortland's Henry Steck describes the days of growth in colorful terms: "you had to wade through the money."[63] Others fondly recalled raises of 15 percent one year and 15.5 the next. In the minds of many faculty, these were the best of times.[64]

By 1970, however, the state was experiencing a severe budget deficit, and the flood of dollars stopped flowing into the university. While millions in public tax dollars in the form of the Scholars Incentive Program (the predecessor of the Tuition Assistance Program, TAP) and Bundy money flowed into the coffers of private institutions, at SUNY talk of layoffs and retrenchments replaced promises of better salaries. As the struggle for scarce state resources took center stage, faculty became less accepting of the governance process and the ineffectiveness of their advisory role. Even the usually compliant Faculty Senate groused to Chancellor Gould about the university's lack of responsiveness to its advice and counsel. One issue that they found particularly annoying was the university's failure to keep a promise it had made regarding salary increases. In 1969 the Faculty Senate had reached an agreement with the chancellor's office to distribute unspent funds to campus administrators and professional staff. But that never happened. The university reneged on the agreement, leading the Senate to criticize SUNY's central administration.

The simmering frustration of giving much advice with minimal results led one senator to publicly tell Gould that in speaking for the Senate, "I must say that we have been terribly frustrated in terms of the results . . . and [are] getting some kind of feeling that we were being reasonable and yet being completely ignored."[65] At that same meeting, the chair of the Economic Status Committee, faculty senator James Reidel, resigned. Citing the university's lack of cooperation with the Senate and its unwillingness to share important information, Reidel warned the chancellor that when the advice and counsel of first-rate faculty are ignored, the best faculty members will walk away and their replacements will be faculty "who have nothing better to do."[66] The chancellor attributed the university's recent unwillingness to share information or otherwise cooperate with the Senate to the requirements of the Taylor Law, which mandates that a union negotiate terms and conditions of employment. But this explanation was unacceptable to Reidel and his colleagues, who reminded the chancellor that the Taylor Law was three years old and there was still no union. Morale was slipping, and the far-from-independent Senate was becoming increasingly frustrated. Even though SUNY still did not have a bargaining agent, the chancellor's office anticipated the establishment of collective bargaining and was carefully taking terms and conditions of employment away from the Senate.

Impact of SUNY's Grievance Process and
Other Managerial Policies

The perceived arbitrariness of salary increases and promotions was just a small, albeit significant, part of the terms and conditions of employment at SUNY. Prior to the formation of a union, SUNY faculty lacked real control over almost every part of their professional lives. They might be consulted from time to time, but they had no redress when management ignored their recommendations. The creation and implementation of the university's pre-union grievance process illustrates the weakness of the faculty's position.

The issue of a grievance procedure became a topic of discussion in the Faculty Senate following an August 5, 1955, gubernatorial executive order mandating all state agencies to create a grievance procedure "to establish more harmonious and cooperative relationships between the state and its employees."[67] SUNY's position on the governor's mandate was predictable. According to chief counsel John Crary, the university already had a procedure for its civil service employees. The Faculty Senate routinely discussed issues outlined in the mandate, and that was sufficient. In other words, SUNY's president did not think it necessary to establish a grievance procedure for faculty, because Senate deliberations already served that function. Before finalizing SUNY's position on the grievance issue, Crary wanted to hear the faculty's opinion. They concurred that they didn't need a civil service–like grievance process, voting at a special meeting of the Senate in January of 1956 to add the following passage to the minutes of their previous meeting: "It was pointed out that the real reason a faculty does not need a . . . grievance procedure is that it is traditional in American universities for each professional staff member to have the right of appeal and access to the highest administrative official of the university. President Carlson agreed with this statement and pointed out that he hears such direct appeals as a matter of course."[68] The senate then unanimously agreed that it should not serve as a grievance forum to resolve the problems of individuals, but concern itself only with policy decisions. President Carlson concluded the special meeting with comments on the need to establish personnel committees on campus to hear grievance claims, but he reminded the body that the personnel committees are purely advisory "and the head of the institution is ultimately responsible for whatever personnel decisions are made."[69]

Not all members of SUNY's faculty took such a sanguine view of the Senate's uncritical acceptance of the president's position on a grievance process. New Paltz faculty, for instance, submitted a statement to the Senate criticizing the administration's position that the Senate's role in the grievance process fulfilled the governor's mandate. Questioning the ability of the Senate to effectively serve as a hearing board with personnel issues, the New Paltz faculty stated that "formal grievance machinery constituted the individual's only recourse in case of unfair treatment by local administrative personnel."[70] The Senate, they claimed, was simply not up to the task.

In response to this criticism, SUNY counsel Crary reminded the Senate that the State Grievance Board agreed that the Senate did constitute a body to hear grievances. If they had declined to assume this role, he continued, "a faculty member is deprived of a grievance procedure and is thus left at a disadvantage."[71] Crary further noted that he had advised the Grievance Board that the question of a grievance procedure for academic personnel would be reviewed by the Senate's personnel committees on each campus, and these committees would serve as auxiliaries to the Faculty Senate. The November 1959 meeting of the Senate then referred the issue of a grievance procedure to its Committee on Personnel Policies for study.

The grievance process evolved slowly, with the Senate playing an increasingly active role in its often tumultuous evolution. In May 1960, the Senate, acting under the authorization of the Trustees Policies, Article VIII, Title F, gave its Personnel Policies Committee the responsibility of hearing appeals of grievances not successfully resolved on the campus level. In support of its new charge, the committee initiated a fact-finding investigation of the campus grievance committees authorized by the Trustees Policies, Article X, Section 5. A year later the Personnel Policies Committee reported a wide variation in the practices and procedures of campus personnel committees, the committees that actually heard the grievances, and discovered that some campuses did not even have these forums. These findings supported the Senate's charge to the Personnel Policies Committee to serve as the forum for appeal by aggrieved faculty. If a faculty member appealed to the committee, the committee would then conduct an investigation to determine if a hearing were warranted. If so, they held one to resolve the issue. Failure to resolve the problem at this committee level would bring the issue before the entire Faculty Senate with a recommendation for action. The Senate would then "make a formal recommendation to the President of the University for his guidance."[72] The president then noted that the final appeal of his decision rests with the Board of Trustees—in other words, the people who hired him and for whom he works.[73] The university president also promised to work with campus presidents to promote uniformity in the admittedly ineffectual grievance process.

The growth of the university had a significant impact on the grievance process. As faculty numbers increased, the number of grievances grew. Great disparities regarding the treatment of grievances on the campuses also remained. Some campuses had clear and effective procedures; others did not. Consequently, in 1967 the Faculty Senate, following the Policies of the Board of Trustees, Article 10, Section 5, developed a formal grievance process. The new process had a strong bias in favor of management. It worked as follows: any professional employee could submit a grievance *after* it had been identified as one through informal discussions with the appropriate chairperson, director, dean, or other administrative officer of the college. If the issue were not resolved at this informal level, the appropriate administrative officer referred the matter to a higher authority on campus. This authority forwarded the complaint to the campus grievance committee, which reviewed the issues and made recommendations to the college president. The president made the final campus determination. A grievant could appeal the president's decision by applying to the chairperson of the Faculty Senate's Personnel and Policies Committee and the chancellor for a review of the college's decision. It was now up to the chair of the Personnel Policies Committee to determine if the grievance was appropriate for the committee to hear. If so, the committee would conduct a hearing and send its recommendations to the chancellor for final action.[74]

The new procedure rationalized the grievance process at the university level. But the number of grievances grew so much that the workload became too heavy for a subcommittee of the Personnel Policies Committee to handle, leading the Senate to establish a separate Grievance Committee. Nevertheless, the lack of uniformity among the campus committees persisted, even after the Grievance Committee, with the chancellor's blessing, offered workshops to promote uniformity in the procedure. Indeed, as late as 1970 the chair of the Grievance Committee characterized some campus grievance committees as "inoperable."[75] Some were inoperable because of overly complex procedures, others were operable but unproductive, and on some campuses faculty simply chose not to use the procedures.

The experience at the college of Oswego provides a good example of an operable but ineffectual procedure. The Oswego College president apparently disregarded the grievance process. In a special report about grievances at the college, most of which resulted from the reorganization of the language department, a member of the campus Personnel Policies Committee blamed the college administration for problems with the process. The administration, he claimed, "has shown itself unwilling to cooperate with the committee either by implementing the committee's recommendations or by taking part in the Grievance Committee's hearings."[76]

Oswego's experience was far from unique. Professor Sam Wakshull, who later became president of the faculty union, claimed that the local committee at Buffalo State, although elected by faculty, was really a presidential committee because it reported to the college president, who made the final decision on campus. The committee lacked power and was mostly ineffective.[77] Of course, Wakshull continued, employees could appeal to the Faculty Senate Committee, but the chancellor still had the power to say no. Without any real appeal to independent arbitration, the process had only moral suasion, and that was limited.[78]

There were problems in implementing the new process at the local campus level. The new, more bureaucratically rational procedure was designed to give faculty a forum to air their grievances by providing an appeals process to a level above the college president, but did not question or undercut the chancellor's "final say" power. To do so would have required a change in the Trustees Policies, a change the trustees were not inclined to make. As the number of grievances mounted and the chancellor's decisions tended to differ from the Grievance Committee's recommendations, the committee brought a proposal to the full Faculty Senate that would create a professional arbitration board independent of SUNY and the chancellor. The committee chair justified the use of an independent arbitration board on the grounds that the chancellor frequently ignored the committee's recommendations. Members also contended that when he accepted the committee's analysis of the issue, the chancellor often imposed a solution different from the recommendation. The committee chair went on to speak of what he characterized as a "double standard" in the application of procedures. The chancellor tended to support campus administrators when they didn't follow procedures, but did not do the same when faculty erred.[79] When asked for data providing the specific numbers of times the chancellor ignored the committee's recommendations, Chairman Goodman responded by saying it was statistically impossible to provide such numbers. The issues, he claimed, were far too complicated. How, he asked, do we define a response? For instance, the committee may recommend a specific cash payment, but if the chancellor provides a different amount, does that constitute a response in agreement or disagreement? This example was not atypical. The Senate proceeded to vote overwhelmingly in support of the resolution requiring arbitration, with only one vote in opposition.

Several months later SUNY's new chancellor, Ernest Boyer, promised to consult and confer closely with the faculty on grievance matters and expressed a willingness to work jointly with the faculty in resolving any differences. He also had the final word on the proposed arbitration board. Boyer had no objection to a review panel that studied the issues prior to his final decision. He objected to the establishment of any board that served as an appeals body, and concluded his remarks on the issue by reminding the Senate that "the final action regarding this matter of grievance as the structure now exists is the responsibility of the chancellor and it cannot be transferred to another party."[80] The Senate could still recommend and give all the advice it wished. But SUNY's chancellor would have the final say.

Lacking any procedures giving the faculty real power and control over the terms and conditions of employment, issues negatively affecting faculty continued to surface and, most of the time, faculty had little or no recourse. Nontenured faculty, for instance, might learn of their nonrenewal just days before the start of a semester. In 1968 the Trustees Policies finally addressed this problem by amending the policies to provide a formal notification process. But implementation on the campus level remained an issue, and nonrenewed faculty had no recourse if the procedures were violated. Other issues abounded. The Faculty Senate, for instance, frequently petitioned the university for tuition waivers for dependents, but was repeatedly turned down.[81] On some campuses—Cortland is a good example—administrators denied faculty access to their personnel folders. This presented a significant problem in that a faculty member could be denied a merit raise or promotion on the basis of a document in the personnel file that the individual did not know about and therefore could not refute. Nothing in the Trustees Policies prohibited faculty from viewing their files. The restriction came from college presidents who claimed that nothing in the policies prevented them from imposing such a restriction. The Faculty Senate discussed this issue at length, but it remained unresolved until confronted by the force of collective bargaining.[82]

Faculty who were neither civil service employees nor instructional staff faced their own set of difficult problems. These employees, classified as nonteaching professionals at the time, served in a wide variety of jobs in a number of different types of institutions. Their jobs ran the gamut from goat herder and lab technician to radiologist at a hospital and assistant dean. While the jobs of professional staff differed greatly, the lack of job security was something they all had in common. Unlike faculty members and civil service employees who could earn tenure or its equivalent, salaried professional staff, in the words of one admissions officer at Morrisville, "served at the whim of the President."[83] This complaint was echoed by professionals throughout the university. Tom Matthews of Geneseo, Robert Potter of Brockport, and Josephine Wise of the University at Buffalo, distressed over the lack of job security for professional staff, reported various tales of what they perceived as unfair dismissals.[84] Cobleskill's Henry Geerken put the lack of job security in the context of arbitrary behavior by campus presidents when he observed that a professional staff person with good evaluations could still be axed because the administration found someone it liked better.[85]

Much evidence exists supporting claims of arbitrary firings of professionals. As early as 1966 the Faculty Senate addressed this issue, with no immediate results. By 1970, however, as the state's budget squeeze brought an end to the good times of the early Rockefeller years, job security for professionals again became a major issue. On one campus, management fired five professionals, prompting the Senate to recommend the establishment of continuing appointment for professional staff following a process of several years of evaluations.[86] The Senate recommendation was rejected and professional staff worked in a precarious "at will" capacity for several more years until the issue was resolved in collective bargaining.

Job security was the major concern of professional staff, but there were other issues too. Workload—what constituted a day's work; in other words, a person's professional obligation, and how to compensate professional staff for work beyond their professional obligation—presented significant issues to professional staff and SUNY managers. Early in its history, the university decided that the standard nine-to-five workday enjoyed by civil service employees was not applicable to professionals.[87] After all, they were professional employees and often worked jobs requiring long hours. This created important problems regarding compensation. Take the case, for example, of college admissions officers who travel for days at a time to high schools across the state to recruit students. Since the obligations of professional staff were not defined in terms of the standard workday, they were not entitled to overtime pay. Some campuses made informal arrangements providing compensatory time instead. But that was not always the case, and great inconsistencies existed in how the university compensated professional staff.

In 1972, SUNY vice chancellor Kenneth MacKenzie tried to bring uniformity to the issue by promulgating a memorandum clarifying compensatory time across the campuses. Needless to say, some campuses never implemented the terms of the memo and others enforced them sporadically. On campuses where it was implemented, new problems arose. First among these was the question of what constitutes compensatory time. How is it calculated? Some professionals reported that they did not receive all the "comp time" they deserved. Much confusion and significant disparities existed across campuses on this issue. A number of professional staff also complained of their inability to use their compensatory time; in other words, they were granted the time due to them but could only use it at their supervisor's discretion. Whatever the merits of the complaints, the campus president decided whether the professional staff person was treated fairly in accordance with the Mackenzie memo, which was not legally binding. If a staff person disagreed with the president's decision, there was always the grievance process in which the chancellor made the final decision. Lacking job security, professional staff tended not to initiate grievances.

If workload was a complex issue for professional staff, it was equally complicated for instructional faculty. The assistant to the president of SUNY in 1960 reported on the complexities of trying to explain workload to government policymakers. "[T]he concept of workload," he said, "is complex and difficult to interpret to legislative leaders and others responsible for making final decisions."[88] The data, in fact, are extraordinarily complex and mainly unavailable, primarily because the evolution of workload was similar to Hegel's view of the unfolding of history: it took place behind our backs. In short, it was evolutionary and developed differently on each campus, and in each division and department on a campus. This diversity of workload practices across the university helps explain why neither SUNY nor the union wanted to negotiate workload subsequent to the unionization of the university.

It is possible, however, to make some general observations and still gain an accurate understanding of teaching load at SUNY prior to unionization. For budgetary purposes, the university viewed faculty workload in terms of student-faculty ratios. At the third Faculty Senate meeting in 1954 President Carlson conceded the existence of a wide variety of student loads on the campuses and announced that a fifteen-to-one student-faculty ratio was acceptable to the university. A year later the chancellor called for studies of teaching load and the possibility of reducing the load as a prerequisite for faculty to substitute research activities for classroom teaching. The chancellor's target for the university was "a class teaching load of 240 student credit hours and a laboratory load of 200 hours."[89] At the time of Carlson's comments on teaching load, workload varied from campus to campus and from department to department within each campus. In the 1950s, in terms of classes taught, at the university centers the load usually ranged between three and four courses a semester; at the college level it usually ran from four to five courses a semester. The agricultural and technical colleges usually ranged between five and six courses a semester. The term "usually" is important here. Some faculty taught more and some taught less.

During the expansionary Rockefeller years, as the university hired more faculty and research became a higher priority, classroom teaching loads declined, particularly at the medical schools and university centers. Research became an important aspect of faculty obligations at these institutions, generally reducing teaching obligations to two or three courses a semester, sometimes even less. At the colleges where prior to expansion many faculty functioned within an academic division rather than a department, academic departments were created and workload was determined by departmental colleagues, with, of course, the consent of the appropriate college administrative officer. The growth of departments in the four-year colleges with their own specific cultures, needs, and histories further complicated the issue of teaching load. Mirroring the centers, many departments at the four-year institutions had differing loads. But in general, most faculty at this time taught three or four courses a semester. Many faculty at the agricultural and technical schools still worked within a division, such as social sciences, rather than a department. With much less emphasis on research at these two-year institutions, faculty there usually taught a load of four or five courses. Still, essential to understanding workload at SUNY is its general lack of system-wide uniformity. Binghamton's Morris Budin put it most succinctly. When referring to campus and departmental workload, he noted, "There are thirty-two campuses and everyone's got their own arrangement."[90]

Teaching load, like virtually everything else at the university, was ultimately determined by the chancellor through the campus president. This meant that load could be a rational way to allocate work and promote the educational interests of the institution or it could be used as a tool to satisfy the whim of a campus dean or president. In general, departments usually relied on the collegial process to determine workload and teaching schedule. The results of the process were usually accepted, particularly during the fiscally prosperous years, but not all the time. Department chairs, with the approval—tacit or explicit—of an administrator, sometimes increased the teaching load of an unpopular or "unproductive" faculty member. The faculty member had no real forum to appeal such actions.

In the fall of 1970, when the state's budget squeeze began to affect SUNY, student-faculty ratios increased, even though the university changed the faculty count to include departmental chairs,[91] which made the student-faculty ratio look smaller. The following winter the budget situation worsened, leading Chancellor Boyer to announce that "workload will be slightly invaded," thereby placing pressure on local campuses to do more with less, which often resulted in faculty teaching additional sections.[92] As subsequent chapters will show, workload became an increasingly significant issue as SUNY's funding began to shrink. It is also important to note that after SUNY and the new union agreed not to negotiate workload, provisions of the Taylor Law kept the university from arbitrarily increasing workload. Past practice, then, would determine workload.

A clear understanding of what it was like for faculty at SUNY prior to its unionization must also take into account the university nepotism policy and its treatment of women. The Trustees Policies contained a prohibition against the employment of relatives at SUNY. The policy had an escape valve that allowed SUNY's president to waive the prohibition when warranted by special circumstances. According to many faculty members, the waiver was often used to hire the wives of male faculty members. In 1961, for example, Faculty Senate minutes show that Binghamton's Harpur College was handicapped in faculty recruiting and should consider "a number of competent faculty wives to fill these positions."[93] Given the restrictions of the nepotism policy, when a waiver was granted and the faculty wife hired, she was usually placed on a temporary line and generally remunerated at a lower rate than her male colleagues. Admittedly, much of the data supporting this contention is not available. But ample anecdotal evidence, including personal testimonials, is available to support the notion that the university treated women less fairly than it treated men at this time. Stony Brook's Judith Wishnia recalls the secondary status of women regarding salaries,[94] tenure, research, and basic career opportunities, as does Cortland's Jo Schaffer, among others.[95] The Faculty Senate recognized the unfair treatment of women as a problem when the Committee on the Economic Status of the Faculty discussed the need for equal pay for women faculty, although they admitted that they lacked any hard data substantiating the claim of gender-based salary inequities. The issue does gain credibility with the filing of gender-based lawsuits in the early 1970s, some of which were successful. Almost immediately after the formation of the United University Professions, the union helped finance pay equity lawsuits for women at Stony Brook, New Paltz, and Farmingdale.

Equal pay and continuing appointment were not the only issues negatively affecting women. At Brockport a female "faculty wife" was "nonrenewed" shortly after becoming pregnant and seeking maternity leave. After unsuccessfully going through the university's grievance process, she took her case to the courts. By the time the court heard her case, the union had come into existence and helped finance her successful litigation against the university.[96] A New Paltz faculty member tells of being hired on a temporary line. When her time expired, a male colleague doing the same work resigned, yet the college, which was satisfied with the woman's work, hired another male as a replacement. At the time of her initial hiring, the woman faculty member was the only woman in a ten-person department.[97] She later joined other similarly situated women on her campus in a lawsuit, which ultimately failed. Stories like this are endless. Certainly the perception of gender discrimination existed at SUNY at the time, and given the deep-rooted cultural sexism of the times, it undoubtedly existed. In any case, this tough issue might best be understood by the observations of a faculty activist who noted that the "many discrimination cases after the formation of UUP suggests management was getting away with much prior to the union."[98]

On the eve of the unionization of the university, SUNY managers had the final say on virtually every issue affecting the professional lives of its employees. Due process was nonexistent as long as those who made the rules had the power to determine their enforcement. With the election of Rockefeller, in a little over a decade SUNY had undergone drastic change. The physical plant grew tremendously, and new facilities continued to be built; an upgraded faculty body had undergone significant growth; the very culture of the university changed. What had previously been a fragmented, paternalistically managed university with a less-than-sterling reputation had become, at least in terms of enrollments, the major university in the state with well-respected campuses, medical schools, and specialized colleges. Some faculty complained that the growth brought bureaucratization and the emergence of a cadre of permanent administrators who replaced the faculty colleagues who had previously temporarily served in such positions.[99] By the early 1970s university growth was ending. The state faced serious fiscal issues and SUNY could no longer count on generous budgets. In fact, faculty layoffs were anticipated, and the money that had previously papered over problems facing faculty was no longer available. As long as substantial pay raises were an annual occurrence and faculty had the resources to pursue their professional interests, the issue of control over one's professional life could easily be placed on the back burner. Tough budgets, however, pushed the issue of professional control higher up in the order of faculty priorities. These conditions all contributed to the formation of what would become the nation's largest higher-education union.

Chapter 2

The Right to Bargain Collectively, 1967–73

New York's fiscal prosperity papered over the complaints of SUNY's faculty concerning the often arbitrary and capricious behavior of campus managers. But an end to the state's prosperity brought the faculty's concern to the surface just as it became possible for all state workers to unionize. While many still opposed collective bargaining, SUNY's faculty and professional staff eventually joined other public workers in forming a union. But the sheer size and complexity of SUNY made organizing an extremely complicated and difficult task.

The first question focused on the size of the bargaining unit. Would the new bargaining unit be a series of campus-based unions or one university-wide unit? When the governor's office ruled in favor of a single bargaining unit, the issues became even more complex and troubling. Different campus types, for instance the medical schools and university hospitals, had different interests than the colleges of arts and sciences. A single bargaining unit meant the new union would have to represent an extraordinarily broad range of occupations, running the gamut from shepherds at the agricultural and technical colleges to brain surgeons at the medical schools. A single bargaining unit would have to address the crucial issues of professional staff, many of whom believed they needed a union separate from the faculty. Then, of course, the essential question arose: what union would best represent SUNY's professionally diverse faculty and professional staff? After a series of conflicts, false starts and ineffectual representation, UUP finally emerged in 1973 as the result of a merger between the Senate Professional Association (SPA) and State University Federation of Teachers (SUFT). This chapter chronicles the difficult and complex struggles that culminated in the formation of the United University Professions, and in so doing provides a foundation for understanding the internal struggles the union would face for its first several decades.

Public Workers Organize

The right for public workers to organize came after years of labor unrest. In New York City especially, elected officials were unwilling as well as unable to enforce provisions of the Condon-Wadlin Act, the law that prohibited public employees from striking. Given the growing spate of illegal strikes, as well as a taxpayer suit that voided the law, Governor Rockefeller in January 1966 established a five-member panel, chaired by Dr. George Taylor of the University of Pennsylvania's Wharton School, to recommend a means to remedy labor unrest among public employees.[1]

With remarkable speed, the Taylor panel submitted its report in March. It recommended that public employees in the state and its subdivisions be granted the right to collective bargaining; the creation of a Public Employment Relations Board (PERB) to mediate between public labor and management; and the revision of the Condon-Wadlin strike penalties, concentrating on financial penalties for the unions involved, while relying on the Civil Service Law's Article 78 for sanctions against individual strikers. After considerable political backing and filling, the Taylor Law was passed and signed by the governor.[2] In return for the right to collective bargaining, the law prohibited public-sector workers from striking. Nevertheless, collective bargaining for the public sector was now in place and deemed the primary means of allowing public employees to attain equitable treatment.

New York State's public employees embraced the promise of the Taylor Law with an enthusiasm and militancy not initially shared by their counterparts in higher education. While there had long been a very small cadre of faculty, including such luminaries as Albert Einstein and John Dewey, who believed in collective bargaining as the only truly effective way to control their professional lives, most academics deplored the notion of unions. Indeed, for most professional employees and administrators in SUNY, the opportunity for collective bargaining "was a surprise, a puzzle and a threat."[3] Most clung tenaciously to the concept of "collegiality," even though almost no one had ever really experienced it. Few in the ranks of academe saw themselves as "employees." For example, when President John F. Kennedy's Executive Order 10988 in 1962 enabled federal employees, many of whom were "professionals," to bargain collectively, it was not embraced by faculty and had little impact in higher education. The staff at the Merchant Marine Academy at Kings Point, New York, tentatively began to organize in 1966.[4] This was followed by modest efforts to move toward collective negotiations at the City University of New York, Central Michigan University, and Southeastern Massachusetts University in 1968 and 1969, but for the most part the opportunity was largely ignored.[5] It should be noted that these earliest efforts toward collective bargaining came in areas of the country with strong union bases in the private sector. In fact, when public-sector bargaining became law, faculty unions in public institutions followed, almost because they had no real choice in the matter. Where such legislation was absent, little unionization took place.[6]

Collective Bargaining and Higher Education

By 1970, one-third of all government employees were covered by collective bargaining, providing a real incentive for faculties to move in this direction.[7] Organized public workers were effectively staking their claims to large portions of the state budget, threatening the economic base of public higher education, as well as the opportunity for salary increases for faculty and staff at the university. In New York, after the passage of the Taylor Law, it became increasingly clear that faculty and staff at the public universities, colleges, and community colleges could no longer ride the coattails of the Civil Service Employees Association or Local 2 of the American Federation of Teachers (the AFT local in New York City, led by Albert Shanker). Historically, when either of these organizations succeeded in convincing the appropriate legislature that pay raises for employees were justified, the increase was extended to all other employees in the jurisdiction. Under the new order of things, each unit would have to bargain for itself or go without. This was now seen as an intolerable situation, made more painful by the runaway inflation that continued to undermine the middle-class status and comforts of faculty and staff. Clearly, passage of enabling legislation that gave birth to effective unions on every level in New York's public sector became a powerful incentive for faculty to get over the distaste for unions and begin the long road toward collective bargaining for the State University of New York.

Still, while most faculty seemed to support the idea of collective bargaining in higher education in principle, they continued to be reluctant to see it introduced on their own campuses. "Unionized scholars" was a disconcerting notion because of the independence and professional status normally associated with work in a university or college.[8] Many faculty, the beneficiaries of the middle-class life afforded them by their unionized fathers and the GI Bill that saw them through graduate school, were determined to leave the blue collars and lunch pails behind. Unions were not for them. They were "professionals." Administrators and even representatives of the American Association of University Professors frequently played on this snob appeal in fighting off unionization. One college president publicly asserted that "Trade unionism has no place among the faculty of a great university."[9] The changing economic realities and declining political support for higher education took a toll on faculty confidence in the long-term stability of the home for their vocation as teachers and scholars. Academic managers overextended their role in campus decision-making. State legislatures began to intrude into the academic world, claiming a need to ensure "accountability" for the taxpayers' investment. The traditional role of faculty in determining academic policy was clearly under assault.

Initially, unions seemed to offer an opportunity for strengthening faculty participation in college governance. For the nonteaching professionals in the State University of New York, collective bargaining offered a power base from which to wedge their way into the governance of their institutions. A survey in 1967 of "faculty discontent" found governance a primary issue.[10] As late as 1982, a new study found a direct link between growing support for collective bargaining and dissatisfaction with the state of collegial governance on campus. Indeed, one of the very first accomplishments of the unions in California's community college system was the establishment of college senates.[11] The same motivation seemed to apply to the conversion of faculty at the complex multicampus universities. State governing structures had encroached on institutional independence, and faculty were treated just like other state employees, not as self-starting, self-supervised scholars. The large unions established at the City University of New York and Rutgers University were a reaction to the perceived overextension by their academic managers in campus decision-making.[12] However, there is a reason to believe that the administration at Rutgers quietly supported the unionization drive as a means of preserving its own autonomy against the intrusion of state government.[13] Austerity budgets endowed collective bargaining with added appeal. Talk of layoffs involving tenured professors was another common concern precipitating unionization. Research indicated that the strongest early supporters of collective bargaining were the more vulnerable, lower-paid untenured faculty, more often than not in the departments of social science or the humanities.[14]

The appearance of aggressive public employee unions during the 1960s helped to channel the growing faculty discontent into unionization drives. Among the most assertive exponents of unionization among state employees was the American Federation of Teachers (AFT), whose membership expanded from 56,000 in 1960 to 400,000 by 1974.[15] The AFT had pioneered genuine unionization of teachers in primary and secondary schools. Under the leadership of Albert Shanker, New York City teachers had walked out on strike on November 7, 1960.[16] While the strike lasted only one day, it was sufficient to disrupt the school system and catapult the AFT (Local 2) into the leadership position in city schools, placing it in the prime position to become the sole bargaining agent for the city's 40,000 teachers when the collective bargaining election was finally held. Such militancy did result in major advances in the terms and conditions of employment for primary and secondary teachers, but it tended to frighten and alienate many in higher education who were more comfortable with traditional professional associations.

However, the problems would be compounded when the economy began to contract sharply in the late 1960s and 1970s. The declining birth rate cast a long shadow on the prospects for continuing growth of demand. The size of the traditional college cohort, after peaking at 17.1 million in 1979, was expected to decrease by 24 percent over the next fifteen years.[17] The long-term wave of higher-education expansion came to an abrupt halt by 1975. Few new institutions were founded and 250 actually closed.[18] In addition, runaway inflation drained the actual buying power of consumers and institutions alike, even as dollar appropriations were rising. For faculty, the problem was acute, because salaries suddenly failed to keep pace with inflation, averaging a drop of 2.5 percent annually in the 1980s.[19] As more and more of the nation's resources were being invested in the military and social services, popular support for education began to wane. Taxpayer revolts focused on the one area where the public could strike back: the annual local school district budget vote. State and local governments were forced to steer more and more funding into elementary and high schools, which left considerably less for investment in higher-education budgets. Administrators began to talk of cutbacks, sharp reductions in expenses, salaries, tenured faculty and even retrenchment of staff. Discontent among faculty and staff grew as a result of the progressively bleaker picture facing people who had been recruited to the academy in the halcyon days of the 1950s.[20] As the outlook for higher education became progressively grimmer, managers began to sharply reduce operating expenses, capital maintenance and improvements, employee benefits, and the filling of vacant positions; eventually there was even retrenchment of tenured and untenured professors.[21]

Professional Organizations Prepare

The National Education Association (NEA) and the American Association of University Professors (AAUP) began as professional associations and devoted their activities almost exclusively to the broad needs of the profession of teaching, rather than to advancing the concerns of individuals. The leadership of both organizations was adamantly opposed to unionization, seeing it as highly unprofessional. While both moved into collective bargaining, it was with great reluctance. They were unalterably opposed to affiliation with the American Federation of Labor–Congress of Industrial Organization (AFL-CIO), which the AFT and its affiliates embraced with enthusiasm. The AAUP, to this day, has a continuing internal struggle between those who are committed to and involved in collective bargaining and those who wish to focus the organization's energies and resources on upholding professional standards, protecting governance, and fighting for academic freedom and tenure.[22] It finally rationalized its involvement in the process in 1973 when it declared that collective bargaining was just another tool to advance the traditional concerns of the organization: "the enhancement of academic freedom and tenure, of due process; of sound academic government."[23] The fierce competition among the three organizations for recognition

as the sole bargaining agent for the faculty and staff of the State University of
New York after the passage of the Taylor Law would prove to be costly in the
extreme and delay the coming of bargaining for several years.

Nonclassroom Professionals Organize

While public higher education in New York State rapidly evolved from free-stand-
ing teacher-education institutions into a system of loosely linked multipurpose
liberal arts and technical colleges, university centers, and medical schools and
healthcare training centers, faculty struggled to establish traditional governance
practices and procedures to ensure peer involvement in curriculum matters and
the hiring and tenure of colleagues. Under the collegial model of participatory
governance advocated by the American Association of University Professors,
senates and faculty councils were adopted with which academic personnel were
comfortable, convinced that they guaranteed a meaningful and collegial role in
the governance of their institutions. In every case, these bodies were exclusively
made up of academic faculty. The so-called "nonteaching professionals" (NTPs)
were excluded.

The nonclassroom professionals of SUNY were caught between a rock and
a hard place. They did not fit comfortably into a unit of clerical and maintenance personnel because, as "professional," they were "unclassified personnel." In
point of fact, they "served at the pleasure of" their supervisors, which effectively
denied them the civil service protection that afforded job security after successful completion of a probationary period of one year. If the SUNY nonclassroom
personnel had a written job description, and many did not, it included phrases
that, in essence, required that they perform all tasks assigned to them by an
immediate supervisor, in addition to those specified. People in this category had
no defense against abuse of authority and no access to a grievance mechanism.
The academic faculty had effectively barred them from participation in governance, closing this route as well.

Unclassified personnel performed essential functions for the university.
They were the people who recruited students, handled transfers, directed student
unions, operated the financial aid offices, and kept all the records. They ran
laboratories and gymnasiums, staffed many departments in libraries, arranged
athletic programs, supervised the student teaching programs, and the like.
Clearly, the institution could not survive without them. But they had no real
job security and could be fired at whim, with little or no notice and no sever-
ance pay. Their professional obligation, unlike that of the academic personnel,
was a full calendar year, and they believed that their compensation lagged well
behind that of the faculty, unlike their counterparts at the City University of
New York, who enjoyed a unified salary schedule with the academics. To a

person, they felt like second-class citizens in their universe, convinced that the faculty believed members of the professional staff who do not hold academic rank "are somehow inferior and of lesser importance in their ability to contribute to the University."[24]

Efforts to redress these grievances began at Stony Brook in 1968–69 with the creation of the State University Professional Association (SUPA), which was designed to become a statewide organization that could "effectively represent and promote the interests of professionalism in the upcoming [collective bargaining] election."[25] Simultaneously, professionals at SUNY–Buffalo established the Association of Professional Non-Academic Employees. These two organizations sent out a call for delegates to meet at the Albany campus in October 1969 to create a statewide organization to promote the interests and general welfare of the nonacademic personnel of SUNY, "in order that they make a more meaningful contribution to the university and hence its educational mission."[26] SUPA leadership also sought to ensure that the NTPs took advantage of the prospective election of a collective bargaining agent, which they believed provided an opportunity that would not come again to achieve recognition of the NTPs' interests and goals and eliminate their second-class status. Initially they sought legal counsel to investigate the possibility that the organization could enter the Public Employees Relations Board hearings as a potential bargaining agent for the NTPs in SUNY. Meeting with Edward Brookstein of the Albany firm of Brookstein, Kahn, and Karp, Joel True and Neil Brown were advised that the cost of legal fees alone put the effort beyond their potential resources. As a result, all subsequent efforts of the organization were devoted to playing a powerful, even determining role in the coming selection of the exclusive bargaining agent.[27] The leadership committed itself to playing that role, provided that the organization it endorsed would give airtight guarantees that the collective bargaining process would result in genuine redress of the many grievances professionals had to live with.[28]

Unit Determination Struggle

The Taylor Law, or more properly the Public Employees Fair Employment Act, required that the governor's office define the appropriate collective bargaining units for personnel in state service. It also established a Public Employment Relations Board to act as arbiter to ensure proper implementation of the provisions of the enabling legislation. The appropriate unit for collective bargaining was to consider the genuine "community of interest" of the members of the potential group. Such factors as "substantial mutuality of interest in wages, hours, and working conditions," "[c]ommonality of employment practices and working conditions, geographic separation, functional integration, [and] degree of interchange among the employees" were also to be taken into account.[29]

From the outset, the governor's office was determined to create the largest feasible units to prevent balkanization and to limit the number of contract negotiations that must be undertaken.[30] Consequently, the state-operated campuses of SUNY were constituted as a single "community of interest" in 1967. Community colleges, although a part of the state university, were excluded from the unit because of their local sponsorship and operation. Similarly, contract colleges, such as the Agricultural College, the School of Veterinary Medicine, and the School of Industrial Relations of Cornell University and the College of Ceramics at Alfred, were excluded because of the special funding arrangement with the state that they enjoy. Neither community colleges nor contract colleges negotiated directly with the state.

The SUNY unit as initially proposed consisted of approximately 15,000 professional employees, located on twenty-six highly diverse campuses, scattered in the far reaches of the state. Only the common purpose of making available to the citizens of New York quality higher education at a price they could afford bound them together. As defined, the system included four medical centers with three hospitals, four research universities, ten four-year, multipurpose liberal arts institutions that had evolved from their teacher-training roots, six agricultural and technical colleges, and five specialized colleges ranging from the Maritime College to the College of Environmental Science and Forestry. Each of these institutions, with the exceptions of Stony Brook, Old Westbury, and Empire State College, had a long and independent life prior to incorporation in the SUNY system. (At the time of the unit determination hearings, the colleges at Purchase and Utica-Rome were still on the drawing board.) The campus cultures at all of these institutions were highly specialized and unique products of that history.

The personnel in the proposed unit included all unclassified employees of the state-operated campuses of SUNY, all full-time, part-time, and casual persons who were teaching, doing research, or were professional or technical employees. Department chairs were included in the unit because, while they perform an administrative function, they were not considered "management confidential." Excluded were management, clerical, and maintenance personnel and employed students.

This definition meant that the certified collective bargaining agent would be negotiating a statewide contract that would determine the terms and conditions of employment for people ranging from Nobel Prize and National Book Award winners to shepherds, from astrophysicists to financial aid counselors and gymnasium managers, from medical doctors with annual incomes of several hundred thousand dollars to librarians who made less than $20,000 a year. It meant that the bargaining agent would be responsible for reconciling the diversity of professional obligations, which saw research university personnel as responsible for only three or six classroom hours a semester, while their counterparts at ag and tech colleges had a fifteen-hour obligation. There was also the problem of rationalizing the ten-month obligation of the academics with the twelve-month requirement for nonteaching professionals, librarians, and faculty at the medical colleges. Bargaining for such a unit promised to be a formidable task indeed.

SUNY faculty and professionals were the last state employees to enter collective bargaining after the passage of the Taylor Law. It was not until 1971 that appeals from the governor's original unit determination and litigation over the nature of the bargaining unit and which organizations could compete to fairly represent its members were completed, and PERB was able to hold an election and certify a bargaining agent.

Competition to Represent

Few university and college personnel embraced the opportunity opened by the enabling legislation with any enthusiasm. University people are trained from the outset to work as individuals, not collectively. Henry L. Mason, an early student of faculty unionism, put it succinctly when he stated that "By practice and tradition, the members of the faculty are masters and not servants."[31] Sam Wakshull, a leading figure in the union movement in SUNY, suggested that the development of a scholar militates against working together for the common good, because they are taught to compete for such things as merit pay and promotion. He also noted that a major block in recruiting faculty to collective bargaining organizations was the broadly held notion that "unions were for people who swept floors and worked with their hands." College and university people "worked with their minds."[32] As a result, there was little grassroots demand for immediate participation in the process.

Furthermore, no statewide organization existed that was prepared or equipped to seize the day. The Senate was chaired by the chancellor and only advisory to him. It was not a membership organization and was funded by the university budget, making it, in the minds of many, a creature of the employer. The State University Professional Association appeared to understand the opening afforded by collective bargaining, but its membership was limited to nonteaching professional staff. Its leadership looked into the possibility of entering the race for certification, but found out almost immediately that it did not have the financial wherewithal to compete. The American Association of University Professors had chapters on twenty campuses and met regularly on a statewide basis to facilitate communication. Its membership was strictly limited to academic personnel, and as a traditional "professional" organization, it originally rejected collective bargaining as incompatible with the professional culture its members espoused. A Faculty Association of SUNY (FASUNY) existed, originally created to serve the schools of education out of which a large part of the system was ultimately forged, but it failed to expand or adapt to the new reality of SUNY.

While it was a membership organization, its resources were extremely limited and it would quickly fade from the scene.[33]

A small percentage of the members of the unit had joined the Civil Service Employees Association (CSEA), more often than not to avail themselves of group life insurance rates and other organizational benefits, but they did not seem to be committed to it for this new purpose. The overwhelming majority of CSEA's state members were clerical and maintenance personnel. While some professionals were originally included in that large unit, neither group was really comfortable working with the other. (The professionals in CSEA would eventually break off and create the Public Employees Federation when they found that the great diversity in the unit was incompatible with their economic and professional welfare.) In addition, for personal or professional reasons individuals had joined the National Education Association and the American Federation of Teachers, but neither national organization had a real base in SUNY in 1967 when collective bargaining came.

The first issue that the Public Employment Relations Board had to deal with in relation to the university was whether the academics and the nonteaching professionals were properly assigned to the same unit. The matter was complicated by the number of organizations seeking certification as bargaining agent, at least one of which was disinclined to represent nonacademic personnel. Others claimed to represent all professionals, but had few nonacademic personnel in their ranks.

The University Senate Emerges

When it became clear that PERB would order an election, the University Senate immediately asserted its primacy. A poll was undertaken in the spring of 1968 to determine if there was faculty support for bargaining.[34] With the outcome 1,558 for and 761 against, the Senate voted to seek certification at its Oneonta meetings on May 3, 1968.[35]

The leadership of the Senate argued that from the origins of the university as a system, it was charged with representing the welfare of the faculty. In July 1965, the Senate adopted bylaws that set forth, in broad terms, the responsibilities and activities of its members and committees and gave it the "sole and exclusive authority" to adopt and amend the bylaws. The incorporation of the Senate's constitution in the bylaws of the Board of Trustees was designed as "official recognition of the Senate's status as the representative for the university's professional staff."[36] Following the passage of the Taylor Law, the article was amended to formally reaffirm the Faculty Senate's status as "an independent and viable representative of the University's professional staff." Its Personnel Policies Committee was charged to "represent and promote the improvement of personnel policies obtaining in the University on behalf of the University staff." It served as the highest appellate body for resolution of grievances raised by members of the professional service.[37] Further, the Economic Status Committee would "function as the negotiating arm of the Faculty Senate," since it already prepared annual proposals for improving the economic status of the university's professional staff, encompassing salary scales, grievance procedures, fringe benefits, conditions of work, and other items suggested by the Senate and its committees as deemed appropriate for negotiations under the Taylor Law. The new bylaws charged the Economic Status Committee to serve as the official bargaining agent for the Senate and "refer back to the Senate for ratification any proposed agreement resulting from bargaining with the appropriate employer."[38] Under this authority, the committee had made an official presentation to the Governor's Negotiations Committee for the fiscal year 1969–70 and at the time of the unit determination hearings was drafting a proposed contract to be submitted to the governor's office upon certification of the Senate as the exclusive bargaining agent for the staff.[39] The new bylaws also changed the governing structure of the Senate. The chair of the Senate was now to be elected from its ranks, eliminating the role of the chancellor. From its inception, the chancellor had served in that capacity. In addition, the nature of representation was changed to include "all professional staff," not just academics. Many saw this move as an attempt to "blanket in" the NTPs to create a broad membership for purposes of collective negotiation under the Taylor Law.[40] The NTPs, however, did not embrace this move with any enthusiasm.[41] The rapidity with which the Board of Trustees acceded to these changes forces the conclusion that if collective bargaining was to come, the Senate was the preferred vehicle for the operation.

Other Contenders

The Faculty Association of SUNY also indicated that it would participate in the projected election, anticipating that it would not be subject to the charge of being a "company union" as the Senate clearly would be. Its leaders believed that the Senate would not qualify as an employee organization.[42] AAUP, through its New York Council, continued to maintain an interest although it originally asserted that it would not seek a place on the ballot. Membership in the association was strictly limited to academics, and the national office remained completely hostile to collective bargaining. But in November 1968, the New York Council took what was characterized as "a radical and revolutionary action" and voted to seek a place on the certification election ballot.[43] The Civil Service Employees Association claimed to be a viable alternative to the newcomers in the field. It had ample resources and would be courted by several of the contenders to form a coalition for the campaign. In the background emerged a new element, the rapidly growing membership of the American Federation of Teachers, organized

as the State University Federation of Teachers (SUFT), affiliated with the national
AFT and the AFL-CIO.

Members of the American Federation of Teachers were strongly committed
to the collective bargaining process and had no doubt that it was the opportunity
to empower faculty and staff to shape and control their professional lives. On
five campuses, locals were chartered between 1967 and 1969. Efforts were made
to forge a statewide platform through the creation of the SUFT. These locals
were dynamic and effective in making the case for unionism on their respective
campuses. They undertook to defend faculty and staff in grievance procedures
and to render legal assistance as needed. They produced regular newsletters
and accompanied personnel in meetings with administrators as witnesses and
moral support. One activist reported that his president had come back from a
statewide administrators' meeting to report that "we were up half the night last
night figuring out how to organize the Senate to oppose the Union."[44]

It was this group that in May 1968 challenged the single-unit determination by presenting five petitions to the Public Employees Relations Board asking
that AFT locals at the five campuses be certified as exclusive bargaining agents
for the professionals on those campuses. [These campuses were Cortland, New
Paltz, Brockport, Buffalo State, and Delhi.] Hearings on these petitions began
in the summer of 1968 and continued well into 1969, delaying a representation
election for two years.

Unit Determination Hearings

Supporting the original decision of the governor's office, spokesmen for SUNY
management asserted that the university was a single system that had made
unprecedented progress since its inception in 1948 in service to the citizens
of the state. By demanding campus-based negotiations, the Federation was in
effect petitioning "to change the basic structure and character of the university
from a unified University to that of a loose confederation of campuses of individual educational institutions." This proposition had been rejected by the state
legislature in 1950, and the Taylor Law had no power to revert it back to the
situation that existed in 1948.[45] An uninformed or precipitous unit determination occasioned by a misunderstanding of the inherent character of an academic
institution and the state university system could significantly change the course
of that progress and deter the continued evolution of what McGeorge Bundy,
president of the Ford Foundation and chair of the Select Committee on the Future
of Private and Independent Higher Education in New York State, characterized
as "a veritable education revolution," which has "begun to overcome decades
of neglect."[46] This progress and dramatic development, it was argued, had been
fostered by the "uniqueness and oneness of the State University System," which

by 1975 was projected to enroll more than 300,000 full-time students, more than the entire population of the State of Nevada. "State University will stand unique; the largest single University System in the world."[47] Clearly, the single bargaining unit was required.

Faculty traditionally held that they are the university and tend to identify themselves with the entire educational enterprise. Henry L. Mason, an early scholar of collective bargaining in higher education, asserted that "By practice and tradition, the members of the faculty are masters and not servants."[48] Most were extremely uncomfortable associating with industrial organizations or other public employees. Out of this attitude or culture came the creation of the notion of a "community of scholars" who share a common "community of interest." A definition of a bargaining unit that fostered divisive and fractional grouping of the university's professional staff on a campus-to-campus basis "would give rise to a chaotic condition capable of destroying the unity of the State University of New York."[49] If the professional staff elected to negotiate collectively, the chancellor's office asserted, it "is imperative that this be done on a university-wide basis if the essential character of the State University as a University is to be maintained."[50] In opposition to this position the AFT locals stood alone. All other parties to the hearings agreed with the single-unit determination made by the governor's office.

The AFT argued that there was ample justification for campus-by-campus bargaining. SUNY ranged geographically across the state and included a host of different and diverse institutions with a wide range of purposes. Maritime College, for example, educated deck officers, while Upstate trained doctors. In addition, it included two-year colleges, four-year institutions, and university centers. A single unit would create a "bureaucratic monstrosity." The chancellor himself had indicated that he did not want to be part of a system "where the individual identity of an institution was smothered."[51] The chief administrative officer of each campus had effective control of budget and personnel decisions. The AFT argued that moving bargaining away from the campus would increase the alienation that a faculty member felt in trying to determine who is responsible for what is going into the university. Evidence was presented that both graduate and undergraduate programs, departmental organization, grading systems, calendars, governance, and definition of faculty were not standardized. There were no SUNY-wide athletic programs; admission policies, student fees, and alumni associations were all determined locally. While final say on budgets was vested in the central administration, the local president largely prepared it, and budgets differed from campus to campus.[52]

During the hearings, the AFT modified its original position and sought a "dual-unit" bargaining structure that would allow each campus to choose its own agent to negotiate local issues and a council of local representatives that would represent the subject employees on statewide issues. Concern was expressed for the well-being of small campuses that, in statewide bargaining, could easily see their demands become subservient to the demands of the larger and more powerful campuses.[53] Differences between the campuses were real and material. All other parties to the hearing rejected the dual-unit concept and insisted that only a state-wide unit would be appropriate.[54]

The AFT also maintained that the Senate was not a genuine employee organization in the meaning of the Civil Service Law because it was "entirely beholden to the employer for its very existence."[55] It was not a membership organization, its budget was provided out of the university's funds, and its constitution was subject to the approval of the Board of Trustees, thus giving management effective control of the institution.[56]

PERB's director of representation ruled in August 1969 that the single unit originally defined by the governor's office was most appropriate for purposes of collective bargaining in SUNY. He did, however, agree with the argument made by the AFT that statewide issues and local or campus issues would evolve, but did not find that the "dual unit" called for by the AFT was necessary or desirable to deal with the dichotomy, because it seemed to lack "the stability and responsibility necessary in the negotiating relationship."[57] He also rejected the AFT charge that the Senate was not a proper "employee" organization under the law, accepting the state's argument that evidence led to the conclusion that the Senate had tried to improve terms and conditions of employment over the years. It had long represented the faculty to the administration on such matters as tenure, faculty self-governance, academic freedom, admissions policy, class size, physical conditions of work (including secretarial support for faculty and space for offices), sabbatical leaves, grievances, recruitment, retention, promotions, retirement, accident insurance, health insurance, and relocation expenses. To the director of representation, these matters seemed to be a primary function of the Senate. The charge that it was an employer-dominated organization was improper and would have to be adjudicated in a separate forum.[58] Shortly thereafter, the full Public Employment Relations Board sustained his decision. SUFT then appealed the Board's ruling.[59] The case was transferred to the Appellate Division of the State Supreme Court on April 1, 1970, which upheld the earlier rulings on November 10, 1970. PERB moved immediately to order a representation election.

Certification Election

During the almost two years between the designation of a single bargaining unit for all the unclassified professional employees of SUNY and the announcement of the election procedures to certify an exclusive bargaining agent in the fall of 1970, all interested parties scrambled publicly and behind the scenes to find resources and expertise to undertake a very expensive statewide campaign. None

of the activists in any of the organizations had practical experience in either collective bargaining or the type of campaign needed to win certification. Financial
resources were extremely limited. Coalitions were sought with potential allies,
accepted, and then rejected.

The Faculty Association of the State University of New York (FASUNY)
had been established as a statewide organization when most units were teacher-
training institutions. It was designed to accomplish four basic objectives: communicate among the various units, provide benefits, advance the economic and
professional well-being of the faculty, and promote professional growth.[60] Like
many professional organizations, its ranks were open to administrators and other
management-confidential people, which raised questions about its viability as a
bargaining agent for faculty and staff. It was quickly overwhelmed by the legal
costs of involvement and travel expenses to attend the unit-definition hearings
in Albany. Its Board of Directors decided to withdraw from the hearings, but
reserved the right to appear on the ballot should matters "take an unforeseen
turn." The leadership believed that the Faculty Senate would not qualify as an
employee organization and the Board "voted unanimously to back the SUNY
AAUP Council to be certified as negotiating agent" and to cooperate with the
council in a campaign to this end.[61] President G. A. Cahill did, however, make
a presentation before the Governor's Negotiations Committee on December
21, 1968, to make known the organization's views on terms and conditions of
employment.

Professionals Prepare

The State University Professional Association (SUPA) used these months to develop
a membership campaign that succeeded in enrolling approximately 1,000 persons
across the state by the opening of the fall academic semester. It also utilized the
opportunity to reach out to all conceivable candidates for certification to find
a partner that would guarantee nonteaching professionals equal voice in the
determination of terms and conditions of employment, if PERB did not allow
them to have their own unit.

Motivated by the passage of the Taylor Law, the nonteaching professionals
on several campuses had felt the need to form a coordinating organization to
begin the struggle to redress their common grievances and ensure that their needs
were not ignored at the bargaining table. Intercampus communication began in
1968, and an organizational meeting was held on the Albany campus in the fall
of 1969. The session brought together sixty individuals informally representing
fifteen campuses in the system. Guest speakers were invited from the New York
Council of the AAUP, the Faculty Senate, and the AFT to discuss their respective
philosophies of collective bargaining and the place of the nonacademics in their

organizations. A steering committee was established with representation from university centers, four-year colleges, medical centers, the Maritime College, and the College of Environmental Science and Forestry. The committee worked until a meeting on December 12, 1969, which attracted seventy delegates from seventeen campuses, when it presented plans for an organizational structure, statement of purposes, and membership eligibility. Articles of organization were adopted and officers elected immediately. The State University Professional Association was launched, determined to militantly represent its constituents.

From the outset, members of the SUPA designed a program that they viewed as an essential part of any negotiating platform of any organization they would endorse in the coming election. Unlike most of their academic colleagues, NTPs truly understood the opportunity afforded by collective bargaining to redress long-standing grievances, which were quite real. Nonacademic employees of SUNY were the only state employees who had not received regular cost-of-living increases since 1969. Members held that basic salary scales were depressed below those of comparable positions in the industrial sector and at other academic institutions. Furthermore, SUNY's NTPs were the only people in state service who had no job security, since they could be terminated at will.[62] The response to the call for organizing was positively received and the leadership looked forward to having a "decisive" role in the election, possibly determining which organization would emerge victorious.

Immediately after formally establishing itself, the SUPA president, Neil Brown, communicated to the chancellor the growing dissatisfaction of NTPs with the status quo and the efforts of the Senate to broaden its own membership to include professionals in order to qualify as a representative of all the members of the designated unit. Brown complained that the proposed amendment to the Faculty Senate bylaws was merely continuing the "seeming superiority" of voting faculty to professional staff without academic rank. It was completely unacceptable to his members, who felt that they were "second-class citizens in comparison to the teaching faculty." This feeling was particularly intense on the agricultural and technical campuses, where governance did not exist or was in its infancy, and NTPs were totally excluded from participating. Here the non-academic professionals felt they were merely "junior partners" in the work of the university. They viewed themselves as the "disenfranchised portion of the professional staff" that had been overlooked for years in regard to compensation and conditions of employment. Across-the-board salary adjustments in 1966, 1967, and 1969 had been different for the two categories of employees, and discretionary or "merit" moneys were denied to the whole category. SUPA members felt that conditions of employment for persons with academic rank should also apply to the noninstructional professional staff.[63]

SUPA leaders were willing to accept that the intentions of the Senate might be "honorable," but the lack of "appropriate means by which we might participate in University governance tends to negate all such good intentions."[64] Robert Granger, who would emerge as a major player in the collective bargaining scenario, denounced the proposal, stating "I believe it ludicrous of Faculty Senate to relegate the professional staff member without academic rank to a position where he 'shall have the opportunity to participate meaningfully in the process of governance.' This is the same bromide the Senate proposes for students in the same revision." To Granger, the proposed revision perpetuated the faculty view that professional staff without academic rank "are somehow inferior and of lesser importance in their ability to contribute to the University."[65] The chancellor was urged to oppose the proposal because the nonteaching staff deserved an equal role in governance.[66] Gould replied that he would not recommend the revision to the trustees, but instead was creating under their aegis a committee on governance that SUPA was invited to join.[67]

Throughout the spring of 1970, while awaiting the ruling of the Appellate Court on the appeal of the AFT locals, SUPA contacted the leadership of the State University Federation of Teachers (AFT), CSEA, the SUNY Council of AAUP, the Executive Committee of the Faculty Senate, and even the SUNY Librarians Association. Each organization was questioned about what guarantees it would give to SUPA that the interests of the noninstructional staff would not be sublimated to the needs of the faculty. It also insisted that if SUPA was to become a partner or form a coalition with any of them, the nonacademic professionals would have to have equal representation on a bargaining committee when certification came, and dual membership with SUPA.

By mid-February, a membership drive was in high gear with formal chapters on seventeen campuses and in Central Administration. Reasonably effective lines of communication were in place.[68] These developments, with the growing numbers of vocal members, placed the organization in a solid position to negotiate with potential coalition partners and to play a significant role in the outcome of the certification election at the end of the year. Consequently, all potential contenders were hospitable to SUPA's overtures when they were approached.

SUPA drafted a series of minimum conditions to be submitted to each contender for its endorsement. These were nonnegotiable and included equality of the NTPs in all collective activities; equality of the NTPs in local chapters; and joint membership in SUPA and the potential agent for all SUPA members.[69] The potential bargaining agent was expected to formulate propositions designed to remove inequities unique to SUPA members, and above all recognize that the NTPs "will no longer accept the second-class citizenship which has been traditional." The leadership recognized that while the academic personnel had unique "indigenous problems," the NTP situation required immediate and vigorous representation.[70] Dealing with the American Association of University Professors was problematic in the extreme because its national convention had once again rejected a constitutional amendment to permit nonacademic personnel to

join the organization. Fully 25 percent of the members of the SUNY bargaining unit would thus be excluded from full participation in the agent's activities,
including bargaining and ratification of an agreement, should AAUP prevail. The
New York State AAUP Council voted in November 1968 to seek certification
and encouraged SUPA to continue organizing with the promise of proportional
representation on any AAUP negotiations committee, even though they would
not be members of the organization. At the unit determination hearings, AAUP
continued to call for a division of the bargaining unit into one for the academics
and one for the professionals and testified that it would seek to represent only
the academics if the division was made. It maintained that while the appropriate
unit was SUNY-wide, it should consist of only the academic staff and exclude
the NTPs.[71] Clearly, SUPA had no choice but to seek a different ally.

The Civil Service Employees Association (CSEA) originally promised to
establish a chapter for all professionals on each campus of the university. It
agreed to consult with SUPA as the sole representative of NTPs, but declined to
submit to the Board of Directors several of the nonnegotiable minimum conditions for contenders adopted by SUPA, and equality of the NTPs in all collective
bargaining activities, including representation at the negotiation table.[72] The use
of such words as "consideration" and "consultation" was entirely too reminiscent
of the commitments of the Faculty Senate and recalled to SUPA activists the
"second-class" citizenship they fought. Firmer guarantees were required. CSEA
also sought to create coalitions or consortiums with the Senate, the New York
State Teachers Association (NEA), and FASUNY.[73]

The AFT was blunt in its response to SUPA's overtures. It "respectfully"
pointed out that SUPA could have no official status in collective bargaining as an
organization in terms of negotiation and ratification of an agreement. Its advice
and support were welcomed, but "The best way for the interests of non-teaching
professionals to be advanced is for them to join our organization en masse and
become active in the affairs of the locals."[74] The AFT stood uncompromisingly
for the principle of "one man, one vote," which precluded "equal representation"
in all collective bargaining activities for the minority of the unit represented by
SUPA. This position was read as lack of genuine concern for the problems of
the NTPs.[75]

The Senate Adjusts

The Faculty Senate presented a very different challenge to the NTPs. From its
inception, it had excluded nonacademic personnel from the ranks of governance,
although it claimed to represent all SUNY professionals. In spite of its "sincere
intentions to represent all professionals equally, vigorously and effectively," it had
a long history of, at best, neglect or at worst, paternalism in its relations with the

nonclassroom personnel, including deans of students, librarians, and admissions officers.[76] James Reidel, chair of the Economic Status Committee of the Senate, which was charged with collective bargaining responsibility, anticipated the expansion of the Senate's constituency by amendment of the Trustee Bylaws. He urged the senators to establish channels of communication on each campus to determine what NTPs wanted, emphasizing, "They are now your constituents."[77] Some programs had to be developed that would illuminate the different roles played by professionals, "hopefully giving some the chance to discover pride in other titles than 'professor.' "[78]

In its brief presented to the appellate court in opposition to the AFT's position, the Senate did assert that all professionals in SUNY, academic or nonacademic, had a common mission, namely "the educational mission of the University." It further argued that the Senate's commitment to the governor's initial unit determination was motivated not by a desire to expand its constituency to conform to that designation, but by its independent determination that the governor was correct as a matter of labor-relations law.[79] These sentiments left the door ajar for further negotiation with Senate personnel as the mailing of ballots approached. Leaders of the Senate carefully courted their counterparts in SUPA throughout the waiting period.

The Senate had other problems that complicated its desire to be certified as sole bargaining agent for the SUNY faculty and staff. Almost immediately after the passage of the Taylor Law, the Faculty Senate passed a resolution asserting that from its origins, it had "undertaken to represent the University Faculty in all the areas of its interest, including wages, grievances and conditions of employment," and that Board trustees had recognized the Senate as the representative agency of the university faculty. It also undertook a study of the new legislation to determine "the role the Senate will have as the representative of the University Faculty within the meaning and purposes of the Act."[80] At the unit determination hearings, the president, John M. Sherwig, had presented a petition supported by almost 4,000 signatures, approximately 30 percent of the members of the university staff, seeking recognition as agent.[81] Recognizing some of its limitations as a potential bargaining agent, the Senate undertook a "joint venture" with CSEA on June 3, 1969, to vie for representational rights for the SUNY professional staff.[82] The leadership rejoiced when PERB decided that the Faculty Senate "is a legitimate agency within the meaning of the Taylor Act and is, therefore, entitled to a position on the ballot, jointly with CSEA."[83]

But the Senate was not a voluntary membership organization whose rank and file paid dues, giving it an independent source of revenue. The budget for its operations came from the university appropriation, which clearly could not be used for "political purposes." Legal fees and travel expenses were piling up with no remedy in sight. Financial support from the larger organization was clearly the primary motivation for undertaking an alliance with the Civil Service

Employees Association, which had earlier characterized it as a "company union."[84] Not surprisingly, the relationship lasted only until March 17, 1970, when the CSEA Board of Directors severed ties, declaring that the two organizations were unable to "achieve the viable working arrangements" within the confines of the Memorandum of Understanding executed by the two on June 3, 1969. Senate expectations that the CSEA would help pay for a "very substantial bill they incurred" could not be realized because an appropriation for Senate debts had never been approved by the CSEA Board. The bill referred to was approximately $70,000 of legal expenses incurred by the university body in pursuit of its claim to be the appropriate collective bargaining unit for SUNY professionals. Clearly conflicting cultures and expectations prevented the development of a working arrangement and required the end of all joint efforts.[85]

At the same meeting, the CSEA Board agreed to deal with SUPA because it could "deliver upwards of 3,000 votes to CSEA" in the forthcoming election. In a resolution adopted by the Board, CSEA recognized that the noninstructional personnel had been treated as less than professionals in terms of salary, tenure, appointment, leave status, and other areas of professional standing, and pledged itself to "pursue the attainment of improved status for all employees teaching and non-teaching alike." To this end, it offered the "full use of all of its efforts, strength, experience, organizational structure and manpower as the collective representative of the entire professional staff."[86] More importantly to CSEA, unlike the Senate, SUPA was "asking practically nothing of us other than that we allow them to maintain their organizational integrity." It sought only that CSEA work "to raise their status to be equal to the teaching people."[87] The SUPA overtures to CSEA were undertaken in spite of the fact that it continued its negotiations with other contenders, including the Senate.

The Senate Professional Association Created

By the spring of 1970, it had become very clear that the Senate was not constituted to carry out the responsibility of collective bargaining despite the PERB ruling that it was eligible to compete as an employee organization. However, the leadership was determined to prevent the intrusion of any other element into the governance of the State University of New York. In other words, they were determined to keep out an organization affiliated with the labor movement. The possibility of unionization was anathema to them. Plans were quietly drawn, behind the scenes, to create a wholly independent organization that would be a voluntary, dues-paying membership body, designed for collective bargaining. Senate leadership undertook a campaign to create a foundation of support for this alternative to actual Senate participation in the process. Recognizing the potential cost of the coming election campaign, the National Education Association (NEA) was approached for advice and support.

On January 10, 1970, the Senate formally disassociated itself from the Civil Service Employees Association (CSEA) and cleared the way for finding another mechanism to "continue on an active basis to contend for the privilege of representing the professional staff in collective negotiation under the terms of the Taylor Law."[88] The Executive Committee of the Senate was authorized to explore the feasibility of establishing an independent, self-funded, membership organization designed for collective negotiations. It was also authorized to explore "affiliation with other organizations whose resources, personnel and expertise" might assist the professional staff in the attainment of its objectives, thus legitimizing the outreach to the National Education Association.[89] The new organization would be called "the Senate Professional Association," preserving the mantel of traditional governance and the aura of "professionalism."

Throughout this period, Senate leaders took public action to allay potential hostility among the NTPs to the new organization they planned. A resolution recognizing the right of the NTPs to share in the governance of the university was passed on February 13, 1970. Representatives from their ranks were invited to join the Faculty Senate Committee on University Governance, under the aegis of SUPA. The president of SUPA was invited to sit with the Faculty Senate Executive Committee in a continuing role. In a letter to the governor dated February 16, 1970, the Senate recognized that the noninstructional staff were the "disenfranchised portion of the professional staff" of the university, which had been overlooked in improvement of compensation and terms of employment for a number of years. Its authors argued that the NTPs were always excluded from consideration for "merit" pay increases, putting them at a serious disadvantage over a lifetime of state services. The governor was urged to establish conditions of employment for these professionals "similar to those that apply to persons with academic rank," and in particular that the noninstructional staff of SUNY be granted term appointments of one to three years, timely notification of nonrenewal, continuing appointment after several years of full-time employment, and provision for professional leave for educational purposes after seven years of service.[90] All these demands addressed the long-standing grievances of the NTPs and helped to raise to a very high degree their expectations about what would come from collective bargaining. At the same time, broad circulation of this Senate letter to the governor encouraged the rank and file of SUPA to support the new Senate Professional Association, despite the long history of Senate negligence of their interests.

The incorporation of SPA was designed to meet most of the objections of SUPA leadership to cooperate with the Faculty Senate. They were aware of the effective structure the NTPs organization had already created, giving them a potential stable base of political support in the coming certification election.

First, the draft bylaws guaranteed equal representation of professionals and academics on each campus, although professionals constituted only about 25 percent of the bargaining unit. Article IX provided equal representation at the state level in the earliest stages of organization by requiring one academic and one professional representative to the central body, regardless of membership numbers. It allowed for additional representation as SPA membership grew. This provision addressed the long-standing NTP fear of the potential "tyranny of the majority." The draft bylaws also ensured continued life for SUPA by allowing dual membership for professionals and providing that half of SPA dues paid by professionals earning less than $15,000 would be rebated to its treasury. Most important of all to the professional organization's leadership was the commitment to equal representation in all bargaining activities, including the drafting of demands and the actual negotiations team.[91]

Draft documents of a constitution and bylaws were quickly distributed to all senators and representatives of "other appropriate organizations" for review and commentary. Senate president Frank Erk proceeded to recruit individuals, all close to the Senate, to incorporate the new professional association. This self-selected Board of Incorporators would function as "interim officers" until local chapters were chartered and representatives to a statewide council elected. The council would then elect officers of the new organization. The new body would have close ties to the Faculty Senate, which the president characterized as "an umbilical cord," but it would not BE the Senate. He insisted that "as soon as it is born it will be on its own."[92] Any further relationship between SPA and the Faculty Senate would have to be the result of written agreements between the two organizations.

Senate President Erk continued the courtship of SUPA, with its membership now well over 1,500, announcing that the "Faculty Senate will be pleased to work with your organization as a strong colleague-in-arms in helping to bring this idea to fruition."[93] He also indicated that if SUPA decided that the new association was "the best possible way for the professional staff to be fully represented," several members of the SUPA governing board would be invited to become incorporators of the organization, "thus guaranteeing that they will play an important role in the early stages of implementing its organization structure."[94] In fact, the night before the crucial Senate vote to authorize the creation of the new organization, the Senate Executive Committee held a joint meeting with the Executive Board of SUPA and forged an agreement "in principle" that would guarantee the support of SUPA to the Senate Professional Association in the coming designation election.[95]

On the next day, February 6, 1970, the full Senate voted without dissent to create a dues-paying membership organization whose purpose would be to act on behalf of the Senate for Taylor Law purposes. Immediately after the meeting recessed, leaders of the Senate, now authorized to seek affiliation with other professional associations at the state and national levels, met with representatives of the New York State Teachers Association/National Education Association (NYSTA/NEA) to discuss relationships between the projected Senate Professional Association and the NEA.[96]

The constitution and bylaws, which had already been drawn up, were unanimously approved by the Senate Executive Committee and sent out to its constituents for review. Favorable responses were received from the majority of the senators, which President Erk saw as authorization to proceed further. Members of the Executive Committee and "representatives of other appropriate organizations," functioning as individuals, went ahead and incorporated the Senate Professional Association. The Board of Incorporators followed the original plan and functioned as interim officers, pending the creation of local, representative chapters.

Professionals Accommodated

Given the failure of other potential contenders to meet the basic, nonnegotiable demands of SUPA, the newly created Senate Professional Association was highly attractive to its activists. SUPA had the numbers to demand a strong voice, and it got one. From the SUPA point of view, the NTP block of votes would be the "answer to defeating SUFT [AFT affiliate] and keeping SUNY affairs within SUNY."[97]

The leadership of SUPA responded to the draft constitution and bylaws by proposing several revisions to bring the organizational structure into closer alignment with their minimum conditions for endorsement. The most significant proposal was the election of representatives from teaching and nonteaching ranks by their "appropriate constituencies" and none at-large. Six members of SUPA, including President Neil Brown, acting as individuals, became incorporators of SPA.[98] Clearly, in the coming election an organizational structure that recognized the duality of the members in the bargaining unit and incorporated it into its constitution made SPA the most attractive alternative to the minority of unit members, the NTPs. In urging the NTPs to support SPA, Robert Granger insisted to them that SPA and its academic members had shown "good faith in both action and speech." They had forged an organization that met all the demands of the NTPs and was the only potential contender to do so. Formal affiliation with SPA was held up until the proposed amendments were adopted by its Representative Council.[99] Skepticism about the ability of SPA to provide full participation by NTPs waned when the SPA constitution was adopted with SUPA's proposed changes included.

Each campus chapter was required to have at least one representative from each of the two types of professionals. The constitution also established a vice president of each category and an executive board that would reflect both groups proportionately. Most convincing to SUPA members was the provision that the Committee on Terms and Conditions of Employment and any bargaining team would have equal representation of the two groups. Academic objection to the disproportionate representation of professionals in these functions was countered by stressing that the final draft of the negotiated agreement must be submitted to the full membership for ratification. Here, it was asserted, the professors had a substantial majority and could easily vote to reject an unfair agreement.[100] However, it should be noted that these negotiations between the Senate people and SUPA took place in the summer months when few academics were focused on such developments.

The alliance between the two organizations made practical political sense. Faculty could gravitate toward the Senate and the professionals toward the SUPA wing of the new association, but when the blending happened, the SUPA people had a decided advantage. Its leaders were thoroughly organized and they "knew what they wanted in bargaining demands," which could not be said for the Senate element.[101]

SUPA leaders urged its members to join SPA and send delegates to the Representative Council in October to ensure approval of the equality gained in proposed amendments to the original draft. It was argued that if the rank and file of SUPA failed to support SPA in the efforts to win a place on the ballot, due to insufficient membership, the NTP "will once more be relegated to the back of the bus and forced to live in the ghetto of the university."[102] Such rhetoric, promising harmony between the factions, created an initial partnership, but it would not be long before tensions between the two would become almost unbearable.

SPA and the National Education Association

Up to this point, major expenses for SPA had come from membership dues, but these had been kept extremely low to attract membership. Its limited treasury was a clear threat to success. In fact, at the first Representative Council meeting in October 1970, the organization had only 761 members and $4,000 in the bank.[103] It received no financial support from SUPA despite the close cooperation between the two organizations and the many concessions the original Board of Incorporators had made to the noninstructional staff association. Given its extremely narrow membership base, SPA simply could not go it alone. A stable, affluent partner was needed. NYSTA and NEA volunteered aid because they did not want AFT to win. The two immediately paid for printed materials and indicated their interest in future affiliation but did not make it a requirement for their assistance.[104] This arrangement allowed the leadership of SPA to continue to assert that they were wholly SUNY and free of outside interference or control. But considering the fact that a four-person committee established to develop the organizing campaign, consisting of two SPA people (Robert Hart and Robert Granger), one NYSTA person (Ronald Bush), and one NEA representative (Philip Encinio), with each "vested interest" having one vote on policy issues, the claim was somewhat disingenuous.[105] In fact, in a letter to the editor of the *Chronicle of Higher Education* immediately after the runoff election, James H. Williams of the NEA asserted that SPA's bargaining experience will come "not from some alleged tie to the Senate, but from its relationship with the National Education Association and the New York State Teachers Association."[106] Later, commenting on the unimplemented proposals made to the national office early in the NEA/SPA relationship, Philip Encinio argued that additional financial relief was essential to his attempts "to assert to a coquettish higher education constituency the strength and security that accrues from a marriage with NYSTA and NEA." This reflects the true nature of the professional staff perception of the relationship.[107]

Representing fellow SUNY employees and improving their terms and conditions of employment did not alone determine the course of action for Senate activists when they established SPA. Like the financial angel, defeating the "fast growing SUFT [State University Federation of Teachers/AFT/AFL-CIO] forces" was paramount.

In fact, by the fall of 1970 with the certification election looming, in terms of membership and visibility, it looked like the AFT affiliate was the front runner. Herman Doh, who would become academic vice president of the SPA, candidly reported "There is little doubt that SPA incorporators from the Senate were anti-union and SUFT was a local of the American Federation of Teachers (AFL-CIO)."[108] Although it is hard to document, the domination of the AFT in New York by the leadership of Local 2, the United Federation of Teachers in New York City, also played a role. Charles Santelli, a professional from Cobleskill and later NYSTA staff assigned to work with SPA, observed that faculty on upstate campuses "were just scared" of the idea of a union, especially because of the strikes in New York City. He went on to say that most were "absolutely frightened of labor strife and didn't want to be considered in a blue-collar type union."[109] Some conjured up images of Jimmy Hoffa controlling their destiny.[110]

But hostility to unions was not totally irrational. This was the era of the Vietnam war, and the academy was often the center of antiwar sentiment. This would play a real role in shaping some people's sentiments toward unions. George Meany, president of the AFL-CIO, was a "cold war warrior," absolutely anticommunist, absolutely supporting the war. Albert Shanker also supported the war. He was viewed as a "cold war liberal," that is, a liberal in social policy, but a superconservative in foreign policy. Many simply could not abide the foreign policy of the general union movement, and this added to or justified antipathy to the AFT and SUFT.[111]

If collective bargaining had to come, SPA seemed to be a more acceptable alternative to a "union," because it was "kind of an offshoot of the Senate," traditionally acceptable (i.e., acceptable to the administration), "the lesser of a number of evils."[112] Sensitive to these feelings, throughout the designation campaign,

SPA always stressed its professional culture and independence from all outside influence and control. It insisted it was wholly SUNY-based, owing allegiance only to SUNY and its own members. This campaign rhetoric was all well and good, but as SPA would face the realities of negotiations and representation for the 13,000 members of the unit, it would have to develop a degree of militancy like a real union. In the process, the core of traditional academics would become disillusioned and the initial unity of the organization would fracture.

Mutual hostility to unions in general and the AFT in particular made the approach to the NEA a natural. In fact, NEA agents were waiting in the wings at the Faculty Senate meeting that authorized the creation of the new association, and they met with the leadership immediately after the meeting was adjourned. Given the paucity of economic resources available to SPA at its inception, its founders' only choice was to find a financial supporter. SPA's actual membership stood at 760 when the first Representative Council met. At least 1,400 valid signatures were required to place it on the ballot.[113] An alliance with the American Association of University Professors (AAUP) had failed.[114] The Civil Service Employees Association (CSEA) had rejected a joint venture. The NEA alone offered the promise of the financial and organizational support necessary to stem the tide toward the AFT. However, potential NEA cooperation and support promised that an outsider would have influence, if not control.

Minutes of the Board of Incorporators of July 19, 1970, record that the SPA had already received considerable support in the form of money, manpower, and office space from NYSTA, but that there had been no formal deal made between the two organizations.[115] The NYSTA Board recognized that it was in its best interests to support SPA, however quietly, if for no other reason than it would block the advance of the AFT in New York State. Affiliation of SPA with the NEA, it was agreed, would come only after bargaining rights had been won.

In the meantime, the organization continued to accept aid of many kinds. In early November, NYSTA set up a bank account for the campaign with the sum of $12,000. An Albany office was established for coordination of operations; it was occupied by NYSTA representative Ronald Bush, SPA representative Robert Granger, characterized as chief coordinator of operations, and Philip Encinio, NEA representative. Equipment and secretarial support were provided by NEA. A questionnaire on terms and conditions of employment was sent out to the staff, and NSYTA facilities were made available for regional meetings around the state.[116] NEA members within the SUNY system received a letter from Bush explaining that NEA was endorsing and supporting the SPA because of its "commitment to a professional and responsible position and dedication to serve the interests of both the teaching and non-teaching professionals of SUNY." He promised that SPA, NYSTA, and NEA would provide potential voters with "a rational and accurate presentation of the issues involved in a choice which will have momentous ramifications," unlike the "propaganda" anticipated from the competing organizations. NEA pledged to provide the required resources and personnel for the election and future negotiations with the state to ensure that professionals of SUNY would be represented by a competent, experienced, and informed team.[117] An example of the comprehensive support NYSTA rendered is the personal involvement of its president, Thomas Hobart. He made a point of reaching out to faculty leaders, particularly people elected to key positions in professional and discipline organizations, not in any way involved or interested in the collective bargaining campaign. Convinced that "people like to be asked," Hobart traveled around the state and met with them to recruit them to work for SPA. His personal outreach was hugely successful in recruiting otherwise disinterested parties to accept membership and commit to vote for SPA.[118]

Certification Election at Last

With his support, interim president of SPA Robert Hart communicated to the director of PERB on September 11, 1970, the organization's commitment to the Taylor Law, including the required rejection of strike action, and asked to be placed on the ballot. Under separate cover, he transmitted 1,400 dues-deduction and authorization cards, roughly 10 percent of the unit membership.[119] Robert Granger, at that time SPA first vice president for professionals, reported that "SPA was a distinct underdog and one which was not considered a serious threat."[120] But the widespread fear of "unions" on the part of many in the unit would give the lie to this perception.

Also qualifying for the ballot were the American Association of University Professors, New York Council, the Civil Service Employees Association and the State University Federation of Teachers, AFT. A fifth alternative, "NO AGENT," was also made available. To many the last-mentioned was the greatest threat because, it was feared, people simply did not want to accept the idea that collective bargaining was needed. Professionals operated on an individual basis, one on one with their president.[121]

The decision of the Appellate Court on November 10, affirming the ruling of the Public Employment Relations Board that the professional employees of SUNY were to constitute a single bargaining unit, cleared the way for a certification election. The campaign to win the votes, if not the active support of the members of the unit, began immediately. In terms of membership and statewide visibility, SUFT was clearly the front-runner.[122] Most academics were unaware of the emergence of SPA because most of the work was done during the summer months when most faculty were not on campus, but it was able to build on the base of support provided by SUPA. Throughout the campaign, NEA professionals assigned to SPA reported that their biggest problem was faculty apathy regarding the entire prospect of collective bargaining.[123] Arguing that it alone provided an internal professional association compatible with the collegial traditions most professors were comfortable with, SPA was able to garner 1,400 signatures, barely sufficient to earn a place on the ballot. PERB announced that the election would be held by mail ballot during the week of December 1.

A vigorous campaign on the part of the SPA and SUFT followed. According to Herman Doh, the SPA academic vice president, NYSTA-NEA support was "carte blanche." The extent of its investment "surprised even the SPA leaders," guaranteeing that if they carried the day, they would have no choice but to recommend to the membership affiliation with the national and state branches of the NEA.[124] Organizing and communications personnel were assigned to help the leadership prosecute the campaign. A similar investment was made by the American Federation of Teachers. SUFT was originally in a better position than SPA because it had conducted collective bargaining elections before and was better organized. It also had the successful history of the United Federation of Teachers (Local 2) in New York City to build on, although the militancy of that organization proved to be a handicap. Many upstate unit members still feared the "monolith" and militancy, believing that unions were simply not "respectable" and would bring down all the standards.[125] Before the final days of the campaign, the two national organizations had spent more than half a million dollars.[126] CSEA and AAUP hardly engaged in the fight.

Victory for SPA

None of the contenders achieved the required clear majority. Much to everyone's surprise, nearly 10,000 votes were cast, with the AFT emerging as the front-runner.[127] A runoff in January between SUFT and SPA resulted in a SPA victory (5,491 to 4,795).[128] "The upstart SPA had won the largest representation election ever held in higher education."[129] PERB certified it as the negotiating agent on January 29, 1971.[130]

Although some leadership emerged that helped to pull things together for SPA, at base its victory was attributable to antiunion hostility. SPA spokesmen pandered to this emotion, arguing that in the initial vote, nearly 70 percent of SUNY faculty and professional staff voted against AFL-CIO trade unionism and domination by union bosses and for professional organizations concerned with the welfare of the individual and the university.[131] People who had voted for AAUP and no agent seemed to have turned to SPA as the lesser of two evils. According to Charles Santelli, SPA won the election because there were more upstate than downstate or transplanted faculty, and these voters opposed SUFT because of the UFT and the AFL-CIO connection and the industrial model of representation they feared. There was also a real identification with the Faculty Senate, and many felt the SPA was the Senate.[132] SUFT activists believed that it lost because SPA "did not exist as a real organization." "It was created just to have an alternative to us!" They believed that many SPA supporters did not want a real union but rather an association like the Faculty Senate, a halfway house between a union and voting for no agent at all.[133]

Throughout the certification campaign, SPA spokesmen had insisted that the organization was formed "to provide a vigorous, responsible organization of the professional staff under the Taylor Law," that it was fully concerned with the rights and welfare of all staff members "as well as the future of the University," and possessed a determination to obtain "just treatment" for all.[134] They promised widespread consultation on all proposals, which would be communicated to the appointed committees charged with developing SPA positions on all terms and conditions of employment. Translating the rhetoric into reality proved to be almost impossible.

From the start of its life, SPA had recognized that the single bargaining unit established by PERB was "a magnificent delusion."[135] The university consisted of twenty-eight campuses scattered across the state from Fredonia in the west to Stony Brook on Long Island, from Plattsburgh in the north to Maritime and Optometry in the south. The educational purposes, histories, and functions of the campuses differed dramatically, and over the years had determined basic terms and conditions of employment in very different ways.

Average salaries for full professors ranged from $15,000 at the agricultural and technical colleges to $22,500 at the university centers. Teaching loads averaged fifteen hours at the ag and techs to six to nine hours at the centers. Most instructional staff worked the academic year (ten months), while nonteaching professionals worked the full calendar year. The Board of Trustees Policies guaranteed term and continuing appointment for academics and defined criteria for promotion and tenure, but granted no such protections to the nonteaching professionals. They worked "at the pleasure" of their supervisor and could be dismissed at will with no appeal. Consequently, the basic agenda for collective bargaining of the two wings of the unit would prove to be radically different, and in some real ways mutually exclusive. To address the fears of the NTPs and win their support for the certification election, the SPA constitution guaranteed them equal representation on all key committees. Such an obligation would pose serious difficulties as negotiations with the state neared. Granting special identity and representation to the NTPs countermanded the PERB definition of a single "community of interest" in the university. Additionally, the effort to accommodate the "special" needs of the medical and health-science units further fractured the single-unit concept.

As it approached negotiations, SPA was not a real organization. It had no staff to speak of. For the 15,000 people it represented, it had no political structure, no accountability, no track record, no traditions, a constitution that had yet to be interpreted, a series of unresolved issues, and a number of very strong-minded personalities. Personnel were loyal to campus and discipline rather than to the organization. SPA did not even have chapters at every site. All these factors militated against cohesion and success at the table. "Everybody was loyal to their own particular little area, and very few saw the bigger picture."[136]

Another problem faced by SPA leadership was the definition of "employer." The negotiations committee would not meet with fellow university personnel to address the terms and conditions of employment, but rather with representatives of the Office of Employee Relations (OER) who did not share the culture and psychology of the academy. Robert Granger, chief architect of the final package of demands, would later assert that OER representatives viewed SUNY as merely another state agency, similar to the Department of Mental Health or Corrections, resulting in conflicts between the state and SUNY interests. He believed that when OER achieved final authority over what went into the agreement, it produced decidedly mixed results for his constituents.[137]

Few in SPA's ranks had any experience with the bureaus and agencies representing the state at the table. One speaker at the Representative Council meeting while negotiations were underway characterized the situation as "playing poker under the pressure of very high stakes."[138] It was feared that OER's primary concern would be budgetary, with the other matters neglected because of the growing fiscal crisis of the state. In fact, when an impasse was declared, it was over noneconomic matters that the state initially refused to bargain about, arguing that they were covered by the Board of Trustee Policies.[139] This position was unacceptable to SPA, because the terms of the policies could be changed at will by the trustees themselves or by the legislature with no consultation with faculty and staff, and would not have the legal protections of a contract.

Such fundamental problems were compounded by the leadership's total inexperience with collective bargaining and the severe limitations of its resources. The dues structure of the organization was designed to attract members, not fund an expensive negotiations process that could last for months. SPA had no organizational leave for its officers or negotiations personnel and no money to pay full-time officers. Consequently, meetings were forced into weekends, with sessions lasting long into the night.[140] Adding to these difficulties was the fact that neither SUNY nor SPA knew exactly how many people were actually in the bargaining unit. Printouts submitted contained the names of 14,000 to 18,000 unit members. Some persons were administrators on faculty lines and some were faculty funded by the Research Foundation. SUNY's data collection was "a mess."[141]

The state legislative calendar was problematic. SUNY employees were already three years behind the other units in the bargaining process due to the delay caused by court proceedings regarding unit determination. The governor's 1971–72 budget was already completed with the legislature, whose approval of any funding was required by an agreement, but they were planning on adjournment by June. Clearly, time was at a premium.

First Round of Negotiations

Under these circumstances, it was essential that a package of negotiations demands be compiled and presented to OER as quickly as possible. To expedite the process, the SPA Executive Board appointed its members (twelve) and eight others to be the negotiating committee. NYSTA and the NEA provided financial support and two trained personnel to make the operation effective. One of the assigned men, David Graham, became the chief negotiator and the other, Philip Encinio, SPA's executive director, bringing as much experience in collective bargaining in higher education as was available at the time.[142] Jerry Strum, an NEA lawyer, would become chief negotiator after an impasse had been declared. He had been largely responsible for negotiating the first agreement for the faculty and staff of the City University of New York and so brought new expertise to the table.

From the outset, it became obvious that there were too many cohort groups to establish clear priorities. Not only were there major differences among academics depending on which type of campus a person represented, and between the NTPs and the academics, but members of the committee did not even agree on the nature of collective bargaining itself. Senior academics, nurtured in the (real or imagined) collegial traditions of the university, were uncomfortable with making "demands" "that seemed to them to be dishonest." They had problems understanding "how or why a truthful man could attempt to elicit from the State something he did not expect to get or which was obviously impossible and unrealistic." They simply did not comprehend the theatrical nature of the process. Above all they believed that the SPA victory had been a repudiation of the traditional bargaining model promulgated by the SUFT/AFT. According to Herman Doh, it would be this philosophical difference on the Negotiations Committee that would result in the walkout of two key players before the final SPA package was presented to the state.[143]

NTPs, on the other hand, were willing to ask for everything since they had begun with nothing and were determined to acquire from collective bargaining "the rights and prerogatives that their ivory tower colleagues had long enjoyed." They were "the most underpaid and over employed people in the University," unprotected by the legacy of tradition that academics enjoyed.[144] Their passionate advocacy exacerbated the natural tension between academics and NTPs.[145] Many academics came into the process with the attitude that "we've got the power, we want to keep it," but they were seriously divided between the two-year and four-year colleges and university centers. There was additional tension between persons with tenure and younger colleagues who had not yet achieved it, and between those who had attained the rank of full professor and those who had not.[146] In fact, a "curious coalition" between instructors and assistant professors and the NTPs emerged, because they identified with each other in opposition to associate and full professors, who wanted to retain full control over who got tenure.[147] One full professor from Binghamton actually argued that it would destroy the university if the faculty did not decide who was to get tenure and who was not. Similarly, the conservative senior academics were opposed to continuing appointment for NTPs. They lost on all these issues.

The first round of discussion proved to be extremely heated, so to facilitate the drafting of the negotiations package, the committee was divided into small subcommittees to develop proposals in specific areas. Robert Granger, vice president for NTPs, deemed the level of debate to be quite normal "within the University community."[148] But confrontations were continuous and sometimes quite ugly. Discussions over workload, work week, work year, continuing appointments, evaluations, the promotional system, and job security for the NTPs were "explosive" but did result in acceptable compromise. The academics who were all opposed to defined workload language in an agreement accepted the concept for inclusion in deference to the need of the NTPs, but with the understanding that in the final contract they would be excluded from the definition.[149] The economic package would generate the "most violent debate and the most trouble."[150]

Internal Conflict Breaks Out

Conflict between senior academics and the NTP representatives, which had surfaced over job security and workload definitions for the nonteaching staff, reared up again over the compensation issue. Proposals were made for separate salary schedules for NTPs and academics; for a uniform schedule for both; for a salary schedule for academics by type of institution, with a special schedule for medical faculty; and for uniform compensation by rank regardless of type of campus. The most violent disagreements were over the uniform schedule for all members of the unit, academic or professional, and over the concept of uniform compensation for academic ranks regardless of type of campus. University-center personnel found it difficult to accept that a full professor at an ag-and-tech college should earn the same salary as his counterpart at the university center. On this issue, an acceptable compromise could not be reached. The break came when the subcommittee on compensation, chaired by an economist from Binghamton, a member of the conservative minority, presented a proposal that was somewhat larger than what the state would accept but called for increases of about 15 percent. It was reasonable and based on sound economic principles. Almost immediately a substitute proposal was offered by Robert Granger, a professor from an ag-and-tech college, calling for a 30 percent increase and the university-wide uniform salary schedule. The proposal was based on the logic of the single-unit designation affirmed by the courts. All professionals, be they academic or noninstructional, in the community of interest should have comparable terms and conditions of employment. Debate raged.

When pushed to a vote, the substitute carried (eleven to four), and so advocates of the new model of bargaining for higher education had lost. The issue was not about actual salary increases, but rather the nature of bargaining itself. The SPA had embraced the "hard line adversary posture and was getting ready to do battle with the enemy."[151] Two members of the committee, one of whom was the SPA president, walked out of the meetings, disillusioned with the course that collective bargaining for SUNY had taken. Robert Hart and Alfred Carlip would issue a joint statement making it clear that their alienation was a consequence of the manner in which collective bargaining was evolving, not the particulars of any item in the proposed demands.

Robert Granger, who became acting president when Hart resigned, played a key role in finalizing the compromise demands. He would later assert that several policies were adopted to deal with the problems of a diverse university where there were honest philosophical and pragmatic differences, most important of which was the principle that no group would suffer loss of current status or privilege and could gain at the expense of another. He believed that this commitment solved much of the conflict in the development of the proposal.[152]

On March 15, an eighty-eight-page package, "a political document" from which to bargain, was drafted and formally transmitted to the state to open talks.[153] According to the state, SPA demands would have cost $193 million, or about 94 percent of payroll.[154] Meetings were held on a weekly basis, several days a week from March to early May, without significant progress. SPA declared an impasse in May because the state insisted on settling the economic issues before addressing such essential matters as job security, professional standards of collegiality, and proposals that would undermine and invalidate the Policies of the Board of Trustees.[155] A mediator was appointed but was unable to resolve the problems. Fact-finding was the next step, with discussions between the parties about the appointment of a panel taking place in July, but talks resumed in early August with a new chief negotiator for SPA, Jerome Sturm.[156] Agreement was reached on August 12, 1971, providing for across-the-board salary increases of 6 percent and 2.7 percent in annual increments. Provision was made for additional reopeners on salary only in the second and third years of the *Agreement.*[157] Many of the thorniest issues, such as promotion and continuing appointment for noninstructional personnel and the special economic issues of the medical campuses, were deferred to study committees empowered to make recommendations that could be ratified by the parties at a later date.

SPA leadership was relatively pleased with the outcome of negotiations. It had won a 9 percent salary increase and other contractual stipulations, particularly for the NTPs, which had much to recommend them. Robert Granger, now president of SPA, celebrated the fact that now all SUNY faculty and staff had a voice in university governance, a long-desired NTP reform. He also insisted that the Agreement guaranteed academic freedom, a viable procedure, and binding arbitration on economic and noneconomic matters. He viewed the job-security clause for noninstructional staff as a significant "breakthrough which offers, for the first time, an opportunity for this group of employees to discuss and make recommendations affecting their positions."[158] But it was not continuing appointment or tenure.

Opposition Solidifies

But not all of his constituents agreed. Twenty years later, Edward Alfonsin, a long-term officer of UUP, would reflect that because the NEA did not have any real experience in higher education in 1971, it negotiated a "collegial" contract, an "almost Faculty Senate kind of contract," which the successor organization was stuck with.[159] Josephine Wise, a professional from the Buffalo Center, would characterize it as "not very good," because you had a group of people to whom unionism "was very strange," who had no real experience, and who continued with "the collegiality mentality."[160]

Almost immediately problems that SPA had no control over presented themselves. As the newly confident leadership looked forward to the opening of the academic year, "the most visible and unequivocal SPA success" (and to many, its only success), was struck down. President Richard Nixon declared a wage and price freeze, which delayed implementation of the pay raises just negotiated. Appeals for exemption were ultimately successful, but when the check was cut in May 1972, retroactive to September 1 of the previous year, it was taxed by the IRS as if it were a normal biweekly payment of an annual salary.[161] Take-home amounts were severely reduced, and members had to wait until they filed their income tax return for refund of the excess withheld.[162] Not surprisingly this created great dissatisfaction in the ranks, which took a toll on SPA credibility.

But there were many other problems with the *Agreement*. People were disappointed because their expectations had been so high. Bargaining promised that problems would be solved, irritations removed, and inequities eliminated, but many of the most serious problems were shifted to study committees to be addressed later by mutually-agreed-on memoranda of understanding. Few appreciated the incremental and cumulative nature of the bargaining process, in which each new contract would build on the progress of one that went before.[163]

SUFT critics were not alone in describing the *Agreement* as "a manager's dream."[164] Fred Burlbach, who was president of both the SPA and SUFT chapters at the Brockport campus, reported that it was "perceived as particularly weak because it didn't have a retrenchment clause and because it gave away the salary schedules, supposedly for the professionals."[165] NTPs had always believed that they had been disadvantaged by the way SUNY applied the schedules over the years. They argued that managers used great discretion in implementation of the program with no redress for the professional if it was not applied accurately.[166] To this day, SUNY faculty and staff are the only state employees who do not have the benefit of an automatic annual salary increment as a result of SPA negotiations. When inflation is high or a new agreement is delayed for any length of time, which has happened many times, its absence becomes problematic. The substantial sum of "discretionary" or "increment money" was characterized as "the straw that broke the camel's back" for many because few campuses established peer recommending committees and many vice presidents used the money for personal advantage, rewarding friends and punishing enemies.[167] Furthermore, local administrators rejected every grievance at step one and SUNY management at step two. Most grievances focused on challenges of judgment rather than procedural issues. Since challenging judgments were no longer acceptable grounds for grievances, this constituted a loss of power that had evolved on several campuses prior to collective bargaining.

The retrenchment clause of the *Agreement* proved to be among the most controversial. Across the university most faculty failed to appreciate that such an article was necessary. Few conceived of the possibility that tenured staff would be "excessed" or contracts broken. Most seemed to have more trust in the administration and fellow faculty members than they did in collective bargaining to protect their place in the institution. They had been recruited in the halcyon postwar days and believed in the AAUP tenure concepts and individual agreements they had struck with the administration. Fidelity to these rubrics would result in tenure and promotion and failure in deserved dismissal. They owed their jobs to the administration.[168] No one anticipated the severe fiscal crisis New York State would face in the next decade, which forced the university to invoke the retrenchment clause and leave the rank and file reeling.

Unit members from the ag-and-tech campuses believed that they had been sold out for the other types. They got no relief from the workload and salary differentials because the Agreement contained no defined workload clause. They were required to work longer hours and were paid substantially less than their colleagues at the four-year institutions. SPA negotiators had refused to include a workload clause in the *Agreement* because there was no way the diverse types of campuses would agree on a single definition, and it was feared that any effort would cement in the inequality for all time.[169] Similarly, members from the four-year schools saw themselves as "step-sisters" sold out to the university centers, which got all the advantages: dramatically reduced loads and high salaries for less work. The professional obligation of faculty at four-year campuses was identical to that of the staff at university centers. They too were expected to engage in research and publication as well as heavy teaching loads, but they got less support for this aspect of their work than their counterparts at the universities. Bitter feelings were generated over these perceptions, and the SPA *Agreement* did nothing to allay them.

The initial Agreement between the Senate Professional Association and the State of New York provided salary reopeners in the last two years of the contract. As the time to begin talks approached, the near-bankruptcy of New York City placed new demands on the state treasury at the same time that state revenues were in decline due to the national economic situation. It was very clear that the free-spending days of the Rockefeller era were over. Furthermore, growing unrest on campuses due to opposition to the Vietnam war fueled public dissatisfaction with higher education. Reflecting the public mood, the legislature in early 1972 entertained a number of bills that called for such limitations on university independence as a moratorium on sabbatical leaves and an increase in professional workload.[170] These circumstances placed genuine constraints on the ability of the parties to negotiate new salary enhancements.

Negotiations began on January 9, 1972, with SPA's presentation of demands. The state estimated the package would cost "in excess of $128 million or more than 70 percent of payroll."[171] Discussions relating to salaries of medical and dental faculty continued under the provisions of Article XX of the original Agreement. Talks continued for seven weeks with little progress. SPA declared an impasse on March 7, and Dr. Eric Lawson was appointed mediator. Agreement amending salary provisions in the initial *Agreement* was reached on April 17, providing for an across-the-board increase of 3.5 percent for faculty and 4.0 percent for NTPs with an additional 1.5 percent for merit.[172] Continuation of the medical and dental talks was also provided for.

The differential between the two wings of university personnel would haunt SPA for the rest of its short life. While it could be justified or rationalized by noting the long periods of neglect NTPs had experienced, the absence of a promotion system, and their historic deprivation of merit money awards, faculty did not see it that way, a point of view that is understandable considering the inflationary pressures of the day. Many teaching faculty publicly regretted "the day that we allowed SUPA to come in on an equal footing with the faculty because it gave them such more power than their numbers reflected in the organization."[173]

Tensions between academics and NTPs were further exacerbated by the provisions for distribution of the 1.5 percent merit pool. Thirty percent of faculty and 25 percent of the NTPs on each campus were eligible for an award. Faculty were unaccustomed to sharing the merit money with the noninstructional personnel, and the NTPs felt aggrieved because 5 percent fewer of their number were eligible, once more making them "step-children" of the system. The main beneficiary of the "inequitable" distribution of funds would prove to be the AFT local, which had been defeated in the runoff certification election but waited in the wings to challenge when the law permitted.

Talks on the second salary reopener began on December 12, 1972, with the SPA presenting demands that the state argued would cost in excess of $110 million, or more than 60 percent of payroll.[174] Sessions were held regularly through early spring with little progress. On April 4, without notification to the state, SPA declared an impasse, which OER first heard about through inquiries from the Gannet News Service and the Associated Press. Across-the-board increases were a real issue, but SPA was equally concerned about the so-called "merit pool" (1.5 percent of payroll) insisted on by the state. SPA characterized such a pool as a "slush fund" to be distributed at the discretion of management and rejected the idea of salary improvements solely dependent on administrative goodwill.[175]

Further shocking the state representatives, the SPA, "in a completely unorthodox move," went into mediation with increased salary demands.[176] Mediation was unsuccessful, so PERB appointed a fact-finding panel, which issued its report on May 18. The fact-finders recommended 5 percent across the board and 1.5 percent "merit money," a settlement comparable to that negotiated by other state workers represented by CSEA. SPA accepted the recommendation, but the governor's office did not, and resorting to the final step provided by the Taylor Law, the problem of a settlement for SUNY professional employees was pushed into the legislature. The governor asked for 3.5 percent in across-the-board and 1.5 percent in "merit." A legislative hearing panel of six was established to deal with the matter in the special session in July but reached no conclusions before adjourning for the year.[177] The matter was not resolved until after the merger of SPA and SUFT.[178]

There was, however, a successful outcome of the second salary reopener. Discussion with the medical and dental faculty caucus, agreed on in the salary *Agreement* of April 17, 1972, were concluded with a tentative agreement providing salary increases for the faculty at the health-science centers, together with a comprehensive plan for the management of the clinical practice and income derived from it. The faculty in these talks were represented by their own counsel, Jerome Sturm.[179] The clinical practice plan articulated in these talks would become the basic frame of reference for dealing with one of the most contentious and problematic matters in the operation of the SUNY system for at least a decade. Financing university medical facilities, personnel, and equipment was always problematic.

Clinical Practice Plan Background

Common practice in American medical schools has been a limitation on clinical practice activity to ensure the primacy of the physician's commitment to education. Most U.S. medical schools chose to limit income as the most effective method of accomplishing this goal. In 1951, the SUNY Board of Trustees unilaterally adopted such a limit on professional income from sources other than state salaries, declaring that it was the best method to encourage clinical practice and research and would attract and retain quality personnel, "so as to upgrade the level of instruction." The resolution also stressed that it was the trustees' intention to ensure that the primary attention of the faculty of the medical and dental colleges would be focused on their teaching obligation.[180] Faculty earnings from private practice were restricted to 50 percent of an employee's budgeted state salary. If additional income was generated by research grants, the limit was set at 20 percent of that salary. The "privilege" of engaging in private practice and research required university approval, which could be revoked at any time it was "judged not to be in the best interests of the Health Sciences Center."[181]

Little was done to strictly implement this policy when funds were plentiful. The university was new and expanding in every direction at a very rapid rate.[182] The trustees revisited the issue at its meeting on June 18, 1959, adopting a series of resolutions (#59-74 through #59-77) that refined and expanded the earlier policy and outlined the scope and procedures related to clinical practice and research income arrangements. The main resolution allowed faculty to organize as a group on a college, department, or sectional basis for the purpose of conducting private practice and disposing of income earned.[183] Reiterating that it was the desire of the university to have a full-time faculty "primarily devoted to education and research, and professional practice related thereto," the trustees once again adopted the income cap. Faculty members could determine the configuration of the authorized practice groups, with the approval of the president of the center.[184]

The same action established a series of priorities for the disbursement of income generated by the clinical practice groups. The absolute priority was "reimbursement of State University on a fair and equitable basis for the use of Medical Center facilities and for services rendered by University personnel." Next came payment of premiums on medical malpractice insurance and other expenses accepted by the Internal Revenue Service as usual and necessary for the practice of medicine. The third priority was supplemental income to the members of the practice plan, limited only by trustee policy. Any remaining balance was to be used for "purposes consistent with the objectives of the Medical Centers."[185] With the exception of Upstate Medical Center in Syracuse, almost no progress was made in implementing these policies.[186]

New reporting requirements imposed by the state in 1972 on all hospitals within its jurisdiction forced the university to pay new attention to the practice plans.[187] Audits completed in 1973 revealed weaknesses in the handling of revenue and expenses at all four centers. Subsequently, the state legislature amended the Education Law by adding a section specifically directed to the dormant practice plans. In the statement of legislative intent, the framers noted that the current methods of managing clinical practice operations "are inadequate and fail to serve properly the need of the medical and dental schools, the state university system, or the people of the State of New York." The amendment outlined a mechanism for governing the operation and authorized the trustees to create at each medical and dental school "a clinical practice income management corporation for the purpose of collecting, managing and disbursing clinical practice income."[188]

When collective bargaining came to SUNY, management of the clinical practice plans was no longer the sole property of the SUNY Board of Trustees. The Governor's Office of Employee Relations and the certified bargaining agent for the faculty and staff had to deal with the dissatisfaction of the executive and legislative branches with the operation of the health-science-center clinical-practice plans. As a term and condition of employment, clinical practice income was a mandatory subject of bargaining.

Faculty at the medical centers viewed themselves as unique academics and feared that their more traditional colleagues knew nothing of their special situation and had little sympathy for their needs. Most of the physicians were convinced that this ignorance and lack of empathy made non–health science faculty totally unfit to bargain for the doctors. Some of their number flirted with the possibility of petitioning to be established as a separate bargaining unit, but this idea got little support, so their leaders chose an alternative route. During the lengthy months of litigation for unit determination, the medical faculty at the four centers established lines of communication and created a caucus to ensure that their interests and special circumstances would be protected no matter who was certified as bargaining agent.[189] Members solicited contributions of $25 from each colleague to fund its operations. Considering that the dues for members of SPA started at $10 annually and topped out at $25, the sums collected at the centers gave the caucus a real advantage. Immediately on certification, Dr. Michael Horowitz, an active member of the SPA and an activist in the caucus, contacted SPA leadership to remind them "of their commitments with respect to the medical and dental school faculties." He reported to his members that "In my opinion, they are to a man, in their leadership, good and honorable people."[190] He went on to urge his colleagues to enroll in SPA and to recruit as many of their cohorts as possible to join them, because only dues-paying members could vote on a contract that he was confident would produce "exciting and fruitful means" of resolving outstanding problems of the medical and dental schools.

At the first meeting of the SPA Representative Council after certification, the agenda of the health science centers occupied "an excessive amount of time." The effective organization of the caucus had proved invaluable in capturing the attention of the representatives charged with drafting a package of demands for negotiation with the state. Additional evidence of the influence of the medical caucus can be seen in the fact that when subcommittees were established to discuss specific areas of concern to be included in the proposed agreement, none was established for the medical and dental schools.[191] From the outset, the independent organization was instrumental in drafting the SPA position on health science center issues. However, when the first contract was finally produced on August 15, 1971, categorical and specific solutions to most of the principal questions plaguing the system had not been produced. Like many issues, health science problems were deferred to a joint committee to "study the adequacy of salary schedules" and a second to "consider . . . aspects of the medical program."[192]

Pressured by the well-funded and militant representatives of the four centers, the Executive Board of the SPA, on January 25, 1972, accepted the notion that "the community of interest of members in the bargaining unit in Health Sciences Centers is essentially discrete from the community of interest of the core chapter," effectively separating the two wings of the university centers and facilitating the coalition of the healthcare-related campuses. In the process, it cast a shadow on the viability of the single-unit designation by the Public Employment Relations Board.[193]

The medical caucus seized the opportunity to "study" key issues. Representatives from its ranks were elected from each center and then SPA appointed them, with their lawyer, Jerome Sturm, as the negotiations team to meet with the state. Reflecting the state's deep interest in clinical practice income and procedures, the state's side consisted of representatives from the Governor's Office of Employee Relations, the Bureau of Budget, the Bureau of Audit and Control, the state attorney's office, and senior administrators from each center. Genuine negotiations on behalf of the full-time employees having academic rank at colleges of medicine and dentistry began under the provisions of Article XX of the *Agreement*. Talks began and continued until the medical caucus declared an impasse in April 1973.[194] Agreement was finally reached in June and became effective on January 3, 1974, by which time SPA had already merged with SUFT to form United University Professions, but the agreement that resulted from these protracted talks became the framework for the governance of clinical practice in the university for almost a decade.

Clinical Practice Plan Framework

The "Plan for Management of Clinical Practice at SUNY Health Sciences or Medical Centers" called for the establishment of nonprofit corporations in each center where clinical practice resulted in a fee for professional services. All employees of rank who engaged in clinical practice were required "as a condition of employment [to] be members of the corporation" and to be subject to the operating procedures developed by the Governing Board established and approved by the Board of Trustees. Plans could be college-wide or by department, with the decision on which structure would be adopted made by majority vote of department members. Operating procedures would be developed by the Governing Board of the corporation, consisting of one representative of each clinical department and one representative from among the basic science departments elected by secret ballot. All ground rules for operation of the plans required approval by the SUNY trustees. The chief administrative officer or his designee was an ex officio nonvoting member of the Governing Board.

The Governing Board was charged with administering all matters concerning the day-to-day operation of the clinical practice plan. The not-for-profit corporations enjoyed a large degree of autonomy within the restrictions established at the bargaining table and incorporated into the University Board of Trustees Policies. A fiscal officer, paid by the corporation and appointed jointly by the Governing Board and the center chief administrative officer, was responsible for operations. The university and the state were not liable for any of the activities of the plans. Collection of fees, set by the individual practitioner, would be through a process established by the Governing Board and approved by the Board of Trustees and the state comptroller. Standard accounting, auditing, and reporting systems were mandated.[195]

The *Agreement* established a priority of disbursements. First, the state was to be reimbursed for the "regular and customary costs of a practitioner," including use of facilities, personnel, and supplies and equipment provided by the state. Second was payment of all costs and expenses related to clinical practice, legally deductible, in accordance with Internal Revenue regulations. The cost of malpractice insurance and any legal service required was included. The plan also required the establishment of a fund, equal to 5 percent of the residual income of the plan controlled by the CAO or his designee, to be utilized "for the benefit" of the home institution. Employees required to participate in the program could retain an amount from net clinical practice income equal to 75 percent of the state salary.[196] After all of these distributions, remaining clinical practice income was to be distributed in accordance with guidelines established by the Governing Board for the benefit of the particular faculty.[197]

Maximum base salaries for each rank were agreed on. The SPA medical caucus's key role in these matters was recognized when it was required that the chief administrative officer would undertake "consultation" with the local caucus before distribution of the $1.5 million incorporated "for the purpose of adjusting salaries . . . so as to strengthen the medical and dental schools." Priority was to be given to meritorious service by faculty members whose salaries were below the average salaries at equivalent ranks at the university centers.[198]

Dr. O. M. Lilien, a urologist from Upstate Medical Center and a member of the SPA negotiations team, urged his colleagues to ratify the proposed agreement. After carefully weighing the constraints placed on faculty, he said "it is my best judgment that you should vote for acceptance" as it represented "a fair and reasonable resolution of extremely divergent initial positions" and established significant principles and precedents that would be highly beneficial. Reconciliation of basic differences between the faculty, the state, and the university came about as a result of "a serious attempt on both sides to understand our separate concerns, address these concerns, and find reasonable solutions which could be mutually acceptable."[199] The independence felt by the medical caucus is reflected in the willingness of Dr. Lilien to communicate directly with Leonard Kershaw of the Governor's Office of Employee Relations, bypassing the SPA hierarchy, when he became concerned about the impact on faculty morale resulting from confusion and misunderstandings about "our painfully negotiated" Article XX in the contract.[200] When consummated, the *Agreement* was signed by Dr. L. DeLucia for SPA/UUP and Drs. O. M. Lilien and Z. Taintor for the medical caucus.

The Agreement forged by SPA and GOER in 1973–74 was in conformity with the expectations of the legislature when it added Section 8-AA to the Education Law and specifically included SUNY programs under its provisions. But while the new law empowered the trustees to create public benefit corporations and mandated promulgation of plans, the initiative was placed in the Governing Boards at each center. Consequently, SUNY believed that it was never within the authority of the Board of Trustees to proceed unilaterally to full implementation of the law. Little was done to create plans and otherwise operate in conformity with the legislation.[201] Failure to move vigorously on this front would create serious problems for the United University Professions when the comptroller's office undertook a massive audit in 1981 and the Governor's Office of Employee Relations determined to force conformity.

Impact of Merger on Clinical Practice Plans

The merger of the Senate Professional Association and the State University Federation of Teachers created a different kind of problem for the union. The health science centers, accustomed as they were to controlling negotiations regarding their unique situation, took a dim view of the new leadership, which was fully committed to the unity of the system and the integrity of the bargaining unit as originally defined. Fearing the "balkanization" of the university, UUP grew wary of continuing the practice that gave "special interests" control of any part of the bargaining jurisdiction. The SPA concession faded and the doctors felt betrayed, calling on the New York State United Teachers, with which the union was affiliated, for assistance in restoring their autonomy at the bargaining table.

The good offices of NYSUT resulted in an agreement between the central administration of UUP and the four local chapters of the health sciences centers. They forged a compromise that preserved the basic constitutional authority of the UUP president to negotiate the statewide contract, but assured that the drafting of the demands relating to such matters as patient care and clinical practice would remain in the hands of elected representatives of the centers. The brokered deal ensured that UUP would maintain the current practice that no clinical practice plans would be implemented "unless there is clear evidence of acceptance of the plan by the local membership." Ratification of negotiated issues affecting patient care at health sciences centers was to be by a majority of the members of the centers.[202]

When the university finally moved to implement the provisions of the contract in August 1975, a group of doctors at Downstate Medical Center brought suit, challenging SUNY's right to capture fees generated by private practice. They argued that such fees were not employment-related and that Article 8-AA of the Education Law effects "an unconstitutional taking of property in violation of the due process and equal protection clauses of both State and Federal Constitutions." Injunctive relief was sought restraining the university from requiring the physicians to become members of a clinical practice income management corporation, from placing any limitations on their outside income, and from taking action against those who refused to join. By March 1977, because of this resistance by the faculty, for all practical purposes, SUNY had abandoned the necessity to implement Article 8-AA.[203]

The Downstate Medical Center suit (*Kountz et al. v. SUNY*) wended its way through the judicial system. The initial decision rendered in January 1977 held that the Article 8-AA did not regulate or control private clinical practice earnings, basically supporting the Downstate doctors. Reversed on appeal, the court held that a trial was necessary, which took place in September and October 1980.

On March 17, 1981, the State Supreme Court ruled on the Kountz case, upholding the constitutionality of Article 8-AA. The court declared that the provisions of the amended Education Law are "applicable to all patient care services rendered by the teaching professionals (i.e., doctors) employed at SUNY medical colleges, including the services rendered by the doctors, and the fees earned therefrom, to patients in their private practice." The decision also concluded that the Law did not violate any of the plaintiffs' constitutional rights and that the enactment of clinical practice plans and the inclusion of a teaching doctor's private practice within the purview of the plan are reasonably and rationally related to the legitimate state and university interests of fostering full-time devotion to teaching duties. In the opinion supporting the state's mandate, the court concluded that an excessive outside practice might interfere with the educational duties of a faculty member and that therefore it was not unreasonable to place a limit on income as a way to ensure the primacy of the educational objective of a faculty member's professional obligation.[204] A spokesman for SUNY indicated that the real significance of the decision was that it upheld SUNY's right to regulate the outside income of employee physicians under the collective bargaining agreement.

During the period of litigation, UUP, now the certified bargaining agent for the SUNY professional staff, and the Governor's Office of Employee Relations undertook discussion to refine the existing clinical practice article of the contract. Throughout these discussions, UUP's chief negotiator, Evelyn Hartmann, was joined by Murray A. Gordon, representing the medical caucus. Gordon had been retained as a consultant to the caucus in the context of the role "authorized" by the union.[205] UUP committed to pay the costs of the consultation on behalf of the Health Sciences Centers Caucus. On March 4, 1981, their work resulted in a change of the income limitations from state and other sources to 175 percent of the maximum state salary for an employee's rank. Heretofore the limit was 175 percent of the *employee's* salary. Creation of a corporation was not mandated, and the organizational and operational details of a clinical practice plan were left to local development. SUNY indicated that this agreement would increase the potential for genuine implementation of the mandated clinical practice plans.[206] In June 1981, the State Department of Audit and Control undertook a comprehensive review to determine if SUNY had complied with trustee resolutions and the Education Law.

NEA and AFT in New York Talk Merger

The spring of 1971 witnessed the beginning of a series of events that would have a profound effect on the history of public-sector collective bargaining in New York State. To garner support for Governor Nelson Rockefeller's budget, Republican legislators negotiated a series of deals with their most conservative colleagues, who were holding out because the proposed budget included more spending and taxing than they were comfortable with. Pet legislation was offered to the most reactionary among them, including a series of "antiteacher" bills that had long been the heart's desire of Assemblyman Charles A. Jerabek of Long Island. The front page of *Newsday* headlined the action as: "GOPers Agree on Budget Cuts/Teacher Benefits Traded Away." The four bills were later characterized by one teacher activist "as an alarm that woke up a political giant that had been sleeping in the state for well over one hundred years: teachers."[207] Eliminating the due process protections of tenure made teachers vulnerable to arbitrary firing by local hacks or school politics, an intolerable situation for most. From one end of the state to the other, teachers came out fighting. Two major developments flowed from the Jerabek challenge: political activism and peace and reconciliation between the two major teacher unions in New York, both of which would have a direct impact on higher-education collective bargaining in general and the Senate Professional Association in particular.

Albert Shanker, president of Local 2, United Federation of Teachers (AFT), long believed that the political impotence of teachers in New York was the result of the warfare between the two major organizations, AFT and NEA, which went beyond disliking and distrusting each other. They exaggerated their differences, demonized each other, and were involved in institutional warfare for dominance in the field. In March 1971, Shanker and NYSTA president Emanuel

Kafka found themselves in substantial agreement on all major educational issues when interviewed for a report for the New York State Education Department's monthly magazine, *Inside Education*. When confronted with this reality, Shanker asked Kafka when merger discussions would begin.[208] While Kafka personally supported the proposal, he could not convince his board to go beyond discussions. However, the annual NYSTA convention in Syracuse in November overwhelmingly endorsed a resolution demanding that the organization continue and expand discussions leading to a possible merger of all teachers in the state into a single organization. Under the leadership of the new president, Thomas Hobart of the Buffalo Teachers Federation, conversations did continue, and with great difficulty a deal was ultimately struck creating the New York State United Teachers (NYSUT). The absurd cost of the jurisdictional disputes between the two organizations had taken its toll. The hundreds of thousands of dollars invested in the struggle to best each other could have been better invested in advancing the status of the profession and improving the quality of education in the state. Above all, however, merger would allow teachers to speak with one voice in the political arena and to champion the cause of teachers and education generally.[209] Although it was not easy, common sense prevailed and unity was affected in spring 1972.

Merger of the affiliates created problems for both the Senate Professional Association and the State University Federation of Teachers. SPA, with collective bargaining rights, was a member of the statewide organization, NYSTA. SUFT, waiting in the wings to challenge SPA when the law allowed, was affiliated with the United Teachers of New York (UTNY), which Shanker had created to pursue the anti-NEA struggle in upstate areas and Long Island and ultimately pressure NYSTA into merger. Now the two higher-education rivals were members of the merged organization, an embarrassment for NYSUT, whose leadership remained sympathetic but "confused" about what course of action to pursue regarding its two SUNY affiliates.[210] The NYSTA-UTNY merger was completed in March 1973. SPA's members were affiliated with the AFT, "whether they liked it or not."[211]

SPA and SUFT Merge

Merger of SPA and SUFT was acutely problematic because in the time since the runoff election, the AFT affiliate remained active and extremely hostile. Many of its members were strongly committed, and continued to be "angry and bitter," seeing SPA as a "phony union." In their view, too many of its members really wanted a union that was like the Faculty Senate, for which true unionists had nothing but contempt.[212] In spite of its diminished numbers, SUFT remained a "fierce adversary" on several campuses.[213] Under the leadership of Edward Wesnofske, a sociologist from the Oneonta campus, SUFT systematically criticized every move and accomplishment of the certified agent. It took the lead in demanding action to appeal the application of the Nixon wage freeze to SUNY increases. Irregular newsletters were circulated attacking the agreements negotiated, the alleged staff domination of the organization, and the essential lack of democracy built into the structure of the rival.

First and foremost, attention focused on the contract failures, particularly the weakness of the retrenchment clause. In addition, academic unionists could not forgive SPA for surrendering, in 1972, the increment system that provided additional dollars added to base for each year of service, and negotiating a half-percent more across the board for professionals than academics. These grievances caused unionists to stress their consistent demand for "one person, one vote" as the true shape of democracy, not the 50-50 division incorporated into SPA that gave the nonclassroom personnel an edge not merited by the numbers.[214] Basically, the SUFT rank and file distrusted the SPA people as "not true unionists," and continued to see them as quasi–Faculty Senate types, more inclined to accommodate the administration than to stand up and fight aggressively for members' rights. In fact, many saw SPA as a "sick and corrupt organization with a company union philosophy" and longed for the date (September 1, 1973) when SPA's unchallenged representation would expire and SUFT could call for a new election.[215]

SPA people remained convinced that SUFT members were "militant unionists," trying to bring an industrial model of unionism into the academic world where it simply had no validity; that they distorted and twisted things to try and make that model fit. As the more traditional academics, SPA loyalists were distinctly uncomfortable with the ideology of the unionists and refused to be defined in this fashion.[216] They saw the SUFT members as sore losers who should cease and desist their hostility and work for a unified SUNY professional staff. Many felt that since SPA had bargaining rights and was a viable organization, there was no need for merger.

Once again, statewide developments affected the SUNY reality. Shortly before the consummation of the statewide organizations' merger, a "big scare" came out of New York City. The AFT higher-education local was planning to challenge the certified bargaining agent for the faculty and staff of the City University of New York (CUNY), which was affiliated with NYSTA. Because the salaries of CUNY employees were tied to the negotiated pay of the United Federation of Teachers (UFT, Local 2, AFT), many members felt a greater affinity to the UFT people than they did to the upstate teachers who had no ties to their agreement. Most did not have the fear of Al Shanker that characterized many outside the city. Preliminary reports indicated that the AFT would carry the day and CUNY would be lost to the NEA. To avoid this confrontation, the CUNY organizations agreed to merge, forming the Professional Staff Congress (PSC). This development, and the admitted weakness of its agreement with the state, encouraged SPA leaders to be very quietly promerger. They figured that in merger there would be survival.[217]

SUFT's president suggested to his executive board that attacks on SPA were probably counterproductive and supported talks to initiate merger.[218] By the spring of 1972, SUFT attacks had "diminished somewhat," and by the fall, informal talks between leaders led to a decision by the SPA Representative Council that the executive board "could talk seriously with SUFT about merger," but insisted that costs and benefits of merger with other organizations be investigated.[219] In fact, if merger with SUFT had not been affected, there would have been a certification election, because the academics in the university, the vast majority of the unit, never forgave SPA for what happened in the 1972 agreement.[220]

Informal talks became formal and a merger document was drafted. SPA had an internal struggle over the preferential treatment of nonclassroom professionals built into the constitution and bylaws, but many of the leaders had come to feel that the perception of NTP domination of the organization had inhibited the recruitment of academic members and so were willing to compromise.[221] When presented to the Representative Council meeting in February 1973, however, the proposed constitution was rejected because there had not been adequate investigation of the costs and benefits of potential merger with AAUP and CSEA, as well as concerns for the representation of the nonclassroom personnel. The officers met again with the SUFT negotiation team and succeeded in getting a commitment that at the first Delegate Assembly of the merged organization, the first order of business would be entertaining amendments to the document that could address all doubts and concerns.[222] Two weeks later, at a special meeting of the Representative Council, it reversed itself and accepted the board's recommendation that the proposed merger be submitted to the membership for an advisory referendum. With 50 percent of those eligible responding, the Representative Council accepted the overwhelming advice of the membership, and on April 14 adopted the proposed constitution and bylaws of SUNY/United. The merger was accomplished and the first Delegate Assembly of the successor organization was held on May 14, to finalize the agreement and elect officers.[223]

SUFT members had an easier time of it. Early in the discussions of potential merger, its leaders had agreed on a few essential "non-negotiable demands" for the shape of a new organization. It saw itself as a "viable local" within SUNY, with SPA, the accredited bargaining agent, ruled by "an unacceptably undemocratic constitutional structure." When merger of the affiliates was completed, the AFT leaders believed that SPA would have to reorganize along the lines required by the new state organization or get out, losing its vital NEA subsidies and staff, paving the way for SUFT's ascendancy.[224] In March 1972, the board empowered the officers to pursue merger talks with SPA after the announcement of the UTNY-NYSTA merger. They dealt with the NTP question by asserting that "future distinctions between teaching and non-teaching professionals should be abolished" and that all members of both SUFT and SPA would be received into membership on an equal basis. On the local level, they insisted that new chapters be formed, with an executive committee composed of the officers of the merging chapters and new elections to be held within one year of merger.[225] SUFT negotiators never wavered from these commitments, giving them a strong basis for bargaining. Wesnofske continued to reach out to Robert Granger, SPA president, urging merger as in the "best interests of the SUNY staff" and expressing disappointment that earlier conversations had brought such negative responses. He insisted that "the increase in hostile and divisive attitudes" would fuel organizational competition and solidify attitudes among staff and members of both organizations that would harm the welfare of SUNY professionals.[226] He was particularly eager to begin discussions so that the SUNY representatives could carve out a positive place for themselves in the new statewide organization.

Negotiations began with SPA represented by Granger and Philip Encinio, executive director, and SUFT by Edward Wesnofske and Sam Wakshull. A draft document was proposed that was very much a compromise between the traditions and cultures of the two organizations. For example, it was agreed that the two wings of the professional staff would have proportional representation in the Delegate Assembly and that the two categories would be guaranteed a certain number of seats on the executive board, reflecting the concerns for NTP sensitivities.[227] SUFT appointed a Merger Implementation Committee on November 18, 1972, and sent the proposal to referendum on February 8 in conjunction with the ballot to elect delegates to the NYSUT Representative Assembly.[228]

Both parties came to the May 14 Delegate Assembly with proposals for constitutional amendments and slates of candidates.[229] Almost immediately political caucuses emerged. Although delegates from the SPA chapters far outnumbered those from SUFT, the demand for "one person, one vote" attracted many of the conservative SPA academics to the SUFT camp, resulting in an almost equal distribution of strength on the floor. Intense politicking, caucusing, and lobbying characterized every action the assembly took, from modifying the draft constitution to electing officers.

The modification of the proposed document with the greatest long-term significance proved to be efforts to strike down term limits for the executive board and the officers. According to Dorothy Gutenkauf, the first secretary to the new organization, agreement had been worked out before the meeting opened that the three-term restriction on elected representatives, a legacy of the NEA affiliation, would be eliminated on the floor. The appropriate motion dealing with the terms of Executive Board members was made and carried, but the assigned person who was supposed to introduce a parallel motion dealing with the officers failed to respond to the call from the chair. It was suggested that he was out in the hall politicking, so the constitution went into effect with no limitations on terms for Executive Board members, but a three-term restriction on the officers.[230]

The SPA nominee for president was the incumbent, Robert Granger. SUFT avoided an outright confrontation by placing in nomination a compromise candidate who had not been up front in the fierce struggle between the two rivals, Lawrence DeLucia, an economist from Oswego with impeccable academic credentials. DeLucia's most effective platform for winnowing away the support of SPA traditionalists was his insistence that consultation was the key to good labor-management relations. He won them over in that he found "jawing preferable to 'warring,' " with the result that he was elected by a comfortable margin. Some SPA leaders believed that he won because the SUFT people had "just done a better job of preparing," even though he was not perceived as a strong leader by most people.[231] It must be noted, however, that the fact that Granger was a nonclassroom professional contributed significantly to his defeat.

The SPA caucus recognized the impact of this first ballot defeat and proposed Fred Burelbach for vice president for academics. Burelbach was an extremely wise choice because he not only had strong academic credentials, but most important of all was a member of both organizations, a SPA activist and an officer of the SUFT chapter at the Brockport campus. His election set the tone for the rest of the day: cooperation and balance between the two camps to ensure success of the merger.[232]

The leaders of the two caucuses met behind closed doors, and it became apparent that the SUFT delegates could control the remaining elections and sweep all offices, denying the SPA wing any leadership role in the merged organization. But SUFT leaders "felt this was not a particularly good thing to have happen," so the two groups agreed to alternate the elections, with SUFT getting a slight majority.[233] A common slate for the remaining members of the Executive Board was proposed and duly elected. "Having come to the Assembly with twenty-six delegates, 'SUFT' had the better of the day."[234]

Although many of the early SPA activists would continue to be involved in the successor organization, SUNY/United (later United University Professions), original SUFT members would slowly emerge to dominate the leadership of the new organization. They frankly embraced collective bargaining as a positive good, clearly articulated their goals and objectives, and organized effectively to accomplish the agenda. SPA leadership always suffered from the fact that they were not fully committed to the often adversarial nature of collective bargaining and were uncomfortable with it when reality forced them to act like a "union."

Evaluation of SPA's Work

Partisan passions have clouded the effort to evaluate the contribution of the Senate Professional Association to the welfare of the faculty and professional staff of the university. First, the cachet that the organization's proximity to the traditional governance institutions of the academic world helped many reconcile themselves to collective bargaining, which, particularly for academic personnel, was extremely foreign but essential to their economic well-being. The coalition the SPA leaders forged with the nonclassroom personnel helped them begin to work effectively with the academic element of the unit, from which they had been historically alienated. It also eased the route to inclusion of the NTPs into governance on many campuses, a long-desired goal of the group. SPA negotiators established the framework for the establishment of clinical practice plans, which once they were up and running have operated successfully for more than three decades. In the process, they required local determination of the corporate structures and the democratic process in the selection of governing boards and operating procedures, once again preserving traditional academic governance ideals, all of which have been continued by UUP.

On the other hand, many SPA activists became involved mainly to block the ascendancy of the American Federation of Teachers locals and were extremely uncomfortable with the whole collective bargaining process. When reality forced them to act like a "union," they could not, and the first president resigned for that reason. As Herman Doh sadly commented after the merger: "Whatever the distinction between SPA and SUFT might have been in campaign rhetoric, it did not materialize as SPA proceeded with the work of representing the 15,000 SUNY professionals."[235]

The SPA partnership with the professionals was a mixed blessing. It led them to deny the fundamental democratic principle of one person, one vote, when they guaranteed one-quarter of the unit equal representation on all major committees, such as negotiations, causing serious problems for the organization down the line. Deference to the professionals' claim that the existing salary schedule, which included increases for each year of service up to a set maximum for rank, discriminated against them, SPA surrendered the schedule, leaving the members of the university unit as the only state employees with no raises when an impasse occurs and no recognition for longevity of service. Similarly, the negotiation of slightly more across the board for professionals was long remembered by academics; the retrenchment clause of the early agreements were extremely weak, giving little protection to endangered staff in times of financial stress. Finally, in establishing the original grievance procedures, SPA accepted a process that excluded the right to grieve "substance," something that had been achieved on several campuses and limited its operation to "technical" details.

After a series of false starts, representation battles, and seemingly endless internal disagreements, in 1973 SUNY faculty and professional staff formed a new complex organization. On its creation, the United University Professions was internally balkanized and scarred by past bargaining concessions and bitter internal battles. These conflicts would remain an important part of UUP's political culture for years to come. Indeed, SPA's give-back of salary schedules haunts the union to this day. But over the next several decades this nascent higher education union would gradually mature, transforming from an internally con-flicted organization of limited power and significance into the most formidable higher education union in the United States. The following chapters chronicle the evolution of UUP's growth.

Chapter 3

The Emergence of
United University Professions, 1973–81

SUNY academic and professional employees now had a new union, but that newly formed organization would face many challenges on its road to stability. The issue of representation was not fully resolved. Constituencies within the organization threatened to break from the parent group, and outside groups mounted representational challenges. New contracts and salary reopeners had to be negotiated by a union with minimal experience, and at the outset, with only a minority of members among those it represented. Clearly, increasing the membership would have to be a high priority. The union also faced inadequate budgets for the state university, as well as some significant retrenchment of staff. Additionally, there were internal disagreements over how the union should operate and who should run it; given those concerns, would there be orderly transitions of leadership? Over the next several years, the organization addressed these challenges with a fair amount of success and established its position as an effective advocate for its members.

Among the earliest problems that needed prompt attention by SUNY/United was its name, since the state objected to the use of "SUNY" by the union. A list of potential names was compiled, which was cleared by NYSUT's attorneys and the office of New York's secretary of state. At the July 13–14 meeting of the SUNY/United Executive Board, it was decided to recommend that the Delegate Assembly choose one of four names for adoption. At its October 12 meeting, the assembly passed a motion to change its name to United University Professions (UUP) and to amend its constitution and bylaws to reflect that change. The name officially became United University Professions on January 24, 1974, and the next month the Public Employment Relations Board (PERB) amended the union's certification to reflect the change in name from Senate Professional Association to United University Professions.[1]

Another issue that needed to be resolved as a result of the merger concerned dues. With UUP as the recognized bargaining agent, dues formerly paid to SPA and SUFT now needed to be remitted to UUP through payroll deduction. On May 31, 1974, UUP President DeLucia wrote to Melvin H. Osterman, Jr., who was the director of the State of New York's Office of Employee Relations (OER), requesting that the state "take such steps as may be necessary" to have payroll dues deductions for SPA and SUFT transferred to UUP.[2] Osterman notified the state's comptroller that this should be done.[3] At about the same time, UUP's executive director, Frederick J. Lambert, wrote to Leonard Kershaw, the OER assistant director, informing him that "UUP and the State of New York have an agreement on exclusivity of deductions," and that UUP is "taking the position that deductions for any organization other than UUP for members of the bargaining unit constitute a violation of our Contract."[4] UUP's bylaws had established that dues were to be 1 percent of each member's annual salary, with a maximum payment of $250; however, prior to the merger, SPA members were paying 0.9 percent of their annual salary in dues, and SUFT members paid dues at a flat rate of $91 a year. In a memorandum to chapter presidents, UUP secretary Dorothy Gutenkauf noted that while the dues increase to bring SPA members up to 1 percent was made shortly after the merger, "it has taken one year to convince the State to adjust dues for former SUFT members." Not only did this delay cause financial problems for UUP, it resulted, Gutenkauf pointed out, "in a situation which is absolutely unfair and inequitable." She informed the chapter presidents that the problem had been resolved, and that beginning June 27, 1974, "former SUFT members will be transferred by the State into UUP's deductions and the State will deduct dues at the correct rate of 1 percent."[5]

Unit Representation Problems

The merger of SPA and SUFT to form UUP would appear to have resolved the representation issues, but that was not entirely clear. There was a movement among the nonteaching professionals to split from UUP and to have separate representation. In July of 1973 a petition was being circulated to have the NTPs split from the academics, and also to be represented by the Civil Service Employees Association. A July 27 letter sent to members of the bargaining unit by Larry DeLucia and vice president for nonteaching professionals Patricia Buchalter urged that such a proposal needed "careful study and review." They admitted that these constituencies had "diverse concerns," but they did not agree "that cleaving professionals from teaching faculty is the best way to represent those concerns." They pointed out that by being represented by SUNY/United, "academics and professionals will not be competing with one another for the same pot of money as they would be if they were represented by two agents."[6] Also, to address the issue, the UUP Executive Board, at its August 11 meeting, unanimously passed a resolution proposed by Patricia Buchalter that "an Ad Hoc

Committee on NTP Concerns be established, to actively reflect the concerns of the non-teaching professionals within the unit, and to develop recommendations for action by the Executive Board, the Negotiating Committee, and other relevant committees."[7]

On August 31, CSEA filed a "Petition for Certification and Decertification" with the Public Employment Relations Board.[8] But since PERB had earlier (August 12, 1969) determined that the academic and NTP staff were to be considered a single unit, CSEA was informed by the state's director of public employment practices and representation, Paul E. Klein, that it would have to submit evidence to convince him "of the necessity for a hearing" on the matter.[9] Apparently, the submission was convincing enough for PERB to schedule a hearing. Klein notified CSEA, NYSUT, and OER that he had "determined that this affidavit does allege significant circumstances that have changed since the date of this Board's initial uniting decision, as well as other relevant facts not addressed during the earlier proceeding."[10] DeLucia announced Klein's ruling at the October 12 Executive Board meeting. Following DeLucia's announcement, a resolution was proposed that would have had UUP notify PERB that it did not object "to the formation of a separate bargaining unit within the University for those members of the professional staff of the University who do not hold academic rank or qualified academic rank." On request, DeLucia ruled that such a resolution would be in violation of UUP's constitution. A substitute resolution was introduced affirming that UUP "continue as an integrated bargaining agent for the State University professional staff, and particularly that United University Professions actively reaffirm its commitment to achieve equitable rights and benefits for all members of the professional staff of the State University." The substitute resolution received the overwhelming approval of the Executive Board.[11]

By December, the American Association of University Professors was involved in the unit determination case, having filed as an intervenor on December 6. In a memorandum to "AAUP Chapter Presidents in SUNY, and Other Interested Association Members," Martin Lapidus of AAUP's Northeastern Regional Office noted AAUP's intervention in this case, and stated, "Because of their different interests, the AAUP believes in the merit of separate units for faculty and the nonteaching professionals."[12] CSEA was optimistic that PERB would decide in favor of separate bargaining units,[13] but on January 21, 1974, the PERB hearing officer ruled "that CSEA has not sustained its burden of establishing that PERB's prior unit determination, made after extensive litigation, should be altered." CSEA's petition was "dismissed in its entirety."[14]

There also was an active group within SUNY's health sciences centers seeking separate bargaining status for those units. The health sciences centers claimed they were different than the other SUNY units because of "patient care around which exists a special time frame entailing year-round, twenty-four hour responsibility involving life and death situations." Moreover, it was argued because "clinical practice is an essential component of education in the health sciences it is neither possible nor desirable to separate patient care from educational programs," and this meant that the professional staff of those units were faced with "response times so compressed as to conflict with the normal administrative practices of a university."[15] In 1971 SPA had set up a separate negotiating unit for the health sciences centers,[16] but some members of these centers wanted to have a distinctive bargaining agent within UUP. A resolution from Stanley Goldstein, M.D., was submitted to UUP's Executive Board on June 4, 1973, requesting UUP to petition PERB "to create, for the Health Science and Medical Centers in the State University of New York, a separate bargaining unit for negotiations under the Taylor law," which would negotiate a contract "ratified by the membership in the Health Science Centers and Medical Centers separately from ratification of agreements for other segments of the SUNY/United bargaining unit." The resolution argued that the terms and conditions of employment at those centers were significantly different from those at other SUNY units, and could "be addressed only by individuals with an in depth comprehension of the mission, organization, and function" of those centers.[17] That resolution was discussed at the Executive Board meeting of July 14, and it was decided to "refer the resolution to the Negotiating Committee for study and report back to the Executive Board at the August meeting."[18] At that meeting Leland Marsh, reporting for the Negotiations Committee, noted that the committee failed to achieve a quorum at its last meeting and "suggested that since the meeting of the Board unanimously passed a strong unity resolution, there was no need for the committee to consider a resolution referred to it earlier considering separate negotiations for health sciences centers." The Executive Board resolution he referenced stated "that SUNY/United will immediately take all steps necessary to preserve a united collective bargaining unit," and that "an Ad Hoc Committee be established to implement this resolution."[19]

Meanwhile, the joint SPA-State committee, which had been established under Article 20 ("Medical and Dental Salary Review") of the 1971–74 *Agreement* with the State of New York (which was the union's contract), had reached a tentative agreement on May 31, 1973. The tentative agreement was sent to the membership of the medical centers for a vote. That vote turned out to be very close, and DeLucia was asked by the president of the Buffalo Health Sciences chapter to review the eligibility requirements and voting procedure for the ratification.[20] At the Executive Board meeting of September 14, a resolution to set aside that vote and carry out a new referendum was passed.[21] The ballots from this new referendum were counted on November 9, and the tally showed that 176 were in favor of ratification of Article 20 and 147 were opposed. The main opposition had come from the Downstate Medical Center.[22]

Although the July 14, 1973, Executive Board resolution made it quite clear that the union was serious about preserving bargaining-unit integrity,

John Valter, a member of the Stony Brook Health Sciences Center faculty, on behalf of the "Congress of the Health Sciences," wrote to Janet Axelrod of the Public Employment Relations Board on November 1, arguing that there should be a separate negotiating unit for employees of the health sciences centers. He maintained that in the opinion of the Congress of the Health Sciences, "the case for a separate unit is so pervasive as to be capable of resolution under far less formal circumstances than a hearing."[23] On the same day, he sent a copy of this letter to Lawrence DeLucia, stating that "both the Executive Board and the Negotiating Committee have declined to work out a mechanism under which the unique needs of the health sciences centers can be resolved by persons able to understand them."[24] DeLucia reported on this to the Executive Board at its November 10 meeting, whereupon the board went into executive session and decided to establish a special committee "to investigate the problems posed by the Valter inquiry to PERB, and to develop and recommend appropriate action to the Executive Board."[25] The recommendation came in the form of a motion submitted to the board at its January 1974 meeting, that the board "approve the principle of expanding those issues subject to negotiations (i.e., Article 20 and Article 38 [Health Sciences Centers]) previously negotiated for and by medical and dental faculty at the Health Sciences and Medical Centers to include all the personnel of those Centers." The motion carried.[26] Clearly, the Executive Board was concerned about the possibility of losing members at the health sciences centers, and at its May meeting it decided to forward to the Delegate Assembly a motion stating that that body authorized "representatives of the Health Science Centers, in the future, to engage in full, proper and independent negotiations on all issues peculiar to those centers, for all faculty members eligible for U.U.P. representation."[27] When that motion was brought to the floor at the May 1975 Delegate Assembly, it was passed unanimously.[28]

Still, the problems with the health sciences centers were far from over, and they continued to be prominent in the discussions of the Executive Board. At the October 25, 1974, meeting of that body, a motion was passed providing that the board set aside time at its December meeting "for discussion of the problems of the Health Sciences Centers," and "that the presidents of the four UUP Health Sciences Center chapters be invited to attend or to send a designee."[29] But on November 12, DeLucia was informed that a "caucus of UUP chapter leadership at the four Health Sciences Centers" considered "past and present arrangements" for their representation "undesirable and unrepresentative." Also, in the upcoming renegotiation of Article 29 [Clinical Practice], they insisted that only representatives from the health sciences centers be involved in the negotiations, and that only personnel from those centers be involved in all subsequent negotiations and ratification of any agreements affecting those centers. Further, they demanded that the union provide appropriate funding for those negotiators. DeLucia was informed that they "require a response from the Union Executive by November

20, 1974." DeLucia was told that if their conditions were not met, the centers "will not participate further in negotiations and will consider ourselves unrepresented."[30] The specifics of what the health science centers caucus wanted in Article 29 were never delineated; the issue was who would do the negotiation.

Earlier, on October 12, the UUP Negotiations Committee had adopted two motions: first, that "The Committee reaffirmed the constitutional mandate to serve as the sole vehicle of negotiations for the entire bargaining unit"; and second, that "Ratification of any agreement negotiated by UUP will be by the entire membership." Both these motions were adopted without dissent. When the committee met on November 14 and found out about the position of the health sciences center caucus, it passed a resolution deferring its decision to reopen negotiations on Article 29 "until such time as the Health Sciences Centers advise us further on the reaffirmation of our October 12, 1974 position, and clearly advise us on the propriety of reopening." In the spirit of compromise, they passed a second resolution resolving "to provide mechanisms for Health Sciences Centers" to have input into the negotiations on Article 29, should those negotiations take place. But on November 18, DeLucia was informed that the health sciences centers found the Negotiations Committee resolutions "unacceptable."[31] DeLucia informed Eli Friedman, the president of UUP's chapter at Downstate Medical Center, that if the health sciences centers wanted UUP to reopen negotiations on Article 29, they needed to inform him of that by the close of business on November 27.[32] The reason for that deadline was that UUP would have to notify the state no later than December 1 if they wanted to reopen negotiations, and the UUP office would be closed on November 29, the Friday after the Thanksgiving holiday. The health sciences centers representatives were to be meeting in Syracuse that Friday evening and Saturday morning to see if they could reach a consensus on the Article 29 reopener. UUP secretary Dorothy Gutenkauf agreed to have Friedman call her at home at the conclusion of the meeting on Saturday to let her know whether they wanted UUP to reopen the negotiations, and if they did, she agreed "to notify the State in a timely manner."[33] As promised, Friedman called her that Saturday, but informed her that the representatives from the health sciences centers wanted to delay the request to open negotiations until after the December 13 Executive Board meeting. She told them "that would be risky," since it was doubtful the state would agree to the extension, but they said they would take the risk. DeLucia contacted Melvin Osterman, Jr., the director of the Office of Employee Relations, who turned down the request for the delay. Gutenkauf called Friedman to tell him the request for delay had been denied, whereupon Friedman "stated definitely that they did not want to reopen." [34] At the December 12 meeting of the Negotiations Committee DeLucia informed the committee that "there will be no reopeners under Article 29 for the medical professional staff."[35]

In conformity with the resolution passed at the October Executive Board meeting, time was set aside at the December meeting to discuss the problems of the health sciences centers. Several members of the Upstate Medical Center were in attendance to make presentations on some of those problems. Following that, the board entered a protracted discussion of these issues and UUP's involvement. This discussion finally concluded at 1:00 a.m., although no formal action resulted.[36] At the May Executive Board meeting, however, a resolution concerning the role of the health sciences centers in negotiations was passed and sent on to the May Delegate Assembly, which also adopted it. That resolution provided that "negotiations on all issues affecting patient care be carried out by elected representatives of those centers with appropriate professional support. Agreements arising from such negotiations must be approved by a majority of those affected prior to inclusion in a master contract." To prevent any impact on university-wide issues, the Executive Board would appoint someone to monitor these negotiations.[37]

Negotiating Contracts

Not only did the fledgling union have to deal with challenges to its position as sole bargaining agent and with dissention within its own ranks, it faced a reopening of negotiations of salary, as provided by SPA's 1971–73 *Agreement* with the state. The union had asked for a 9 percent compensation increase, which would include 3 percent for cost of living, 3 percent per employee for "an equal service recognition sum," and 3 percent for the beginning of "a more equitable salary program." The state offered a package of 5 percent, which would be composed of 3.5 percent across the board and 1.5 percent for "merit increases at the discretion of the Chancellor." The two proposals were taken up by a PERB fact-finding panel, which on May 12, 1973, recommended that the compensation increase by 6.5 percent, of which 5 percent would be an across-the-board salary increase and the remainder would be a sum equal to 1.5 percent of the payroll "for the sole purpose of salary increases for meritorious performances."[38] Governor Nelson Rockefeller informed the state's legislature that he agreed with the panel's recommendation of 1.5 percent for merit and that he agreed with its denial of inequity salary increases, but perhaps reflecting his recent attempt to appear fiscally conservative, he did not agree with the recommendation of a 5 percent across-the-board increase; instead, he proposed a 3.5 percent increase.[39] For his part, DeLucia accepted the 5 percent across-the-board increase, as well as the additional 1.5 percent, although he stated that it "should be made available to each employee in the bargaining unit in an equal per capita amount." On the other hand, he disagreed with the panel on salary inequities, contending that "money should be made available to correct salary inequities within each rank."[40] Since the two sides could not agree, an impasse was declared, and the issue went before a select committee established by the state legislature. That committee held hearings at which it heard from both sides, and finally, on January 21, 1974, it recommended to Governor Malcolm Wilson an increase of 6 percent of payroll, with 4.75 percent allocated for across-the-board increases and 1.25 percent for "discretionary increases for meritorious performances." The increase would be retroactive to July 1 or September 1, 1973.[41] A bill was introduced in the legislature, and it was passed by the third week of March.[42] While the union was not satisfied with the final salary decision, DeLucia told the May 1974 Delegate Assembly that they could "take consolation in the fact that the OER felt that the final decision was a defeat to them."[43]

With the *Agreement between the State of New York and the Senate Professional Association* due to expire at the end of June 1974, UUP began to prepare for negotiating a new contract. On June 5, 1973, DeLucia informed Leland Marsh of the College at Oswego that the Executive Board had approved his nomination to be chair of the Negotiating Committee.[44] On July 31, Marsh informed the Negotiating Committee that its first meeting would be held on August 7 to deal with "organizational details and the ways in which the Negotiations Committee can best operate."[45] With the goal of strengthening SPA's position in negotiations, the union began a major drive to recruit new members on each campus.[46] DeLucia expected that negotiations with the state would begin somewhere around November 1, and he asked Marsh to have his committee come up with a final list of demands to be ready by October 25.[47]

On October 11 DeLucia wrote to the director of the Office of Employee Relations, Melvin Osterman, Jr., requesting that the collective bargaining process begin on October 31.[48] But Osterman was reluctant to proceed with negotiations while CSEA'S challenge to SPA's representation status was before PERB. He suggested, though, that "to expedite the negotiations when they do commence, we would be pleased to receive your demands in writing as soon as they are ready."[49] Not surprisingly, DeLucia did not agree with Osterman's position, pointing out that "SPA is the duly elected and duly recognized bargaining agent until June 30, 1974." The union was ready to negotiate, and he urged Osterman to meet "without delay."[50] Nonetheless, Osterman declined to meet with the union,[51] and the first negotiating session was not held until February 4, 1974, by which time the CSEA challenge had been dismissed by PERB.[52]

The expiring contract had few defenders within the union, and its negotiations team tried to win back some things it had lost under that contract. In particular, prior to unionization faculty received automatic salary increases tied to longevity, but the 1971–74 *Agreement* did not provide for a continuation of that practice. The union's negotiators tried to win back that longevity pay, but they were not successful.[53] They did manage to achieve a two-year contract that provided for a salary increase of 6.5 percent across the board, with another 0.75 percent for discretionary increases that would be awarded for merit and to correct inequities. For the second year of the contract the salary increase was to be 6 percent across the board, with an additional 0.75 percent for discretionary merit increases and 0.25 percent for discretionary correction of inequities. The union had wanted to have provisions for cost-of-living increases, as well as regional cost-of-living adjustments, but they failed to achieve them.

A very important goal for the union was to establish a system whereby NTPs could achieve permanent appointment, something academic employees already had. The union was successful in this. NTPs were now eligible for permanent appointment if they had completed seven years of service in the university and had been in their title for two years. If these criteria were met, the appointment would need to be recommended by the campus president and then approved by the chancellor.[54]

The *Agreement* did contain a retrenchment clause, which the AAUP was later to criticize as lacking a requirement that "the University demonstrate to the faculty that it is faced with a bona fide financial exigency which can only be met by termination of faculty." AAUP believed the definition of retrenchment was "overly broad," and it could be used by "a malevolently intentioned administration to undermine the principles of academic tenure."[55] Still, the union membership clearly was pleased with the contract, with 2,317 voting in favor of ratification and 547 against, a ratio, as DeLucia pointed out the union's Executive Board, of better than four to one.[56]

Internal Dissention

Not only did DeLucia have to deal with a contract, representation challenges, and controversy within the union's ranks, he had to contend with staffing problems. Shortly after the union's first Delegate Assembly in May 1973, executive director Philip Encinio notified DeLucia that he was resigning, effective September 5. By the end of that summer, the assistant executive director and the special assistant to the executive director also had resigned. Fortunately, DeLucia and Secretary Dorothy Gutenkauf were able to work out an arrangement with NYSUT to have Fred Lambert work with UUP as executive director on a temporary basis.[57] Gutenkauf maintained that without that "the outfit would not have survived."[58] DeLucia also ran into difficulties with some members of the union's leadership. In part, this was because the disagreements between the SPA and SUFT factions were not completely ended by the merger. Much of the opposition to DeLucia came from the former SPA people. But some complaints about DeLucia emerged. The UUP presidency was a full-time, salaried position, but since DeLucia commuted from Oswego, he was only in the union's office for part of the week.

Partly because of that, some felt he was not a very effective leader, and former Executive Board member Doris Knudsen, for example, considered him to be a "wishy-washy individual with no backbone."[59] Others were concerned about his having worked as an arbitrator for school district management.[60] Further, DeLucia became involved in a controversy with UUP treasurer Joseph Drew. In addition to serving as treasurer, Drew chaired the union's Budget Committee. At the September 15, 1973, Executive Board meeting, Drew had pointed out that holding both those positions was a potential conflict of interest, and so the next day DeLucia wrote to Drew relieving him of the Budget Committee position, and informing him that he had replaced him with Richard Hyse.[61] A few days later, Hyse sent a memorandum to the members of the committee stating that Drew had resigned and that DeLucia had appointed him to chair the committee, and that the scheduled September 28 meeting of the committee would be held.[62] But Drew did not accept DeLucia's decision, and sent his own memo to the Budget Committee members, asserting he was still chairing the committee, claiming that he hadn't resigned the position and contesting DeLucia's action because it did not have the approval of the Executive Board.[63] DeLucia held firm, informing Drew: "My letter of September 16, 1973, is to be implemented."[64]

Matters came to a head at the October 12 Executive Board meeting, when an attempt was made to include a resolution of no confidence in President DeLucia on the agenda. A roll call vote revealed that the board was split, and so the motion was defeated.[65] Nonetheless, it appeared that a motion for impeachment might come to the floor of the October Delegate Assembly. This was of great concern to the NYSUT leadership, and so NYSUT Vice President Dan Sanders appeared at the Delegate Assembly and convinced people that an impeachment vote would be disastrous for the fledgling union. He was successful, and impeachment never came up for a vote.[66] But DeLucia's time in office would soon come to an end. At its January 1975 meeting DeLucia notified that Executive Board that he would not be a candidate for election that May.[67]

A Change in Leadership

With DeLucia not running, Samuel Wakshull, from the College at Buffalo, who had been elected vice president for academics the previous year, ran unopposed. Nicholas Harding, from the Farmingdale campus, defeated incumbent secretary Dorothy Gutenkauf.[68] There had been some discontent with Gutenkauf. A number of union activists believed that part of the problem with DeLucia's administration was that he relied too much on her, and there were accusations that she had visited at least one campus while intoxicated.[69]

The fledging union that Wakshull took over was beset by many needs and problems. It had an inadequate staff and a membership that amounted to only a small proportion of the SUNY employees it represented. In his first few years in office, he had to deal with challenges from rival unions, retrenchment, and negotiation of a contract. Wakshull quickly negotiated with NYSUT to provide another staff member, and the person he brought in was Evelyn Hartmann, who was made UUP's director of staff. She went on to play a major role in most of UUP's activities, and she and Wakshull later were married.

Retrenchment

It did not take long before UUP's new administration was faced with probably its greatest challenge, and there was not much it could do about it. New York City's fiscal crisis in 1975 and its impact on the state led to financial belt-tightening. Governor Hugh Carey proposed a $10.69 billion budget, which was cut by the state legislature, so that the 1975–76 fiscal year budget passed in late March was for $10.4 billion.[70] On March 31 DeLucia informed the union's membership that the increase proposed for SUNY would not even cover half the inflationary increases. The union, he claimed, "together with New York State United Teachers, is working hard to restore all of these cuts in the supplemental budget, which will be considered by the Legislature after the current recess."[71] But although the legislature added another $38.7 million in the supplemental budget, no additional funds for SUNY or CUNY were included.[72] The result was staff retrenchments in both university systems. The City University of New York was faced with a very serious financial exigency, and was forced to reduce its staff substantially; in doing so, however, it did not retrench any tenured faculty. SUNY, on the other hand, faced with a no-growth budget rather than a reduced one, chose to include faculty on "continuing appointment" among those retrenched. Instead of reducing staff based on seniority, SUNY chose to eliminate some programs.[73] The rather open-ended definition of retrenchment in the 1974–76 *Agreement* permitted SUNY to take this course of action. Article 35 defined retrenchment as "the termination of the employment of any academic or professional employee . . . as a result of financial exigency, reallocation of resources, reorganization of degree, or curriculum offerings or requirements, reorganization of academic or administrative structures, programs or functions University-wide or at such level of organization of the University as a campus, department, unit, program or such level of organization of the University as the chancellor or his designee deems appropriate."[74] In fact, SUNY's vice chancellor for faculty and staff relations, Jerome B. Komisar, in a June 23, 1975, memorandum to campus presidents, informed them that the "decision to retrench and the determination of what programs and activities are to be reduced or ended rests with the campus president." Further, he noted that the *Agreement* provided "a great deal of discretion in deciding upon the campus organization to be retrenched."

In actuality, as an investigation undertaken by the New York State Assembly's Committee on Higher Education concluded, retrenchment resulted more from management's desire to maintain flexibility and to rid itself of troublesome units or individuals than from fiscal shortfalls.[75]

The retrenchments were most extensive at the State University at Albany, where the departments of Art History, Astronomy, Comparative and World Literature, and Speech Pathology were among those eliminated. At Stony Brook the School of Education was terminated, and several other campuses also lost programs and faculty.[76] This was, in the words of longtime UUP activist Edward Alfonsin, a "bloodbath."[77] The Assembly committee noted that the union "has acted as vigorously as possible . . . but there are severe limitations placed on it by the Taylor Law and the structure of the system."[78] Moreover, as Sam Wakshull later recalled, the only staff person UUP had at this time was Evelyn Hartmann.[79]

Membership Building

Building the membership was the primary goal of the early years of the Wakshull presidency; but it was very difficult. Academics in particular were hard to recruit as union members. Many saw themselves as individual entrepreneurs, whose fate was in their own hands. They believed that if they excelled in their scholarly fields and taught well they would be rewarded, and they did not need a union to advance in rank and salary. They saw themselves as perfectly capable of negotiating working conditions on their own. So while UUP was recognized by the state as their bargaining unit, many saw no reason to become members. The big breakthrough came in 1977, when legislation was passed requiring nonmembers to have a fee equal to union dues deducted from their paychecks.[80] Obviously, agency fee was important not only to UUP, but to all of the public employee unions. NYSUT was very active in pushing for passage of the bill, as were CSEA and other unions.[81]

Membership development was important not only to UUP, but to NYSUT. NYSUT saw higher education as its "greatest potential for increased membership" and so increasing UUP's membership would be one of its "top priorities."[82] A meeting of NYSUT staff with UUP's statewide officers and chapter presidents was held in Syracuse on April 29 and 30, 1977. A NYSUT staff member, Tony Ficcio, found that meeting to be "totally unproductive." Rather than fulfilling its purpose of working with UUP to develop a program to increase membership, he claimed it "turned out to be bullshit session concerning grievances and local problems." He saw the meeting to have been "very poorly organized," and to have had "no structure."[83] In July, Ficcio complained of a lack of cooperation with NYSUT in the membership campaign on the part on the part of Wakshull and Hartmann.[84] But by September Wakshull reported to the UUP Executive Board that due to the passage of agency fee legislation, the number of payers had tripled, and so "a massive organizing campaign, even beyond what had been contemplated for this fall, was being planned."[85] That plan met with some success, and by the end of November UUP reported that membership had increased by 2,000 and stood at more than 6,000 members in a unit of approximately 14,000.[86] Wakshull claimed that some of this growth came because they "were taking on the grievances," and they "were showing people that we really were interested in doing things, and we would communicate it with them. We started putting out a newspaper which went out once a month." They also made an effort to visit the campuses.[87] Doris Knudsen, who served as a NYSUT field representative assigned to UUP, recalled that signing up members was "essentially what I attempted to do. And I think that that was the major charge of every single rep that was hired at that time." They worked not only to sign members, but to make them committed members.[88] By May 11, 1978, membership had grown to 7,800.[89]

Challenges to Representation

Organizing was especially important because UUP was facing potential challenges as a bargaining unit. The relationship between NYSUT and NEA had not been very cordial, and when NEA began promoting itself in New York and also pressuring NYSUT to adopt the secret ballot (which was the practice with NEA, but not with NYSUT), the relationship worsened. NEA began to lure staff members from NYSUT and set up rival offices at several locations in the state. By March of 1976 NYSUT had essentially disaffiliated from NEA, and UUP did the same a month later.[90] The possibility of NEA challenging UUP's bargaining rights was of some concern, and there were indications that it was a distinct possibility. On October 8 of 1976, Wakshull informed the Delegate Assembly that UUP had not received any official notification of such a challenge, but a challenge would have negative consequences no matter what the outcome. He stressed that "Nobody wins in such a situation . . . except the State."[91] But by January, NEA officially began its challenge of UUP as the bargaining agent, and they had mailed signature cards to all members of the unit.[92] Further, NEA had made overtures to AAUP about sharing bargaining rights.[93] In February another challenge began as the Faculty Senate on the Stony Brook campus endorsed a petition from the "Stony Brook University Professional Association" to split the university centers from the rest of SUNY for the purposes of negotiation. That petition was distributed to other university-center senates to solicit their support. Soon after Wakshull got wind of this, he wrote to Donald Wollett, director of the New York State Office of Employee Relations, and demanded that "all State funding of the [Stony Brook] faculty senate cease without delay, as otherwise the State would be guilty of financially supporting a union." He further demanded that "appropriate action be taken against the faculty senate for their use of State stationery and services in carrying out their union activities." Lastly, he demanded "that the faculty senate be disbanded as presently constituted, since otherwise the State would be condoning a union conducting its business under the guise of governance."[94] In the next few days he wrote to Wollett to protest making any campus facilities available to AAUP or to NEA, "for to do so would be recognizing a competing union during the period when we are the exclusive agents of the bargaining unit in question."[95] And when Wakshull was informed that the Faculty Senate at the University at Buffalo would be using one of their meetings "for the purposes of discussing formation of, as well as endorsing, a competing union," he wrote to Wollett demanding that the Buffalo Senate be disbanded.[96] Not surprisingly, neither of those Faculty Senates were disbanded, but Wakshull was on record defending UUP's exclusive bargaining rights.

On April 4 a letter went out to SUNY faculty informing them that an organization had been formed, known as the SUNY AAUP Representation Committee (SARC), which had "only one purpose: to replace the United University Professions, Inc. as the official bargaining representative in the SUNY system." They argued that UUP had signed very bad contracts, and the latest one permitted "the violation of virtually every major AAUP principle." They asked people to join with them to help lay the groundwork for a representation challenge, and hopefully to contribute money.[97] Evelyn Hartmann reacted to this letter by writing to Leonard Kershaw, who was OER's assistant director, pointing out that the authors of the letter had listed their university phone numbers as a way to contact them. She stated that UUP questioned "the propriety of allowing state phones to be used for AAUP matters." She insisted that Kershaw's office "advise all SUNY AAUP leadership involved that AAUP activities are not to take place on campuses as UUP is the legal bargaining agent."[98] A few days later she again wrote to Kershaw complaining that the New York Higher Education Association (NYHEA, the NEA division formed in New York to try to become the SUNY bargaining agent) had been scheduling organizing meetings on the Canton and Potsdam campuses, and demanded that OER see to it that similar events were "not repeated anywhere in the University."[99] Protesting letters from Wakshull and from Hartmann to Kershaw continued to be written whenever UUP learned that AAUP was scheduling on-campus meetings.[100] Finally, in late September of 1977, these letters appear to have made some impact. Kershaw sent a letter to Jerome Komisar, vice chancellor for faculty and staff relations at SUNY, asking for his "cooperation and assistance in insuring that State University facilities are not approved" for an AAUP-sponsored roundtable scheduled to be held at the University at Buffalo on September 27.[101]

In December 1977 and January 1978 the possibility of a merger between AAUP and UUP was being floated, and on February 29 Wakshull sent a proposed merger agreement to AAUP general secretary Morton S. Baratz.[102] On March 10

Wakshull reported this to the UUP Executive Board, but stated that he had not yet received a response.[103] He did hear from Baratz on April 18, who informed him that "any joint venture in SUNY must be discussed on its own merits, not as part of an affiliation between AAUP and AFT at the state or national level." Baratz went on to insist that a new organization would have to be created, which would be "organized as SUNY is organized, with autonomous subunits for the colleges, for the university centers, for the agricultural and technical colleges, and for the medical center." Furthermore, those "subunits must retain a substantial portion of the dues income."[104] These, of course, were conditions that ran counter to UUP's stated positions. Nonetheless, Wakshull informed the Executive Board on May 5 that a "meeting was scheduled for 15 and 16 May with AAUP representatives to discuss a possible merger."[105] The meeting did not prove fruitful, though. On June 3 Wakshull informed the Executive Board that the talks had broken up, since "AAUP representatives had pressed demands which they said were 'non-negotiable.' "[106]

In May UUP had commissioned Louis Harris and Associates to conduct a poll of SUNY staff members concerning their preference for a bargaining agent. UUP emerged as the first choice, but was favored by only 33 percent of the responders. The runner-up was "no bargaining agent at all" with 21 percent; AAUP was favored by 13 percent and NYEA by 11 percent; and 22 percent indicated they were uncertain how they would vote. This was especially significant since UUP only had a 12 percent advantage over those who favored no bargaining agent.[107]

By August, NYEA had filed a petition with PERB to decertify UUP as the bargaining agent for the SUNY Professional Services Negotiating Unit, claiming that "A majority of employees within the unit desire representation by petitioner."[108] A few days later, the UUP/NYSUT Strategy Team received a "Confidential Campaign Overview" from Charles Baker and Associates. It concluded that the no-bargaining-agent choice was a serious threat, and that a barrier must be kept between NYEA and AAUP, pointing out that "AAUP's 13%, if allied with NYEA's 11%, could produce a formidable contender." The advice was to "do an intense job of acquainting SUNY employees with UUP accomplishments and services" and to "project UUP as an open, democratic organization in the process of change"[109] (emphasis in original).

In September, the Steering Committee of NYEA's Organizing Committee sent a letter to Wakshull pointing out that hearings before PERB might be prolonged, and that would delay contract negotiations. They proposed that "instead of either of our organizations using the negotiations process as a campaign ploy, we join together and form a joint negotiations team to bargain with the State." They indicated that they intended to make that proposal public,[110] which they did in a September 15 letter to SUNY staff. They argued that while there probably were "people at UUP itself who welcome the NYEA/NEA offer," UUP was not really self-governing; rather, "major decisions are all made by someone outside UUP: by Albert Shanker, the New York City teacher-union leader who is also a vice president of the national AFL-CIO."[111] Clearly, NYEA was convinced that many SUNY staff had negative feelings about Shanker and his New York City connection, and that they would not want to think of themselves as traditional union members. Charles Baker advised that UUP not respond directly to the NYEA letter, but rather call for a bargaining-unit election to be held before the end of the year, so that the bargaining process could proceed.[112] On September 21, UUP put out a press release stating that the Delegate Assembly "unanimously adopted a resolution calling for 'the earliest possible' representation election." The release quoted Wakshull as having said, "We have just been informed by PERB that the formal hearing scheduled for Friday, September 22, has been postponed indefinitely. I am extremely concerned that such delays will have a harmful ripple effect, in that we cannot begin negotiations with the State on a new contract until after the representation election has been held and the matter of who the bargaining agent is has been determined."[113] The goal was for having the election before the end of the year, and ballots were to be mailed out in December.[114]

But in October, UUP learned that NYEA/NEA wanted to be designated on the ballot as "NYEA/NEA SUNY as endorsed by AAUP." Wakshull forcefully objected to that designation in an October 31 letter to Harvey Milowe, who was director of public employment practices and representation at PERB. He objected to this for several reasons. Not only was "NYEA/NEA" the "organization that had petitioned for the challenge," it was also the organization designated on the authorization cards seeking an election. Moreover, he pointed out that "the official acronym of the State University of New York is SUNY and therefore inappropriate for any organization other than that agency." (Indeed, that was the reason "SUNY United" had to change its name to "United University Professions.") Lastly, he claimed that "any endorsement statement is a campaign statement and totally inappropriate for a voting ballot." In conclusion, he insisted "that the challenger be notified that the appropriate official name on the ballot [be] the name under which they petitioned for a challenge and solicited cards and that being the name NYEA/NEA."[115] The state agreed with Wakshull's argument, and the Governor's Office of Employee Relations notified PERB that they objected to NYEA/NEA's requested designation on the ballot as "wholly inappropriate."[116]

Albert Shanker, in his "Where We Stand" column in the November 19 *New York Times*, urged that when SUNY faculty vote for a bargaining agent "they would do well to push aside the campaign slogans and the instant political promises." The only question they should ask is "which organization has the size know-how and power at the state and national levels to prevent disaster and bring about needed improvement—the miniscule NYEA or the UUP, backed up by the NYSUT, AFT and the 14 million-member AFL-CIO?"[117] A few days later, *New York Times* writer Damon Stetson reported on the upcoming bargaining agent vote at SUNY. He pointed out that for NEA a victory would provide "a major thrust in its effort to expand its representation among professors and non-teaching professionals at colleges and universities nationally." A NYEA representative claimed that there was "general frustration with United University Professions as bargaining agent," which negotiates a single contract for all of SUNY, while NYEA had "put out a model for decentralized bargaining." For UUP and AFT, Stetson noted, "the election is a critical challenge to past performance and future potential." UUP claimed that "the salary increases negotiated this year were the highest ever negotiated for the State University staff," and a UUP spokesperson pointed out that "locals affiliated with the American Federation of Teachers now bargain for more faculty members at both four-year and two-year institutions than the combined totals represented by the National Education Association and the American Association of University Professors at such institutions."[118] On the day before the ballots were to be mailed, Shanker again commented on the impending election in his "Where We Stand" column. He maintained that "New York State is spending a disproportionate share of public tax dollars to support private colleges and universities and is not giving enough to CUNY and SUNY," and argued that a vote by the professional staff to retain UUP as their bargaining agent "will put them in the best position to join with the Professional Staff Congress at CUNY for an effective battle to restore the proper balance between private and public higher education in New York."[119]

On December 23 the *New York Times* reported the election results: UUP received 6,067 votes, NYEA 4,092, and 1,156 voted for no union. Wakshull, of course, was delighted with the election results, "but he said that the long campaign by his group in its successful effort to retain its representation rights had taken its toll in time and energy, which could best have been devoted to serving faculty members and nonteaching professionals in the State University system." UUP now could concentrate on negotiating a new contract.[120]

Considering that UUP won a substantial victory in this election, how serious had NYEA's challenge been? Reflecting on this years later, some who were in UUP leadership at the time argued that there was a strong possibility that NYEA might win the election; others disagreed, but expressed the view that UUP had to act as though the threat was serious.[121] There certainly had been some discontent with several of UUP's positions and sympathy with some of the views expressed by NYEA, but as Paul Lauter recalled, "what was decisive was that after a while . . . we might not agree with a lot of what NYSUT was really committed to but whatever else was true, NYSUT was strong."[122] Whatever the reasons for the UUP victory, longtime UUP activist Harvey Inventasch, who was present at the vote count, recalled, "We felt very good about it." He pointed out that the substantial vote margin "really strengthened our hand for the next negotiations, allowed us to go out now to the membership or to the bargaining unit and indicate that those who had voted for us now ought to join as well."[123]

Negotiating Contracts

During these many months of representation challenges, UUP had been faced with negotiating a new contract. The *Agreement with the State of New York* that had been negotiated during Lawrence DeLucia's presidency was due to expire at the end of June 1976. Wakshull asked Harvey Inventasch, a professor at the SUNY College at Cortland, to chair the negotiations committee. Inventasch agreed, but he declined to be the chief spokesperson for the union at the negotiations. That role was assumed by Evelyn Hartmann, and she and Inventasch worked very closely together. Both Inventasch and Edward Alfonsin considered her to be a good choice, since she had contract-negotiation experience and was, according to Alfonsin, "a strong speaker in just about any forum." Inventasch recalled that he had an "excellent team," and he particularly singled out SUNY Binghamton economics professor Morris Budin as being "outstanding." Budin, he claimed, could "cut through the financial nonsense to whatever the important matters are and be able to see and project them very easily."[124]

UUP had established an Advisory Committee to the Negotiations Committee, and on October 17, 1975, Inventasch sent a memorandum to all chapter presidents to remind them of a meeting of the Advisory Committee in Syracuse on October 25. He also reminded them that each campus was "to select two representatives (one academic and one NTP) to attend the meeting to submit in writing to the Negotiations Committee any suggested changes of, additions to, and/or deletions in contract language for forthcoming negotiations." UUP had not devised a uniform method for directly soliciting membership input concerning contract issues; rather, that was left to the individual chapters. Inventasch's memorandum stated, "We trust that as President of the Chapter, you have set up the means by which Chapter members can give their input to their representatives to the Advisory Committee."[125]

The Office of Employee Relations also had established an advisory committee to its negotiators. The SUNY Negotiations Advisory Committee was composed of vice presidents, deans, and other administrators from throughout the SUNY system. That committee held its first meeting on October 7, 1975, to discuss the negotiating process and the role it would play in that process. Among other tasks, the committee would develop management proposals and review and analyze union demands.[126] A second meeting was scheduled for November 3, the purpose of which was to discuss the "most frequently addressed areas of managerial concern." These were continuing and permanent appointment, job security review procedures, retrenchment, personnel files, retirement age, leave provisions, and notice of nonrenewal.[127]

The first negotiations meeting between OER and UUP took place on December 16, and the OER contract proposals were presented at that meeting.

The state's proposals clearly were unacceptable to UUP. The UUP Negotiations Bulletin pointed out that there was no salary proposal, and the state wanted "continuous administrative review and evaluation of all tenured academics," "parking fees for all employees," a requirement that academics "work on campus during instructional recesses," and that professional employees' vacation leave would be "at the discretion of and with the approval of the campus President," among other demands (emphasis in original).[128] The state was presented with UUP's initial negotiating demands at a meeting on January 14, 1976.[129] As expected, several issues were contentious from the start. Basic to any agreement is the issue of employee salary. UUP, of course, proposed an increase in direct compensation, but rather than asking for an across-the-board percentage increase in pay, UUP had put forward a plan for specific dollar amount increases to July 1, 1976, salaries, with those at the lowest compensation levels receiving the largest increases.[130] The union also proposed that the state assume 100 percent of the cost of medical and dental insurance for employees and their families, and that librarians be converted from calendar-year obligations to academic-year obligations, without reduction in salary. The state rejected these and other increases associated with payroll, claiming that to accept them would result in a payroll increase of 81 percent.[131] Another contentious issue was that of retrenchment. UUP wanted to at least modify some portions of the state's retrenchment clause (Article 35) proposal concerning reasons for retrenchment, prior notification of retrenched employees, and length of period of eligibility for reemployment after retrenchment, among other provisions. Also related to job security were the union's demands for more extensive reviews of negative recommendations for reappointment, continuing appointment, or promotion.[132]

The state's negotiators were playing hardball, however, and by May 1976 little progress had been made. On May 4, NYSUT's director of field services, James Conti, met with UUP leadership to develop a plan to move the bargaining process forward. One element of that plan was to call for picketing on SUNY campuses at various times. Conti instructed NYSUT's field representatives who had higher education responsibilities to work with UUP chapter presidents to plan and help with picketing.[133] Still, when interviewed in 1990, Wakshull claimed that NYSUT tried to discourage UUP from picketing. He claimed that NYSUT was fearful that too few people would show up for the picketing, and also that they were much more concerned with K–12 issues.[134] But UUP's contract was to expire on June 30, and it was clear that a new one could not be in force by then. What would happen then? SUNY Chancellor Ernest L. Boyer consulted with Donald H. Wollett, director of the Governor's Office of Employee Relations, who informed him that "the provisions of the 1974–76 Agreement between the State of New York and United University Professions . . . will remain in effect until we are otherwise notified." On June 29 Boyer notified campus presidents of that ruling, and he also informed them, "As in the past, where the provisions of the agreement are different from the provisions of the Policies of the Board of Trustees, the provisions of the agreement shall be controlling."[135]

By the end of October it appeared that progress was being made on some issues, especially those related to personnel files and special consideration for retrenched employees. By the October 28 negotiations session, UUP hoped that a conclusion to the process was near, but at that meeting the state presented a revised retrenchment proposal and a money proposal. The latter included something UUP had been requesting for some time—a fourth academic rank for librarians, although with no money attached to it. After a three-hour caucus, the union's negotiators returned with a counterproposal. The state's team then caucused for some time, and returned to inform UUP that they were withdrawing their offers for a fourth rank for librarians and for minimum salaries.[136] In a negotiations update, Wakshull informed UUP's members that the state negotiators then walked out, with the parting words that they had "negotiated to a conclusion and that's it." No further bargaining sessions were scheduled, but UUP intended "to press on in our efforts to negotiate an acceptable contract."[137] UUP staged demonstrations and informational picketing on most campuses, and several thousand signatures were collected on petitions supporting the UUP negotiations team. The union also tried to enlist state legislators to apply pressure to OER to resume negotiations. UUP was successful in convincing Senator Ronald B. Stafford to write a letter to OER director Donald Wollett requesting that OER make every effort to bring contract negotiations to a conclusion. Finally, it was agreed that bargaining sessions would resume on January 7, 1977.[138] This round of negotiations was successful, and on March 11 Wakshull announced that the *Agreement* had been ratified, with more than 69 percent of the votes cast for approval.[139]

While UUP, obviously, did not achieve all its goals, there were some significant gains for the union in the 1977–79 *Agreement*. A fourth academic rank for librarians was agreed on, and minimum salaries for each rank were established. Some limitations were imposed on the nature of materials that could be placed in an employee's personnel file, and employee access to those files was broadened. The retrenchment article in the contract had engendered a considerable amount of discussion at the bargaining table. In the final agreement, management still retained considerable flexibility, with retrenchment being defined essentially as it was in the previous contract, as "the termination of the employment of any academic or professional employee during any appointment, other than a temporary appointment, which may be terminated at any time, as a result of financial exigency, reallocation of resources, reorganization of degree or curriculum offerings or requirements, reorganization of academic or administrative structures, programs or functions or curtailment of one or more programs or functions University-wide or at such level of organization of the University as a College, department, unit, program or such other level of organization of the University as the chancellor, or his designee, deems appropriate."Nonetheless, UUP did manage to expand the provisions determining the order of retrenchment of employees. It increased the recommended time for notification of retrenchment for those holding permanent or continuing appointments from one semester to two and won a requirement that such notification be sent to the affected individual by certified mail stating the reasons for retrenchment, with a copy to be sent to the local UUP chapter president. Clauses dealing with special consideration for placement of retrenched employees within the university and for reemployment were also expanded.[140]

As with all union contracts, the provision for salary increases was of paramount importance to the union's members. Past salary increases had come as an across-the-board percentage increase paid to all employees, but this meant that employees earning larger salaries received more money than those on lower salaries, increasing the monetary gap between lower earners and higher earners. UUP, as has been noted, proposed larger dollar amounts for the lowest paid and smaller amounts for the highest paid. While Article 20 (Direct Compensation) of the *Agreement* did not go that far, it did provide that lower-paid employees would receive salary increases that represented a higher percentage of their base salaries than did those at the top.[141] As it turned out, this displeased those at the higher levels, who thought they should have received more, while those at the lower levels complained they did not get enough. This method of distributing increases was never attempted in subsequent contracts.[142] When interviewed in 1990, Nuala Drescher, who had served as a president of UUP, maintained that this was a good contract, and that the method of allocating salary increases was "long overdue." Still, she noted that "it was not popular because everybody didn't get the same."[143] Those who were unhappy with this arrangement could hope that things would change the following year, since Article 20 provided that UUP could reopen negotiations on salary for the next year of the contract by notifying the state of its desire to do so by November 1, 1977.

UUP did notify the state of its desire for a negotiations reopener, and the first meeting was held on November 15, 1977. At that meeting UUP proposed that the basic annual salaries of those holding positions in the negotiating unit as of June 30, 1978, should be increased by 15 percent. The proposal also included minimum salaries for all academic and professional ranks.[144] At the next meeting, on December 7, the state claimed that UUP's salary demands would cost the state $43.5 million, but UUP contested that figure.[145] By the third meeting the state offered its proposal, which would provide for a 4 percent across-the-board increase, with an additional 2 percent "to be distributed in the discretion of the State University Trustees." The offer on salary minima was significantly lower than that proposed by UUP, and the state's proposal was not acceptable to UUP.[146] At a subsequent meeting, the state argued that UUP's proposal was unreasonably high, while that offered by the state was in line with previous settlements with UUP. The union maintained that the state's offer was unacceptable—the percentage increase was too low, and the discretionary portion was too high, while the salary minima also were too low. In a January 25, 1978, memorandum to bargaining unit members, UUP claimed that the state "has refused to add one single penny to its original salary offer, even though the union reduced its own proposal in hopes of spurring the talks."[147] The sides remained far apart, and when Inventasch presented the Negotiations Committee report to the Delegate Assembly on February 4, he pointed out that before there could be any agreement on discretionary money there would have to be a satisfactory addition to an across-the-board increase. He also pointed out that a recess in negotiations had been called.[148] Negotiations meetings resumed on February 22, but while UUP had reduced its salary increase demand to 13 percent, the state still found that unacceptable. The March 8 meeting appeared to show some motion. UUP's chief negotiator, Evelyn Hartmann, reported that " 'for the first time since the talks began, four months ago, the State is beginning to change its position. It is too early to say that the State is prepared to make a reasonable offer . . . but things are finally starting to open up.' "[149] But that was not to be. Negotiations dragged on through April, and although UUP reduced its salary demand, both sides remained far apart.[150] Union members were frustrated, and at the Spring Delegate Assembly a resolution was proposed by the Oneonta Chapter calling for the recall of the negotiating team and its chief negotiator and replacing them with "a new and competent team led by a professional negotiator." The resolution was tabled.[151] Not only were UUP's negotiators convinced that the state's proposal for an across-the-board increase was too low, they were especially concerned about the amount the state wanted to be available for discretionary money. Moreover, the union was convinced that doling out discretionary money presented a strong possibility for abuse, and they wanted safeguards to minimize that. Things remained stalemated, and by mid-May UUP sent a telegram to Governor Hugh Carey "alerting him to the situation," and chapter presidents were "alerted to the possibility of special action if we do not shortly get the bargaining back on course."[152] After many sessions during which offers and counteroffers were exchanged, agreement finally was reached during the twenty-third negotiations meeting, which took place on June 7 and 8, 1978. The package provided for a 6.5 percent across-the-board salary increase, an additional 1 percent "to be distributed in the discretion of the State University Trustees," and a 1.5 percent across-the-board increase on March 1, 1979. Salary minima were to be: professor, $19,500; associate professor, $15,000; assistant professor, $12,000; and instructor, $10,000. There was a similar scale for librarian ranks. A guideline for the distribution of discretionary money was included, but it was rather weak: "Upon the request of a department or professional area committee, the President or his designee will meet to discuss the criteria upon which the President based his recommendation to the Chancellor for discretionary increases."[153] Still, Sam Wakshull saw this as " 'a breakthrough for accountability on discretionary increases.' "[154] The wage settlement was submitted to the membership for ratification, and it was approved by 93.2 percent of the votes.[155]

But it was not long before UUP would be back at the bargaining table, this time to begin negotiations for an agreement to cover the years 1979–82. On January 19, 1979, Wakshull wrote to Meyer S. Frucher, the director of the Governor's Office of Employee Relations, to request a negotiations meeting on February 28, and Frucher agreed to that date.[156] But by April 6, Negotiations Committee Chair Harvey Inventasch reported to UUP's Executive Board that while the "atmosphere in session with the State is cordial and business-like," there had yet "been no money proposals . . . submitted by the State."[157] Talks continued to move slowly, and on May 10 a UUP "Leadership Bulletin" pointed out that there were "only seven weeks left in the current UUP contract," and that the UUP negotiating team was "unhappy about the rate of progress in current negotiations." It reported that talks were "bogged down over several issues, among them uncertainty on the part of the State about exactly who should or should not be in the bargaining unit."[158] Concerned about the lack of progress, Wakshull complained to the governor's office and the Office of Employee Relations. By the end of the month things began to move rapidly, with the UUP Negotiations Team and the state entering round-the-clock sessions, and Wakshull was able to "report tentative agreement on a large number of articles."[159] On Friday, June 1, negotiations were completed and a "tentative agreement on a new contract" was reached. This was to be a three-year contract that provided for a 7 percent across-the-board salary increase in the first year, plus an additional discretionary increase of 1 percent of the payroll. For the second and third years there would be a maximum 7 percent salary increase, "gauged to the rate of inflation." Other features included a new tuition assistance program, improved medical and maternity benefits, and a "retraining fund to assist employees whose jobs may be affected by reductions in force."[160] On June 7 a special meeting of UUP's Executive Board was called to inform that body of the details of the tentative agreement. The Negotiations Committee already had recommended a "yes" vote by the union's membership, and the Board now made the same recommendation.[161]

Still, there was some opposition to the contract. On July 3, a letter was sent to bargaining unit members by Sharon Villines, chairperson of the SUNY Alliance Steering Committee. The SUNY Alliance claimed to be "Endorsed and Supported by NYEA, NEA and the SUNY-AAUP Representation Committee (SARC)." She stated that the SUNY Alliance "analysis of the UUP contract and the reactions of SUNY academics and professional faculty continue to emphasize the need for an alternative organization. It is clear that UUP has again failed to obtain significant contract improvements." The contract, she asserted, contained "almost no major non-economic benefits and fewer economic benefits than other OER-negotiated agreements."[162] But her letter seems not to have garnered much support for her organization's position. The votes were counted on July 10, and 73 percent favored approval.[163]

Advocating for SUNY Funding

From the founding of UUP, one of the union's greatest concerns was the state's budget, and especially the portion allocated for the state university. UUP recognized that it was important to interact with the state's legislature, and as early as July 1973 its Executive Board passed a resolution to have the chairman of the Legislation Committee register as a lobbyist and pay the requisite $5 fee.[164] Hoping to have a friend in the governor's office, in September 1974 the Delegate Assembly overwhelmingly passed a resolution endorsing Congressman Hugh Carey for governor and state senator Mary Ann Krupsak for lieutenant governor.[165] But as noted earlier, New York City's fiscal crisis led to the state's legislature cutting Carey's proposed budget. It was clear that UUP needed to take an even stronger position in advocating for funding for SUNY.

Despite UUP's endorsement, Carey did not turn out to be a staunch supporter of SUNY. After studying the executive budget proposed in January 1977, Wakshull, in a memorandum to chapter presidents, the Executive Board, and the Legislation Committee, noted that it showed "how serious the Governor is in diminishing the State University of New York." He pointed out, however, that the budget "is not final and is in a sense, a negotiating document between the Executive and the Legislature." UUP, he stated, intended "to impact the Legislature to save the SUNY system." To begin, he asked for four people from each chapter to come to Albany on the evening of Monday, February 28, and remain through Tuesday afternoon, to lobby for the SUNY budget and also for a statutory tenure bill.[166] At the February 5 meeting of the Delegate Assembly, the chair of the Legislation Committee said that the "top priority" items on the program for the March 1 "Legislative Day" would be the statutory tenure bill and restoration of cuts to the SUNY budget.[167] It is not clear what impact UUP's efforts had on March 1, but Wakshull thanked those who attended, and he remarked that: "This was only the first step in establishing UUP as a recognizable political force for public higher education."[168]

State budget allocations for SUNY remained a concern. In his report to the UUP Executive Board on February 1, 1979, Wakshull expressed his concern of possible retrenchments, and he reported that he already had contacted SUNY's administration about that. Another worrisome item was a proposal to increase funding for private colleges. Wakshull told the board that he had already met with the chairs of the higher-education committees of the state's Assembly and Senate.[169] Reporting to the Fall Delegate Assembly on lobbying activities for 1978–79, John O'Neil, chair of the Legislation Committee, noted that UUP's "Lobby Day" was attended by "nearly one hundred chapter volunteers—our most successful effort yet." He told the delegates that the principal area of concern was funding for SUNY, but next in importance was the state's support for private colleges, known as Bundy Aid, "and our plan to ward against it." The Legislation Committee "realized the near impossibility of eradicating Bundy Aid," and so it proposed having it "administered and awarded on a basis of equity." Bundy Aid was distributed to private colleges based on the number of degrees they granted. As a result, some colleges and universities would try to attract transfer students from SUNY and CUNY schools, for which they would receive full Bundy Aid when they graduated from those private institutions. UUP proposed having Bundy Aid "granted on a pro rata basis, so that a qualifying institution would receive aid only for that prorated part of the student's degree preparation for which the institution was directly responsible (years of full-time attendance)."[170]

On November 27, 1979, Michael Finnerty, deputy director, Division of the Budget, wrote to SUNY chancellor Clifton R. Wharton, Jr., informing him that the SUNY staff was to be reduced by 475 positions by June 30, 1980.[171] Wharton replied that this position reduction would be "devastating," and would make "program reduction and personnel retrenchment totally unavoidable." He pointed out to Finnerty that "the University cannot be viewed as a single unit with a 32,000 person work force, all performing similar interchangeable tasks and easily reassigned from one campus to another or from one department to another on the same campus." "What is extremely aggravating," he exclaimed, "is that in 1980–81, Bundy funding will go up by $20 million and TAP funding by some $13 million for previous commitments to funding increases for private sectors of higher education, and there will be no reconsideration of the $33 million decision, while the State agencies, including State University, continue to be reduced." SUNY was "willing to take a 260 job freeze and a funding reduction, with that eventually becoming permanent by September 1980," but did "not see any possibility of a 475 job reduction." Wharton asked for a "reconsideration of this cut level."[172] Sam Wakshull concurred with the chancellor's position on staff reductions. In a December 19 letter to Governor Carey, he referred to Wharton's letter, and added, "I am bewildered at the suggestion of the D.O.B. [Division of the Budget]—a suggestion which ignores the reality of staffing a university system and which can only lead to a dismantling of quality public higher education in SUNY." As did the chancellor, he complained about the increase in Bundy Aid, which, he pointed out, was "given to subsidize private colleges on the basis of degree granted even if the student has been enrolled for only six months." He called on the governor to direct his staff that "SUNY shall be minimally maintained at the cap of 32,245 lines set by D.O.B.," and that "any lines lost through attrition be replaced."[173]

On the same date, Wakshull addressed a letter to SUNY's faculty, in which he enclosed a copy of his letter to the governor, pointing out that this was "only a first step in what will be a hard and bitter fight to stem the tide which has seen State aid to private higher education increase steadily at the expense of public higher education." He informed them that UUP will be involved in several actions, one of which will be "the staging of 'Save-SUNY Day' on January 29 at the State Capitol in Albany. UUP will be sponsoring this mass gathering of faculty, staff and students to dramatize our efforts to, literally, save SUNY." He asked for their support, noting that UUP would provide free transportation from each campus.[174] On January 11, 1980, UUP and the Student Association of the State University (SASU) issued a joint press release announcing a protest of SUNY budget cuts and plans for the January 19 lobbying day.[175] Two days after the rally, Wakshull reported to the UUP Executive Board that attendance had been estimated at between 2,500 and 3,000. He noted that there would be follow-up meetings with SASU, and that during the Delegate Assembly recess that Friday night he would convene a meeting of chapter presidents. That meeting would discuss circulating petitions, letter-writing campaigns, holding meetings with legislators, issuing news releases, working with SASU chapters, and coming to Albany in February and March, as well as additional lobbying.[176]

Apparently, the "Save SUNY" campaign was having a positive impact. A February 25 UUP news release stated that petitions containing approximately 83,000 signatures of " ' concerned New Yorkers for Public Higher Education' were delivered to the office of Governor Hugh Carey Monday, protesting $27 million in budget cuts the Division of the Budget proposes to impose on the State University of New York."[177] In April, Wakshull informed the Executive Board of the continuing lobbying effort, noting that "he had requested people from five chapters to come to Albany each day the Legislature was presently in session."[178] This constant pressure on state legislators was to bear fruit. On April 29, the *New York Times* reported that the "Assembly voted today to restore the money for the State University–$22.3 million. And it warned the Carey administration against impounding the funds." That vote, it was noted, was unanimous. The Senate was expected to pass the bill. But while there was no indication of how the governor would respond, the *Times* reported that a "top Assembly aide said that if the Governor vetoed the appropriation, the Legislature would override that veto."[179]

UUP's Delegate Assembly was so pleased with this turn of events that it passed a resolution expressing its "appreciation for President Samuel Wakshull and Executive Director Evelyn Hartman [sic] for their foresight and persistence in the planning and execution of the SAVE SUNY campaign."[180] But the euphoria was short-lived, since Governor Carey vetoed the budget restoration and the Senate failed to override that veto. Following that, the Speaker of the Assembly, Stanley Fink, along with some colleagues, introduced a separate appropriation bill to restore the SUNY funds, which was approved by both the Senate and the Assembly. This time the governor signed the bill, which became law on May 12.[181]

The "Save SUNY" campaign had been effective, and years later some of those who took part in it remembered it as a high point in the union's perennial struggle to obtain adequate funding for SUNY. Longtime activist Alan Shank from the Geneseo campus related, "I recall getting in a bus with several other people and a lot of students and we drove, I guess we left about 5:00 in the morning and we drove all the way, it was over 200 miles. We drove from Geneseo to Albany and we lobbied all day long. We wore these big 'Save SUNY' buttons and it was really, it was very impressive to me that that kind of effort would be organized."[182] Malcolm Nelson from the Fredonia campus, not usually one of Wakshull's supporters, claimed the campaign "was Sam's high-water mark and I think he did it very well. I think the union came out very well."[183]

Internal Politics

At the May 1977 Delegate Assembly, Sam Wakshull stood for reelection as president of UUP. Having successfully negotiated a contract that received strong approval from the membership, it perhaps was no surprise that Wakshull was unopposed for the president's office at those elections. Also unopposed were the candidates for secretary (Edward Alfonsin) and membership development chair (Bruce Marsh), as well as all but one of the candidates for seats on the Executive Board. The only contested seat was won by Edward Wesnofske, who was chosen over Constantine Yeracaris, although by only one vote.[184]

From the outset, though, UUP members had differing views concerning the direction in which the union should move. In the early years, the most noticeable distinctions were between academics and professionals, and there were "caucuses" formed to represent these groups. By about 1977 the caucuses were becoming more formalized. The supporters of Sam Wakshull gravitated to the United Caucus, while his opponents were organizing into a group that called itself the Reform Caucus. The political activities of the Reform Caucus became evident in the 1979 union elections, when Sam Wakshull was challenged for the presidency by Edward Wesnofske of the Oneonta campus, and the incumbent secretary, Edward Alfonsin, was challenged by Diane Ciminelli from the Cobleskill campus. Both Wakshull and Alfonsin were easily reelected.[185] The Reform Caucus leadership tended to come mostly from the agriculture and technology units and some of the four-year colleges. Their vision of the union differed in substantial ways from the United Caucus view. In particular, they wanted to see more power centered in the campus chapters, and they wanted to have UUP be less reliant on NYSUT. They did not believe UUP received a sufficient return in services and representation for the dues paid to NYSUT, and they argued that UUP should hire its own staff, lobbyists, and attorneys, rather than being dependent on those who were on the NYSUT payroll.[186] The Reform Caucus also was formed in opposition to Wakshull, who they perceived as autocratic.[187] As early Reform Caucus member Malcolm Nelson put it: "I don't think Sam had very good ears. He tended to want to control absolutely everything."[188] The Reform Caucus made a significant inroad to United Caucus leadership of the union when, in May 1981, their candidate for vice president for academics, Paul Lauter of Old Westbury, narrowly defeated the United Caucus candidate, Richard Teevan of Albany, by a vote of 93–89, and

Charles Hansen of Stony Brook defeated Donald Wenzel of Brockport for vice president for professionals by an identical tally.[189]

The election of 1981 was to be of considerable significance. Sam Wakshull, having completed three consecutive terms as president, was prohibited by the UUP constitution from running again. It was pretty clear that the Reform Caucus candidate would be Paul Lauter, and the United Caucus needed a strong candidate to oppose him. At the February 1981 Delegate Assembly, the United Caucus met to choose their candidate. It was widely assumed that Wakshull was supporting John ("Tim") Reilly of Albany as the caucus choice to succeed him, but Nuala Drescher of the college at Buffalo challenged Reilly for the nomination—and she was successful.[190] She also succeeded in defeating Lauter in a hard-fought election that May by a vote of 106–96. United Caucus candidates also won the other officer positions on the ballot that year: secretary, William Cozort of Cortland; membership development officer, Edward Alfonsin.[191]

UUP's First Eight Years

In its first eight years of existence, United University Professions faced many challenges. It was charged with representing two-year agricultural and technical colleges, four-year colleges, university centers, and medical schools; within those units there were teaching and research academics, librarians, nonteaching professional staff, and a variety of medical professionals. Each campus had unique characteristics, and each of the staff types had different needs. There often was a lack of trust between academics and professionals, and the medical personnel saw their situation as distinct from that of other SUNY employees. Much of the union's time and effort was spent trying to reconcile these different interests. At the same time, and partly as a result of intraunion disagreements, other organizations contested UUP's status as sole bargaining unit. There were challenges to UUP from the National Education Association, the American Association of University Professors, and the Civil Service Employees Association, but UUP won out in each of them. While under this constant pressure, UUP successfully negotiated three contracts with the State of New York and two separate salary agreements. Although the official representative for SUNY's academic and professional employees, only a small fraction of them were actually members of the union at first. With some assistance from NYSUT, UUP embarked on a largely successful campaign to increase its membership. The union managed to survive declining state financial support for the university and serious retrenchments. These cuts might have been worse, though, were it not for UUP's efforts to marshal public and legislative support for the university. Increasingly, UUP was becoming effective in bringing its issues before the state's lawmakers. Most significantly, UUP twice was able to achieve orderly transitions of leadership. By 1981 UUP was a rapidly maturing organization, and it was ready to meet new challenges in the ensuing years.

Chapter 4

Organizational Structure, Internal Disagreement, Innovation, and Growth, 1981–87

As UUP approached the constitutional term limit of President Sam Wakshull, the organization found itself in a markedly improved situation. The base in the chapters was stabilizing. Membership was growing, and by the tenth anniversary had increased to 13,000.[1] Overt hostility to unionization had been allayed to a large degree by the SAVE SUNY campaign Wakshull had designed. While enthusiasm for collective bargaining was not widespread, there was a growing appreciation of the union's usefulness in preserving the system and keeping the "bean counters" at bay. Evidence of this maturation is the fact that when volunteers were needed for political action in Albany on behalf of the SUNY budget, or even for informational picket lines when contract talks bogged down, a respectable turnout could be expected on most campuses. In addition, the number of agency fee protests declined each year, so that by the spring of 1983, it was down to eighty-seven.[2]

New Stability, New Directions

The new reality permitted development of activity in new and creative areas. Outreach was made to other unions. More than 100 members participated in the massive Solidarity Day rally in Washington, DC, to protest the Reagan cuts in health and safety enforcement and funding for the Departments of Labor and Health and Safety. They also protested the destruction of PATCO, the air traffic controllers' union.[3] Representatives of the two-year agricultural and technical colleges regularly attended the NYSUT-sponsored community college conferences, opening new lines of communication and cooperation.[4] In an effort to position itself as the intellectual reservoir of the New York labor movement, UUP designed and executed a political action educational conference for the state AFL-CIO, held at the United Electrical Workers retreat in Bayberry, Long Island, in 1985.[5] It took the lead in creating a Coalition to Save Public Higher

Education and worked cooperatively with the Student Association of the State University (SASU) to defend against regular raids on the SUNY budget.

UUP worked with the SUNY Senate to cosponsor a three-day conference celebrating the life work of the novelist James Baldwin when the university conferred an honorary degree on him. It brought together leading African American writers and scholars of African American literature; UUP's chief negotiator, John (Tim) Reilly, a nationally recognized scholar of the work of Richard Wright, delivered the keynote address. The organization paid for 50 percent of the cost of participants.[6] UUP also successfully initiated the nomination of Toni Morrison, one of the outstanding African American novelists and later winner of the Nobel Prize for Literature, for a Schweitzer Chair to be placed in the English Department at the University at Albany.[7] Collaborating with the university, UUP cosponsored a symposium on excellence in the curriculum, which included such luminaries as Diane Ravitch of Columbia University, Maurice Easch of the University of Illinois, and James MacDonald of the University of North Carolina.[8]

The organization also was able to work with the New York State Senate Higher Education Committee chair, Kenneth LaValle, and the central administration to develop a program to permit cooperative use of SUNY facilities by regional small businesses; the program protected both the facilities and the patent rights of unit members.[9] In the long run, these activities resulted in the creation of a viable patent policy for the university, giving effective protection to inventors and authors in SUNY, which made them the only public employees in the nation shielded from the implications of the US Supreme Court's revitalization of the Eleventh Amendment to the Constitution.[10] Innovative programs were inaugurated to promote the general prosperity of the university and the economy of the state of New York on which it depended. Most notable of these was the work with the Governor's Economic Development Office to prepare the state's proposals to induce the General Motors Corporation to locate its new Saturn Plant in the state. While these efforts were ultimately unsuccessful, the projects did open a new chapter in the state's economic development efforts by involving, for the first time, labor and management in preparing such undertakings.[11]

In response to requests from both its members and the administration at the New Paltz campus, UUP successfully campaigned to overcome the private-college hostility to the creation of two small engineering-degree programs at the college by harnessing the support of NYSUT and consistently pressuring the regents until the programs were approved.[12] When the College of Optometry lost the lease on its Manhattan building, UUP joined the successful effort to ensure that the academic and economic benefits that accrued to the students and the City of New York itself would not be lost if it left for the suburbs.[13] Above all, considerable energy and creativity were invested in the evolution of labor-management cooperation initiatives incorporated into the new agreements negotiated in those years.

Internal Political Stability Evolves

Stability within the political leadership, however, was an entirely different matter. The caucuses in the Delegate Assembly were almost evenly split between "United" and "Reform," as reflected in the one-vote majority on the Executive Board enjoyed by the new president in her first year. Although much of the division was generated by hostility directed at the outgoing administration, there were real philosophical differences between the two factions.

The United Caucus placed primary emphasis on promoting the welfare of the members represented, collectively and individually, through contract negotiations and enforcement to advance that welfare. It was frequently attacked because of the "more practical" orientation it consistently took. While it was by no means opposed to supporting broader social-justice issues, its leaders did not accept the notion that unions were designed to reform the world. They were more than willing to vigorously advance such objectives when they were in harmony with the needs and objectives of the members, but held that the obligation to negotiate a contract, coupled with the annual budget fight that threatened university quality and access to the university, required the focus of all union energies. A quality university was, after all, the first term and condition of employment for the dues payers represented.

However, the United Caucus did not shy away from advocacy of social justice measures when they were in harmony with the basic agenda. It had a long history of support for such progressive programs as provision of quality day-care facilities on site, joining the chancellor in convincing the governor to sign an executive order making day care a legitimate state purpose.[14] Child care was added to the list of legitimate expenses for persons on UUP business in 1985.[15] Affirmative action and the promotion of diversity in the university ranks was always high on the agenda. For example, when resources were extremely limited, it led the call for financial support for the ultimately successful lawsuit of Akira Sanbonnatsu and his wife to overturn the university nepotism rule.[16] The organization sponsored a series of workshops to ensure that local leaders were aware of affirmative-action requirements, to allow their knowledgeable cooperation in recruiting and retaining the protected classes, and to prepare those recruited for active involvement in the union. By 1986, UUP had established a Legal Defense Fund in the annual budget and had already invested more than $150,000 of union funds in grants to individuals and classes of persons in the unit who sued the state for redress of perceived race, gender, and age discrimination.[17]

Against considerable political pressure, United Caucus leadership caused UUP to become the first union in state service to demand the end of discrimination on the grounds of sexual preference. It did so because it was right, and that social change clearly advanced the good and welfare of its members.[18] This demand created a problem for the state. The antisodomy law was still on the books in New York, and representatives of OER felt they could not accede to UUP's demand because it would have put the governor in the uncomfortable position of advocating violation of felony law, although they personally sympathized with the commitment. UUP ultimately agreed that the state could remain silent on the matter, but refused to withdraw the demand, committing itself to the ban in the agreement. Governor Mario Cuomo did respond positively to the growing change in attitude when he signed an executive order barring discrimination based on sexual orientation in the fall of 1983. Furthermore, it was United leadership that responded to requests from Assemblymen Arthur O. Eve and Mark Siegal to call for colleges and universities to divest their trust funds and endowments of South African assets as a strike against apartheid.[19]

The Reform Caucus, on the other hand, saw itself as the more democratic and idealistic element in the organization, committed to using the union's power to uphold social ideals of reform and change.[20] Consequently, it tended to place greater, even primary, emphasis on such matters as litigation for pay equity or the struggle to protect students charging professors with sexual harassment. In fact, Paul Lauter, long a leader of the caucus and its nominee for president in 1981, would later reflect that his involvement in UUP on the state level was an effort "to find a way to keep together an active left in the union which would be interested not only in the narrower issues of wages and working conditions, but also would be interested in issues of affirmative action . . . supporting organizing work that was going on elsewhere among American workers, that took progressive actions." He came to regret the contribution he made to hardening the lines between the caucuses when he agreed to "run against Sam's candidate," because the caucus required that someone run against the "establishment."[21] Throughout its history, checking the "establishment" was a major objective of the Reform Caucus.

A further illustration of the difference between the two factions is to be found in the conflict over representation of the graduate student employees. The United Caucus saw the work done by the members, teaching and research, as its jurisdiction, so defined by the Public Employment Relations Board in the original unit determination decision. Voluntarily surrendering any portion of this jurisdiction would subject the organization to constant efforts to undermine the integrity of the unit, leading to serious "unit erosion." United Caucus members believed that exclusive control of the lines devoted to teaching and research preceded their occupancy by any individual and democratic representation followed the hiring of personnel to occupy them. The Reform people argued that democracy required surrendering the jurisdiction, regardless of the potential dangers, because the current leaders of the graduate students did not want to be represented by UUP. A truly democratic organization, in their view, would voluntarily surrender the jurisdiction.[22] This was one issue that the United Caucus lost, and the graduate students were not accreted to the UUP unit, but were granted their own, which elected to be represented by the Communication

Workers of America.

The rigid division between the two caucuses presented a major challenge to Nuala McGann Drescher when she was elected president in May 1981. For this reason, she made internal organizing the first order of business. Utilizing the presidential responsibility to nominate personnel for the standing committees, she reached out to friend and foe alike to try to create coalitions and cohesion in the Delegate Assembly. The first such appointment was that of John (Tim) Reilly, the candidate she had defeated in the caucus primary, to be chair of the Negotiations Committee and "chief" negotiator in the coming round. His willingness to accept this responsibility was a dramatic signal that a new breeze was blowing. His national reputation as a scholar in two genres, African American literature and English-language murder mysteries, told the constituency at large that the intellectual life of the university was a term and condition of employment as important to the union as the more mundane bread-and-butter issues. It also indicated that the spokesman for the union in negotiations would be a person who would be bound by the agreement to the same extent as those for whom he spoke. Finally, the new president hoped to convince the members of the Delegate Assembly that opposition to her did not mean political suicide, opening the door for contributions of the talented many who had been put off by the partisan division that prevailed.

Similar care was used in other appointments. Members of the Reform Caucus were invited to serve along with United or independent people on every standing committee. Many accepted and served with diligence and creativity, finding that their contributions were welcome and appreciated. The broad diversity of the membership was reflected in the appointment of committee members from all categories of campus, from the ranks of academics and professionals, from the entire geographic range of the state, and from all races and genders.[23] Opposition leaders were not pleased because none of their number had been appointed to chair a standing committee. They believed that the new president was not breaking sufficiently with the past, and that she was keeping things too tightly controlled by a clique of political cronies. But the outreach proved to be a successful strategy. At the next election, in May 1982, the United Caucus widened its margin on the executive board to five.

Financial Crisis: Internal and External

The next six years were dominated by two interdependent issues: negotiations and budget, and the challenges and opportunities that flowed from them. Making progress in these areas, however, was inhibited by the continued division in the Delegate Assembly and a growing internal fiscal crisis resulting from a series of deficit budgets inherited by the new administration. In the spring of 1981, the budget projected a deficit of up to $465,000.[24] Still, new claims on the treasury for an ongoing student recruitment campaign and legal actions against the state on behalf of unit members charging gender, race, and age discrimination were made regularly and successfully from the floor of the Assembly, seriously exacerbating the problem.[25] Adding to the crisis was an order from PERB requiring that UUP refund to agency fee payers that portion of their fee equal to the per-member cost of the union life insurance benefit, heretofore offered only to members. The order cost the treasury up to $250,000 that it could ill afford.[26] The situation was so serious that at one point the auditors suggested that "the union may be unable to continue in existence" and ought to consider bankruptcy.[27]

The Finance Committee, chaired by Harold Cannon of the Albany campus, and the treasurer, Thomas Matthews of Geneseo, worked out an austerity program designed to cope with the growing deficits. It included a restructuring of the dues and caps on chapter treasuries. Members of both caucuses on the Executive Board and in the assembly supported the financial reforms without dissent.[28] The proposal was adopted and the efforts were successful, allowing Matthews to report a year later that the organization had eliminated its deficit for the first time in three years.[29] Financial stability followed, but it was not until early in 1985 that the organization was able to establish a genuine contingency or reserve fund to protect itself against unforeseen financial liabilities.[30] The Executive Board recommended and the Delegate Assembly approved the creation of a $1 million "minimum contingency reserve fund." Access to these moneys required a two-thirds vote of the board and a majority ratification by the next assembly. Finally, in the 1986–87 fiscal year, it was possible to put the two vice presidents on staff full time and create a fund to give relief to the overburdened chapter leaders.[31]

Drastic cuts in the federal budget took a toll on enrollment in the university and consequently on job security for employees. Faculty at the campus schools, some of whom had worked for SUNY for more than twenty years, quickly became the victims of Reaganomics, as one after the other the demonstration schools were closed.[32] Legislative efforts to preserve them failed when Governor Hugh Carey vetoed the bill generated by a vigorous campaign launched by the union. The efforts to override the veto were not successful because the governor threatened to withhold his certification that the budget was balanced, which was required to borrow on the open market. The unsuccessful fight to save the campus schools did bring home to many of the rank and file the potential implications of the state's budget crisis and helped energize the base, creating a willingness to join the next budget battle, which came all too soon.

The waning years of the Carey administration were particularly difficult for the university and the union in other ways. Faculty and staff faced constant downsizing, which the leadership of UUP saw as destroying their university and depriving New York of an excellent, affordable, democratic educational opportunity for all its people. President Drescher reached out to members of the Board of Trustees, urging them to join the union in the struggle to "preserve and protect its greatness."[33] UUP determined to meet every effort to constrict the university with intense opposition until "the imprudent policy" was abandoned and public higher education was preserved at the level that the people of the state deserved.

This time, administration did join in the struggle. Campus presidents joined chapter presidents in petitioning local legislators for relief. Many observers were surprised at the intensity with which both the administration and the union confronted the proposed cuts. The chancellor argued that we are doing more with less and less, and if we want to maintain quality, the university would have to take a hard look at reducing enrollment. "Miffed" by the orchestrated campaign, spokesman for the Division of the Budget, Paul T. Veillette, denounced Wharton's arguments, insisting that demanding additional funds in the current fiscal crisis "borders on irresponsibility."[34]

In response to the executive budget released in January 1982, the chancellor estimated that position cuts called for could range between 700 and 1,000. He believed that the basic mission of the university was in jeopardy if these cuts held. UUP leaders agreed, suggesting that if the cuts were not countered, SUNY "will be crippled."[35] The governor countered by asserting that having proved it could absorb overenrollments while maintaining access and quality in the past, SUNY should do it again. The lead editorial in *The Voice* mocked the governor's thinking by reminding that the "theory that a horse can always pull an ever-greater load with each succeeding whipping has long since been exploded," and that the expectation of substantial revenues from operation of SUNY's hospital and dormitories was "nothing short of a trip up the yellow brick road"[36]

Once again, the political action wing of UUP was called into action to defend jobs, access, and quality. Not only did rank-and-file members travel to Albany weekly to prevail on friends of the university in the legislature to restore funds necessary to maintain the status quo, but a new program of recruiting local businesses partially dependent on SUNY custom was launched. Stickers were distributed that cooperating businesses could display prominently. Their names were then circulated in the campus community, and students, staff, and families were urged to patronize such supporters.[37]

The legislature proved highly sympathetic to the union's arguments because many of their number believed that the Division of the Budget was working to cut the legislature out of the process, except for the appropriation of a single line item for SUNY, leaving the executive in absolute control.[38] In addition, people such as Willis H. Stephen, ranking minority member of the Assembly Ways and Means Committee, were convinced that it was not a genuine economic crisis that motivated the cuts; rather, it was the "apparent policy goal" of the Carey administration to achieve a "balance" between SUNY and all other higher-education segments in the state by "constraining" SUNY.[39] Relief was legislated but Carey vetoed the appropriation. A massive, and this time successful, override campaign ensued, a monumental accomplishment because such overrides never happened in New York. Still, Governor Carey had the last word. He simply impounded the money, and the university was left to muddle along without it, but actual retrenchments did not happen because the administration cut vacant lines, aborted staff searches, delayed maintenance operations, and adopted other cost savings.

Struggle for a New Agreement

Simultaneously, preparations began for the new round of contract negotiations with the state. Fred Day, an experienced negotiator from the NYSUT staff, joined Tim Reilly as an advisor in the process, and the framing of a program began. Efforts were undertaken to launch an open and broadly democratic process that would reach out to the grass roots of the SUNY staff and allow the design of a package of demands that reflected the real needs of the very diverse membership. A survey was constructed and sent out to all members, and an informal negotiations advisory council of experienced people was recruited to help frame the package.[40] Regional negotiations workshops were held around the state to educate people about the process and to continue the solicitation of input from the rank and file. The leadership saw the negotiations process as further opportunity for union building and internal organizing.[41]

UUP entered this negotiation cycle with considerable optimism, despite the prevailing budget-cutting spirit of the Reagan era. The state's economy was slowly but surely recovering. The old adversary on the second floor, Governor Hugh Carey, who had vetoed the campus school legislation and impounded SUNY funds restored by the legislature, was not running for reelection and would soon be replaced. The legislature was counting down to adjournment before the election, and its members seemed to be anxious to get their part of the program out of the way before leaving Albany to campaign.[42] For these reasons, Reilly and the team anticipated that the talks would be tough but reasonable.

The state was notified that UUP was ready to negotiate on November 1, 1981, with proposals exchanged on December 16. Nancy Hodes, deputy director of OER, was appointed chief negotiator for the state, like President Drescher the first woman to occupy her position. This fact would prove significant before the end of talks. Two women, each the first in her position, would quietly agree behind the scenes, when complete breakdown loomed, that they could not allow failure and pushed on to resolve the dividing issues.[43] But it was not going to be easy.

From the outset, the original optimism proved illusionary. An early signal of the inhospitable approach OER planned to take came when chief negotiator Hodes announced at the Baruch Conference on Collective Bargaining in Universities that "We have the right to exploit these casual and part time people because the economic imperative of the state requires it."[44] Presentation of the state's package doomed prospects for a quick completion of a new agreement. The fiscal crisis remained severe and partially explained the rather hardheaded approach of OER to the two seemingly unresolvable issues: workload and clinical practice. In spite of this fact, the governor was willing to make a reasonably generous across-the-board increase in salary in light of the long freeze on employee salaries endured by the workforce. He had already allowed settlements in three agreements with other units for three annual increases in succession, the first of 9 percent and the next two of 8 percent. But the price would be high for this generosity.

OER demanded that any pay raises be tied to productivity increases, "a very sly way of attacking the workload issue."[45] The state was determined to "get more for less," actually celebrating in the budget message of 1982 the fact that increased student enrollment had been accompanied by substantial position decreases with no decline in access or quality.[46] In addition, productivity had become especially problematic for the university, since UUP had won a PERB ruling ordering the state to cease and desist from unilaterally increasing the workload of members in the Morrisville English Department. The decision established a university-wide precedent that workload could not be changed without negotiation, making the rollback of the award an imperative for the state. The clinical practice issue, raised by the failure of the university to implement the earlier agreement governing the system, appeared to be motivated by a similar need to recover the cost of assets given personnel practicing in the medical school clinics and hospitals. Both these issues would be at the heart of the breakdown in this round of talks.

The state's package contained other take-backs, including a two-week lag in the payroll, which amounted to a coerced loan to the state from its workers for the duration of their employment, over and above what they paid in taxes. Other demands were less vacation time for professionals, less sick leave for all, no meeting space on campuses for unions, no organization leave, and in a "cruel turn of events," no retraining money for retrenched personnel. Also demanded were substantial changes in the clinical practice plans at the four medical schools, which were highly advantageous to the state and equally hurtful to unit physicians.

Extremely problematic for the union was the demand for a new definition of eligibility for enrollment in state healthcare programs that would result in the loss of coverage for many part-time and clinical personnel. In fact, most of the people adversely affected by this change when it went into effect had been beneficiaries of an error on the part of the university administration, which had extended healthcare coverage to part-time employees in the clinics who never met the original definition in Civil Service Law.[47] Still, it came as a shock, and the union lost considerable credibility with this cohort.

Negotiations Break Down

Before a new agreement could be consummated, the atmosphere surrounding the talks became toxic. Twenty-seven sessions between the two teams resulted in little progress, with the result that UUP declared an impasse in August. The union representatives perceived a pattern of reneging and withdrawal "which has made a mockery of the bargaining." Citing the continual reduction of state support for the university over the past ten years, the unionists declared, "We fear that the state's position in our negotiations is still another effort to undercut and reduce the state's commitment to public higher education." The declaration of impasse on twenty-nine items was designed to force the Office of Employee Relations (OER) to "justify its strange behavior in bargaining with UUP." Members were informed that the impasse was the result of "OER's antics."[48] In their turn, the chief negotiator for the state denied that there was any impasse, except for clinical practice, and on that issue, "UUP was holding out for a ceiling of $700,000 for medical members of the unit." Labeling the Hodes version of things as a "transparent attempt to anger the public and undercut UUP's bargaining with the members," the unionists denounced it as absolutely "ludicrous," and "farcical in its face."[49]

The hostile rhetoric escalated. Angry phone calls and telegrams were exchanged. At one point, Meyer (Sandy) Frucher, director of OER, accused President Drescher of refusing to negotiate in good faith and threatened to file improper practice charges against the union. He charged that she was deliberately deceiving the members to incite them to disrupt campuses for internal political reasons.[50] The situation deteriorated even further when the chapter at Farmingdale took matters into its own hands. Although cautioned to avoid anything that could be construed as a "job action" under the Taylor Law that would make members subject to the harsh penalties prescribed, between 250 and 400 picketers (depending on whose report is believed) left the line and entered the administration building. Disciplinary action followed, naming five individuals who became known in union folklore as "the Fierce Five of Farmingdale." Such a march through an administration building was a dramatic departure from the usual academic protest demonstrations that had taken place around the state, but it signaled the degree of bitterness the painful negotiation process had engendered.[51]

The two seemingly intractable issues, workload and clinical practice, shared a common theme from the state's point of view: management flexibility, the right to determine the ground rules of operation. In both cases, the union was determined to retain the right to protect the members' interests through grievance procedures and future negotiations.

In relation to workload, the state's demand would have allowed the mix of the professional obligation to be assigned by management without consultation or redress for the faculty members. Initially the state refused to move from its position, which would have required surrendering the Morrisville award, demonstrating little appreciation of problems confronted by an English professor who faced 140 freshman compositions weekly. Resolution was finally achieved by a carefully scripted "table talk" rather than formal language in the agreement. Given the diverse nature of the unit and the widely differing past practices on the various types of campuses, a common workload definition would have created more problems than it solved. The state, in the conversation, referred to the *Policies of the Board of Trustees,* which defined the ingredients of the "professional obligation" and stated that management had the right to adjust it. UUP responded, asserting the right to appeal to PERB when the change exceeded a full professional obligation, or if it was taken without negotiation. It also reserved the right to demand impact bargaining to ensure that any overload would be compensated for if the person in question was willing to accept the change. The state responded that "We agree."[52] This was not quite the status quo, but it did preserve the past-practice principle and assured that the union was able to fight capricious and arbitrary changes when they were identified. It was a neat compromise that survived for more than three decades.

The second of the state's seemingly intractable demands proved to be more difficult to resolve. In June 1981, the state comptroller's office had undertaken an audit directed at determining if the medical centers had complied with the Board of Trustees resolutions limiting the professional earnings of the medical and dental faculty, in the interest of having them concentrate on their teaching obligation.[53] The report noted that in the more than thirty years since SUNY was charged with the responsibility to establish adequate medical and dental faculty plans, this had not happened. Only two centers had such plans (Upstate Medical Center and SUNY–Stony Brook), and even they were defective. It further charged that SUNY had done little to comply with the trustees' resolutions and union agreements, imposing salary caps. It documented the failure of the practitioners themselves to reimburse the state for its investment for equipment, materials, office space, and personnel used by the physicians in their private practices. Finally, the audit called on the governor's office and the legislature to intervene and "establish adequate medical and dental faculty compensation plans."[54]

Given this charge, Director Frucher determined to put an end to the negligence and "correct longstanding abuses" through negotiations with UUP. He asserted that millions of dollars were owed to the state by unit members for its outlay over the years. In addition, he claimed that many physicians had annual incomes that exceeded by "hundreds of thousands of dollars" the limits stipulated by the board of Trustees of the state university.[55]

The union had long accepted the clinical practice plan concept, which was commonplace nationally, and it had been incorporated into earlier agreements, although the doctors, particularly at Downstate Medical Center, were militantly opposed to it. Failure to implement the enabling article of the agreements was the fault of the administration of the centers, not the union. This time around, UUP's team perceived that Frucher's demand would have permitted management to dictate every detail of the plan without consulting with those impacted. It would deny access to the grievance process of any part of the amended article, and effectively bar modifications in future negotiations.[56] Clinical practice plans were a mandatory subject of negotiations under the Taylor Law, and the union team determined that they had no choice but to hold out until they were able to ensure that the two fundamental principles of negotiation and grievance were preserved. The union also insisted that the plans must be democratically conceived, arguing that a plan imposed by the chancellor or OER violated the precepts of local governance and self-determination that are the primary factors in making an operation successful in a university. An acceptable plan would also be accountable to local and state auditors and significantly contribute to the educational, research, and patient-care goals of the university.[57]

Compromise finally came, holding the two union fundamentals sacrosanct. Dr. Norman A. Haffner, vice chancellor for professional programs, "described the agreement as a 'minor miracle' in view of the prior history of faculty opposition."[58]

Settlement

With this article settled, the agreement was finalized and sent off for ratification, which carried 5,920 to 1,098. Few were surprised at the lopsided outcome considering the wage freeze that had prevailed in the university for three years. It was a three-year pact that included annual raises to base pay of 9 percent, 8 percent, and 8 percent, a vastly improved dental plan operated by the union, a $2 million disparity fund to deal with salary inequities, a $1.5 million fund for professional development and quality of work life to be administered by a joint labor-management committee, a one-time payment of 0.6 percent to recover the lag COLA from the previous agreement, and a 1 percent discretionary fund for each year.[59] The agreement was retroactive to July 1, 1982. A major innovation was the provision of Article 35.7, which gave to retrenched nonclassroom professionals the right of reemployment in the same position at a similar college, should an opening for such employment arise, and committed the state to investigate ways to extend this preference to academic personnel.

The Continuity of Employment Committee was continued, and a new, funded, joint committee, the Professional Development and Quality of Working Life Committee, was established. Membership of both parties in these forums was equal, which encouraged cooperation because either side could veto the ideas of the other. Joint committees were also provided to address safety and health issues in SUNY, a professional employee promotion system, medical center issues, and health benefits. The purpose of these forums was to provide a place to "discuss, consider and attempt to resolve matters of interest to either or both parties."[60] The disparity fund was to be disbursed, following the recommendations of a similar joint committee.

The Continuity of Employment Committee was charged with studying employee displacement due to economic and technological changes. On the basis of its investigations, it was to recommend solutions and make available funds for retraining affected employees. Eligibility for such fellowships was extended beyond those who had already received notice of termination, to those who perceived that they were at "high risk" of retrenchment. To fund its operations, $500,000 per year was provided for the life of the contract.

The Professional Development and Quality of Working Life Committee received a similar annual appropriation to undertake jointly agreed-upon programs designed to enhance personal professional growth and the improvement of general working conditions. Individual grants would provide funds for study and travel leaves, health and safety, health benefits, day-care facilities, employee assistance, affirmative action, medical malpractice insurance, and other problems unique to the medical centers.[61] Librarians benefited from a $150,000 fund earmarked for study leaves and other professional development activities. UUP and OER sponsored a workshop at Lake Luzerne to introduce chapter leadership and local managers to the program and encourage their exploitation of it. Chancellor Wharton gave the keynote address, entitled "Retraining: Putting Our Own House in Order," signaling his appreciation of the opportunities flowing from collective bargaining.[62] Almost immediately proposals were approved for professional study leaves, new faculty development programs, experienced faculty travel awards, individual study grants, and training programs in such areas as grant writing, computer technology, and leadership seminars.[63] Due to the financial constraints imposed on the university by the decline in state appropriations, operation of the Professional Development Committee very quickly emerged as the only source of subsidy for individuals to pursue travel to professional meetings and other activities essential for their career development.

Of special note was the Disparity Fund, the first recognition by the state that there were serious inequities in the salary system in the university. The agreement provided for $2 million to address the problem and established the joint committee to make recommendations for the distribution of the fund. Under the leadership of John Carney of Oneonta, the UUP half of the committee did internal and external research to help identify salary disparities and the degree of inequity involved. "Shadow committees" were established in each chapter to help collect data and identify persons potentially eligible for an award. The joint committee's final report was "voluminous," recommending awards to 3,000 staff members. Both parties agreed that it would take more than $8 million to redress all of the inequities identified but only $2 million was available.[64] The chancellor recognized the difficulty faced by the committee, but praised its members for the cooperation and understanding that characterized the deliberations, noting that "although the individual desires of some may not have been met, we have been well served by the Committee."[65]

In the judgment of President Drescher, it was the smooth, effective, and harmonious operation of the joint committees in the next two years that was responsible for overcoming the mutual hostility that characterized the negotiations that created them. In addition, the committees provided a new opportunity for internal organizing, and so each chapter appointed a "shadow committee" to explore what programs should be invested in by the jointly managed committees, bringing new people into union activity. Exploitation of the openings presented by these committees would occupy union activists until the next agreement, when work would begin all over again.

The agreement included an additional innovation for New York State, the provision for a salary reduction program allowing the sheltering of a percentage of an individual's annual income from federal income tax, to be invested in an account for retirement when taxes on withdrawals would be lower. OER and UUP worked cooperatively to promote the needed implementation legislation. UUP's insurance committee, chaired by Harvey Inventasch of Cortland, devised the program and identified firms willing to serve as common remitter to any plan or fund in which the members could legally participate.[66] This program, when authorized by the legislature, was later extended to all units of state service, including that of the management-confidential personnel.

Budget Fight Once Again

But before the euphoria over what was a remarkably good contract under the circumstances could fade and UUP members begin to implement and benefit from it, a devastating financial challenge to the university threatened its quality and access, if not its very existence.

The new governor, Mario Cuomo, for whom the unionists had fought long and hard in the Democratic primary and then the general election, submitted his first budget. In it he cut appropriations to SUNY massively, including substantial reduction of the workforce, on top of those sustained under his predecessor. Even Chancellor Wharton conceded that the budget was bad, describing it in a press release as "shocking" and "appalling." He suggested "that with these cuts we can barely accomplish our mission," declaring that "an institution, even one as large as SUNY, cannot continue to absorb such major reductions over a long period of time without sharply affecting its ability to educate." He predicted that tuition would have to be increased substantially and total employment cut by more than 2,500, concluding it would be extremely difficult to preserve academic integrity without major programmatic reductions or elimination and reduction in size and diversity in the university.[67] Student support services and student life would be seriously eroded, whole departments eliminated, high-demand programs curtailed, new programs frozen on the drawing board.[68] For no apparent reason, SUNY was scheduled to suffer a 12.1 percent cut of personnel, while only 5.1 percent was cut from other state agencies, and the university's share of the general fund continued to shrink from 5.4 percent in 1975 to 4.2 percent in the new fiscal year, a reduction of 22 percent. Student enrollment increased by more than 8,000 in the same period.[69]

Accepting that the president of the union could say things that a member of the governor's cabinet could not, President Drescher respectfully disagreed with the chancellor. She excoriated the practices of the Division of the Budget, insisting that they produced "chronic uncertainty and frankly, demoralizing chaos," and "totally frustrate the constitutional budget-making process." She and her colleagues in the union genuinely believed if the projected cuts held, the university would be ruined, totally unable to perform its basic function. They saw that cuts of this magnitude would constitute a "massive breach of faith" with the hundreds of thousands of New Yorkers who hold SUNY degrees and the 150,000 presently enrolled, not to mention the generations to come. The university, in their view, simply could not sustain the projected losses of personnel and remain viable.[70] The time had come to protect the investment the taxpayers had made in the university or lose it all. The nation was facing a total restructuring of the economy from an industrial to an information-based economy, so it made no sense at all to bleed the institution of the very people who would give the state the engineers, programmers, and others necessary to accomplish the painful transformation and facilitate the rebirth of the state into the new economy.

The union also saw some serious philosophical problems, which added to the imperative to fight against the new priorities established by executive decree. These flew "in the face of major social decisions which have been made in the last two decades."[71] The executive budget drastically cut appropriations for both public systems without a commensurate adjustment of state funding for private colleges and universities. UUP had quietly accepted the general principle of equity in the relationship between support for public and private institutions that had been adopted after lengthy public debate. Now it was threatened by executive action alone. In fact, state aid to the private colleges had increased by 65 percent since 1975, while support for SUNY had risen only 43 percent at the same time—and this when total state spending had risen by 104 percent.[72] Unionists characterized this as "warfare" on public higher education. Therefore, the fight to save jobs in the university took on an additional imperative. It became a commitment to preserve the democratic process and protect public higher education from well-placed and well-funded hostile advocates of the alternative system.

The substantial tuition increase in the two public universities was a further change in public policy by executive decree. It altered the principles on which public higher education in the state had been based, by repealing the concept that cost would be kept to a minimum. The budget introduced, for the first time, the idea that a set percentage of the cost should be borne by the student and that "affluent segments of the student population in public as well as independent institutions should not be unduly subsidized by less affluent taxpayers."[73] Compounding the problem was the introduction of new "user fees" that would not be covered by tuition assistance, thereby adding a new "tax" on the students and their families. While modest in 1983–84, it was feared that the universal computer fee constituted the beginning of a new method of financing the university, like the California model, where "free" tuition was supplemented by extensive mandatory fees.[74] Again, public policy was being transformed by an executive department without public debate or legislative action.

UUP leaders feared the psychological and emotional impact of the proposed massive personnel cuts, because the governor's office demanded the names of those projected to be retrenched. Circulation of "hit" lists would cause untold agony and suffering. In fact, before the struggle was over, the vice chancellor and provost, Jerome Komisar, reported to the UUP president that his office had forwarded the names of deceased members of the staff to fulfill that requirement and protect others from the anxiety engendered by a layoff notice that later might be rescinded, a quiet and decent thing to do. Some administrators aborted searches, eliminated all temporary appointments, and added in nonrenewals to meet their assigned totals. Travel money was eliminated and all dollars squeezed from student services, temporary employee, and graduate assistant funds. On some campuses, such as Alfred and Geneseo, the administration predicted the worst but anticipated that the union fight would save the day.[75] Other managers simply accepted the inevitable and began the notification process. But everywhere, there was "great apprehension and fear," intensified by the long wait before resolution.[76]

Program of Defense

Believing that "There's little excuse for permanently wounding the University while seeking solutions to what the Governor has termed a temporary problem," the union designed a program of intense action to educate the public to the danger and to obtain legislative relief. The situation called for the creation of a militant mindset on the part of the members, which would prevent any thought of accommodation.[77]

First and foremost, President Drescher warned against "renegotiation," or what people were calling "retrieval bargaining." She characterized the idea as "double tom-foolery" and reported that she had received petitions with hundreds of signatures, hate mail, and anonymous angry phone calls demanding the re-opening of negotiations to give back some or all of the recent pay raises. Acknowledging the acute difficulty of living with colleagues who had been notified of the premature end of their careers, she suggested that there was no guarantee that any surrender of negotiated increases would actually accomplish the desired end. Giving back the long-overdue raises might not save a single job. The surrendered funds could easily be placed in the general fund to be used for whatever priority the Division of the Budget established, and not remain in SUNY at all. There were other problems with the idea. For example, whose job would be saved? Who would actually decide among the many threatened? Even the director of OER, Meyer Frucher, agreed that state workers enjoyed "less than 'very generous' pay," making a give-back even less justified.[78]

Most delegates to the 1983 Winter Delegate Assembly reinforced the official UUP position, supplying evidence that various administrators were willing to accept the disintegration of SUNY and the proposed ways of apportioning the disaster. Some reported talk of cannibalizing the system. The executive committee of the Faculty Senate at Albany endorsed its administration's proposal for differential tuition to bridge the gap created by the proposed budget, thus accepting the "balkanization" of the SUNY system. William Wiesner of the Stony Brook campus reported that his president had talked openly about closing some upstate campuses. A similar report came from the Oswego campus with word that President Virginia Radley had spoken of closing the Buffalo State and Brockport colleges.[79] Farmingdale delegates suggested that their president had been ordered to fire a set number of people and had already done so. Clearly, defeatism was in the air.

On the other hand, some delegates had come to the Assembly already in a fighting mood, wearing the "SAVE SUNY" buttons from the old campaign, when the fight had saved 2,200 jobs. Plattsburgh representatives wore the buttons created to fight the campus school closing, which warned that "Retrenchment is contagious!" Geraldine Bard from the Buffalo State chapter reported on its program, which had already saved thirteen jobs and distributed buttons recalling the Pogo philosophy: "We have met the enemy and he is us!"[80] Clearly, leadership at the base of the union was ready for constructive action to avoid tragedy.

Coalitions to Fight

Under the leadership of Dan Sanders, Executive Vice President of NYSUT, a coalition of the presidents of UUP, the Public Employees Federation (PEF), and the Professional Staff Congress (PSC) had been created to call for an alternative to the governor's approach to dealing with the budget deficit. At the press conference, the four called for "revenue enhancement," frankly, a tax increase in the form of a temporary surcharge on the income tax, to sunset when the crisis had passed as anticipated. In New York, this was a time-honored method of dealing with such extreme fiscal problems, having been utilized twice before in recent memory.

A massive education program was adopted to "overcome the horrors of the Governor's proposal." Designed to be "obvious but not obnoxious," it called for rallies; visits to the Legislative Office Building in Albany and local legislative offices; press conferences and media events on campus; meetings between labor and management; approaches to and coalitions with students; outreach to families, alumni, and friends of the SUNY community; and mobilization of businesses in the areas adjacent to campuses that depended on student and staff patronage. The campaign was to be done in a controlled and reasonable fashion because tax increases of any kind were a very sensitive issue.[81]

The delegates endorsed the plan and allocated funds to subsidize it. The next six weeks were spent carrying out the program. A regular bulletin was produced throughout the season that excoriated the cuts as calling for the "destruction of the university," and sought to energize the chapters to join the campaign. Twice a week on "lobby days," between thirty-four and seventy-five people walked the halls of the Legislative Office Building, meeting with legislators and staff and distributing prepared materials documenting the damage that would be done if funds were not restored to the SUNY budget. They were always visible, but never obnoxious. To the leadership's great satisfaction, legislators expressed appreciation for the campaign, suggesting that it was "one of the most sophisticated and consistent lobbying campaigns any group has ever undertaken."[82]

UUP worked closely throughout the campaign with the Student Association of the State University (SASU). On February 23, between 2,500 and 3,000 students traveled to Albany on busses provided by the union to take part in a well-coordinated operation. Every legislative office was visited by several delegations of constituents. The students produced a mass of letters and cards appealing to the governor. The students were enthusiastic participants in the campaign because they were even more horrified by the proposed cuts than the unionists were. A spokesman for SASU characterized the proposed cuts as "mauling" and "crushing" the system, leaving it "a mere shell of its former self." They feared that under Cuomo's budget plans, tuition would increase annually until SUNY was "competitive with the private colleges," placing an unjust barrier between the uneducated and opportunity, between personal and professional advancement in a real world that required advanced education.[83] Both NYSUT and the Professional Staff Congress (PSC) worked closely with UUP in the struggle. The PSC had ready access to Assembly Democrats from New York City, while UUP worked with Republican Senators from upstate and Long Island. Members of the two organizations spoke with one voice, making an effective case for both systems. A public-employee coalition in opposition to the proposed retrenchments was created that included the Civil Service Employees Association (CSEA), UUP, the Public Employees Federation (PEF), the Fraternal Order of New York State Troopers, and Council 82 of the American Federation of State and Municipal Employees (AFSME, corrections officers).[84] Representatives of the several organizations met weekly to facilitate cooperation. One concrete outcome of these efforts was creation by UUP, PEF, and SASU of five-minute radio spots dealing with the consequences of the proposed cuts, which were distributed to appropriate markets.[85] A deal was actually struck with central administration to work cooperatively on two issues. UUP would work to support sponsored research in the university, which management needed, and management would support the union request for $1 million for the SUNY awards program., desired by the union.[86]

By early March, the campaign seemed to be working. The legislators seemed sympathetic. The governor was petitioned directly to join the call for the temporary surcharge on the income tax, a time-limited increase in the maximum tax, or a combination of the two, because it was the earlier narrowing of the progression of the income tax that had created the crisis in the first place. While it had provided a windfall for 12 percent of New Yorkers who earned the highest incomes, few of those who faced layoff benefited from the tax cuts of the past five years.[87] Legislators seemed to feel that taxpayers would understand the necessity for revenue enhancement to provide services for the sick, the mentally ill, the disadvantaged, and students. Senator Joseph L. Bruno, majority leader of the Senate, suggested that as budget negotiations intensified, creative new ideas would emerge and "we will not need to be faced with the layoff of thousands and thousands of workers as previously predicted."[88]

Resolution of the Crisis This Time

He was right. By mid-March, central administration had drafted a new budget proposal shaped by the prospect of the huge number of position cuts, massive contraction of academic programs, and large enrollment reductions implicit in the executive budget. The revised financial plan was designed to produce dollars that could be used to avoid the personnel reductions. Included were savings from utility and fuel outlays due to lower-than-projected utilization and reductions or elimination of building repair and equipment replacement. Enrollments would still be curtailed and new programs implemented only if they were deemed critical to the state's economic development.[89] New revenues for the state were generated by increases in gross receipts from the tax on oil companies, the institution of a real estate capital gains tax, and increased "sin taxes" on liquor and cigarettes.[90] When the budget was finally adopted, more than $13.5 million was restored to SUNY. Coupled with the administration's alterations in its original projections and the increase in tuition, the restoration was sufficient to avert actual retrenchments. On April 8, UUP was able to inform the members that "Once again, our efforts have paid off and our friends in the Legislature have come through for us." Most important of all, layoffs had been avoided and the quality and diversity of the academic programs preserved.[91] UUP and its allies had played a significant role in the success, and many considered it to be "UUP's greatest test." Chancellor Wharton expressed his appreciation for the union's work when he wrote thanking the organization for all it had done on behalf of the university, which had been "vital to our efforts to achieve a high level of educational opportunities for the people of the State."[92] The Executive Board voted to recognize the work of Assembly Speaker Stanley Fink with its Friend of SUNY award for 1984, noting that "he was without peer in his efforts to persuade his colleagues in both houses that the budget and personnel cuts which plagued SUNY last year had to be reversed," while working tirelessly to sustain the quality of and access to public higher education.[93] Speaker Fink attended the banquet in his honor on May 11 to receive the award.

Struggle for SUNY Flexibility

Having lived through the dangers of dramatic decline in state support for the university initiated by two governors, which had led to serious talk of downsizing and even closing some campuses, Chancellor Wharton was determined to find a way to free SUNY from total dependence on the vagaries of the political world. Above all, he sought freedom from micromanagement by the Bureau of the Budget. Treating the state university as simply another branch of state operations, subject to the many layers of bureaucratic oversight, had in his estimation reached the point of no return. The "excessive oversight and control" deprived the institution of "a significant part of its great potential" and increasingly, though unintentionally, "frustrated or compromised the objectives set by the Governor and the Legislature."[94] Piecemeal efforts to remedy the problem had proved inadequate. Consequently, Wharton appointed a fifteen-person commission to help SUNY evaluate its role and mission. Called the Commission on the Future of the State University, it was made up of prominent New Yorkers and national education leaders who had no relationship to the university. Its mission was to look at the size, governance, and accountability issues, academic quality, finances, and other factors that determined the institution's ability to properly serve the people of the state. What the chancellor and the Board of Trustees sought from the Independent Commission, as it came to be known, was the members' best judgment on all issues involved in running a major university, that is, a "thorough review of current circumstances and future potential" of SUNY. The prime factor in creating the commission, which was funded by grants from the Ford, Carnegie, and Rockefeller Foundations and the Ford Motor Co., was the problem of meeting the university's financial difficulties without constantly raising tuition. "Decisions have to be made," Wharton asserted, "as to whether SUNY will continue as the accessible, broadly based institution envisioned by its founders, or have it efforts redirected toward narrower, less comprehensive objectives."[95]

The operation of the Independent Commission presented a dilemma to the union. It could threaten UUP's relationship with the state by moving collective bargaining to the Board of Trustees, something the administration lobbied for assiduously.[96] Such a change would prevent the union from sitting down at the bargaining table with the people who had the real power to set terms and conditions of employment for the members. Increased financial flexibility and less administrative oversight could result in cannibalizing the system, pitting one campus against the others in the fight for primacy and resources that the union had opposed for all of its history. Some feared the commission was designed to pit university centers against each other and then against the four-year institutions, with marching orders to enrich some and close others—in short, that it was merely a cover for downsizing. But it could also be the only opportunity on the horizon to promote the preservation of the institution to which members devoted their lives and protect it from the continuing machinations of the unelected bureaucracy, which took an intolerable toll on staff morale, preventing them from delivering the level of excellence they aspired to deliver.[97]

It could work out to be a singular opportunity to create new allies in the struggle for adequate funding, if the commissioners stressed the need to stabilize and enhance the financial picture and to help guarantee that planning for the future was rational and long-term.[98] Consequently, members were urged to participate in the commission hearings on local campuses to reinforce in the minds of the commissioners "the most positive impression of the University that is possible, stressing the unique mission and the accomplishments of each individual campus."[99] Chancellor Wharton took pains to involve the union in the work of the commission, indicating that he felt UUP was a very valuable asset to the university. The commission conducted 190 interviews, held public hearings in Albany and New York City, reviewed more than fifty staff studies, visited eighteen campuses, and held nine plenary sessions, making twenty-nine recommendations on a multitude of topics in its final report, *The Challenge and the Choice.*

The chief focus of the commissions' work was the perceived "overregulation" of the university, which had " 'its roots in the legal conception of SUNY as a state agency' when the university was founded in 1948." Declaring that SUNY had the least flexibility of all systems studied, the commission concluded that "state government does not trust SUNY's Board of Trustees, Chancellor, or campus presidents, with even the most elementary administrative decisions concerning the institutions that they have been asked to manage."[100] There is a clear choice before New York, the report asserted: "The state can decide that New York is not going to get a public university of high quality, or it can change the rules." Consequently, the major recommendation was the transformation of the university into a "public benefit corporation," empowered to manage its budget and academic and personnel affairs, free of many of the restrictions currently imposed by state law. Crucial to its success would be lump-sum appropriations, rather than the minutely detailed external determinations that restricted SUNY's expenditures and its ability to allocate and manage its available resources. To UUP's great relief, the commission rejected campus closures and the dismantling of the system, arguing that closing even the most inefficient of the campuses would generate "only limited gains," would greatly reduce student access, and at the same time would produce great political divisiveness, "all of which outweigh any potential benefits." The report stressed that, in spite of its problems, SUNY represented powerful advantages for the state, which could serve "in full partnership with the independent sector and the City University of New York as a magnet for industry and a force for community and economic development, benefits that other states now enjoy from their state universities." In sum, the Independent Commission believed that the university's activities had been stunted by overregulation and inadequate support and that every citizen of the state had been the victim of that neglect. It argued that a weakened SUNY meant a weakened tax base, less vitality in the economy, and lost opportunities to stem migration from New York.[101]

Governor Cuomo was unenthusiastic about transforming the university into a public benefit corporation. Consequently, he introduced a "flurry" of legislative proposals that would give both public university systems greater flexibility and power to manage their own finances, expanding purchasing authority and the ability to shift funds, within limits, from one campus to another without seeking approval for each move, and encouraging the development of endowments and financial support from outside. Legislators were slow to react to either approach to reform, fearing limitations on legislative oversight while not diminishing the authority of the Division of the Budget.

While the governor, legislature, and SUNY management hammered out a mutually acceptable response to the commission's recommendations, UUP took a stand that backed away from the public benefit corporation but supported major new flexibility in financial operations. This was consistent with the organization's long-held belief that a radical restructuring of the relationship between the university and the unelected state agencies was essential to improved service to the people of the state.[102] While supporting proposals to free the university from excessive and truly unnecessary regulation, characterized by the commission as "tragically inappropriate," the organization opposed any proposal that would artificially insulate the institution from sensitivity to the social, economic, and political needs of the people served. Basically, UUP called for changes that would eliminate what was inhibiting and wrong, but retain adequate financial accountability and oversight responsibility as appropriate. Essentially, the commission's report was seen as "a ringing endorsement" of what the staff of SUNY and its union had been trying to do since its foundation, against insurmountable odds.[103] The political arm of UUP prepared to "lobby" for a reform package that did not artificially insulate the members from their "paymasters," the elected representatives of the people served, that preserved the system as a whole, and that facilitated the development of quality in and broader access to the institution.[104]

The Senate and Assembly Higher Education Committees reached an accord on management flexibility for SUNY in June. The public benefit corporation was scrapped, but most of the other recommendations of the commission were incorporated into the legislation, which was rapidly adopted and signed by the governor. UUP supported the legislation and asked for and received the active efforts of the affiliate, NYSUT, in promoting its passage.[105]

Almost immediately the struggle for SUNY flexibility paid off. When the state budget was adopted in April 1985, many of the debilitating austerities proposed in the initial executive budget message had been ameliorated by legislative action. More than 133 positions were restored, and funds were added in such vital areas as temp service, engineering equipment, computer upgrades, recruitment of minority students, organized research, restoration of child-care centers, establishment of the engineering baccalaureate at Farmingdale, and enhancement of EOP and EOC programs. But union leaders took equal satisfaction in the requirement that the university management report to the legislature on such matters as staffing levels, early retirement plans, reallocation of vacant positions with timetables for filling them, and the like. UUP saw this requirement as a "clear message to the un-elected bureaucrats that the legislature will be served. There was flexibility, but also accountability.[106] UUP's executive board was so delighted that it voted the Friend of SUNY award to the Independent Commission on the Future of the State University of New York at the May 1985 Delegate Assembly.[107]

Activities to Promote the General Welfare

Dealing with the annual budget crisis and efforts to stem its impact were not the only activities that occupied the organization in these years. Preparations for a new round of negotiations with the state were underway, while efforts to exploit the opportunities built into the existing agreement and the ordinary business of representation continued. Prosecution of grievances resulted in some significant victories. An arbitration award clarified the definition of the "unit" for retrenchment, and a physician who had been excluded from the implementation of the clinical practice plan at his center and was severely hurt as a result was made whole by a check for $346,861.[108] A class-action grievance was filed when it was determined that minimums under the contract had not been honored for a substantial number of unit members. An AIDS committee began operation to preserve the civil liberties of victims of the epidemic, some of whom were members. Efforts were undertaken to support the campaign the American Federation of Teachers had undertaken, at UUP's request, to convince the US Senate to pass the Pepper Bill abolishing mandatory retirement for college professors, the only "non–first responder" category of workers still forced to retire at age seventy. High on the political agenda was repeal of the Tier III category in the state employee pension system, which required those hired after July 1, 1976, to contribute 3 percent of their salary to the system. Also fought for and achieved in those years was the extension of the New York State income tax exemption to public employees in the TIAA-CREF retirement system, a singularly important contribution to the retirement well-being of members of the unit.[109] A benefits specialist was added to the staff to meet a growing need for coordination of member inquiries on three pension systems, the new dental and optical plans, and the salary-reduction program then under way. NYSUT was prevailed on to assign an assistant director of staff to the UUP office to help coordinate the evolving activities of field staff around the state, continuing the growing sensitivity of the affiliate to UUP's importance in the organization. Participation in the Employee Assistance Program was initiated, involving recruitment of members on each campus to help frame and implement the program on the local level. [110]

Innovative Student Recruitment Activities

Student recruitment, a major project begun in the previous administration, was significantly expanded in these years. An ad hoc committee, renamed the Public Education Committee, was once again appointed. It was charged with developing innovative methods of advertising the quality and diversity of the university and attracting new cohorts of young people to SUNY. Substantial appropriations for its activities (between $50,000 and $100,000 annually) were provided.[111] Under the leadership of Geraldine Bard of the Buffalo State campus, the committee developed programs focused primarily on New York City, where the bulk of the state's population resides, with the full cooperation of the central administration admissions office, the NYC Urban League, and the United Federation of Teachers (Local 2, AFT). At UUP expense, groups of academic counselors and representatives of the league were brought to campuses in western and central New York and the Hudson Valley to see for themselves what the various types of SUNY colleges had to offer. To avoid "canned" presentations, the counselors met with New York City students at each site, often resulting in excited reunions.[112] A typical trip involved four campuses, such as the University at Buffalo (an urban university center), Buffalo State College (an urban four-year liberal arts institution), Alfred Tech (a rural two-year agricultural and technical institution), and Fredonia State

College (a rural four-year liberal arts college). All of these projects were operated with the cooperation of the appropriate NYSUT K–12 locals and branches of the Urban League. Other projects subsidized by UUP included overnight bus trips of minority students from Rochester and Syracuse to campuses such as Plattsburgh, Canton, and Potsdam; telephone banks to follow up with accepted applicants, using faculty and students to provide personal contact and encouragement; participation in vocational fairs and advertising campaigns; a poster competition; and distribution of promotional videos funded by the union.[113]

The reaction of participants seemed to emphasize the fact that for many New York City educators, "SUNY is a well-kept secret!" And the plans had a positive impact on student recruitment, which was reflected in the invitation from the president of Maritime College to the president and secretary of UUP to join the training cruise up the Hudson to Albany, as a result of the flood of applications resulting from the union's activities on its behalf. Brockport, which had experienced a unique decline in applications and expressions of interest, enjoyed a similar increase following special attention to its needs.[114]

Part-Time Colleagues Come to the Forefront

New activities to redress the use and abuse of part-time colleagues, initiated during the Drescher years, would have a long-term impact on the organization. The Wakshull administration demonstrated UUP's commitment to part-timers when he prevailed on the state to extend negotiated raises to them, a modest relief they had not enjoyed before. Now new energy was brought to the attack on their serious and long-standing grievances. The campaign began in June 1982, when UUP alone protested, unsuccessfully, the Board of Regents's proposed policy changes to allow an institution of higher education to have "a majority of faculty to be other than full time."[115] The UUP argued that part-time faculty make important, indeed essential, contributions to higher education, and that they are an auxiliary support for full-time staff; they urged outright rejection of the proposal. The UUP felt that both the substance and reputations of colleges and universities would be seriously impaired if financial exigency dictated the unlimited expansion of the numbers of part-time personnel.

An internal program to deal with the long-standing exploitation of this staff began shortly thereafter. Dr. Gerald Schiffman, a highly distinguished faculty member at Downstate Medical Center, wrote an article for *The Voice* identifying the nature and extent of the problems. In it, he castigated the state for failing to use part-time personnel creatively to enrich offerings, increase badly needed flexibility, promote heterogeneity, and improve the state of the art of instruction, particularly in science and technology. He argued that present practice virtually precluded the translation of the great potential of the pool of part-timers into reality because the recent practice is "too irrational and reactive.[116] The first ad hoc committee on part-time concerns was appointed in June 1983, chaired by Barbara Andrews, a part-time member of the English Department at the Utica-Rome campus. Immediately, a questionnaire designed to identify primary problems of the cohort was drafted and sent to all persons listed on the payroll as earning less than the negotiated minimum.

More than 700 replied. Of these, more than half indicated they had been employed for more than three years at the same campus, a strong indication that they were not "casuals," as many in the administration had maintained. Slightly more than a majority were invited and actively encouraged to attend department meetings, but many were not permitted to vote. A majority were not given control over what they would teach, and only 65 percent were permitted to write their own syllabi once a course was assigned. Among professionals, one-quarter did not have required performance programs and only 53 percent had performance evaluations. Sixty-five percent reported membership in UUP, but only 3 percent attended meetings. Needless to say, improved compensation and job security were vital concerns.[117]

Plans were drawn up for the first statewide conference to consider the results of the survey and ways and means of involving part-time colleagues in the work of the union. High on the agenda was preparation of contract demands to improve the basic terms and conditions of employment system-wide. Forty-one colleagues from twenty-one campuses attended the weekend workshop. Guest speakers included people with highly successful programs at other institutions advancing the interests of part-time staff. "Best practices" were identified and potential options for SUNY discussed.[118]

The work of the ad hoc committee demonstrated the real need for greater attention to the problems of the part-time workforce. To demonstrate the commitment of the organization and ensure regular and consistent attention to their needs, the Executive Board introduced an amendment to the UUP constitution to establish a standing Committee on Part-Time Concerns, charged with encouraging the membership and involvement of part-timers in the work of the union, to propose ways and means to redress their grievances and improve the general terms and conditions of their employment. In addition, it was called on to educate full-time members on the important role of part-timers in the life of the university.[119] As a signal to the state of how important the leadership of UUP considered the issue, President Drescher appointed Barbara Andrews to the new negotiating team, the first time a part-time member had served in that capacity.

Actual progress in addressing problems of adjunct faculty and staff would prove to be extremely difficult and slow-going, but their grievances and issues were put on the UUP agenda in these years and have continued to be of major importance ever since.

Joint Committee and Medical Malpractice

Of particular significance in the ongoing activities of UUP was the work of the joint labor-management committee dealing with establishing and operating the clinical practice plans so painfully worked out in the negotiations of 1982. The most serious problem faced by New York's medical profession as a whole was the out-of-control escalation of medical malpractice insurance premiums. There were actually predictions that if something was not done to cap escalation of premiums, the future of medicine and medical education in the state would be in jeopardy. In turn, the cost of medical delivery would skyrocket, influencing what all citizens paid for insurance, drugs, and dentistry. Responding to the danger, Governor Cuomo initiated a package of bills designed to address the problem. The state Senate responded quickly, but all efforts were blocked in the Assembly, which took a very strong position in defense of consumer rights. UUP doctors, in partnership with the New York Medical Society, inaugurated efforts to lobby for major change, because all agreed that only a substantive breakthrough could forestall disaster. At their request, UUP joined the campaign.[120]

Because of their threefold mission of teaching, research, and patient care, clinical faculty have historically been less active with patients and therefore less at risk for charges of malpractice than full-time practitioners. Insurance companies, however, declined to take this fact into consideration in setting premiums. Consequently, it was estimated, the SUNY clinical practice plans regularly paid $12 million annually for $3 million in awards, hardly a cost-effective investment of resources. The joint labor-management committee tackled the problem and worked constantly until 1990 when a solution was devised. A reciprocal insurer, "Academic," was established and licensed in New York with a charter sensitive to the realities of academic clinical practice. A similar corporation, Academic Medical Professional Insurance Exchange, was licensed in Vermont to insure medical students and residents in all fifty states. It is estimated that the operation of these two companies, initiated through collective bargaining, have saved SUNY and its practice plans more than $150 million since they were established.[121] The major architect and driving force behind these efforts was Peter Kane, M.D., of Upstate Medical Center, who represented the SUNY physicians on three negotiation teams and consistently served on the joint committees.

Efforts for Professionals

Nonclassroom personnel in SUNY had always felt themselves to be second-class citizens in the university community. UUP had responded successfully to their primary problem, job security, when it negotiated permanent appointment for their ranks in the Wakshull years. Nevertheless, they continued to suffer from the rigidity of the system that retained caps on salary in ranks and the absence of

a career ladder and genuine promotional opportunities. Many deserving professionals, even though recommended, were precluded from receiving discretionary
awards for excellence in service because they were already at the top of the grade.
(It should be noted that these caps were imposed by the Board of Trustees and
not negotiated by the union.)[122] Lew Herrod, a delegate from Downstate Medical
Center, was typical of a professional suffering from the limitations of the system.
He had been a PR (Professional Rank) 1 since 1968 when he spoke at the assembly
in 1982. He argued that the absence of promotional opportunities denied committed employees any "sense of accomplishment on the job."[123] Throughout the
Drescher years, redress of these problems was high on the agenda, and the joint
labor-management committee approach was utilized to study and find solutions
to the seemingly intractable handicaps professionals faced.

In 1979, a joint committee had been established to review the evaluation
system for professionals, and when its report was issued on July 1, 1981, the
three parties left the basic structure of the oldest statewide evaluation system
intact. The required performance program was to be designed by the individual
and the immediate supervisor. Evaluations were to be based on that program.
While pay was not directly tied to it, these judgments were a factor in presidential consideration for renewal, promotions, and discretionary awards. Several
minor changes were also agreed on that reflected irritants professionals still had
to live with. For example, many professionals had never been informed who
their immediate supervisor was, the person who was required to discuss areas
in need of improvement before annual evaluation.[124] Satisfaction with the evaluation process, however, did not relieve the great dissatisfaction with the absence
of a career ladder and promotional opportunities.

In preparation for new negotiations, Charles Hansen, vice president for
professionals, drafted a questionnaire seeking information on the status of his
constituents. The instrument focused on whether all employees actually had
an updated performance program, the individual's role in its creation, and the
evaluations based on it. It also sought to document the reality of a career ladder
and promotion system, the operation of the grievance procedure for professionals, and the availability of sabbaticals for them.[125] The results of this investigation and further outreach of the negotiations committee in 1981–82 found
that there was no rhyme or reason to the placing of professionals in PR ranks.
Many people were PR 1 on one campus while their counterparts with the same
skills, training, and responsibilities on another were PR 2. The union had put a
demand in its package for a set number of promotions in a discrete period of
time, but was convinced to accept the state's proposal for a complete evaluation
of job titles and the rank system, to be undertaken by a fully funded outside
consulting firm. Since there had not been a classification study in SUNY in
twelve years and the rankings seemed to make no rational sense, a dispassionate
evaluation seemed to be in order. Consequently, the new agreement called for

the establishment of a joint labor-management committee to ensure UUP input into a reclassification study which by statute was the exclusive jurisdiction of the executive department.[126] Many professionals were extremely disappointed in this outcome, because studies had been going on since the days of the Senate Professional Association with no real remedy for their frustration. The negotiations team agreed to this approach because it seemed to be an opportunity to solve the problems once and for all, with the joint committee approach ensuring that the union had real input into the choice of consultant and the implementation of the ultimate recommendation. The study of promotion and classification and changes necessary to implement career advancement opportunities was funded by an allocation of $100,000.

The union's preparation for effective operation of the study included a statewide workshop that attracted sixty-seven members. Under the leadership of the new vice president, Barbara Wiedner of New Paltz, participants focused on job security and evaluation, compensation, leaves and fringe benefits, and recruitment and the involvement of professionals in the recruitment process.[127] Particular attention was focused on elements of the new agreement that clarified professional access to study leaves to improve skills or preserve licenses, compensatory time policies, and cooperation on health and safety issues, which were of vital concern to professionals, particularly those at hospitals.[128]

The diligent preparation in the weeks before the scheduled meetings of the joint committee enabled the UUP delegates to have maximum impact on the agenda for its work. The state's representatives came to accept the concept that the job classification, compensation, and promotion were inextricably entwined, long the union's position, and therefore must be considered as a package. One dimension of the unions' preparation was the Survey of Professional Employees, which so impressed the OER members that they offered to reimburse the union for the cost of administering an instrument.[129] Fully 21 percent of the unit responded to the initiative, making available extremely valuable information for the committee. Interestingly enough, among those who applied for and failed to win promotion, 79 percent were denied locally, giving the lie to the excuse generally circulated by management that it was the Division of the Budget that denied the move. Analysis of the survey results revealed that the nonclassroom personnel desired a promotion system analogous to that of the academics: movement from rank to rank based on increase in expertise, growth in the profession, and longevity.[130]

But solving professional problems proved to be slow going because SUNY record-keeping was abysmal. The personnel data system (PDA) on which analysis and recommendations must be based was filled with errors. It included management-confidential people, groundskeepers, security police, academics, erroneous professional titles, and changes in rank and department that had never happened.[131] The Arthur Young Company was the successful bidder for the study. Starting in December 1984, its agents fanned out across the state to interview 300 professionals, a number representing the twenty-seven to thirty more populous titles. In the interviews they sought to collect information on the duties and responsibilities associated with the job titles and the promotional process and opportunities available. It should be noted that the Young representatives cautioned that the data on which the classification system was based was inaccurate and inadequate, confirming the suspicions of the UUP committee members at the outset.[132] The result would be further delay in the resolution of professional issues until a new agreement would ensure funding for implementation of the results of the Young Study.

New Negotiations

Beginning in the early spring of 1984, UUP began preparing for the new round of negotiations with the state. The leadership anticipated a much easier time because relationships with the representatives of both OER and SUNY management had been increasingly cordial. The operation of the joint committees had successfully addressed some of the most difficult, long-standing problems, or were in the process of doing so. UUP's initiatives in addressing student recruitment were highly regarded. Cooperation in achieving the SUNY flexibility legislation and with the state's economic development proposals was publicly appreciated and led the UUP leaders to believe that the congenial atmosphere would continue and an agreement would emerge without delay and rancor.

The Negotiations Advisory Committee began meeting in April to inaugurate the process of soliciting grassroots involvement in drafting the package to be presented to the state in the new year.[133] A broad questionnaire was sent to all members, and eight months of intensive analysis and outreach followed. More than 4,200 replied to the instrument, and approximately 200 additional persons took the time to write lengthy letters articulating their hopes for the new contract, yielding a wealth of information on the needs of the unit.[134] Actual negotiations were scheduled to start on January 9, 1985, with the exchange of packages. Two additional meetings were planned for the same month, reinforcing the conviction that the agreement would be settled with alacrity.

By February, external developments began to dim the sense of optimism. *The New York Times* reported on the opening of negotiations with all of the state's workers, noting that the governor's budget for the new fiscal year allowed for public-employee raises of 2 percent. In addition, Thomas Hartnett, now the director of OER, cautioned that the state needed to negotiate greater flexibility in job assignments, among other things, to cope with the negative effects of the Reagan budget cuts, and this would clearly impact negotiations with the state workers.[135] Escalating healthcare costs, particularly the highly inflationary increases in the price of drugs, became a major issue for all units in state service. The Public Employee Benefit Trust, established after the last agreement to handle such insurance as prescription drugs and dental plans for UUP and the Public Employees Federation (PEF), faced serious deficits. Additionally, the state proposal for the new Empire Plan, which would radically change the entire approach to state-provided health insurance programs for its workers, created a double problem for UUP, which represented both consumers and providers.[136] The results of UUP's outreach to various state medical associations and members of the unit for an assessment of the potential of the Empire Plan were uniformly pessimistic.[137] Rates of compensation to physicians were projected to be below those of Medicare, creating uncertainty about whether New York medical practitioners would sign up to participate, impairing delivery of healthcare for state employees.

Other items in the state's package that UUP's negotiating team found problematic included demands for parking fees; the absence of any attention to "operational" items such as the professional career ladder and promotional opportunities for professionals, issues that were still unresolved; and willingness to deal with restoring a salary schedule, longevity increases, grievance procedures, retrenchment, and part-time issues. But above all, the demand for "renewable tenure," which would compromise tenure and permanent appointment in the university, simply stunned the UUP team.[138] All saw it as a frontal assault on academic freedom, the essential ingredient in promoting vitality and creativity in the American university.

Over time, the divide between the parties widened and solidified as time passed. Little progress was made, in spite of regular, even daily, sessions. UUP declared an impasse on June 27, 1985, which lasted until March 4, 1986.[139] Mediators were appointed. Fact-finding began, but little progress was made. Once impasse was declared, the battleground shifted from the table to the media.

In discussing responsibility for the failure to consummate a deal, the chief negotiator for the union, Tim Reilly, declared that "the State does not understand union language," arguing that the other side's "people don't grasp meaning if their minds are encoded for a different set of assumptions." He believed the state's negotiators were concerned almost exclusively with preserving the managerial status quo or with "helping managers do their job easily," with no concern for the quality of education or professional excellence so long as employees stayed on the job.[140] Director Hartnett countered by insisting that the state's offer was" a reasonable one" and that he would not go back to the table "unless the union is through talking 'nonsense.' " At one point he characterized the union's proposals as "a pile of manure," which resulted in the UUP Executive Board entertaining a motion to consider delivery of a quantity, preferably a truckload, of the same, to his front yard with a note explaining the difference between the UUP demands and the substance delivered.[141] It seemed that it was not the issues themselves that Hartnett and the OER team had problems with, but rather, in their words, "the manner in which they are presented which is so fog like." In fact, posturing by both sides created the stalemate with what the director characterized as the state's "best paid worker union." He insisted that this dispute was the "most serious in the last four rounds of negotiations" and threatened to lobby the fact-finders not to recommend that raises be retroactive. He further suggested that OER would refuse to bring up for consideration issues dear to the union's heart, such as the promotion and reclassification study.[142]

The union viewed fact-finding as a ploy on the part of the state to delay further, asserting that UUP had no fear of public scrutiny of their concerns and demands. The "antics" of the state were a "war of nerves," and members were urged to "Hang Tough!" An ad was placed in *the New York Times* arguing that the faculty and staff of SUNY needed a contract that provided for basic minimum wages, at least equal to entry-level salaries for New York City public school teachers, rewards for career employees, a clear and sensible promotion system for professionals, protection of employees against arbitrary personnel policies and layoffs, and an end to the exploitation of an underclass of part-time workers. Absence of these basics inhibited recruitment of top-quality staff and access to SUNY for the citizens of New York State. Similar advertisements were placed in *the Legislative Gazette*, the Albany-based publication tor the legislature.[143]

Both assessments of the situation were close to reality. The sides, representing two entirely different cultures, were talking at and not with each other.

Declaring "Unity Day," the union staged a series of events around the state calling attention to the frustration members felt. Informational picket lines were set up on each campus and support was solicited and received from other unions, such as several locals of the American Federation of Federal, State and Municipal Employees (AFSME), the Public Employees Federation (PEF), the United Electrical Workers (UEW), the Albany Police, and the Troy Labor Council, among others.[144] A Crisis Committee was established to plan a concerted program of public education on the impasse and issues still unresolved. The union inaugurated a "Cuomo Watch" so that wherever in the state the governor visited, a handful of UUP representatives picketed his appearances, calling for a fair agreement. The Delegate Assembly authorized the creation of a war chest or "Defense Fund" to raise nondues money in case any of the planned activities were deemed a violation of the structures of the Taylor Law, characterized as the "Drescher bail money." The Crisis Committee designed an action plan that incorporated a "work to rule" program.[145] Staging a referendum on more "militant action" was discussed. For the first time in its history, the central administration building in downtown Albany was picketed by union activists, resulting in a "lockout." All external doors were closed and barred to the public. The protests were noisy, with participants carrying placards reading "Get Serious with UUP," "Mario, Aren't We Family?" "Talk's Cheap. So, Talk!"[146]

In late November, the state informed UUP that if it did not resume talks within three weeks, it would appeal to the Public Employment Relations Board to investigate the union's intent to engage in "good faith bargaining." Two sessions were quickly held, but no progress was made, resulting in the commencement of the investigation.[147]

In the meantime, the state circulated a memorandum to members of the unit declaring that participants in the statewide and GHI health insurance plans would be automatically transferred to the newly created Empire Plan in November 1986, in spite of the absence of an agreement. The union countered with the threat of an improper practice charge, arguing that the state's action was inconsistent with its obligations under the Triborough Decision, which required maintenance of benefits in the gap between contracts.[148] Similar fears were raised about continuation of prescription and dental benefits for the duration, but quiet talk behind the scenes, resolved the problems.[149]

On February 19, 1986, UUP organized a statewide demonstration day to protest the continued lack of productive talks. Campus demonstrations at Upstate Medical Center and Albany, which included picketing and parades of members, attracted citywide television and print coverage in Syracuse and Albany. "Work to rule" activities were undertaken at Farmingdale, Canton, New Paltz, Plattsburgh, and Fredonia. Resolutions in support of the union were adopted by the senates at Fredonia and Geneseo. At Environmental Science and Forestry, cars parked on campus lots were blanketed with flyers explaining the union's position. In addition, staff threw up an informational picket line around the campus. All-day picketing took place at Potsdam, and rallies and picketing took place at Downstate, Binghamton, Delhi, Alfred State, and Optometry. Several thousand calls were made directly to the governor's office, and legislators were contacted in their home offices. At Alfred, a picket line wound its way through the campus, picking up new participants as it wended its way around the buildings, so that by the end, fully one-third of the faculty and staff were participating. Maritime's executive board called on members to "work to rule" and petitioned the admiral (campus president) for his support.[150] John Carney, chapter president at the Oneonta campus, when interviewed on the picket line, indicated that he had heard talk of strike on this "fairly moderate campus," and called on the governor to intervene to move things forward.[151] Throughout the impasse period, UUP produced more than fifteen negotiations bulletins distributed unit-wide to keep members abreast of all developments or lack thereof. The president said that "we are not at fault for failing to negotiate a contract, unless you want a contract that will embarrass us."[152]

An open letter to Governor Cuomo was drafted and signed by members of chapter executive boards deploring the continuing stalemate and urging him to personally examine the union's proposal, "since it is obvious that your representatives do not understand the university and its unique problems." It pointed out that a minimum salary of $13,500 at this point in time was unrealistic, and that delay and uncertainty regarding tenure had a direct impact on recruitment and retention of staff. The union concluded its appeal declaring that "we are trusted with the State's most important resource: its citizens seeking a quality education. Therefore, your full attention is required to resolve this impasse."[153] Unfortunately, in a call-in radio show, Cuomo seemed to wash his hands of the problem, suggesting that "you people wanted your University to yourselves. We gave it to you and now you cry for help," obviously referring to the union's role in the struggle for SUNY flexibility.[154]

The comprehensive action plan worked, at least to the extent that membership in the union increased from 13,600 in October 1985 to 14,250 in February 1986, the highest it had ever been.[155]

By mid-February, it appeared that the appointed team did not apprehend just how serious the state was about charging UUP with failure to bargain in good faith and that it would be unable to consummate an agreement. OER representatives said publicly and privately that the state had gone as far as it could go. At a special meeting of the team, after convincing most of its members that it was a "do or die" situation, President Drescher exercised her constitutional responsibility and took control of the situation. She asked for and received a list of which areas members felt were essential to an acceptable deal. After consulting with close advisors, she met with the OER director and worked out modest advances in all of the areas identified by the team except one. The state continued to refuse to restore the salary schedule surrendered in the first round of collective bargaining by the Senate Professional Association, long a demand of UUP.

But there was improvement on the others. The movement, however, was a compromise between the absolutist positions taken by both sides up to that point. Like all such compromises, they satisfied no one, but did make an agreement possible. For example, the new minimum starting salaries were elevated, but remained unrealistic for the time, although no full-time personnel earned less than the new minimums. The state's demand for parking fees, ending a long-standing past practice agreed to by other units in the university service, was modified so that UUP agreed to negotiate such fees on the local level, with the tariff to be based on the actual cost of maintenance of the facilities. Not perfect, but it did give the UUP unit a genuine say in the imposition of the costly annual parking charge. However, as it worked out, most chapters were able to protect their members from it by vigorously prosecuting this clause through grievance to arbitration. Very quickly thereafter a memorandum of understanding was wrapped up and a tentative agreement finalized.[156]

Agreement and Ratification Problems

Almost immediately, opposition to the pact emerged. Barbara Andrews, representing part-timers on the team, could not accept the very limited advance for her constituency and so resigned from the negotiations team. John Hunt, chapter president at Farmingdale with 700 members, deplored the failure to restore the salary schedule, and he also resigned. Both refused to sign the pact when it was finalized. William Wiesner, chapter president at the Stony Brook main campus, representing 1,300 members, denounced the settlement to *Newsday*, the major Long Island newspaper. He and Hunt announced that they would oppose ratification "because the terms are inadequate and were reached without their consent." Salary increases were too small and improvements for part-time staff pitiful.[157] Hunt stated that he had been "devastated" because Drescher had agreed to the settlement without consulting the negotiating team. This assertion was not exactly true in light of the meeting when she asked the team to list areas of improvement essential to an agreement. But even if it had been true, the UUP constitution charges the president with the responsibility to negotiate the contract, based on a package of demands worked out by the Negotiations Committee. The team was a surrogate for the president, and had no constitutional standing.

However, the defection of two team members and lack of enthusiasm on the part of others who shared the disquiet of the defectors placed a heavy burden on the president to sell the contract, lest the union be found guilty of "bad faith" bargaining. The tentative agreement was published, with an explication of all changes from prior agreements, and Drescher spent the next six weeks traveling around the state meeting with the leadership of every chapter, holding town-hall type sessions on every campus, and generally educating the members on the opportunities afforded by the pact.

It was a three-year agreement, with 5 percent across the board salary increases and 1 percent discretionary money each year. The first year was retroactive to 1985, and to protect the members from the rigid rules of the Internal Revenue Service, the state agreed to annualize the retroactive check so that the federal withholding would be less burdensome.[158] Professionals were to receive a performance award of $500 when they achieved permanent appointment. One percent of payroll was to be allocated to implement the Young reclassification study recommendations. Since 1 percent of payroll amounted to more than $8 million, professionals were afforded a major economic gain. Librarians were to be placed on the same pay schedule as the academic faculty, a demand articulated by their association since 1968.[159] Long-term part-time employees gained new protection through term appointments, requiring notification of nonrenewal. Ample funding was made available for initiatives to be undertaken by health and safety, day care, employee assistance, and affirmative action joint committees. Two million dollars were provided for the joint Quality of Working Life Committee, $3 million to deal with disparity in salary, and $900,000 for the Continuity of Employment Committee.

Health insurance was to be provided through the Empire Plan, which did include psychiatric coverage and additional moneys to improve dental and prescription plans and to initiate an optical program for unit members. A valuable innovation in health insurance was the inclusion of an opportunity to tailor aspects of the plan to the specific needs of the unit.[160] A New York State/UUP Joint Committee on Health Benefits was established to be "a consumer advocate at the ready," carefully and continuously monitoring the operation of the plan and taking actions to improve its functioning.[161]

Ratification ballots were sent out to the members, and the American Arbitration Association counted them on May 8, just in time for the results to be available at the Delegate Assembly, which met the following day. Fully 87 percent of those voting (7,312) favored the pact, with only 1,119 dissenting.[162]

Leaders of the organization came to believe that the long struggle to achieve this agreement had strengthened the organization internally, in spite of the dissent of some involved. Not only had UUP fended off the frontal assault on tenure, but the fight had given birth to a new momentum that could be harnessed to exploit the opportunities incorporated in the agreement. What had not been accomplished would become the agenda for the future. In the editorial announcing ratification, Drescher thanked the members for their patience, solidarity, and persistence, which were deemed essential to the breakthrough. The visible expressions of support, large and small, that came throughout the trying months, she said, "constitute the nutrition that sustains resolve, without which courage and strength can wither and die."[163]

Contract Opportunities Exploited

The hallmark of the new contract might be "opportunity," but exploitation of that opportunity would take a great deal of creativity, militancy, and hard work. Expansion of the labor-management cooperation model, with adequate funding, was the key to the evolution of healthy improvement in individual and group terms and conditions of employment. UUP became a true partner in resolving serious problems, rather than an actor on a stage that allowed only the illusion of participation. All parties—UUP, the state, and SUNY—had a proprietary stake in the successful outcome of plans into which the committees invested their appropriations. The union's experience with such committees in the past had been very positive, and so the leadership looked forward to continued amicable operation of the expanded program.

One of the more positive and promising innovations in this area was the creation of a joint committee to address the rather dismal record of SUNY in recruiting and retaining members of the federally protected classes in its workforce. Programs authorized by the joint Affirmative Action Committee were to be funded by the Professional Development and Quality of Working Life Committee. Under the leadership of Tim Reilly, now chair of UUP's standing committee, the committee created a diversity fellowship program, funding leave time for women, minorities, Vietnam-era veterans, and the disabled, for the year or so before a tenure decision must be made to "insure that the candidate has free, unencumbered time to complete research necessary for the successful outcome of the peer review process."[164] It is a unique program in higher education and is deemed to be a remarkably cost-effective way to promote diversity in the workforce. At the suggestion of OER director Thomas Hartnett, it was named for President Drescher and has functioned effectively for thirty years, particularly in the recruitment and retention of women to the faculty and staff of the university.

Internal Growth and Development

In light of the expanded programs incorporated into the new agreement and the growing financial stability of the organization, the Spring 1986 Delegate Assembly considered the proposal of the Executive Board to make the two vice presidents full-time staff members. This was an important decision because it ensured the continued primacy of the elected representatives of the members. The work of a truly democratic organization, the leadership asserted, should be carried out by persons accountable to the membership and not hired professionals, as valuable and essential as their assistance was. The Executive Board felt that oversight of the work generated by the new agreement, particularly the projected creation of thirty-two chapter "shadow committees" to gather ideas for the development of programs to be funded by the joint committees, was simply too much for one person. Oversight of almost $15 million of negotiated, members' funds was a grave responsibility that should be undertaken by people directly responsible to the members. Work to be assigned to the new full-time vice presidents included statewide training of volunteers to exploit the new opportunities, coordination of all committee meetings, data assessment, and travel around the state to encourage participation in the new programs. Of particular concern were the opportunities opened by the contract to finally address the grievances of professionals, which required continuous monitoring. All of this was in addition to the regular activities of the central office of the organization, not the least of which was organization of the new round of fighting to protect the SUNY budget.[165] In short, by adopting the proposal, UUP rejected the potential for a "staff-dominated" organizational structure.[166] After lengthy debate, the assembly agreed to place the two vice presidents on staff at a salary comparable to that of the secretary.[167]

Following elections, the new vice presidents, John Crary of Canton, a Reform Caucus member, for academics and Thomas Corigliano of Plattsburgh, a United Caucus member, for professionals, took full-time status on July 1.[168]

The remaining year of the Drescher administration was invested primarily in implementing development of the new agreement, particularly in resolution of professional problems. By fall, major advances had been made in developing a promotion program and establishing clear overtime procedures.[169] Compensatory time problems were resolved by the end of the year and "on call rates" determined at a mutually satisfactory level. In addition, in the new year, campuses became directly involved in creating a locally sensitive promotion program patterned on one adopted originally at the Albany campus.[170]

The work of the now full-time vice presidents was vital to completing efforts to resolve these long-standing problems. In addition, their presence on staff allowed the president to undertake a number of projects that helped advance the organization's status in the labor movement in general, which had not been possible in the past. UUP became directly involved in the NYSUT and state AFL-CIO political endorsement process. She was also able to spend time in Illinois, working with the United Professors of Illinois on organizing faculty at Northern Illinois State University, in a sense paying back the AFT for its assistance in UUP's struggles with the NEA. Several hundred members benefited from the initiation of a class-action grievance on their behalf to rectify serious miscalculations in their retroactive paychecks and those of professionals whose continuing appointment bonus had been improperly withheld.[171]

One of the major developments in the life of the organization was the introduction by the Albany chapter, a United Caucus stronghold, of an amendment to the UUP constitution establishing the direct election of its officers. Interestingly enough, direct election of officers was supported by the leadership of both caucuses. Because the proposal was an extremely complex measure, the Delegate Assembly recessed to a "committee of the whole," chaired by Edward Alfonsin, a delegate who was also a professional parliamentarian. Adopting this approach allowed flexible rules of debate not possible with the formal strictures of Robert's Rules of Order that governed regular sessions.

Arguments centered on the appropriateness of expanding the democratic process in UUP in spite of the logistical and financial difficulties of implementation, as opposed to preserving the present representative system. Debate was lengthy and passionate. When returning to regular session, the delegates chose to preserve the power and responsibility of the Delegate Assembly and table the motion, with intent to kill.[172] Resuming the chair, President Drescher indicated that while she was disappointed in the decision of the Assembly, she felt that the debate had been the most "far-reaching, intelligent debate" in the history of the organization and was proud to have faced the issue in a "four-square" way and on a level of statesman-like behavior that did the union credit.[173]

Other activities in the waning months of the administration involved the annual budget battle to preserve access and quality in the university, the expanded student recruitment activities, new outreach and programming with the Student Association of the State University, and work with the shadow committees and the joint labor-management operations. Full implementation of the Employee

Assistance Program was a major achievement. In the election of May 1987, the chief negotiator, Tim Reilly, was elected to succeed President Drescher, and she was elected to the Executive Board to continue service to the organization as an "elder statesman." A farewell banquet was held to celebrate her efforts, attended by more than a hundred, including representatives of SUNY central, OER, NYSUT, and AFT. Proceeds of the affair were donated to the union scholarship trust.

Nuala Drescher made significant contributions to the life and stability of the organization. She brought new energy and creativity to the office, which allowed UUP to build on the solid foundation of her predecessor, who had been her early union mentor. In these years, the organization coped successfully with serious fiscal problems that might have driven it into bankruptcy. Working with treasurer Thomas Matthews and the finance committee, a new element of transparency was added to fiscal operations, which continued to be the hallmark of the operation for the next several administrations. Her willingness to work with political opponents, both in her own base and outside of it, allowed for coalition-building and a new degree of civility internally. The success of external political activities, which were significantly regularized and expanded, helped allay the overt hostility to unionization and collective bargaining in general. Similarly, expansion of training workshops for chapter leaders helped broaden the base of activism and involvement on the local levels. During her years, membership steadily increased. Emphasis on joint labor-management cooperation, not limited to the funded committees, helped create reasonably cordial relationships with the SUNY administration and the Governor's Office of Employee relations, in spite of militancy at the table and independence in the budget battles. Attacks on tenure were thwarted, traditional governance was protected, particularly at the medical schools, and democratic control of the governance of the union itself was preserved.

Chapter 5

Expanding the Role of UUP, 1987–93

With Nuala Drescher barred by UUP's constitution from running for another term as president, the United Caucus threw its support to John M. "Tim" Reilly, who Drescher had defeated as the caucus standard-bearer six years earlier. The Reform Caucus choice was John Crary. In the election at the May 2, 1987, Delegate Assembly, Reilly soundly defeated Crary, with 136 votes to Crary's 73.[1] On assuming office, Reilly indicated that his goals were to increase membership and chapter participation, strengthen the union's lobbying effort, and make the university more accessible to minorities. As noted in UUP's publication, *The Voice*, he told news reporters, " 'I want UUP, together with its affiliate, the New York State United Teachers (NYSUT), to secure the necessary state funds to move SUNY into the front ranks of the nation's colleges and universities.' "[2]

Negotiating Contracts

But these were goals; a more immediate need was to begin negotiations for a new contract. The current Agreement with the state was due to expire on June 30, 1988, and the union needed to develop its demands for its replacement. Involving the membership in this process was deemed important, and so on September 8, 1987, William (Bill) Scheuerman, who had been designated chief negotiator and chair of the Negotiations Committee, informed the union's members that the committee would be "spending the next several months sampling opinion and eliciting suggestions" from them, "so that UUP's efforts are directed toward solutions of problems and improvements of conditions our members identify as important to them in their professional and academic careers." To gather that information, a survey questionnaire was developed. Additionally, each campus would have a representative on the Negotiations Committee and two members on the Negotiations Advisory Committee, and those committee members would "be holding meetings, organizing visits from the Negotiating Team to your campus, and generally working to see that you, and all other members, have the chance to participate fully in the effort to win our new contract."[3] Subsequently, over a four-month period, the committees held numerous lengthy meetings, reviewed the thousands of questionnaires that were returned, reviewed input from UUP committee chairs, and held several hearings, while Negotiations Team members visited twenty-seven of the union's chapters.[4]

On November 2, Reilly informed Elizabeth D. Moore, director of the Governor's Office of Employee Relations, that UUP desired "to begin negotiations for a successor agreement to the existing contract," and that those negotiations "should begin as soon as practical."[5] It was agreed that the initial negotiations meeting between UUP and GOER would be held on December 18 at UUP's offices.[6] The purpose of that meeting was to discuss ground rules and set dates for future meetings. Among other housekeeping issues, it was agreed that a forty-eight-hour notice would be given before going public on any issues. The date for the next meeting, at which contract proposals would be exchanged, was to be January 21, 1988. After a two-week period, during which both sides would examine the proposals, they would meet again on February 11–12.[7] Meanwhile, Reilly created an Action Advisory Committee (AAC), which was "charged with developing and coordinating campus-based political actions in support of . . . negotiations efforts." Scheuerman informed chapter presidents that at the first AAC meeting the committee's members "agreed to explore the possibility of taking symbolic actions on each campus shortly after we exchange packages," and that "a committee member will contact you concerning the options your chapter may wish to pursue."[8]

When exchanging proposals at the January 21 meeting, Scheuerman noted that the UUP package was "derived from rank-and-file democracy and input gained through endless meetings and visits to individual campuses." Christopher Eatz, the state's chief negotiator, stated that their proposal (which totaled 145 pages) was "committed to the principle of accountability to the taxpayers of the State of New York and to UUP."[9] The UUP Negotiations Team met with the union's Negotiations Committee two days later to review the proposals. The February 11 clarification meeting was held, but the meeting scheduled for the next day had to be postponed until February 18 as a result of a winter storm. Clarification continued at that meeting, and supplementary demands were exchanged at a February 23 meeting. Weekly negotiations meetings were scheduled through March.[10]

What was UUP trying to achieve in the contract? The item of most interest to members in any contract usually is salary, and for this one UUP was asking for an 11.7 percent annual increase. But they also sought higher minimum salaries and the elimination of maximum salaries that were never negotiated but imposed by the trustees. Benefit improvements also were sought, especially having health insurance premiums being fully paid by the state. Professional development proposals were geared to both academics and professionals, but more so for the latter. For professional employees the demands were for sabbatical leaves, continuation of the reclassification process, promotion and peer evaluation, and a reduction of the probationary period. There also were several affirmative action items and the elimination of mandatory retirement. Stronger job security provisions were proposed, as was a complete renegotiation of the language of the Clinical Practice Plan. The UUP proposal contained several items to address the needs of part-timers, in particular that salary increases and health insurance benefits would be applied pro rata for them.[11] The March 28 UUP "Negotiations Update" reported that the weekly meetings of the negotiators "to define and clarify their demands" and to "justify the proposals" were, Scheuerman noted, "fruitful and edifying." Meetings would now continue weekly through April. Scheuerman was quoted as saying, " 'We're ready to move into intensive negotiations and we have made that intention clear to the state.' "[12]

After nineteen negotiations meetings and nine private meetings,[13] a mailing to UUP members from John M. Reilly and William E. Scheuerman of June 14 reported that a tentative Agreement had been reached between UUP and the State of New York that would be effective July 1, 1988, to June 30, 1991. Recipients of the mailing were told that the tentative Agreement "improves our terms and conditions of employment and opens new opportunities to redress long-standing problems. In addition, we have achieved innovations eliminating serious salary inequities within our unit." Members were informed that across-the-board salary increases would be 5 percent in the first year, 5 percent in the second year, and 5.5 percent in the third year, for a total compounded raise of 16.3 percent. There also would be a longevity award of $300 added to base for those holding or achieving continuing or permanent employment during the life of the contract, 1 percent for discretionary increases in each year of the contract, Excellence Awards of $3,000 each added to each recipient's base salary, and location stipends for full-time employees working in New York City and its suburbs, as well as several other salary-enhancement provisions. There would be increased funding for affirmative action and day care, and for Professional Development and Quality of Working Life awards. While there would be a small increase in the copay for medical office visits and some other outpatient services, that was offset by a reduction in the major medical deductible and in the maximum out-of-pocket expense under major medical, and an increase in lifetime major-medical coverage. Also, there was a 43 percent increase in the state's contribution to the UUP Benefit Fund. An important victory was achieved for part-time employees, who would now receive health insurance if they taught two or more courses. The two-course criterion for healthcare coverage replaced a more restrictive standard that varied campus by campus and excluded many who taught two courses. There also were improvements in the clinical-practice provisions of the contract.[14] The Albany *Times Union* reported that UUP President Reilly "called the $1 million allotted for excellence awards a 'crucial innovation' because it expresses the union's commitment to recognize superior service."[15]

On June 21 a final negotiations session was held to formally sign the contract. At that meeting, Elizabeth Moore stated, "I would like to say that I am very, very pleased that we are here today . . . and I think the contract is a good one and the cooperation, in the end, led to an environment in which to accomplish good things." Tim Reilly responded by noting that they had achieved "a contract that is fair for all and provides a basis for pursuing the mutual interests of the State and UUP through the years." Moore added that she appreciated Reilly's "commitment to affirmative action," which she considered "an important component of the contract."[16] UUP's members were now to vote on ratification of the contract. The process would be conducted by the American Arbitration Association, with ballots to be mailed on July 25 and returned no later than 5 p.m. on August 11, and to be counted the next day.[17] UUP's Negotiations Team held regional meetings to brief chapter leadership and respond to questions, and they also visited several chapters. When the ballots were counted on August 12 it became clear that the membership overwhelmingly approved the new contract. Of the ballots cast, 88 percent were in favor, which was the highest percentage of yes votes for any UUP contract. UUP's chief negotiator, William Scheuerman, claimed one reason for membership support was that the "bargaining demands were constructed through an open process; we sought and received high levels of membership input so that the proposal we gave to the State last January truly represented the rank-and-file." He also pointed out that "the contract breaks new ground in a number of areas." Among those he listed were affirmative action, longevity recognition, part-time issues, and a geographical stipend.[18]

By the fall of 1990, UUP began preparations to negotiate a successor contract. For the first and only time in UUP's history the president decided to serve as chief negotiator. On September 14, Thomas A. Corigliano, the Negotiations Committee's chair for that contact, sent a notice out to the membership soliciting suggestions for the new agreement. Once again, members received a survey instrument that would provide "a confidential format for members to indicate new and specific ideas about the issues and benefits we should work to achieve." Also, as was the case with the last contract negotiation, each chapter would be represented on the Standing Committee on Negotiations and on the ad hoc Negotiations Advisory Committee; in addition, regional meetings and meetings with constituency groups would be held to gain further input.[19] On February 7, 1991, UUP and the state exchanged contract proposals. Notably absent was any specific salary increase proposal from either side. While UUP did list a number of changes it wanted in Article 20 (Direct Compensation), including a continuation of the $300 addition to base salary for those who attained continuing or permanent employment, which had been a feature of the expiring contract, the state's text for Article 20 simply stated that it was "prepared to consider the union's proposals in the compensation area and to respond to such proposals in the context of the State's fiscal environment." Another of the innovations in the expiring contract was the Committee on Excellence, and UUP proposed that it be continued and that $500,000 be allocated to it for 1991–92, while the state proposed that it be eliminated. The union's proposal contained several changes to Article 39 (Health Insurance) to lower costs and improve benefits for its members, but the state proposal simply stated general principles and its desire to keep costs down.[20]

Contract negotiations proceeded very slowly. By June 21, although UUP's team had met with the state's negotiators eleven times, and subcommittees had been working for two months, it appeared likely that a new contract would not be in place by July 1. The state had yet to pass a budget, even though the budget year began on April 1. The governor and the legislature were disinclined to institute new taxes, and the governor had made it clear that he would not support any increases in the costs of union contracts. What would happen if a new contract were not in place when the old one expired? Fortunately, what is known as the "Triborough Doctrine," which had been codified in the Taylor Law in 1982, would come into play. This meant that as long as the union continued to bargain in good faith, the provisions and protections of the old contract would remain in force. Of course, there would be no salary raises and there would be no money for any specifically funded programs. Most disconcerting, though, was that the Benefit Fund, which provided for dental care, prescription drugs, and the vision plan, would no longer receive funding. Meanwhile, negotiations were to continue, and the UUP team "resolved to work as hard as it takes, as long as it takes to get a good agreement."[21] In an effort to save the Benefit Fund, UUP's negotiators met with those from the state on June 27, and by 5:15 a.m. the next day worked out an arrangement to do that.[22] This agreement was announced by Tim Reilly in a July 2 memorandum to all members of the bargaining unit, who were told that it would preserve the Benefit Fund as well as "the range of health services in Article 39 with no increase in premium cost and with little change in out-of-pocket expense." Members were assured that there was "no longer any reason for anxiety," since the Benefit Fund would "continue to receive regular payments," and would "be supported by additional money that should cover inflationary cost increases in prescription drugs, dental care, and vision care." More details would be provided soon, they were told.[23] Those details were summarized in a "Negotiations Bulletin" on July 16.[24]

Eighteen months after the start of negotiations the state finally put forward a money offer, but it was hardly one the union would accept. It called for a three-year contract, with no raise in the first or second years and only 1 percent across the board in the third year. It also called for all employees to pay a minimum $11-a-month parking fee where there had been no parking fee, and stated that the state would no longer pay malpractice insurance for UUP physician members engaged in clinical practice. CSEA, which had gone through impasse, mediation, and fact-finding, had come up with a tentative agreement.

But, as was pointed out in a UUP "Negotiations Bulletin," that agreement was "a largely self-funded contract—that is, one in which the salary increases come in large part from money the state saves as a result of certain contractual changes." UUP's negotiations team and leadership remained committed to not accepting "an agreement that is funded by give-backs." They were "prepared to go into the fall semester if it [was] necessary in order to secure a fair contract."[25]

Finally, on June 26, 1992, a joint press release from UUP and the Governor's Office of Employee Relations reported that a tentative settlement had been reached. It was for a four-year contract, effective July 1, 1991, through July 1, 1995. There were to be no salary increases in the first two years of the agreement, but there would be a 4 percent across-the-board increase effective July 1, 1993, another 4 percent effective July 1, 1994, and 1.25 percent on January 1, 1995.[26] The five-day lag pay that the state had withheld in 1991 in an attempt to resolve budget issues, and that the union had contended was illegal, was resolved. The state agreed to repay the money during the last two years of the contract in three payments at the then-current rate of pay, and the state agreed not to lag the pay of new hires. No new parking fee would be imposed, at least during the first three years of the agreement. After that, any request for fees would have to be negotiated on the campus level. Unfortunately, the Joint Labor-Management Excellence Committee, which had been established in the last contract, would no longer be funded. The breakthrough in negotiations had come on June 19, when President Reilly received a telephone call from the governor's office indicating that if progress toward a contract was not made, several pieces of legislation important to UUP would be in jeopardy. While the union saw this as blackmail, it decided to take advantage of a potential opportunity for settlement. On June 22 a week of intensive bargaining began, culminating in a thirty-seven-hour marathon session beginning on June 25, and a tentative agreement finally was reached. Once again, the balloting would be conducted by the American Arbitration Association, with ballots to be mailed to members on August 10, with a return date of August 27 and a vote count the following day.[27] A special meeting of UUP's Executive Board was held on July 7, at which the Board endorsed the Agreement and "strongly" urged ratification.[28] When the votes were in the tally showed that 78.4 percent of the returned ballots were in favor of the contract.[29]

Parking Fees

One of the issues more or less resolved by this agreement, and one that was very important to many of UUP's members, was the attempt to charge for campus parking in lots where there had previously been no fees. When Governor Cuomo had refused to permit a tuition increase at SUNY, the university looked for ways to make up the difference in the income that would have generated. They came up with the idea of imposing a fee for parking on "all permanent, paved surface lots which are not now subject to a fee." On July 14, 1989, all campus presidents were told to "begin charging a parking fee during F.Y. 1989–90."[30] But Article 38 of UUP's 1988–1991 Agreement with the state provided that "The status quo will be maintained for parking facilities presently provided without charge and no existing charge for parking facilities shall be increased or decreased without negotiations pursuant to this Article."[31] On August 14, SUNY, therefore, formally demanded "that parking negotiations be reopened pursuant to Article 38 of the Agreement."[32] UUP agreed to meet with SUNY representatives, and the first meeting was to be held on September 27.[33] Before that meeting took place, UUP's Delegate Assembly, on September 22, passed a resolution opposing "any changes in the current parking practices throughout the University as well as implementation of any new changes or fees," and urged President Reilly "to consider all of the deleterious ramifications of any such changes in any reopened negotiations on Article 38." The DA also resolved that "no parking fee buttons be prepared and sent to chapters for distribution to members." They argued that parking was "not a benefit but a necessary condition for all bargaining unit members," and that the imposition of a fee, or the raising of a fee, "would constitute a de facto cut in salary."[34] The September 27 meeting with SUNY was short, lasting less than an hour. SUNY asked for a parking fee, in what were then free lots, of $11 a month. The UUP representatives asked for more time to study the issue, and meetings were scheduled for October 4 and 19.[35] The October 4 meeting, which lasted an hour and three-quarters, was devoted primarily to procedural questions. The October 19 meeting opened with a statement from UUP: "We have reviewed your proposal for reopening parking negotiations pursuant to article 38 of the 1988–91 State/UUP Agreement. It is UUP's position that UUP is under no obligation to negotiate with respect to parking facilities presently provided without charge." UUP did agree that it had an obligation to bargain where fees existed.[36] SUNY administration disagreed with UUP's position on the interpretation of the contract, and on January 30, 1990, informed campus presidents that they had notified PERB that they had reached an impasse in their negotiations with UUP and that they had filed an Improper Practice charge with PERB, claiming that UUP had failed to "negotiate in good faith." Further, SUNY administration stated that they had notified UUP "of its intention to convert existing free parking to paid parking in all permanent surface lots on those campuses that impose parking fees as part of the University's parking fee program, subject to appropriate University authorization." (UUP actually was notified the next day.) A fee of $11 a month was anticipated. "The University, of course," it was pointed out, "remains fully ready and willing to engage in negotiations at any time."[37]

Still, before parking fees actually could be implemented, each Campus Council (a primarily advisory body for each campus, whose members are appointed by New York's governor) would have to approve the fee. On February 28, Thomas A. Corigliano, UUP's vice president for professionals, notified chapter presidents that the fee plan had "apparently moved to the campus level." He asked each of them to appoint themselves "or some other UUP activist to assume the role as the lead person on parking" for the chapter. UUP would be holding regional meetings "to discuss the parking issue, and strategies for campus action." He concluded by noting, "The parking fee proposed has little to do with parking and everything to do with SUNY's effort to make employees support the university by returning hard-won salary increases in the form of a tax on autos."[38] The regional meetings, which were held during March, provided attendees with a checklist of activities. That list, in addition to asking for a parking coordinator to be appointed for each campus, suggested forming coalitions with other unions and with student leaders, lobbying with members of college councils, phone banks, letter-writing, and meeting with town officials, among other activities.[39]

These efforts yielded some positive results for UUP. For example, on March 20 the City Council of Oneonta passed a resolution opposing the imposition of parking fees on the Oneonta campus, arguing that "the probable results of the imposition of that fee would undoubtedly impact negatively on the City of Oneonta and its taxpayers by adding immeasurably to the parking problem on the city streets, by increasing public transit needs, and thereby accelerating the deterioration of the roads used for access to the campus and most likely impact negatively on public parking facilities in the city."[40] Several weeks later an editorial in the Oneonta newspaper, the Daily Star, opposed the parking fee, concerned that the city could not "do its job if a decision made by SUNY Central in Albany is going to flood the area with parked cars, all for the sake of a gimmick designed to raise money that should be raised by a tuition increase or some other straightforward measure."[41] Similarly, the mayor of the village of Delhi wrote to the chair of the SUNY Delhi College Council, asking that a parking fee not be charged on the Delhi campus, noting that Village Board members were "concerned that staff and students who commute will park on Village streets and walk or car pool to classes." He related that the village's police chief had stated "that if one fourth of the commuters elect to park on Village streets there will be a serious problem with congestion."[42] Pressure also came from state legislators. Assemblyman Joseph T. Pillitere wrote to the chair of the Buffalo State College Council to express his "strong opposition" to the imposition of a parking fee on that campus. He warned that if the council approved the fee, he was "prepared to draft legislation that will halt the fees from being imposed." He noted that he had "discussed this matter with Assemblyman Edward Sullivan, chairman of the Assembly Higher Education Committee, who also objects to the proposal and will support legislation blocking it."[43] And in the New York State Senate a bill was passed, sponsored by Buffalo-area Senator

Dale Volker, that would block the university from imposing the parking fees. Volker was quoted in the Albany *Times Union* as proclaiming: " 'You can't solve SUNY's financial problems with fees.' "[44] Although SUNY had left the imposition of parking fees up to the campuses, the *Schenectady Gazette* reported that SUNY officials had threatened that the campuses could face layoffs if the fees were not imposed. Campus administrators were told, the *Gazette* noted, "that if they reject the fees, they won't be reimbursed for the money that was expected to be raised by the new charges."[45]

Meanwhile, on March 30, UUP chapter presidents, Executive Board members, and labor-relations specialists were informed that UUP had filed "a Step 2 All-Campus grievance on parking" the previous day. The grievance charged that "SUNY as agent of the State, is violating Articles 38 and 48" of the Agreement by proposing rules for charging parking fees, since that "violates the prohibition against unilaterally modifying the contract." The recipients of this memorandum were urged "to demonstrate directly and plainly to management and the College Council" on each campus their "opposition to the maneuvers by which SUNY is trying to impose the misconceived tax they call a parking fee."[46] While this grievance was moving forward, President Reilly wrote to the director of the Governor's Office of Employee Relations to express his strong objection "to the unilateral imposition of a tax, disguised as a parking fee, on the employees we represent." He pointed out to her that as of that date, seventeen of the university's college councils had met to consider parking fee resolutions and thirteen of them had defeated them. Further, he informed her, "a number of community governments have also spoken out in their opposition to parking charges." He urged her "to reconsider the governor's Office of Employee Relations' position of support for SUNY's tax plan." Copies of this letter also were sent to Governor Mario Cuomo and Chancellor D. Bruce Johnstone.[47] But Reilly's, and UUP's, argument did not prevail. On June 12, a decision was handed down denying UUP's grievance. It was maintained that UUP did not file the grievance within the forty-five-day period required. Further, the decision insisted that "UUP's claim regarding the University's activities is simply without any basis in fact," and that "Article 38 of the <u>Agreement</u> clearly articulates a mutual obligation to negotiate parking fees upon the demand of either party," and that "obligation pertains to <u>all</u> existing parking facilities, regardless of whether such lots are free or paid."[48] UUP may have lost this decision, but it appears to have won in the court of public opinion. The *Chronicle of Higher Education*, which reported on the parking issue, placed a header on the article that read "SUNY's Plan to Pare Its Deficit by Imposing Parking Fees Irks Just About Everyone." The article claimed that "the plan has turned into a political and public-relations disaster."[49] Since SUNY was unable to have parking fees instituted for any SUNY lots where fees had not been charged, an attempt was made to put a parking fee requirement into the next contract, but the effort was not successful. The parking fee issue resulted in a significant victory for UUP, which was the only state-wide union to be successful in resisting the fee. The struggle energized the union's chapters and resulted in considerable cooperation between them and UUP's administrative office, which helped to diminish some of the partisanship that had developed over the philosophical role of the chapters versus the central office.

Retrenchment

One article in the contract of considerable concern to UUP was the one concerning retrenchment. The 1988–91 Agreement defined retrenchment as a termination of employment "as a result of financial exigency, reallocation of resources, reorganization of degree or curriculum offerings or requirements, reorganization of academic or administrative structures, programs or functions or curtailment of one or more programs or functions University-wide or at such other level of organization of the University as the Chancellor, or designee deems appropriate."[50] Applying that definition, SUNY management had significant discretion, and there was little protection for affected staff. UUP was concerned that its members might be co-opted by management into participating in committees that might single out programs or colleagues for retrenchment, so in 1981 the Delegate Assembly had approved a policy opposing such participation. The Winter 1989 Delegate Assembly reiterated that policy, and resolved that President Reilly "communicate this policy to UUP chapter Presidents, to chairs of Faculty Senates on campuses, to the SUNY Faculty Senate, and to other members of the bargaining unit as he deems appropriate."[51]

In September of 1990 fears of impending retrenchments were realized. Officials on the Cortland campus announced that academic concentrations in dance and radio-television were to be phased out by the fall of 1991. They claimed that this was a result of a reduction of state aid and the college's academic priorities. According to a report in the *Cortland Standard*, this would result in the elimination of three tenured faculty positions and the nonrenewal of three term appointment staff.[52] A few days later, it was announced that the Canton College of Technology would be eliminating five full-time faculty positions for the fall of 1991. It was noted that the cuts were "in response to changing student demands and the decreased marketability of certain programs."[53] On September 11, Reilly notified chapter presidents and members of the Executive Board that eight SUNY campuses had announced retrenchments. In response, he had "sent a letter to the Chancellor's office demanding a meeting (under Article 35.3) to get the explanation of these actions." Further, he stated that UUP's field representatives had "been meeting with the individuals targeted by management" and that they would "be filing grievances on any contract violations."[54] At its October meeting, the Executive Board passed a resolution that "UUP mount a campaign of resistance to current and prospective retrenchments and that it communicate the deeper implications of retrenchments to state policy-makers, the public, and members of the university community, using demonstrations, appropriate media campaigns, intensified lobbying, and other appropriate means."[55] By the end of August, eighty-one professionals, forty teaching faculty, and thirty-five classified staff had been retrenched or laid off. The largest number of these, sixty-six, was from the Albany campus, forty-eight of whom were from the New York State Theatre Institute.[56]

The New York State Theatre Institute represents an interesting case where, in actuality, retrenchment had little to do with any financial exigencies, but rather was occasioned by a clash of personalities, and yet could be justified under the vague guidelines of the union's contract with the state. Originally created by the state legislature in 1974, and known as the Empire State Institute for the Performing Arts (ESIPA), it was a unit of the State University of New York, but was located in Albany at the Empire State Plaza's Performing Arts Center, known as the "Egg." But ultimately Patricia Snyder, founder and director of the youth theater, and Barnabas McHenry, who had been appointed by Governor Mario Cuomo as chairman of the Performing Arts Corporation Board, clashed over the organization's mission and operations. So, when the governor submitted his budget proposal for 1989–90, he included a provision that the youth theater, now known as the New York State Theatre Institute, be transferred, along with a budget allocation, to the university's Albany campus. That provision carried through in the final budget.[57] But the Theatre Institute's residence at the University at Albany was to be short-lived. In June 1991, the president of the State University at Albany received a letter from SUNY's provost mandating a reduction of the NYSTI budget by 75 percent.[58] In August, forty-four members of the UUP bargaining unit received retrenchment letters.[59] At UUP's fall 1991 Delegate Assembly, Albany chapter president Ivan D. Steen introduced a motion for UUP to "communicate its extreme displeasure [at the reduction of the Theatre Institute budget] to the Chancellor of the State University of New York" and to "press for legislative action to restore funding for the New York State Theatre Institute to ensure its survival at its current level of activity." That motion was passed without dissent.[60] In the October issue of UUP's publication, *The Voice*, Steen noted that a major effort was under way to save the institute. He was meeting with New York state legislators urging them to intercede, and UUP chapters were sent emails with a request that they contact their legislators. In addition, the Albany County Central Federation of Labor passed a resolution of support, and support also was obtained from NYSUT. A plan by campus management to use the reduced NYSTI budget to rehire some of the staff part-time was opposed by chapter leadership.[61] But by the spring of 1992, SUNY agreed to bring back some of those who were retrenched to finish out NYSTI's season. Originally the plan was to bring them back as "casual" employees, and therefore not union members, but Steen objected and it was agreed that they would be rehired as UUP members.[62] Although UUP had been advocating the retention of the Theatre Institute within SUNY, the organization's director wanted it removed from SUNY's control. The result was that by the end of 1992 it was established as a public benefit corporation, but the union arranged for its members to continue to be represented by UUP.[63] To facilitate the UUP representation, the UUP Executive Board authorized NYSTI's employees to form "a constituent chapter of Local 2190." The board also resolved that they viewed "the action for self-organization of their new chapter as precedential and prophetic of the board's wish to welcome new chapters into the structure of solidarity that characterizes UUP."[64] At the next Delegate Assembly meeting, on January 29, 1993, a motion was adopted welcoming the NYSTI chapter into UUP, and it was also resolved "that the Delegate Assembly further extends a similar welcome to other unorganized workers as they seek to become affiliated with the Nation's Largest Higher Education Union—UUP."[65] This left open the possibility of UUP representing other non-SUNY entities in the future.

Political and Legislative Activities

In Tim Reilly's first report as president to the Delegate Assembly at its September 1987 meeting, he made it clear that the union's political and legislative activities would receive high priority during his presidency. "For contemporary unions," he proclaimed, "one of the conclusive signs of strength is successful achievement in the public arenas of politics and legislation." While this had long been an important activity for UUP, and the union had been rather successful in this area, he was "resolved to see if we cannot create an even more comprehensive participatory structure and program for our efforts." To work toward that goal, he asked Janet Potter, a librarian from the Oneonta campus, who chaired UUP's Legislation Committee, to have the committee work "on campus models for action, taking leads from chapters that have done excellent work already, and on training a cadre of persons for Albany-centered activity that will expand upon plans we have seen presented before." Further, Reilly expressed his conviction "that a union, our Union, must indeed consider its social agenda as inherent in its charge to improve the lives of working people."[66] Acting on that conviction, on January 13, 1988, Reilly sent a memorandum to chapter presidents headed "An Agenda for Labor Solidarity." He asked each chapter to "affiliate with the nearest AFL-CIO labor council" and to "formalize its cooperation with other unions on campus." He also urged them to "seek to develop a relationship with AFL-CIO–endorsed support groups" and "to purchase a union-made UUP chapter banner for use in rallies, on picket lines, and at meetings."[67]

Union solidarity might prove useful in helping UUP battle a proposed state budget that would be harmful to SUNY. A UUP news release on January 25 reported that Reilly spoke at a legislative hearing and "told members of the Senate and Assembly fiscal committees that the governor's budget plan 'underfunds' SUNY to such an extent that 'it will force diminution, reduction and elimination of programs to make up for shortfalls in utility costs and basic maintenance.' "[68] Four days later a "Legislative Alert" was sent out by Janet Potter, announcing that there would be lobbying days in February and March that would focus on the SUNY budget, and in April a lobbying day would be devoted to UUP's legislative program. Chapters would be asked to have as many people as possible to participate in those lobby days. Additionally, there would be weekly lobbying in Albany by a "core group of individuals." She also noted that UUP intended to have greater involvement in NYSUT's Committee of 100, which was composed of activists from NYSUT's locals around the state who came to Albany to lobby with legislators. UUP's chapters were each asked to designate a person to coordinate the chapter's activities and to work with the statewide committee. UUP would provide training, information, and supplies.[69] Yet despite holding three lobbying days and having core lobbyists meeting with legislators every week, UUP's success was, in President Reilly's words, "not stunning."[70] If the state's budget, which was passed during the third week of April, was a disappointment to UUP, things were to get worse. On May 23 the Cuomo administration announced that the state had underestimated revenues and faced a $900 million budget shortfall, and that programs would have to be cut.[71] It was proposed that the SUNY budget take a $43 million reduction, which Reilly noted would result in "serious consequences throughout the university." Both UUP and NYSUT launched a major effort to demonstrate to legislative leaders how devastating the proposed cuts would be to the university. Especially dismaying to both UUP and NYSUT was that the SUNY Board of Trustees, at its July meeting, voted in favor of reducing SUNY's budget by $30 million. NYSUT's Executive Vice President Herb Magidson stated that the trustees' action amounted to "caving in, collapsing, rather than fighting for the university."[72]

But UUP was not about to cave in. On November 10 Janet Potter informed UUP's chapter presidents that the outlook for the 1989–90 budget looked bleak, as the state still was trying to find ways to make up for its large budget shortfall. She called for a well-organized union effort, and reiterated her call for each chapter to designate a legislative liaison person. Chapters would again be called on to participate in UUP events, generate letters to the governor and legislators, meet with local legislators, and work with various groups. In addition, she recommended that chapters "should consider holding some kind of reception for the newly elected legislators in their districts or inviting them to a chapter event."[73] At the December Executive Board meeting Reilly reported that the letter-writing campaign was underway and that regional meetings had taken place. Additionally, he had been working with a public relations firm that was putting a proposal together for UUP.[74] A few days later, a joint press release from the Student Association of the State University of New York (SASU) and UUP announced that the two organizations had "joined forces in a campaign to protect SUNY from damaging budget cuts." The campaign, which would include legislative visits and a letter-writing campaign, was in response to the governor's call "for SUNY to freeze its budget and absorb $92 million in extra costs."[75] A December 15 *New York Times* article revealed that state officials were discussing a SUNY retrenchment that might include closing some campuses as well as tuition increases and layoffs. But, as the article's author, Samuel Weiss, noted, "state officials, legislators and educators generally agreed that closing a campus would be politically difficult. Every county outside New York City has a SUNY campus and legislators protect them because they are often the largest local employers as well as intellectual and cultural centers."[76] Reilly responded to the *Times* article immediately, and noted that the state's fiscal problem was "a result of political decisions on tax policy," and could not "be solved by temporary cuts and reductions," but only by "a delay and reconsideration of future tax cuts and the identification of new sources of revenues."[77] It was learned that the campuses being considered for closing were those at Cobleskill and Potsdam, and Dentistry at Stony Brook.[78] Confirming its earlier prediction of the political difficulty of closing a campus, the *Times* reported that the chairs of the higher-education committees of both the Assembly and the Senate predicted that their chambers would oppose any campus closings.[79] Still, the situation was serious, and at its January 1989 meeting the UUP Executive Board adopted a motion to authorize the president "to spend up to $250,000 for the budget crisis campaign."[80]

On March 15, UUP held a "Lobby Day." The union would be promoting several issues with legislators. One was UUP's opposition to the implementation of a scheduled tax cut, which it maintained would reduce revenue when there already was a substantial budget shortfall, resulting in a decrease in funds available for SUNY and other essential services. Of course, the union also was opposed to any layoffs of SUNY employees. A reduction in funding for the university would further reduce access to education, especially for potential students of lower income. SUNY, it was argued, simply could not withstand any further cuts after a decade of underfunding. Legislators were reminded of SUNY's very substantial contribution to the state's economy, which would make "slashing the State University budget a fake savings."[81] The more than 200 UUP members who attended that event were first addressed by NYSUT leadership and several members of the state's Senate and Assembly before they met with legislators in their offices. An analysis of the reports submitted after these meetings, Janet Potter reported, "indicated overwhelming good will for UUP but opinion was divided" on the idea of rescinding the tax cuts. Still, UUP considered the lobbying effort to be successful, but members were urged not to be complacent. Reilly urged members to write to each of their legislators, the speaker of the Assembly, and the Senate minority leader, and to call the governor to urge him to reconsider his support of the tax cuts. UUP was placing ads in the *New York Times,* the *Legislative Gazette,* and several regional papers. Camera-ready copies of the ads were distributed to chapter leaders, who were urged to place them in local and campus newspapers.[82] Support for UUP's position on the scheduled state tax cuts came from American Federation of Teachers president Albert Shanker in his "Where We Stand" piece in the March 26 *New York Times,* in which he pointed out that SUNY and CUNY were "credited for a large part of New York's economic recovery in the last few years," and yet were expected to take a $115 million cut in the governor's proposed budget. He noted that while the state's fiscal shortfall was largely the result of overestimating tax revenues, it still was insisting on going forward with a tax cut that had been adopted the previous year.[83] Shanker's piece elicited a note of thanks from SUNY Chancellor D. Bruce Johnstone, a copy of which was sent to Tim Reilly and others, who told him that his "presentation of the specifics of SUNY's and CUNY's current budget dilemmas was cogent and effective." Johnstone went on to state, "Putting current budget exigencies and short-term political agendas aside, a strong higher education system isn't a luxury we can enjoy because of national prosperity, it is a major reason why we enjoy that success."[84]

Once again, the April 1 deadline for having a budget in place was missed. On April 18, legislative leaders finally agreed on a budget.[85] At least $48.2 million of the governor's proposed cuts to SUNY would be restored, a significant portion of which would be raised through a $200-a-year tuition increase, which Governor Cuomo had opposed. According to UUP's "Legislative Alert" of April 20, the governor "chastised the legislative leaders for the high priority held by SUNY and CUNY during the final budget negotiations," and noted "the 'strong' organization advocating for public higher education."[86] It would appear that UUP and NYSUT's advocacy efforts had paid off. But the governor was adamant in his opposition to a tuition increase, and he vetoed the bill.[87] Finally, the governor and SUNY found a way to close the gap in the budget without raising tuition, and UUP's May 18 "Legislative Alert" reported it appeared "at this time that, unlike so many other agencies, SUNY will not have to retrench employees or diminish programs."[88]

As early as August, UUP began to plan its activities for the next legislative session. In September, working with NYSUT, it would sponsor a voter registration drive, and at that fall's Delegate Assembly, the Legislation Committee would begin planning for its 1990 legislative program.[89] Early in January 1990, chapters were told to get ready for lobbying activity. Chapters were asked to make appointments for groups of their members to meet with legislators in their district offices. It was the union's goal "to have at least one personal contact by a UUP member with each legislator in the state."[90] UUP also planned to hold a "Legislative Breakfast" for legislators and staff on January 23, which would be followed by core lobbyists spending the rest of the day visiting the Capitol and Legislative Office Building offices of legislators.[91] But the state's serious fiscal problems continued, and the legislature was having a very difficult time passing a budget. Finally, on May 18, nearly seven weeks past the due date, legislative leaders agreed on a budget. Despite UUP's best efforts, that budget included a substantial cut for higher education.[92] This was the third consecutive year that New York's public universities received budget cuts, and so the State University and the City University would, as the *New York Times* commented, "continue to lose teaching positions, put off repairs and reduce purchases of everything from computers to paper clips."[93]

While UUP was unable to prevent the university's budget from being cut, it nonetheless did manage to achieve a couple of its legislative goals. Teachers and most state employees could not be compelled to retire based solely on age, but tenured college faculty were required to retire when they reached the age of seventy. UUP wanted this changed, but university administrators, especially those from the private colleges and universities, wanted to retain the mandatory retirement requirement. On February 12 the New York State Assembly, by a vote of 130 to 1, passed a bill that would make mandatory retirement of college faculty illegal. Similar bills had been passed by the Assembly several times, but as a result of heavy lobbying by private colleges, nothing came out of the Senate. UUP Legislation Committee chair Janet Potter urged the union's members to write to senators urging them to support prohibiting mandatory retirement.[94] Success was achieved. On July 6 Potter informed chapter presidents, "We have won our long campaign to protect tenured college faculty from forced retirement, although the compromise bill passed earlier this week will not include private colleges and universities."[95] The same message from Potter also indicated another UUP success. Most SUNY faculty had opted to have their pensions with the Teachers Insurance and Annuity Association (TIAA), a private pension plan popular at many colleges and universities, rather than with the state-administered plan, Teachers' Retirement System. Those who had been hired years earlier were in the state's pension tiers I and II, but more recent hires were in tiers III and IV. The state contributed the entire amount to the pensions of those in the first two tiers, but those in the later tiers were required to contribute 3 percent of their salaries to their pensions. UUP had pressed for legislation that would have permitted that 3 percent to be tax-deferred. Such legislation was now passed.[96]

Prospects for adequate funding for SUNY in the 1991–92 budget were grim, as President Reilly noted in his report to the Winter 1991 Delegate Assembly. "We must apply all of our political energy and considerable wit to turning that budget around," Reilly wrote, and he proposed "a UUP action plan for a 'Save SUNY Jobs' campaign," which would be put before the Delegate Assembly "to debate, adapt, change, amplify." UUP would be working with the state's other major labor unions in a rally, joint lobbying efforts, and "participation in a new Fiscal Policy Institute developing positions on fair funding of New York's public services." UUP also would work with NYSUT on advertisements, legislative activities, and a "NYSUT Higher Education Lobby Day linked to the visit in Albany of the Committee of 100." Additionally, the union would continue to work with SASU. To reach out to legislators, UUP would be holding a legislative breakfast on January 29 and planning a "UUP Lobby Day" for March 13, as well as, once again, engaging in a letter-writing campaign. He also proposed holding a forum on funding, just prior to the UUP Lobby Day, at which "public policy makers" would be "invited to join in discussion of ways to sustain the university programs and workforce." Additionally, he advocated producing discussion papers providing information and background for UUP's positions, placing advertisements in Albany newspapers and local papers in legislators' districts, and of course continuing with local and Albany lobbying. Reilly urged reaching out to the public to "make clear to our fellow citizens that we have a responsible, positive way to address New York's problems." This might be done by placing advertisements, holding community rallies and forums, writing letters to the editor, leafletting, and holding days on the campuses when the public would be invited "to come and see what we do, to talk about the need for SUNY to stay accessible to the community."[97] To assist in carrying out these activities, the Executive Board passed a motion recommending to the upcoming Delegate Assembly "that the UUP budget for fiscal 1990–91 be amended to take from the reserve fund $250,000.00 to finance the state budget fight and further, to authorize the Executive Board to release additional funds from the same source when the President of UUP finds it necessary."[98] That motion was affirmed by the Delegate Assembly on February 1.[99]

The budget deadline of April 1 came and went, and nearly two weeks later there was no sign of any progress. Clearly, the state had a serious fiscal shortfall. The problem was how to address it—by cutting services or raising taxes? UUP preferred the latter, but there was strong opposition to doing that from the governor and the Senate. The union continued its lobbying activities, especially with members of key legislative committees. Weekly letters were sent to legislators from Reilly and Potter pointing out how New York had fallen behind most other states in support for public higher education, and warning of the dire consequences the proposed cuts would have on enrollment and quality.[100] As directed by the Delegate Assembly, Reilly wrote to American Federation of Teachers president Albert Shanker asking for aid in the campaign to achieve adequate funding for SUNY.[101] On April 30 protests against budget cuts were to be held at SUNY Purchase, Battery Park in New York City, and several other locations.[102]

By early June, more than two months past the legal deadline, the state's legislature finally passed a budget. That budget added nearly $17 million in state aid to SUNY, far short of restoring the governor's reduction, and it also increased tuition by $500.[103] Although the state now had a budget, on June 10 Governor Cuomo vetoed nearly $1 billion in spending, which included more than $16 million that the legislature had restored to SUNY.[104] Finally, on June 29 the governor and the leaders of the Senate and Assembly announced an agreement on a compromise that would restore much of the spending the governor had vetoed.[105] On the same day, though, the State University announced that it was eliminating 900 positions, including 250 teaching faculty.[106]

It did not appear that the 1992–93 budget would be any better. In the "Legislative Alert!" dated December 14, 1991, Janet Potter reported that "key legislative leaders" had noted that higher education was likely to take a big hit in that budget in light of the huge deficit projected for the state. She urged members to immediately contact legislators. It was especially important for UUP to act, since she was told by "legislative leaders" "that SUNY has not defended itself well and has a serious credibility problem."[107] In gearing up for the fight to secure adequate funding for SUNY, UUP leadership met with some leaders of the New York Public Interest Research Group (NYPIRG) to develop cooperative ways to work to achieve that goal. Chapters were urged to "join forces in working with NYPIRG for a letter-writing campaign during the weeks of February 15–26," and also to coordinate district lobbying with them as well as to "explore other types of activities appropriate for your campus."[108]

The governor's budget recommendation would reduce aid to SUNY by $233 million, but that amount could be reduced to $143 million if SUNY would take $20 million from hospital revenues and raise $60 million through a $500 tuition increase. The executive budget also proposed that the Board of Trustees allocate a $60.4 million reduction and be granted the authority to institute a system of differential tuition, which would be based on varying institutional costs.[109] UUP, of course, opposed these cuts, which it claimed would be "devastating to public higher education in New York State."[110]

On April 2 the legislature approved the budget,[111] and it was a harsh one for the university. The *New York Times* reported that the state's contribution was reduced by $143 million, some of which would be offset through the $500-a-year tuition increase. Nonetheless, SUNY officials said they still would have to absorb a reduction of $56 million. The *Times* noted that SUNY management claimed that it would have to cut 1,150 staff positions, and while "the bulk of those cuts are expected to be made through attrition, 250–300 people might have to be dismissed." Chancellor Johnstone was quoted as saying, " 'We are being asked to absorb very deep cuts after having already absorbed a series of deep cuts over the last four years. There's really nothing left to cut except people.' " According to Johnstone the situation was so serious that the possibility of campus closings was being considered.[112] Later in April a *New York Times* editorial claimed that "the reductions imposed on public universities now cut so close to the bone that it's becoming impossible to ask them simply to take the pain. They cannot keep making cuts this deep and fulfill their assigned mission." The editorial went on to point out that "In the last academic year, close to 4 percent of state taxes went to expenses of public colleges and universities. The U.S. average is 7 percent, nearly *twice* that." To illustrate the impact of the cuts, the editorial mirrored arguments that UUP had been making: "SUNY has cut 5,000 faculty and staff positions since the mid-1970s, out of 26,000. Access is threatened by more selective admissions. Some students can't finish in four years because important courses are overflowing, or aren't offered every year."[113]

Angered by the legislature's failure to put back the SUNY funding cut by the governor's budget proposal, UUP embarked on a course of action that would seem to have been rather foolish. In an April 12 news release, the union stated that during that week legislators would "be receiving in the mail . . . exam books and test questions designed to hold them accountable for their failure to restore funds to the State University of New York in the 1992–93 state budget," and that UUP members "would follow up with office visits to administer the test."[114] This approach seemed like it might antagonize some legislators at a time when UUP would be pressing the legislature to restore some funds, and in June the union announced plans to do just that. In a memorandum to chapter presidents and the Executive Board, Janet Potter noted that she had heard from legislative leaders that they would "consider seeking additional funds" if they were to "hear from constituents that SUNY is a priority." UUP was launching a campaign to have letters and postcards sent to the speaker of the Assembly and the Senate majority leader. At the same time there would be "a blitz of radio ads" that would urge listeners to contact their legislators. Potter claimed that the "direct mail appeal will reach over 40,000 people and the radio ad will reach thousands more."[115] Although the union campaign resulted in 11,150 postcards sent to the Senate and Assembly leaders, no additional funds were approved for SUNY.[116]

While UUP was unable to secure the restoration of funds for the SUNY budget, the union did have some success in its lobbying efforts. One achievement was preventing the SUNY trustees' from placing the three SUNY hospitals into a public-benefit corporation. Reilly called that an " 'ill-conceived proposal,' " which he saw as a " 'scheme' to disrupt the benefits currently enjoyed by the employees and a poorly disguised attempt at union busting."[117] At the UUP Fall 1992 Delegate Assembly, Janet Potter reported that as a result of UUP's active opposition, that proposal failed to be considered by the legislature. "Variations of the hospital spin off," she noted, were "expected to resurface," so UUP's fight was "far from over."[118]

Another proposal that UUP blocked from legislative consideration was that of differential tuition.[119] That proposal was based on an assumption that it cost more to educate an undergraduate student at a doctorate-granting campus than at a four-year or technical college. In a memorandum to members of the

New York State Senate and New York State Assembly, Reilly explained the union's opposition to the plan. While not disputing that additional costs were incurred in educating doctoral students, the cost of educating undergraduate students, he claimed, were the same on all campus types. Establishing a two-tier undergraduate tuition policy depending on the type of institution would create the impression that undergraduates would receive a better education at a doctorate-granting campus, and Reilly argued that that was not the case. Rather than reflecting educational costs or quality, Reilly maintained that the proposal was explained by "the universal need for revenue."[120]

UUP also secured passage and the governor's signature for legislation providing for an early retirement incentive for members of the TRS and TIAA pension systems. The reason for proposing this legislation was to reduce the potential number of actual retrenchments resulting from budget reductions. At first the governor opposed the incentive because he believed that it would be costly and that it would not generate more retirements than usual, and thus end up being nothing but a windfall for those who would retire anyway. UUP worked with NYSUT, the CUNY faculty union, and the management of both university systems to bring this legislation to fruition. As Janet Potter pointed out, "No other State agency employees will be offered an early retirement incentive program this year."[121]

By October of 1992 plans had been made for the last legislative effort of the Reilly administration. Once again, there would be district lobbying, but since not all legislators could be reached that way, core lobbyists would meet regularly with legislators in their Albany offices. Plans also were made for dedicated lobby days in Albany, including those sponsored by NYSUT. There were to be invitations for legislators to visit campuses, cooperative ventures with students and other labor unions, as well as letter-writing campaigns and advertisements.[122] Ominous signals were seen in December when the state's Division of the Budget notified all state agencies, SUNY among them, that they should work on plans for 10–15 percent reductions from the current-year budgets. Expecting an uphill battle, UUP planned to continue its practice of "sending frequent correspondence to legislators to maintain high visibility" and to keep its concerns "in the forefront of the debate in Albany."[123] The governor's Executive Budget, released in January 1993, proposed a $50.5 million increase over the previous year for SUNY's operating budget; however, UUP noted, negotiated salary increases were estimated to cost $50.7 million, and SUNY had requested $20 million to cover inflationary costs. The union's budget analysis pointed out that the state's general fund support would now fall to a new low, with only 34.5 percent of the university's budget coming from that source. There was no tuition-raise proposal. To provide an incentive for campuses to increase enrollments a "State University Tuition Reimbursable Account" was established, which would allow SUNY to retain tuition above budgeted levels—something for which UUP had advocated in the past.[124] If UUP was less than satisfied with the Executive Budget, SUNY management seemed to think it was just fine. A January 19 SUNY press release proclaimed that Chancellor Johnstone was "heartened that the Executive Budget" demonstrated "Governor Mario M. Cuomo's continued support for SUNY and *reaffirms the vision* of the University."[125] UUP's efforts to have the legislature restore a $11.8 million "lump sum reduction" to the university's operating budget were not helped by the chancellor's statement, and so the reduction remained in the budget passed by the legislature on April 5. One small item that UUP was successful in having inserted into the budget was $100,000 in start-up money for a University Development Fund. The purpose of that fund would be to "leverage outside funding sources to stimulate application of research and technology, foster innovative programs in work force training and to develop partnerships with government and business."[126]

Looking Beyond Contracts and SUNY Funding

Related to the SUNY budget issues that occupied so much of UUP's time and effort was the question of tuition. This presented a vexing problem for the union. With the regular state cutbacks in financing, the university found itself chronically short of the money it needed for staff, equipment, and services. One way to bring in additional funds would be to raise tuition. But could the union support that? To do so might please some (but certainly not all) of its members, since it might forestall retrenchments. However, it undoubtedly would antagonize students and their parents, and the support of those groups was important in the fight to secure funding from the state. Shortly after taking office as the union's president, when testifying before the Assembly Higher Education Committee in June of 1987, Reilly had expressed concern about student reliance on loans to pay for their education. A result of that, he feared, would be that students would choose careers based on how well they would pay, and that would not only influence curriculum, but it would probably create shortages in some needed fields.[127] In a memorandum to chapter presidents on March 5, 1990, President Reilly stated that UUP had taken "the position that the approach to funding must focus on public investment, not individual payments, because the University is a public resource."[128] By November, though, Reilly appeared to be softening on the tuition question. In a letter to Ivan D. Steen, the Albany chapter president, he wrote: "I'd like to secure some promise from SUNY in return for support of a tuition increase. And I'd like to see the increase be great enough to protect jobs really. That's all confidential for the moment."[129] When testifying at a public hearing of the SUNY Board of Trustees Committee on University Revenue and Tuition Policy on December 7, Reilly maintained that tuition should be free, but he realized that was not likely to happen. However, raising tuition, as was done in the past, because there was a temporary crisis, was not the way it should be done. What was needed, he argued, was "a tuition policy characterized by predictability and uniform applicability." What he advocated was "tying rates to an appropriate price index, either the Higher Education CPI or another appropriate consumer price index." He also recommended that tuition should not be based on the parents' income and that it should be the same for all campuses.[130] Reilly further elaborated on his opposition to charging different tuitions at different campuses in his December 16, 1991, memorandum sent to members of the New York State Senate and the New York State Assembly, and he enclosed a copy of his statement on indexed tuition that he had proposed to SUNY's trustees the previous year.[131] And on January 30, 1992, the UUP Executive Board passed a motion that UUP "resolutely opposes the idea of differential tuition," and that UUP continues "to advocate a tuition policy that is rational, fair and uniform."[132]

UUP's annual legislative agenda went beyond advocating for a good budget for the university, and even beyond other SUNY related issues; it usually included several civil and human rights items for which UUP would advocate. For example, the 1990 Legislative Program called for legislation that "would strengthen civil rights protections and provide criminal remedies against bias-related violence, intimidation, vandalism, and harassment," as well as "legislation to protect employees from secret wiretapping."[133] The 1991 legislative agenda added support for family and parental leave and for "legislation to implement methods of obtaining affordable, adequate housing for all residents of New York State."[134] In 1993 the Legislative Program called for restructuring the state's tax system by addressing the need for revenue "with a coherent and progressive tax system that fairly distributes the tax burden." It also added UUP's support for "the concept of universal health care for citizens of New York State," and it stated that UUP favored banning the use of permanent replacements in labor disputes.[135]

Likewise, a substantial amount of Delegate Assembly time was spent on social justice and solidarity issues. For example, the 1988 Spring Delegate Assembly passed resolutions opposing International Paper's "ruthless labor policies," and supporting cooperation with other groups to "introduce and support a National Health Act, the goal of which is to provide comprehensive and affordable health care with clear and understandable procedures for all citizens."[136] The following spring motions were adopted to "send a message of support to Representative Barney Frank of the Judiciary Committee, in his effort to repeal the McCarran-Walter Act, and to open the exchange between American labor and the organized workers of other nations," and to affirm author Salman Rushdie's "right to speak his mind like any free person," as well as supporting "all those who refuse to limit access to the products of free speech and who preserve freedom's exercise by resisting the terror which would destroy it."[137] At the fall 1989 Delegate Assembly a resolution was passed in support of the soon-to-be-adopted Americans with Disabilities Act, and another condemning Exxon over the Alaskan oil spill disaster and urging UUP's members not to purchase Exxon products, to write to the company to express their displeasure, and for those who had Exxon credit cards, to cut them up and return them to the company. Also, since Eastern Airlines employees currently were on strike, and since the Delegate Assembly was meeting in a hotel located near the Buffalo airport, a motion was adopted for the delegates to "demonstrate support of our brothers and sisters in their labor negotiations by joining the Eastern Airlines strikers on the picket line." Another resolution was passed urging UUP members to write to the CEO of Eastern Airlines "protesting his abuse of unionized workers," and telling him that they would "not fly Eastern or Continental or SAS until the strike is settled to the satisfaction of the Eastern workers." And still another resolution was passed to have the delegates "sign a petition of support for the creation of a commission to investigate the Eastern strike."[138] Subsequently, at that spring's NYSUT Representative Assembly, a special meeting of the UUP Executive Board decided to give $2,500 to the AFL-CIO Fairness for Eastern Fund. The NYSUT board had contributed $10,000 to that fund.[139] Throughout the next few years UUP's Delegate Assemblies passed motions expressing the union's pleasure at seeing the breakdown of apartheid, its concerns about methods of disposing of low-level radioactive waste, its support for the reauthorization of the National Endowment for the Arts, and its support for "the right of every woman to make reproductive choices free from government interference . . ." and several other women's-rights issues. It favored resettlement of Kurdish peoples, supported unionists in Eastern and Central Europe, and opposed discrimination based on sexual orientation, among a host of similar issues.[140] Clearly, UUP was demonstrating a deep concern for issues beyond contracts and university funding.

Reilly wanted UUP to move beyond typical union activities in still another way. A large representative committee was formed to come up with what would be the union's vision for SUNY's future. That committee produced a substantial document entitled *SUNY's Future: Expanding the Mission, Fulfilling the Promise*, which UUP published in March 1990. The introduction to the study proclaimed "In the pages of this document United University Professions calls for a sustained, long-term commitment to a vision of service from a University whose yet underdeveloped strength will be released by enrolling a growing number of diverse students, continually strengthening teaching and research by empowering the professionals whose jobs those tasks are, and expanding the University's influence for economic and cultural development." The publication made recommendations in seventeen areas: access to the state university of New York, diversity and affirmative action, teaching and reform, curriculum, research, libraries, technology, health sciences, economic development, developing an international perspective, serving the community of New York, revitalizing the arts in the university and the community, the university and the schools, the "graying" of academia, improving the quality of life in the university, investing in the university, and the accountable university. All told, there were 101 specific recommendations.[141] To a considerable degree, those recommendations were consistent with one of the goals Reilly had expressed when first taking office: to make the university more accessible to minorities. The publication gained the attention of the *New York Times*, which noted the emphasis placed on the recruitment of a diverse faculty and student body, and on providing services to retain those students.[142]

The report was widely distributed to SUNY managers, legislators, and other public officials, and of course, to UUP's members. President Reilly personally sent a copy to Governor Cuomo.[143] For the most part, the publication was very well received. SUNY chancellor D. Bruce Johnstone sent a memorandum to the university's campus presidents, in which he expressed some of his thoughts about the document. He noted that it was "exceptionally well written, clear and well produced." He considered most of the recommendations to be "sound," and he noted that there were "some very interesting new ideas." He did have some criticism, though. For example, he faulted it for having "virtually no recognition of any achievements or agendas established either by campuses or by the chancellor or trustees." He also criticized it for portraying the chancellor and trustees as "seemingly all powerful," and for not recognizing "any real resource constraints, either in the past or in the future."[144] Most of UUP's members must have had a positive reaction to the publication, since the union's files contain only two examples of negative reaction. A letter to Reilly from a member of the teaching faculty expressed concern about the cost of producing "such a lavish document." He wondered, "wouldn't the message be just as effective if it had been done more modestly[?]"[145] The other negative comment was handwritten by a disgruntled member of the professional staff on a copy of the cover letter that Reilly sent out with the publication: "How much of my dues went into producing this 'trash'? When are you going to do <u>more</u> for the N.T.P.'s?"[146]

Another new UUP project began in January 1990, when Reilly entered into talks with an Albany National Public Radio station, WAMC, to work with them on producing a radio program dealing with higher education. It would be done in a magazine format, and would be composed of about five short segments in each installment. The cost for fifty-two half-hour programs was to be $65,000.[147] Before bringing the issue to UUP's Executive Board, Reilly wrote to Robert Porter, secretary-treasurer of the American Federation of Teachers, requesting financial support for the weekly program.[148] He was successful in receiving some funding from AFT, and also from NYSUT.[149] On March 2 the Executive Board adopted Reilly's proposal to support the program.[150] The program, which was entitled *The Best of Our Knowledge*, was cohosted by Reilly and a WAMC staff member. It appears to have been quite successful. It was carried not only by many public radio stations, but by the late spring of 1991, it was made available to commercial radio stations.[151] *The Best of Our Knowledge* had been airing for more than two years when Reilly's term as president came to an end. In an

April 1993 letter to the AFT secretary-treasurer, Edward McElroy, Reilly notified him of that fact, and pointed out how widespread the audience was for the
program. He claimed that WAMC wanted him to continue with the program,
even though he would no longer be UUP's president, but it was up to the AFT
to decide whether that organization would continue its support under those
circumstances.[152] Clearly, though, since it was a UUP-sponsored program, it was
up to the union, and Reilly's successor, to decide whether it would continue to
be broadcast under its aegis.

Budgetary Problems

UUP's increasing activism did not come without cost. Its advocacy efforts to
secure funding for SUNY incurred expenditures for advertising, printing, and
transportation and accommodations for bringing members to Albany for legislative activities. The union's expanding interest in solidarity with other workers and
in human and civil rights issues frequently involved more than just resolutions
of support. Funds also were expended to produce the document that expressed
UUP's view of a master plan for the university, and for UUP's sponsorship of a
radio program. Staff size also increased, with the addition of a research director
and a health-and-safety specialist.[153] A notable change during Reilly's time in
office was that the union's committees increased substantially in size. While this
may have resulted in more members becoming involved in union activities, it
also resulted in a drain on the treasury. One former statewide officer believed it
was "bankrupting the union."[154] Beginning with the 1987–88 budget year UUP's
expenses exceeded its revenues, cresting at more than $734,000 for 1989–90.
And while the deficit in subsequent years was not that large, UUP's treasurer
reported to the May 1993 Delegate Assembly that he expected that expenses
would exceed revenues at the end of that year.[155]

UUP was going to have to either cut expenses or increase revenue. One
concern among delegates was the large sums of money paid as dues to NYSUT
and AFT, and many wondered what was happening with that money. At the Spring
1989 Delegate Assembly a motion was adopted requiring "the Treasurer of UUP
immediately seek a detailed accounting from NYSUT and AFT of their expenditures of UUP affiliate dues; and . . . That the Treasurer present this accounting to
the Fall 1989 Delegate Assembly; and . . . That the Treasurer continue to provide
a similar accounting to the Delegate Assembly no less often than once a year."[156]
Concern over a large projected budget shortfall took up most of the meeting of
the Finance Committee on March 30, 1990. One proposal was to eliminate the
$6,000 life insurance benefit provided to members of the bargaining unit. "Heated
debate" followed, which "resulted in a decision not to eliminate the policy but
to reduce the amount by $1,000 and thus provid[e] some cost savings." Another

proposal that led to lengthy discussion was to eliminate the dues cap. At that time, dues were assessed at 1 percent of annual salary, with a maximum payment of $450. Although it was argued that this might "not be very popular with the Health Science affiliate members," it was decided to present it to the Executive Board as an alternative to increase revenue.[157] A June joint meeting of the Finance and Constitution Study committees voted unanimously against a constitutional amendment to eliminate the dues cap. Ultimately, the joint committee voted in favor of a constitutional amendment that would keep dues at 1 percent, but would raise the cap over a three-year period until it reached $1,000.[158] The amendment came up for a vote at the Delegate Assembly that fall, but it narrowly failed to get the two-thirds vote needed for approval.[159] However, at the Delegate Assembly's February 1991 meeting, another constitutional amendment that would simply remove the dues cap came up for a vote, and it easily achieved the two-thirds count that it needed. It was expected that this action would increase the union's annual revenue by approximately $330,000.[160] It turned out that it was easier to gain approval for the removal of the dues cap than it was to eliminate the life insurance policy. The Executive Board's October 11, 1990, meeting voted to recommend suspending the life insurance program, with the savings achieved to be used for a "Save SUNY Jobs" campaign.[161] At the Delegate Assembly later that day the recommendation was vigorously debated, and it failed to be approved. Delegates who opposed it argued that it was an important member benefit that should be continued.[162] Still, there were those who considered the life insurance to be a nonessential cost item that would only increase over time. At the April 2, 1993, Executive Board meeting, a motion was adopted to direct the Insurance Committee to "survey UUP membership to determine their views on the future of the life insurance benefit and other in-kind benefits to replace the insurance benefit, and that the Insurance Committee also investigate options that would maintain some form of life insurance." The committee was to report back to the Executive Board by November 1993.[163] By the end of Reilly's presidency, while the union had increased its revenue by eliminating the dues cap and had reduced its expenses in several areas, especially administrative costs and officer travel,[164] UUP's fiscal problems were still far from being resolved.

Internal Politics

The union's financial woes do not appear to have resulted in diminished support for Reilly or the United Caucus; in fact, the United Caucus gained strength during Reilly's terms in office. In the May 1988 elections, the United Caucus candidate for vice president for academics, William Scheuerman, easily defeated the incumbent, John Crary; the United Caucus candidate for vice president for professionals, Thomas Corigliano, had no opposition; and the United Caucus candidate for treasurer, John Hunt, was elected by a substantial margin.[165] The following year Tim Reilly was reelected without opposition, as was the United Caucus candidate for secretary, Jeanne Galbraith. The membership development officer position was contested, but United Caucus candidate Janet Potter received significantly more votes that the Reform Caucus candidate, D. Jo Schaffer.[166] The trend continued in the 1990 election, which saw both William Scheuerman and Thomas Corigliano reelected without opposition. John Hunt did receive serious opposition, but he still managed to defeat his Reform Caucus opponent, Mary Edwards.[167] Since UUP's constitution prohibited any officers from serving more than three consecutive terms in office, Reilly's last candidacy came in 1991. This time he was opposed by W. Roy Slaunwhite, Jr., but Reilly won overwhelmingly by a vote of 170-64. Jeanne Galbraith was reelected secretary without opposition, but in a repeat of the previous contest for the membership development officer position, D. Jo Schaffer managed to eke out a victory over Janet Potter.[168] In the last election of the Reilly years, William Scheuerman easily won reelection over his opponent, Paul Zarembka, and United Caucus candidate Thomas Matthews was unopposed for vice president for professionals. John Hunt again was challenged by Mary Edwards, but defeated her by a greater margin in the rematch.[169]

The provision in the UUP constitution that imposed term limits on statewide officers was a frequent topic of discussion among delegates, both informally and formally. Proponents of term limits argued that it prevented potential corruption and longtime domination by any one individual, as well as promoting the advancement of new talent into administrative ranks. But others argued that it put the union at a disadvantage, since it created lame-duck leadership, which was a problem in the union world, where term limits were not the norm. Moreover, some maintained that it was not democratic, since it limited the voter's choice. In 1990 the matter was taken up by UUP's Constitution Study Committee. At its November 2 meeting, the committee discussed proposed constitutional amendments submitted by the chapters at Albany and the Syracuse Health Science Center to eliminate term limitations for UUP statewide officers. By a unanimous vote it was decided not to support those amendments, since the committee concluded that UUP members wanted to retain the limitations.[170] But the issue would not die, and on February 1, 1992, a term-limit-elimination amendment was brought before the Delegate Assembly, which adopted a motion to postpone indefinitely. Another proposal was put forward that would have changed officer terms from two years to three, with a three-consecutive-term limitation; that, too, was postponed indefinitely.[171]

What had happened to the Reform Caucus, which in the past usually ran candidates for all officer positions and even managed to win a vice presidency? Bruce Atkins, a Reform Caucus member from the Cortland campus, claimed that the caucus had "never been effective" in having enough of its members elected as delegates, and while they attempted to convince delegates of their views through

eloquent speeches, that did not work because United Caucus delegates arrived
at Delegate Assemblies with their minds already made up.[172] Reform Caucus
stalwarts Malcolm Nelson and Susan Puretz saw the United Caucus as being
more effective in mobilizing their members, and Tim Reilly, in particular, as
incorporating some Reform Caucus views into their positions.[173] And perhaps
Reilly succeeded in co-opting some of them. United Caucus members Alan
Shank and William Cozort both claimed that Reilly did not follow a strict party
line when making committee appointments, and so a fair number of Reform
Caucus adherents served on UUP statewide committees. Shank saw this as a very
positive move toward unifying the union, while Cozort saw it as "a very serious
mistake."[174] And then, too, there seemed to have been some internal conflicts
within the Reform Caucus ranks.[175]

Assessing the Reilly Years

In the six years that John M. Reilly served as UUP's president, the union's activities
increased and its influence expanded. The contracts it negotiated for its members
were, from a monetary standpoint, at least as good as those concluded by other
state unions, but also included a number of innovative features not found in those
other agreements with the state. UUP's legislative presence grew substantially,
with its frequent visits to the offices of state legislators. Indeed, the union's "core
lobbyists" became well known in those offices, and many useful relationships
were formed. Some legislators came to rely on UUP for information relative to
SUNY, and UUP's positions on issues were taken very seriously. While the union
did not meet with great success where the budget for SUNY was concerned, it
did garner several significant legislative achievements. Although UUP always
supported other unions in their struggles, its commitment to worker solidarity
grew even stronger during these years. Reilly's commitment to improving minority representation among both students and faculty resulted in some positive
gains in that area, and the union also expanded its role in supporting human
and civil rights issues. Reilly wanted UUP to be seen as something more than
an organization that fought for more pay and better working conditions for its
members, and progress was made toward that goal, most visibly through the
publication of the *SUNY'S Future* document and the airing of *The Best of Our
Knowledge* radio program.

But these gains did not come without cost, and that cost was to the union's
budget. It was expensive to maintain a union presence at the offices of lawmakers,
and staging rallies involved paying for transportation and paraphernalia such as
signs, buttons, T-shirts, and caps. The fight to secure better funding for SUNY
was also costly because UUP expended substantial sums for media advertising.
Union solidarity efforts involved contributions to strike funds, for example, and a

stronger commitment to social causes also frequently resulted in some monetary support. Then too, the production of the *SUNY's Future* document was costly, as was the sponsorship of the radio program. The result of all these efforts was that the union's treasury had been greatly depleted by the time Reilly left office, and it fell to his successor to find a way to put UUP on a sound financial footing.

Chapter 6

UUP Matures: Part I, 1993–2001

The New Administration Does Some Initial Housekeeping

The spring 1993 elections marked a turning point for UUP. Stony Brook's Arnold Wishnia, a leader of the oppositional Reform Caucus, strolled to the microphone and made the unprecedented announcement that the Reform Caucus was backing William Scheuerman,[1] the United Caucus candidate for president.[2] This cross-endorsement of a presidential candidate broke with the past, suggesting that the union might now expend less energy on internal battles and more on its external fights. UUP was maturing as an organization. And mature it did. Over the next decade and a half, UUP underwent fundamental change. While SUNY constantly changed chancellors, UUP delegates removed officer term limits, providing continuity in leadership that allowed UUP to fill the vacuum created by the university's leadership instability. The union became a major player in New York State politics, broke New York's tradition of public-sector-pattern bargaining, made major contractual and extracontractual gains for its members, and eventually took its rightful place as the leading national higher-education union. These achievements did not come easily. The United University Professions initially faced much adversity in the form of an antagonistic gubernatorial administration and university trustees who were openly hostile to SUNY's public mission and its union. The following pages chronicle the maturation and development of UUP as a leading union in the state and nationally.

As described in previous pages, throughout most of its twenty-year history, UUP was rife with internal conflicts. These disputes, which gave birth to the formation of caucuses within the union, arose from the fundamental issues concerning the role of unions and where union power should reside. As already noted, the Reform Caucus thought UUP should become part of a larger social movement, while United Caucus backers wanted the union to focus primarily on terms and conditions of employment. As part of their "movement" mentality, reformers advocated rank-and-file activism and sought greater chapter autonomy and power. After all, they argued, the members are at the chapters. United Caucus supporters believed that the local, as the legal union entity, should serve as the fulcrum of power and authority, while arguing that support of the local did not exclude rank-and file participation. In fact, they contended, it made for a more unified and effective union. The election of Bill Scheuerman in spring 1993 bridged these positions and brought in a "Era of Good Feelings," a time when the desire for unity and commitment began to take precedence over internal differences.[3] This newly established unity would prove essential in meeting the challenges posed by the 1994 gubernatorial election and the policies of the new George Pataki administration. It would also lead to a near-fifteen-year adminis-tration that combined social activism with bread-and-butter unionism.

Since its inception, every UUP administration had increased the union's effectiveness at the bargaining table, in the political arena, in the realm of pub-lic relations, and internally, by building support among the membership. The new Scheuerman administration continued this tradition. But, as with past new administrations, the recently elected president immediately faced some pressing internal and external issues. Internally, UUP faced a budget deficit, a reserve fund that failed to meet delegate assembly requirements, strained fiscal relation-ships with NYSUT and AFT affiliates, a logjam of grievances from the previous administration sitting in limbo as they awaited decisions to terminate or take to arbitration, and important ethical and legal issues concerning chartering of private planes and payment of officers' living stipends. Externally, UUP was preparing to enter contract negotiations, private institutions of higher learning were revving up their efforts to get more state aid, SUNY's hospitals faced the prospect of privatization, and UUP's political operation and VOTE-COPE col-lections needed an overhaul.[4] (Because it is illegal to use union dues for direct political activities such as campaign contributions, unions create a separate VOTE-COPE fund to collect voluntary contributions from members for politi-cal activities.) In 1993, UUP's $13,000 in VOTE-COPE collections amounted to less than a dollar a year per member, placing UUP—NYSUT's second-largest local—last among all NYSUT locals.

Historically, budget issues always haunted UUP. As previously discussed, in 1981 the Drescher administration inherited a major budget shortfall, which President Drescher successfully resolved. The successor Reilly administration began on sound fiscal footing, but it was not long before rising costs and new expenses outstripped revenues, creating a structural deficit. In 1986, for instance, life-insurance payouts for bargaining-unit members cost the union close to $300,000 yearly, but by the early 1990s the cost had jumped to almost $400,000 annually. Release time for chapter leaders, negotiated in the 1988–91 contract, cost several hundred thousand more, and an increase in spending for political ads and a new lobbying program on the federal level in Washington, DC, drained tens of thousands more.[5] Since UUP did not have a "pass-through" provision in its constitution, dues increases by NYSUT and AFT only worsened its financial position.[6] During the Spring 1988 Delegate Assembly, delegates expressed their concern over the budgetary pressures by mandating the establishment of a reserve fund with a minimum of $1 million. But growing expenditures quickly cut into the reserve. On paper the reserve fund usually looked solid, but by the early '90s payment of all obligations would drain the fund. In short, if the union paid all its expenses, the fund would not meet the $1 million balance required by Delegate Assembly policy. UUP's financial situation led at least one delegate to observe that his union was in the hole for "at least a million dollars."[7]

The budget crunch contributed to much finger-pointing. UUP's relationship with its affiliates, never great to begin with, deteriorated as delegates blamed high dues payments to NYSUT and AFT for UUP's fiscal squeeze. They complained loudly about NYSUT's lack of fiscal support[8] and called for nonpayment of dues to AFT. The fiscal crunch also exacerbated the historical tensions between the chapters and the UUP administrative office. Many delegates, still smarting from the previous administration's removal of the dues cap and its failed attempt to terminate UUP's life-insurance payouts, looked at the statewide leadership with distrust. Delegates usually greeted the treasurer's budget report with hostile and accusatory questions, making passage of the budget a time-consuming platform for delegates to vent their anger and frustration. The clash between the chapters and the local led one delegate to publicly observe that "a them-and-us attitude is developing in this body."[9] The issue became so divisive that delegates introduced a motion to shift budget preparation responsibilities from the treasurer to the chapters.[10] Although delegates voted it down, the motion itself clearly indicated that the role of the chapters within the local was an issue not yet settled.

Despite getting cross-endorsements from both caucuses, the newly elected president knew the budget crisis threatened to reopen the union's old internal rifts. Consequently, with UUP facing a deficit of more than $325,000, the administration acted quickly by withholding $150,000 in dues from AFT and negotiating ways to restructure dues payments to the national affiliate.[11] Cost-cutting measures were put in place: instead of mailing proposed constitutional amendments to the membership, they would be published in *The Voice* for a $10,000 annual savings; switching to a new printing company and changing the newspaper's format saved another $16,000–$18,000 a year; and extending the Delegate Assembly to three days saved additional dollars previously spent on additional trips for committee meetings.[12] UUP withdrew its financial support of the WAMC radio program hosted by Tim Reilly, *The Best of Our Knowledge*. The union also imposed travel restrictions on officers and delegates alike. UUP would no longer pay for airline tickets following delegate assemblies, instead requiring delegates to take charter buses for return trips to Long Island and Buffalo. In the past, officers usually flew to distant chapters on commercial airlines or on charter flights. This practice was now forbidden. Officers would have to use their UUP cars to attend meetings within the state. Now they were expected to lead by example.[13] Subsequently, delegates approved two additional money-saving programs in January, 1996. The first was temporarily to switch UUP's two vice presidents from full–time to half-time.[14] The change took effect after the May 1996 elections and saved the union thousands in release-time payments to SUNY. The vice presidents, whose UUP stipends remained the same, were restored to full-time status in 2000, after the fiscal crisis was resolved. The second was a move that took advantage of the Pataki's administration's lack of familiarity with the UUP Benefit Trust Fund. UUP told the newly appointed Pataki GOER director that the Benefit Trust Fund, not union dues, was responsible for paying the union's life-insurance obligations. The new Pataki administration failed to question this assertion, and life-insurance payouts, previously the responsibility of the union, were now paid through the fund with negotiated state dollars.[15] Over the years this move saved UUP millions.

The new UUP administration addressed criticism regarding NYSUT's lack of support by reversing the UUP response to proposed NYSUT dues increases. This move was not as crazy as it sounded. In the past, it was good political theater for UUP leaders to strongly resist any proposed dues increases by NYSUT and AFT on principle, even though they knew they lacked the votes to stop it at the annual NYSUT Representative Assembly. Since UUP did not have a "pass-through" provision in its constitution as required by AFT, these affiliate dues increases would not automatically be passed on to UUP's members. Instead, the union had to pay for an increase out of its operating budget without garnering any additional dues revenue. Not surprisingly, at UUP's Spring 1989 Delegate Assembly, President Reilly openly boasted about UUP's opposition to paying more dues to NYSUT.[16] Opposition undoubtedly made UUP's members feel good, but it only fed into the "them" and "us" attitude some UUPers held toward its affiliates. In short, opposing affiliate dues increases was internally divisive and sent a message to NYSUT that UUP was not a team player.

Scheuerman and UUP's new treasurer, Rowena Blackman-Stroud from the Brooklyn Health Science Center, reversed Reilly's practice of opposing dues increases. They informed NYSUT president Thomas Hobart that they supported dues increases, but they also requested that NYSUT give increased financial support to UUP for its many member services and outreach programs. Recognizing the significance of support from its second-largest local, Hobart agreed to this arrangement. Now seen as a team player, UUP often received extra financial assistance from NYSUT, which exceeded $1 million over the years. By the fall of 1994 Scheuerman was able to report a budgetary surplus that would soon fulfill reserve-fund requirements.[17] Within three years of taking office, the new administration had a reserve fund of over $3 million.[18]

A second pressing problem centered on UUP's lack of an ethics policy. Rank-and-file members frequently perceived UUP officers as acting in their own self-interest rather than in the interest of the union, feeding a growing schism between the campus chapters and the union's administrative office. One such issue was the officers' use of chartered flights. These flights saved on travel time and could be less expensive than commercial flights when officers flew as a group. But charter flights were also sometimes used as an opportunity for a UUP officer to meet the flying requirements needed to maintain a pilot's license with no personal out-of-pocket expenditures, creating the perception that UUP used chartered flights primarily for this purpose. To many, this practice had the appearance of impropriety. Desiring to start with a clean slate, the new administration immediately stopped the chartered flights. Years later, after UUP became fiscally sound, the union occasionally used chartered flights when faced with time restraints on essential travel. But UUP officers did not pilot them.

The new president immediately took on a second ethical question that often rankled the membership. This one involved officers' living stipends. According to UUP policy, full-time officers who relocated to Albany from distant campuses were entitled to a living stipend if they maintained their original residence at their home campus. One officer moved his family to Albany and rented out his campus-based house. For several years he received his UUP living stipend, even though he gained income from this rental. Shortly after taking office, Scheuerman temporarily stopped payment of all officer living stipends and brought the issue to the UUP Executive Board for advice and action. In executive session the Board gave a very broad interpretation of living stipend payments, and the officer continued to receive his monthly stipend along with his rent check. Even though there was no change in the implementation of the policy, Executive Board clarification put the issue to rest.[19]

The final piece of internal housecleaning concerned dozens of grievances from the previous administration left stacked on the president's desk awaiting decisions to terminate or take to arbitration. Grievants generally don't like to be told that their grievance has no merit and cannot be taken to arbitration. Consequently, the Reilly administration often delayed notification of this bad news, and the number of grievances awaiting final decisions mounted up. Some cases were several years old. This too tended to create much distrust and ill will toward UUP's administrative office. Almost immediately following the June 1993 election, the new NYSUT assistant director of staff for UUP, Tina Kaplan, reviewed the backlog of cases and discussed her recommendations with President Scheuerman, who sent final decision letters to the interested parties.[20]

Externally, UUP needed to strengthen its legislative program, increase its VOTE-COPE contributions, and make its legislative agenda more clear and precise. SUNY budgets had been inadequate for several years, leading to the loss of full-time faculty, who were frequently replaced by underpaid part-timers. SUNY viewed the use of part-time faculty as a way to offer a range of courses necessary for graduation at a bargain price. Reliance on poorly paid workers without job security was a band-aid solution to SUNY's budgetary woes. SUNY's finances were so bad that even the pro-private-sector report on the status of higher education in New York by the Riley Commission, which called for increases in Bundy Aid to the privates, also recognized the need to spend more on the state's public institutions—SUNY and CUNY.[21] Additionally, SUNY was attempting to remove the Long Island Veteran's Hospital from the university by converting it into a public benefit corporation.[22] To further complicate matters, SUNY wanted "hospital flex" legislation to allow its hospitals to operate "storefront" facilities that used staff not covered by the Taylor Law and therefore were not in the union. This presented a significant threat to UUP. If passed into law, the proposed legislation would allow the university eventually to replace union personnel with nonunion workers.[23] UUP did not oppose the concept of hospital flex. It just sought to protect its workforce by mandating Taylor Law coverage for all employees.[24]

UUP's new administration addressed these political issues by restructuring its political activities. First, in the past the legislative agenda was often a lengthy wish list addressing a large number of the union's political needs. Union priorities were not always clear, and at the end of the legislative session legislators often said something like, "we tried to help, but didn't know what you really wanted." More, legislators were often overwhelmed with details and requests for aid from many constituents. To cut through these copious demands, they needed precision and clarity. James Biggane, then secretary of the Senate Finance Committee, for example, used to tell Senate staffers, "If it's not on one page don't submit it."[25] The Scheuerman administration shortened the list of legislative items brought to legislators to three priorities. For the 1994–95 fiscal year, these were restoration of 250 faculty lines, protections for the workforce under hospital flex, and new equipment for SUNY's two-year technical colleges. UUP also placed greater emphasis on lobbying in legislators' home districts where the UUP activists actually lived and voted. To implement the latter change, the union divided the state into eight lobbying districts with a coordinator from each. Vice president for professionals Thomas Matthews was assigned the task of recruiting volunteers and coordinating the activities of all districts. The union also appointed several VOTE-COPE coordinators and began aggressive efforts to increase VOTE-COPE contributions, which at $13,000 annually ranked last among all NYSUT locals. The new legislative and COPE programs also served as important means of increasing rank-and-file participation in the affairs of UUP.[26]

UUP's restructured programs combined with monthly breakfast meetings with Mario Cuomo at the governor's mansion and closer cooperation with SUNY's acting chancellor Joseph Burke brought good results.[27] The state's final budget for the 1994–95 fiscal year contained money for eighty new faculty lines and, despite SUNY's opposition, several million dollars to update equipment at the agricultural and technical colleges. The hospital flex legislation did not come up for a vote during the session, and the union blocked an attempt to dump the Long Island Veteran's Hospital.[28] But as UUP was preparing to go to the bargaining table, the election of George Pataki as governor in the fall of 1994 changed everything. For the first time since its inception in 1973, UUP would now function in a political environment openly hostile to unions. It soon became apparent that UUP would be in for the fight of its life.

The Pataki Attack on SUNY and UUP

George Pataki ran on a platform of balanced-budget conservatism, a political program based on the ideology that government shouldn't live beyond its means. Balanced-budget conservatism also recognizes the general unwillingness of tax-payers to part with their money and, consequently, identifies good government with cheap government.[29] Throughout his campaign Pataki echoed these themes, promising to balance the state's budget, reduce the size of the state workforce, and cut taxes. But as the governor discovered on taking office, the realization of these goals would require drastic, even unprecedented actions. After all, New York State faced a budget shortfall of almost $5 billion. This huge deficit made it apparent that balancing the budget while cutting taxes meant that state workers were about to take hits as never before.[30] Proclaiming that he was "overthrowing all the unworkable liberal abstractions of the past and replacing them with a revolution of conservative ideas,"[31] the governor's initial two budgets reduced the state's workforce by 12,000, cutting spending by some $2 billion while reducing the personal income tax by 25 percent.[32]

With a large deficit and promises of severe budget-cutting looming over state agencies, the governor-elect appointed a transition team of sixty-two members to plan higher-education policy. The transition group met at New York University. Of the sixty-two team members, fifty-eight came from private institutions of higher learning. The transition group expressed concern about the 35,000 to 40,000 empty seats at the small private institutions and groused about the difficulty of competing with the state's public universities. One goal, then, was to shift students out of the public institutions, where, to paraphrase a market-conscious trustee, students receive subsidies not unlike welfare, into the private sector where they can take loans and pay them back after they graduate.[33] The threat of massive impending cuts combined with the anti-public-sector attitude of transition members placed the UUP on the front lines of the fiscal battlefield for SUNY's survival.

Prior to submitting his SUNY budget for fiscal 1995–96, the governor imposed a mid year cut of $25 million on SUNY.[34] That was just the initial warning shot over SUNY's bow. The governor's budget for SUNY for fiscal 1995–96 was devastating. Pataki claimed SUNY would take a cut of only 4.8 percent, but that number assumed the university would raise $255 million in new revenue. Consequently, after analyzing all the obfuscating mysteries of budgeting, SUNY was targeted to take an operational cut of 31.5 percent. This prompted recently appointed chancellor Thomas Bartlett to note that the budget proposal "presents budgetary problems of historic proportions for the State University of New York."[35] The governor did not receive Bartlett's comments well. The university's Cuomo-appointed trustees joined their chancellor in resisting the budget when they created a public uproar by publicly stating that the proposed budget could result in as many as eight campus closings, the loss of 2,500 jobs, and a tuition hike of $1,600.[36] Needless to say, they were soon replaced by trustees more amenable to the governor's program,[37] but not before they eliminated 367 full-time-equivalent positions and imposed a hiring freeze on the university.[38] Since Cuomo had left open several vacancies on SUNY's board, Governor Pataki responded to the trustees' resistance by stacking the board with his appointees. The newly appointed "activist" trustees,[39] who now controlled the board and later were to use SUNY as their base to wage a cultural war, almost immediately placed restrictions on Chancellor Bartlett's authority, leading the newly appointed chancellor to resign within a year. Their actions made it apparent to many that SUNY was becoming a political arm of the new governor.[40] With the future of SUNY and many UUP jobs at stake, the union faced an uphill battle.

The state-operated campuses of SUNY were not the only higher-education institutions earmarked for significant budget cuts. CUNY and the SUNY and CUNY community colleges also faced major cutbacks. The privates did not escape the governor's proposed budget cuts either. The governor's proposal slashed Bundy Aid and lowered the maximum tuition assistance by $500. Dropping the maximum tuition assistance award would have a dire effect on the privates, who had more students receiving the maximum award thanks to their higher tuition rates.

UUP would now have to compete with the privates and their lobbying arm, the Commission of Independent Colleges and Universities (CICU), in their struggle for limited funds. Securing legislative funding involved two steps. The first focused on the amount of money the state would spend on all higher education. The second dealt with the issue of how to divide it. Historically, the dollars received by SUNY and CUNY were divided in proportion to the number of students at each institution. But that left open the question of how much should go to the privates. That, of course, was the critical political issue. To make matters even worse for the union, UUP's collective bargaining agreement with the state was about to expire and the union would have to negotiate a new contract within an extraordinarily hostile political and economic environment.

Within weeks of Pataki's inauguration, UUP launched a massive action plan, which continued to develop for years to come. In a frenzy of activity, hundreds of rank-and-file members approached their local businesses with newly printed "SUNY Bucks" to demonstrate the financial impact of cuts to SUNY at the community level.[41] Whenever union activists made purchases at their local stores, after paying for their goods, they presented the owner with SUNY Bucks to demonstrate the important economic role SUNY played in the local community. The message was clear: cuts in SUNY will reduce sales and could even put you out of business. Consequently, many small business owners, most of whom supported the new governor, wrote letters to Governor Pataki in opposition to his proposed cuts in SUNY's budget. In another show of support, business owners placed "Save SUNY" signs in store windows all across upstate New York.[42]

The union also worked with local Chambers of Commerce and formed a coalition of business groups—the Coalition for Public Higher Education—to write the governor in opposition to the proposed cuts.[43] Cooperating campus presidents gave the union lists of campus vendors that profited from SUNY's purchases so the union could write them and ask for their support.[44] The same approach was taken toward parents of students and SUNY's alumni.[45] UUP also initiated a long-term ad campaign; this, combined with Scheuerman's meetings with editorial boards across the state, generated additional publicity for UUP's political position.[46] Based on information attained in debriefing sessions with activist members, UUP formed a war room that kept track of each legislator's position on the issues and their attitude toward SUNY.[47] In addition to its program of district lobbying, the union brought dozens of members into Albany every Tuesday to remind legislators directly of the impact of the proposed cuts on their constituents. Legislative leaders recognized UUP's activism by participating in the union's annual legislative luncheons in record numbers. In fact, rather than sending staff, every year more and more legislators, including legislative leaders, began attending the luncheons.

The Pataki budget onslaught against SUNY, to that point the most serious political fight in the union's history, brought to the fore the critically important role played by politics in the union's and SUNY's existence. UUP's leaders recognized that the union's future depended in large part on its political clout, and argued that restrictive term limits worked against the union's political needs by making it difficult to develop long-term relationships with legislators. Union leaders sought to amend the UUP constitution, not by doing away with term limits, but by extending the number of terms from a maximum of three two-year terms to four. Delegates to the Winter 1995 Delegate Assembly agreed with this assessment. In a clean break with tradition, delegates voted 130 in favor to 64 opposed to change the constitution and allow state officers to serve as many as four two-year terms.[48] UUP members were beginning to recognize the limits and restriction of term limits.

While UUP was building its political program and fighting to save thousands of jobs, its labor agreement with the State of New York was set to expire at the end of June, 1995. This presented the union with even more challenges, for the governor expected all state workers to make major concessions at the bargaining table. UUP's leaders knew negotiations would be difficult.[49] Consequently,

UUP and the other state unions—CSEA, PEF, and Council 82 (later to become NYSCOBA)—agreed to cooperate with each other during these tough times. They agreed to hold regular meetings to discuss bargaining issues and to share information. In February the state presented its proposals to the UUP team, headed by vice president for professionals Tom Matthews. In addition to demanding a four-year contract rather than the traditional three, the state imposed an April 1 deadline for UUP to settle, opposed any salary hikes, and most importantly, sought to undermine the university's tenure system by proposing "the inclusion of language that reflects the needs of the state and its employees regarding the impact on employees of the state exercising its right to contract out."[50] In short, the state wanted the right to replace faculty with non-SUNY employees. For instance, Berlitz teachers of language could replace SUNY faculty who taught foreign languages. The Berlitz teachers would not receive union-negotiated salaries and benefits, they would not be eligible for tenure, and they could be fired at will without any due-process protections. Within this context, tenure at SUNY would no longer exist, and with it academic freedom, the bedrock of American universities, would disappear.

The situation became even more ominous for UUP in mid-March when the new Pataki-appointed SUNY trustees indicated they would not back the faculty and union. Showing their disdain for SUNY and echoing the mantra of the private sector from years past, newly appointed trustee Candace de Russy publicly slammed the university for having what she characterized as unacceptably low academic standards. But she went even further, calling for the closing of SUNY's hospitals and law school. In so doing, de Russy made it clear that graduate education was for the state's private institutions of higher learning, not for the state's public university. Her public comments marked the opening shot in a series of anti-SUNY attacks that she and other trustees would launch against the union and the university over the next several years.[51]

The trustees' hostility to public education and unwillingness to support tenure was bad enough, but the situation worsened when CSEA representatives stopped participating in meetings with other state unions and subsequently announced its acceptance of the state's outsourcing provisions. CSEA, the state's largest public-sector union, had now set the bargaining pattern for all other state unions, and in so doing put UUP in an apparently untenable position. Finally, on the eve of the state's artificial deadline of March 31, after the UUP negotiations team had finished its work for the day and departed from Albany, the governor's office made a new demand, even though the agreed time for amending proposals had long passed. Led by interim director of GOER James Gill, whose three-month temporary service commitment would expire on April 1, GOER demanded an increase in workload of one hour by every faculty member.[52] Gill's vague workload demand did not clarify whether he meant an additional teaching hour or more office time. Since workload at SUNY was based on the Taylor

Law's past practice protections and not negotiated, this was an unprecedented and disturbing demand.[53] More, it was unclear what the demand meant, as even Gill himself conceded.[54] Negotiations broke down.

On April 1, Gill vacated his position and returned to his private law practice in New York City. Governor Pataki did not replace him until September, after he appointed Linda Angello to head GOER. In the intervening four months, GOER lacked a director, and negotiations between UUP and the state were on hold. UUP faced additional pressure after CSEA accepted a contract with similar outsourcing language.[55] PEF and Council 82 shortly followed CSEA's lead, leaving UUP as the last of the large state unions without a new agreement with the state.

As the summer of '95 wound down, UUP still had not reached a new agreement with the state, but on the budget front its political activities were beginning to pay off. Legislative budgetary restorations and a tuition increase kept the SUNY budget cut to about 3 percent, a major victory given the governor's original proposal. The restorations averted massive layoffs and took any discussions of campus closings off the table. SUNY was relatively secure again. The state budget also funded the Theatre Institute for another year, and UUP used its influence to get the legislature to include workers in the optional pensions systems such as TIAA/CREF in an early-retirement bill after they were initially omitted. Finally, working in conjunction with NYSUT and other public-sector unions, UUP helped gain the renewal of agency fee legislation on the very last day of the legislative session.

During this stressful period of the first Pataki budget battle, UUP was involved in a variety of other important activities. In addition to working on budget restorations and negotiating a contract, the union's other significant activities included the settlement of a number of clinical practice grievances through a mediation process established as a consequence of the 1991–95 contract.[56] In short, five physicians at the Buffalo Health Science center had filed grievances primarily but not solely based on moneys they received from the clinical practice plan. UUP, the state, and SUNY had discussed these clinical practice issues during the 1991–95 bargaining cycle and agreed to set up a mediation process subsequent to reaching a contractual agreement. In 1992 the parties met and affirmed that departmental plans are legitimate, chairs' funds are allowable, and the cost of practice reimbursement to an affiliated institution may be on a percentage basis when approved by the chancellor.[57] Finally in 1996, after reviewing the grievances in light of the facts agreed on and after extensive hearings and discussion with all involved, the mediator made recommendations to settle the more than two dozen grievances. All grievants received monetary awards.[58]

The mediation settlement resolved a number of grievances but did not permanently settle future possible issues regarding clinical practice. The fiscally hard-pressed state, for instance, wanted access to the millions generated by clinical practice plans throughout the university. The mediation settlement made clear that after meeting certain negotiated contractual obligations to SUNY, doctors had control of the moneys generated in their clinical practice plans, including setting clinical practice salaries. Nevertheless, some ambiguity remained. Physicians unhappy with their share of clinical practice moneys as determined by their practice plan continued to turn to the union to file grievances. To further complicate matters, some clinicians, particularly departmental chairs, blurred lines by using university letterhead when acting in their capacity as plan members.

Subsequently, in February 2001, UUP and the state entered into an agreement that clarified these issues and, significantly, protected clinical practice funds from state intrusion. In essence, the agreement created a "firewall" between clinical practice plans and the state. It formally stated that practice plans are separate legal entities not subject to the control of the state, except in accordance with the UUP contract and relevant Policies of the Board of Trustees.[59] This meant that money generated by the plans was "wholly owned by the physicians." The agreement also clarified the role of the union. As separate legal entities, clinical practice plans are not parties to the UUP contract, but their actions must be consistent with the contract, Article XVI of the Board of Trustees Policies, and any appropriate memoranda between the state and UUP. Clinical practice income would not be subject to union dues, and the Governing Board, elected annually by plan members, would be responsible for the day-to-day management of the plan, including determining reimbursement to plan members. This meant that UUP could not become legally involved in salary disputes involving clinical practice dollars.[60]

Still working without a successor agreement to the 1991–95 contract, UUP continued to pursue other issues, including a renewed attempt to organize the Research Foundation.[61] If successful, organizing the foundation would greatly restrict the state's ability to outsource to its own nonunion entities, as foundation members would become part of the UUP bargaining unit. Parking negotiations also continued at six chapters.[62] UUP increased its pressure on SUNY by initiating an equal-pay-for-equal-work study funded by a $130,000 grant from AFT.[63] This was in response to claims that the university systematically paid women faculty less than their male counterparts. The report was subsequently submitted to outside counsel, who recommended against action at that time. During this period, UUP also began to emerge as a national leader in the higher-education labor movement by joining forces with SUNY Faculty Senate colleagues, former chancellor Bruce Johnstone, and Senate and NEA union colleagues from the California State system to study the issue of learning productivity, an issue that was fast taking on national significance.[64] Despite all this, with the crucial budget battle out of the way until January of 1996 when the governor would present his budget for fiscal 97–98, the union could now divert more energy into resolving its contractual stalemate.

When the governor finally appointed a new director of GOER, Linda Angello, UUP resumed negotiations in December of 1996, almost six months after its contract had expired. But the contract's expiration within the context of an antiunion gubernatorial administration presented an immediate problem for UUP.[65] The continued funding of UUP's self-administered Benefit Trust Fund (BTF), the fund providing dental, optical, and prescription coverage to bargaining-unit members, was at stake. The union held that funding was covered by the Triborough doctrine, which requires the state to honor all provisions of an expired contract that do not mandate new moneys. The state disagreed with UUP's interpretation, but nonetheless made a one-month payment to the fund in March 1996 as an incentive for UUP to reach an agreement.

At the time, it appeared that UUP might soon agree to a new contract with the state. The union was making significant progress at the bargaining table, extracting "far more concessions on contracting out than the other unions,"[66] according to President Scheuerman. Despite negotiating restrictions on the state's original demand for the unfettered right to outsource jobs at the university, the union could not close the deal because the state's proposal still had provisions allowing SUNY to outsource to itself, or what UUP called "contracting-in." If permitted, contracting-in would be exceedingly detrimental to the union's work-force. It would give SUNY the authority to use existing in-house entities, such as the SUNY Research Foundation, Auxiliary Services, and any other SUNY college foundation, or to create other entities not covered by the Taylor Law to provide services currently performed by members of the UUP bargaining unit. Contracting-in would thus enable SUNY to replace UUP faculty and staff without going through the outsourcing process, thereby rendering meaningless any protections the union negotiated against outsourcing.

Eager to bring negotiations to a conclusion, in March of 1996, Angello made a one-month payment into the BTF[67] while giving assurances that she would address the contracting-in issue favorably. Unfortunately, she ran into a SUNY roadblock. SUNY would not budge on the contracting-in proposal. The university's intransigence was tied mostly to the legislative goals in the hospital flexibility legislation mentioned previously. UUP had successfully blocked the legislation and was now negotiating job-protections language for the bill with SUNY and legislators. Blocked on the legislative front, SUNY sought to realize its same goals in a different forum: the negotiations table. UUP refused to accept a contract sanctioning contracting-in, and, once again, contract negotiations broke down. The state decided to play hardball and responded by stating unequivocally that it would make no additional payments to UUP's Benefit Trust Fund. Faced with the state's ultimatum, Scheuerman and NYSUT director of staff for UUP, Anthony Wildman, made it clear that the union would not budge on the issue of tenure. One state representative warned that union members would not back their leaders on this issue. Twenty-thousand academics are likely to have 25,000 different opinions, the admonition continued, and UUP's leaders would soon come begging for the terms just offered.[68] It was now conceivable that members of the UUP bargaining unit could lose prescription, drug, and optical insurance coverage.

On April 10, 1996, UUP filed an improper practice charge with the Public Employment Relations Board. The union sought injunctive relief on the grounds that loss of prescription drug coverage could do irreparable harm to its members. In some cases funding for prescription drug coverage was a life-and-death issue. The legal question of the filing was whether the expired contract had language that said the fund would sunset at the end of a given period of time or whether it would continue after the contract. PERB ruled in UUP's favor and petitioned the State Supreme Court to give the union injunctive relief. On April 30, the court did just that. But the fund was exhausted and UUP closed it at 11:59 p.m. on May 8. The state appealed the court's ruling and on May 9 unilaterally took over the prescription drug portion of the fund and charged SUNY faculty and professional staff $16 a month. Faculty and staff also lost their dental and optical insurance.[69] To put further pressure on the state's negotiators, UUP sent letters to dental and optical providers advising them that the state's actions would probably lead to a decrease in business and asking them to write the governor in support of the union's position.[70] The union also sent advisories directing bargaining-unit members to hold receipts for out-of-pocket dental and optical expenditures for submission when a contract was reached and the fund restored.

The state's position was clear. All the other major state unions had accepted the outsourcing provisions in their labor agreements, so, state negotiators insisted, UUP would have to do the same. Neither side gave any indication of backing down. Consequently, once the BTF was closed, another long stalemate followed. But SUNY was different from other state agencies, and UUP continued its campaign to influence SUNY college presidents and the chancellor to pressure the trustees and governor to reach an amiable settlement that would maintain the historical practice of tenure. To highlight the devastation outsourcing would bring to the university, the union began holding tenure workshops on campuses, emphasizing the close nexus between tenure and academic freedom. The union also initiated a membership letter-writing campaign to GOER director Angello,[71] generating more than 20,000 letters.[72] Its crisis committee organized informational picketing at the chapters, generating a great deal of media coverage.[73] On the national level, Scheuerman, who by now had become chair of AFT's Higher Education Program and Policy Committee, took to the national stage in advocating for the sanctity of tenure, debating antitenure Harvard Professor Richard Chait, and appearing on radio and television shows across the country.

Campus presidents also wanted a new agreement that preserved tenure. Some even met with their local college council to discuss the gravity of the situation.[74] With no pay increases in sight and the loss of tenure looming as a real possibility, faculty were leaving the university, morale was declining, and recruitment was becoming increasingly difficult.[75] Consequently, campus presidents urged all parties to return to the bargaining table while also making it clear to the trustees that the loss of tenure was unacceptable.[76] In April of 1997 UUP gave members Chancellor John Ryan's email address and urged them to remind him that SUNY needed to settle the stalemate. But the deadlock continued. The governor needed outsourcing, but UUP could not agree to undercut tenure. Speaking before a meeting of the trustees, UUP's Tom Matthews reminded Board members that "[UUP] members have stood firm in the face of adversity" and advised them "to tell the state to drop contracting-out and contracting-in language from its list of demands."[77] Only then, Matthews concluded, would UUP reach a negotiated settlement.

Finally, in August of 1997, the state dropped its demand for contracting-in, and the two sides reached a win-win four-year agreement terminating on July 1, 1999. The governor could declare victory because he secured the outsourcing language he demanded in all state contracts. The language mirrored that found in other state union contracts, a declarative sentence that gave the state the right to outsource.[78] But UUP also gained a victory by defining in twenty-seven pages the conditions under which the state could implement its right to outsource jobs. While both sides declared victory, the restrictions negotiated by the union made the state's right to outsource jobs most unlikely, if not almost impossible. Outsourcing would be far too costly. In this sense, UUP broke the long-held tradition of pattern bargaining in the public sector by becoming the only statewide union that stopped outsourcing. If SUNY decided to outsource, all outsourced faculty and staff on permanent appointment would receive two year's salary plus benefits while retraining or awaiting redeployment. Those without permanent appointment would get a year's salary or receive pay for the duration of their contract, whichever was longer and more costly.[79]

To illuminate the prohibitively high cost of outsourcing, Scheuerman cited the following hypothetical example: if SUNY outsourced a fifty-person department, thirty of whom held permanent appointment and earned an average UUP annual salary of about $50,000 with benefits that cost $15,000 a year, SUNY would have to spend $3.9 million to outsource the department, and the $3.9 million did not include the cost of outsourcing the work of the remaining twenty department members. Given the outrageous expense of outsourcing,[80] the new agreement also prevented the state from contracting-in by prohibiting the state from contracting services in the UUP bargaining unit to any campus foundation. Since clinical practice plans are independent of SUNY, an exchange of letters between UUP and the state agreeing that clinical practice plans fall under the state's ethics law made it illegal for practice plans to contract-in services.[81]

The contract restored the BTF and provided retroactive full reimbursement for out-of-pocket expenditures. New contract language made it clear that payments to the Benefit Trust Fund do not sunset. Since the previous contract had expired two years earlier, only two years remained on the new four-year agreement. During this time, faculty and staff would receive a one-time lump sum payment of $1,250 and two 3.5 percent across-the-board raises, and they would be eligible for an additional 1 percent discretionary increase in each of the two years. Significantly, several campus presidents recognized UUP's growing clout and support of its rank-and-file members by agreeing to chapter leaders' requests that the discretionary funds be distributed equally as across-the-board payments.[82] Employees with tenure or continuing appointment would also receive an on-base payment of $500 retroactive to July 1996.[83]

Other significant gains included an increase in sick leave for family illness from ten to fifteen days; employees could accumulate more vacation time; and those who worked on Christmas would receive 1.5 compensatory days. Employees gained more control over the use of their compensatory time. They could now schedule it any time within twelve months of its accrual. Part-timers, for the first time, became eligible for all raises, and college presidents agreed to attempt to provide yearlong contracts to part-timers, as well as support services and work space.[84]

After facing the loss of tenure and going two years without raises and more than a year without dental and optical benefits, UUP's members overwhelmingly supported the new agreement. With a record ratification vote turnout of 61.4 percent, some 93.4 percent—another record—voted in favor of the new contract.[85] UUP members seemed both relieved and happy, but they faced other problems.

During the two-and-a-half years of protracted negotiations, the governor kept his fiscally conservative campaign promise intact by submitting budgets for fiscal '96–'97 and '97–'98 that again cut SUNY to the core. If the 1980s were years of fiscal austerity for SUNY, the first three Pataki budgets sought to downsize the university as never before. UUP managed to escape most of the damage in the governor's first budget, but the governor's fiscal-year budget for 1996–97 was, as the philosopher Yogi Berra once put it, déjà vu all over again. The governor's second budget proposal aimed at trimming approximately $119 million from SUNY, the equivalent of over 2,000 faculty position.[86] The cuts were real people, not empty budget lines. In fact, as of March 1996, UUP reported that some 150 faculty and staff had already received retrenchment notices, and 129 programs had been targeted for possible elimination. Additionally, the budget failed to fund the Theatre Institute, aimed to privatize SUNY's teaching hospitals, and proposed transferring faculty and staff of the University's Educational Opportunity Centers (EOC), all in the UUP bargaining unit, to the Department of Labor.[87]

The union's lobbying and public information structure continued to develop. In the first two years of the Scheuerman administration, VOTE-COPE collections increased more than fivefold. Campus presidents, recognizing the work UUP was doing to protect SUNY, gave the union lists of campus vendors that profited from SUNY's purchases so the union could write them to ask for their support.[88] UUP took the same approach toward parents of students and toward SUNY's alumni.[89] Additionally, John Mather, a former SUNY vice chancellor of economic development and close associate of the late Governor Rockefeller and former SUNY chancellor Gould, created a new not-for-profit organization with the backing of UUP. The mission of the Preservation of the State University of New York was to oppose the cuts.[90] Preservation adopted as its motto "Drive the vandals from the gate," a charge Mather received directly from Gould. The organization recruited as members some fifteen former trustees and, working in tandem with the union, enlisted the support of former campus presidents and vice chancellors from SUNY Central Administration in an effort to maintain SUNY's mission. Organized opposition to cutting SUNY's budget continued to grow when the mayor of Plattsburgh, Clyde Rabideau, formed a bipartisan coalition of mayors in support of SUNY in the upstate cities where SUNY campuses were located.

Despite UUP's evolving political program and the mounting resistance to the governor's budget axe, the political task confronting UUP was even more daunting than in the previous year. In 1995–96 the Cuomo-appointed trustees tried to build support against the cuts by making sure the public knew the damage Pataki's first budget would do to SUNY and its 400,000-plus students. In contrast, the new trustees threw themselves wholeheartedly behind Pataki's higher-education agenda. In response to the extreme budget cuts proposed by the governor in his first budget, the legislature asked the trustees to submit a plan for the future. Some of the new Pataki-appointed trustees played major roles in the newly formed ultraconservative, antitax organization CHANGE-NY. Trustee de Russy, for instance, was a cofounder. These CHANGE-NY trustees responded with "Rethinking SUNY," their roadmap for SUNY's future. "Rethinking SUNY" had, as former UUP vice president for academics Henry Steck noted, "a 'neo-liberal' market orientation"[91] that would make the university more entrepreneurial and less dependent on tax dollars.

Rather than defend the university, which is the traditional role played by university trustees, the Pataki appointees initially downplayed the impact of budget cutbacks. They did not request additional funding, then understated the size of the cuts, and ultimately announced that SUNY could absorb the bulk of the proposed cuts.[92] The trustees obfuscated the severity of the cuts by constantly making public statements on the budget based on SUNY's all-funds budget rather than its operating budget. The all-funds budget includes all revenue raised by SUNY, running the gamut from hotdog sales in a campus cafeteria to parking fees and clothing sales. The trustees misrepresentation of SUNY's fiscal condition contributed to media coverage that presented the governor's proposed cuts to SUNY in positive terms. In fact, media outlets and newspaper coverage initially reported a $72 million increase in funding.[93] UUP's challenge was to convince the public and the legislature that the budget proposal would hurt SUNY, force the layoffs of thousands of faculty, and prevent many students from graduating in four years because required courses were no longer regularly offered. UUP alerted the media and held demonstrations and rallies across the state. As reported in *The Voice*, these public activities gained "visibility and media attention for the union on both the budget and contract issues."[94]

The trustees also supported the proposal to privatize SUNY's teaching hospitals and went so far as to ban campus presidents from lobbying the legislature for a better SUNY budget. The governor's proposed cuts were so draconian that students began to view SUNY as an unstable institution. CHANGE-NY's research arm, the Empire Foundation, also undermined SUNY's reputation by sponsoring studies specifically designed to show how the university's liberalism was weakening academic standards. The fiscal instability and attacks by CHANGE-NY created a loss of confidence in the university, leading to a precipitous decline in applications for admission. Transfer applications plummeted by more than a third, the number of students seeking admission to colleges of arts and sciences declined by over 13 percent, university center applications dropped by 10 percent, and applications to the colleges of technology fell by nearly a quarter. The massive diminution of student applications forced Thomas Egan, chair of SUNY's Board, to reluctantly rescind his lobbying ban.[95]

However menacing the latest challenge, UUP was up for the fight. When the legislative session finally ended some 126 days after the April 1, 1996, state budget deadline, the proposed cuts were rescinded, the hospitals were not privatized, the EOC remained at SUNY, and the Theatre Institute was funded. UUP made a major political breakthrough by securing language in the state's Green Book of legislative intent stating outright that the fiscal budget for 1996–97 did not intend any layoffs. The Green Book did not have the legal authority of legislation, but it was an important political document that expressed the intent of the legislature. Any state agency, including SUNY, that disregarded the language could expect some form of punitive retaliation from the legislature. Rather than focusing on numbers, this strategy, initially suggested by NYSUT lobbyist Peter Martineau, was goal-oriented. Since SUNY controlled its budget numbers, the union knew that any discussion of the relationship between budget numbers and layoffs was useless. Such discussions, UUP believed, would wind up wrangling about numbers rather than substantive issues. Besides, SUNY controlled their budget numbers and could change them at will with no way for the union to confirm their validity. The trustees' claim to have sufficient resources put UUP in a good position to save jobs using the Green Book statement of intent. Once the trustees told legislators and the governor that SUNY did not need additional funds, legislators generally gave a sigh of relief and looked to channel dollars that might have gone to SUNY to other groups or organizations that lobbied for a share of the state's limited dollars. In a word, legislators would not give

SUNY funds that they said they did not need, especially during a fiscal crisis. UUP's successful efforts to attain language that prevented layoffs—including nonrenewals of nontenured employees—forced the university to maintain the labor force without regard to any budgetary numbers. Trustees abhorred this approach because it forced the university to maintain its labor force and prevented it from using fiscal reasons to justify layoffs.

The Green Book language also sent a strong message to the university concerning UUP's rising political clout, a message that translated into SUNY's decision to rescind some 150 previously announced retrenchments.[96] UUP managed to secure this no-layoff language in the Green Book through fiscal year 2008, when UUP's Smith administration did not pursue the strategy. Significantly, the Green Book language also put pressure on the trustees to request adequate funding for the university, a *bête noire* with the majority of the board. In fact, after submitting negative budget requests for three consecutive years, finally in 2001 SUNY's trustees requested additional new funds for the university. At a time when some 38 percent of SUNY's course offering were taught by part-time faculty, the trustees conceded the need for new full-time faculty positions and actually requested a 13 percent hike in funding.[97]

UUP's Coming of Age

By the end of 1996, UUP's political action plan was coming of age. In the years ahead, the union would face additional budget cuts and battles, but its institutionalized political operation was in place. In addition to playing defense and preventing massive budget cuts and the privatization of SUNY's hospitals year after year, UUP's political operation played an instrumental role in realizing major gains for members of UUP's bargaining unit. In November 1997, for instance, the state authorized spending $40 million without a pay bill to meet obligations of the new contract. This was a first. The following July the legislature passed and the governor signed into law hospital flex legislation. Even though SUNY originally sought legislation that allowed health-science centers to participate in managed care networks, the university ultimately opposed it because of the protections UUP gained for its labor force.[98] Significantly, UUP prevailed in getting a management bill passed that management opposed. The law kept the hospitals in SUNY and accountable to the legislature, provided job security for UUPers, and preserved the teaching and research mission of SUNY's hospitals. At the time of its passage, Scheuerman characterized the new law as "one of the greatest legislative victories in UUP's 25 years."[99]

Delegates to UUP's Fall 1998 Delegate Assembly clearly recognized that UUP was fast becoming an important player in state politics. And they liked it. After a membership drive that brought in more than 1,300 new union memberships,

UUP now had 22,000 members. More UUPers were contributing to UUP's VOTE-COPE fund. Contributions to VOTE-COPE now topped $100,000 annually.[100] With over $3 million in its reserve fund, the union was fiscally sound with sufficient funds to fight successfully in the political arena.[101] Additionally, UUP aggressively continued to protect its members from arbitrary action by SUNY managers. One good example of the union's commitment to protecting its members is an arbitration victory at Buffalo HSC. Scheuerman described to the delegates a case in which SUNY Buffalo HSC fired two part-time dentists on term appointments without a review or evaluation. The union grieved and an arbitrator ruled in UUP's favor. SUNY filed an appeal beyond the ninety-day time limit to do so, but a court of law decided to accept the appeal. The case was still pending in 1998, but the important point was obvious to most delegates: UUP fought and won an arbitration for part-time members, and it would continue that fight for them no matter what. That was significant.[102] Delegates responded, once again, by expressing their support and confidence in the union's leadership by extending term limits from a maximum of four terms to five. The vote of 219 in favor and 64 opposed was even greater than the 1995 term-extension vote.[103]

The extension of terms allowed UUP's president to develop better working relationships with legislators, officials in the executive branch, and even SUNY's chancellor. Over the next few years the union continued to make additional legislative gains for its members. Years of tough budgets dating back to the early 1990s led to the loss through attrition of about 1,600 full-time faculty positions, many of which were replaced by underpaid part-timers. The union addressed the loss of faculty lines by lobbying the legislature for funds to hire additional new full-time faculty. UUP met with some moderate success. For the 1999–2000 fiscal year, the union convinced legislators to add an additional $2.2 million to the budget for new lines, the equivalent of 150 new faculty.[104] The following budget year was even better as legislators earmarked $4.4 million for new SUNY faculty lines.[105] The union also worked with the governor's education chief, Jeff Lovell, to ensure that UUP bargaining-unit members were treated equitably under early-retirement legislation, which sometimes omitted members in the optional retirement systems such as TIAA-CREF, and on one occasion initially excluded SUNY employees at the health-science centers. UUP also won a victory for SUNY over the chancellor's objections when it lobbied successfully for the removal of language in the early-retirement law prohibiting the replacement of employees who took advantage of the legislation.[106]

UUP's increasing political clout put the union in a strong position as it entered negotiations for a new agreement with the state in 1999.[107] This time the state did not demand any significant givebacks from UUP.[108] Once again Tom Matthews, UUP's vice president for professionals, headed the team. The union, which proved itself united and backed by its members, was gradually developing a good professional relationship with the governor and GOER. UUP's internal cohesiveness and effective political activities contributed to the development of a relationship of mutual respect between the union and Governor Pataki. To promote a better relationship with the governor, UUP now chose not to publicly chastise Pataki, as many members wanted. Instead, the union would denounce Tom Egan, the chair of SUNY's Board of Trustees. This decision not to attack the governor publicly gave both him and the union wiggle room to iron out their differences.

Circumstances in 1999 allowed UUP to take full advantage of its growing maturity. In 1999, CSEA, the union that usually set the bargaining pattern for statewide unions, once again became the first of the state unions to reach a tentative contract agreement. Unfortunately for CSEA's leaders and negotiators, the union's membership voted the contract proposal down.[109] As Scheuerman noted in his report to delegates at UUP's May 1999 meeting, two of the other state unions, PEF and Council 82, were in disarray.[110] Council 82 members had decertified their union and PEF had new leadership and staff. All this put UUP in a position to settle first and set the bargaining pattern.[111] UUP's prospects increased, Scheuerman observed, when CSEA and PEF leaders held a press conference publicly blasting Governor Pataki.[112]

Not only did UUP reach a timely agreement, but when UUP announced a tentative settlement with the state that July, for the first time in its history it set the bargaining pattern for other state unions. And it was a good contract. Over the course of the four-year contract base salaries would increase by 12.5 percent. There was an additional 4 percent in discretionary money, two lump-sum payments amounting to $1,750, an on-call pay increase, and a hike in the location stipend.[113] According to the New York City Municipal Labor Council consultants, the cost of the contract to the state would reach 19.83 percent in total after four years. But there was more to the contract than just dollars. The number of UUP leaders eligible for release time increased, allowing the union to offer a program providing additional chapter leaders with release time to serve their members better. In addition to increased funding to enhance member benefits, including significant coverage for dental implants, the union would now offer scholarships of $500 each semester to bargaining-unit members whose children attended SUNY schools represented by UUP. The contract also made major gains for the growing number of part-timers the union represented. In the past, part-time faculty teaching two courses during both the spring and fall semesters would be eligible for full healthcare coverage, but they had to wait forty days prior to each semester for the coverage. The wait was mandatory because part-time faculty were generally hired one semester at a time and, consequently, were removed from the payroll after each semester. In short, they were rehired and starting anew every semester. The 1999 agreement with the state ended that process. It provided a full fifty-two-week health insurance coverage for eligible part-time employees, even though they might not be on the payroll during the summer months or the winter intersession. In 1999, UUP became the only higher-education union in the United States to provide such coverage.[114]

The new contract also addressed structural salary inequities, particularly at the colleges of technology. The contract now contained an agreement (Appendix-31) that allowed the director of GOER and UUP's president to create an executive-level committee to review compensation issues identified at the bargaining table. Structural inhibitors to an equitable salary plan, including campus types, were among the major issues identified. This agreement allowed the union to bypass the contract's "zipper clause," which prohibited it from seeking a legislative solution to issues raised unsuccessfully during negotiations. Appendix A-31 now permitted UUP to seek a legislative remedy for salary disparities at the colleges of technology. Within a short time, UUP used the legislative arena to garner extracontractual salary raises for faculty at the technical colleges.[115]

UUP's members overwhelmingly endorsed the contract. With a voting turnout approaching 10,000 members or some 58.9 percent, the contract was approved by 96.15 percent of the voters, another new record for the union. To make matters even better for UUP's members, the state legislature, apparently confident in UUP's support of the proposed agreement, passed a pay bill to fund the contract prior to ratification. This was still another first for UUP and an indication of the organization's maturity and growing respect from key institutional players in New York's political scene.

Another sign of UUP's growing maturity and ability to make gains for its members outside normal contractual structures is an agreement the union reached with SUNY and GOER on an important workload issue. The union had previously lost an arbitration case on workload at Brockport. Prior to the Brockport decision, the principle of past practice at the departmental level determined workload. The arbitration decision upheld Brockport managers' claim that past practice is based on campus-wide workload. At that college about 20 to 25 percent of the faculty taught twelve credit hours; therefore, the arbitrator ruled, that was the workload. Now everyone would have to teach a twelve-credit load. The union consulted with NYSUT legal staff and decided that it could not win an appeal. It also did not want to lose and set a precedent at a higher level. Consequently, UUP entered into talks with SUNY and GOER. After a year and a half of negotiations, the parties came to an agreement. All agreed to return to the prior standard set in a 1982 Morrisville decision. Past practice at the departmental level would define workload. This was a major victory.[116]

After years of local negotiations and legal hearings, the union favorably resolved an issue raised in the contract settlement of 1991–95 by winning an important arbitration prohibiting the imposition of parking fees at SUNY Binghamton. The 1991–95 contract had a provision mandating local (chapter) negotiations at each campus that wished to impose parking fees. UUP, as noted in chapter 4, stalled in a number of ways. The union wanted to know the size of each parking lot, each parking space, and other such information. SUNY accused the union of failing to bargain in good faith. UUP renewed talks, filed grievances, and eventually took the issue to arbitration. UUP picked Binghamton as the test case to bring to arbitration because it had no other parking fees for employees and there was plenty of land available to park.[117] Parking fees, according to the union's position, were just another means for the campus to raise money. On December 20, 1999, the arbitrator, Joel Douglas, ruled in UUP's favor.[118] UUP became the only state union not to pay a parking fee as negotiated in the 1991–95 agreement with the state. When it appeared that UUP would keep winning arbitrations, SUNY Binghamton threw in the towel and suspended negotiated parking fees for all the statewide unions on campus. After UUP won another case regarding parking at Buffalo State, then winning a similar case at SUNY Buffalo, SUNY abandoned the goal of negotiating new parking fees.

Outside the bargaining table, talks continued to bring good things to members of the UUP bargaining unit. In the spring of 2000, after CSEA finally settled with the state, Scheuerman announced that new talks with state negotiators resulted in several important enhancements to UUP's recent bargaining agreement. For one, the state agreed to pay bargaining-unit members six months earlier than originally negotiated, and salary increases for each of the final two years of the contract would increase from the original 3.0 percent to 3.5 percent.[119] At the Spring 2000 Delegate Assembly, Scheuerman also noted the consequences of the previous contract. UUP, the only union to hold out in the battle against outsourcing, was also the only union that showed an increase in bargaining-unit membership since the ratification of the 1995–99 contract. UUP gained some 4,000 members during this period. On the other hand, CSEA lost about 23,000 bargaining-unit members, primarily to outsourcing.[120]

The union's intervention on an important affirmative action issue at SUNY Stony Brook in 2001 provides another example of UUP's increasing clout. College managers at Stony Brook used what they characterized as "streamlining" to expedite the hiring of personnel. This approach tended to avoid affirmative-action guidelines. Faculty complained to campus officials, but to no avail. Finally, once the issue was brought to UUP, the union discussed it with the Assembly higher-education chair, Edward Sullivan. Sullivan promised to hold public hearings unless the college changed the process to meet affirmative-action guidelines. He even publicly announced a scheduled hearing. With this promise as a weapon in their political arsenal, union leaders met with campus managers and suggested that such hearings might prove embarrassing. Stony Brook leaders got the hint and the "streamlining" process was modified in an acceptable manner.[121] Sullivan cancelled the hearings.

Coming off a contract victory that revealed the cohesiveness of the union, a successful opposition to the imposition of new parking fees, as well as its growing reputation as an important player in the political arena and within the university itself, the union again turned to the legislature to protect and enhance its members' interests. A key issue at this juncture was the growing tendency of SUNY to rely on private funds and private entities to build facilities on various SUNY campuses. When the issue surfaced at Farmingdale and the College of Old Westbury, UUP rejected a "show-business" militant approach of trying to stop the project. UUP did not care whether the funding was public or private. Rather than futilely opposing the expenditure of private moneys and attempting to stop the projects, the union successfully lobbied for legislation that provided all employees in the new entity with protections under the Taylor Law. This meant that employees would be in the UUP bargaining unit, covered by the union contract. It also meant that the operatives of the privately financed entities would be accountable to the state legislature.[122] It was a win-win solution.

UUP successfully used this "keep your eyes on the prize" approach throughout the years of the Scheuerman administration. By the end of 2000, the union's political clout reached a point where Scheuerman reported to delegates at the Winter 2000 Delegate Assembly that chancellor Robert King, the former director of the Division of Budget, conceded that any plan SUNY would bring to the legislature without clearing it with UUP was dead on arrival.[123] It was at this juncture that SUNY began cooperating with UUP on a common legislative program. This new working relationship often involved the chancellor traveling to the NYSUT building to work with UUP and NYSUT political leaders.[124]

As already described, UUP had developed a very effective rank-and-file-supported legislative program. In the year 2000, with VOTE-COPE contributions exceeding $121,000 annually,[125] UUP expanded what political scientist E. E. Schattschneider called the scope of conflict[126] in its favor by developing relationships on the state and national levels with other higher-education organizations. First, with the retirement of Irwin Polishook of CUNY's Professional Staff Congress (PSC), Scheuerman became chair of AFT's Program and Policy Council, an organization representing over 100,000 AFT higher-education members that shaped higher-education union policy in the United States.[127] UUP's president also became the AFT higher-education spokesperson both at home and in the United States and throughout Europe, where Scheuerman frequently traveled to make presentations on the value of unions in higher education. Additionally, UUP entered a relationship with the collective-bargaining unit of the American Association of University Professors. In so doing, UUP controlled the largest number of membership votes and had significant influence on AAUP policies. In fact, shortly after forming the relationship, members of the AAUP Collective Bargaining unit voted the UUP president into an officer position at a meeting the president did not even attend. UUP, the largest higher-education union in the country, had now become a major player in higher-education politics on the national level.

In the year 2000, UUP reached out to public higher-education colleagues throughout the state to form the Public Higher Education Conference Board

(PHECB). The new organization consisted of leaders of the NEA and NYSUT community colleges, UUP, PSC, and both the SUNY and CUNY Faculty Senates.[128] Initially chaired by retired Fredonia campus president Dallas Beal, with Scheuerman serving as the cochair and convener, the Board brought leaders of public higher-education institutions together to work toward better budgets. When Beal suddenly passed away,[129] he was succeeded by cochairs Carl McCall, the former New York State comptroller, and Roscoe Brown, a former Tuskegee airman and retired president of Bronx Community College. Focusing solely on the need for adequate funding for public institutions of higher learning, McCall and Scheuerman met with editorial boards across the state to present opinion-makers with the implications of tough fiscal budgets on public higher-education institutions in the state. McCall and Scheuerman wanted to bring SUNY and CUNY campus presidents into the organization on the grounds that all had a common interest in attaining good budgets, but the PSC, now led by Barbara Bowen, resisted and managers remained excluded.

A crucially important issue that surfaced in the late '90s but remained unsettled until 2007 was pension reform. The stock market peaked in the late '90s, significantly driving up the value of the state's pension investments. The legislature responded to the surfeit of pension funds by passing legislation that benefited employees in the guaranteed retirement system: Teacher Retirement System (TRS) and Employees Retirement System (ERS). The new law used the excess dollars in the state's pension fund to pay for the 3 percent charge employees in tiers 3, 4, and 4A paid into their pensions after those employees had ten years of service. This meant that employees in these categories suddenly received a 3 percent increase in take-home pay. Significantly, while about 22 percent of members of the UUP bargaining unit were affected by the law, the majority of members were not covered because it did not grant the same conditions to people in the optional retirement system, for example, TIAA-CREF. They were not included because, legislators argued, quite reasonably, ORP participants had their retirement money invested in the stock market and they were already benefitting from the market's gains. By picking up the 3 percent payment of people in the ORP, legislators maintained, the state would be giving ORP people a double bite of the apple. In short, ORP members would benefit twice, once from their pension tied to the rising stock market, a second time from the state subsidy. More, the state did not have to reach into its general fund to pay the premiums for those in the guaranteed retirement system. But it would cost the state about $18–20 million to pay the premiums of those in the ORP system

Rather than blocking the pension reform law, UUP supported the legislation, even though it did not include those in ORP plans. But the union made a point of reminding legislators that New York State law required pension equity. The union threatened to litigate but held off, knowing that litigation takes years, and since the issue of what constituted equity was not crystal clear, a litigious route appeared too risky. Instead, UUP lobbied the legislature by appealing to the concept of pension equity. Initially, the union's approach seemed effective. In 2001 the legislature appeared ready to include ORP people in similar pension-payment relief, but the legislature's failure to reach a complete budget agreement prior to the terrorist attack that threw the state's economy into a downspin made any such reform impossible, at least for the immediate future.

The state budget went into crisis mode for the next several years as tax revenues shrunk after the 9/11 attacks. Facing trustees who failed to advocate forcefully for their university amid record-breaking budget deficits, UUP demonstrated its internal unity as it prepared to meet the latest round of challenges. Shortly after the terrorist attack, at the fall delegate assembly, delegates again showed their support and confidence in the union's leadership by debating a constitutional amendment to remove term limits for UUP's officers. Delegate Michael Silverberg praised the union for having such a debate and for giving all delegates a free and open opportunity to discuss such a fundamental issue.[130] The debate was emotionally charged on both sides. Opposition to the amendment was strong. Delegate Judith Wishnia raised the old Reform Caucus issue of the importance of chapter autonomy by arguing "[T]he real work of the union is at the chapters."[131] Other opponents warned delegates of the undemocratic bias of the "power of incumbency." Entrenched incumbency, the argument went, would probably render union elections meaningless.[132] One oppositional delegate even went so far as to claim that the amendment was nothing more than an attempted power grab by the officers. In referring to the officers' quest for term-limit removal, delegate Harvey Axelrod said, "Now, let's talk about what they're really after. This is about power. This is not about leadership. Leadership is just rhetoric."[133]

Proponents focused on UUP's growing ability to serve its members effectively. William Rock, a delegate to UUP's very first assembly, said "I watched this union grow from very weak, very tentative into what is, just a marvelously strong organization fighting for everything that we believe in."[134] Brooklyn's Barbara Habenstreit reminded delegates of the difficult times SUNY and the state faced following the 9/11 terrorist attack. She argued that in times of crisis the union needed proven leadership, not change. Habenstreit, along with several others, also denounced term limits as an undemocratic mechanism "that takes away my free choice."[135] Former UUP secretary and a long-time supporter of term limits, Edward Alfonsin, turned heads when he publicly reversed his position and called on delegates to support the constitutional amendment.[136] With the largest number of votes ever cast at a delegate assembly, delegates approved the removal of term limits by a vote of 190 in favor to 90 opposed.[137] In the end UUP's officers were now clearly in a position to build long-term relationships with New York's key political players in the legislature, in the governor's office, and with their state and national affiliates.

Removal of term limits increased UUP's powers in still another way: it gave UUP's officers greater autonomy from NYSUT staff assigned to the union and increased UUP's independence from the larger teachers' union. By now UUP had an excellent relationship with NYSUT, but the state affiliate would now have to take UUP even more seriously. In the past, NYSUT staff directors assigned to UUP had long-term assignments to the union. Term limits did not apply to them. This meant that NYSUT staff could stay on at UUP while the elected officers were constantly changing. The continuity of top-level NYSUT staff placed them in an advantageous position to influence UUP's officers and policies. After all, they were the experts, and the officers were basically the inexperienced newcomers. This is not to suggest a NYSUT staff conspiracy or to imply that staff manipulated the officers. But the top staff's longevity and experience gave them the ability to a greater or lesser degree to exert control over the elected officers. Scheuerman took this situation seriously. Shortly after delegates removed term limits, Scheuerman had his NYSUT director, Tony Wildman, a personal friend and mentor, transferred out of UUP and back to NYSUT.

UUP's growing political power gained the union considerable legislative support and gave it a forum to push back against the intrusive policies of SUNY's trustees. The union's relationship with the chancellor had improved over time, but its relationship with SUNY's trustees was dismal during most of the Pataki administration. As discussed earlier, the trustees failed to advocate for the university, submitting flat and negative budget requests for several years running. To the union, that was bad enough, but the trustees also developed a method of allocating state funds that ran against the grain of the legislature's and governor's intent. They called it the Resource Allocation Method (RAM). But that wasn't all the activist trustees did. They also attempted to impose a set of conservative culture beliefs on SUNY and its faculty that threatened to undercut faculty governance and academic freedom. UUP joined with the SUNY Senate and ultimately led the way in a successful struggle against RAM and in favor of faculty governance and academic freedom at SUNY.

UUP takes on SUNY's Trustees

In the summer of 1998, at a meeting in distant Plattsburgh, far enough away to prevent significant media coverage, the trustees had quietly adopted the entrepreneurial formula called RAM to distribute legislated funds to the campuses.[138] To increase what they defined as "efficiency," the trustees no longer looked at campus needs and individual college missions as key criteria for funding. Rather, they divided the pool of public dollars from the state budget by giving more to campuses with high student enrollments and low-cost programs and less to campuses with low enrollments and more costly programs. The impact of this formula on the university's structure and academic standards is obvious. First, although both the governor's and the legislature's budget for fiscal 1999–2000 ensured payment of contract costs by allocating funds on a line-by-line basis to each SUNY campus, the trustees, had, without any public dialogue, rejected these guidelines and made a sea change by using these funds to promote competition among campuses for enrollment and cost-cutting. Second, not every campus would receive the amount of support both the governor and legislature intended for covering contract costs. Nineteen campuses received less funding than the budget legislation intended.[139] Some campuses now faced deficits, increasing the possibility of program closings and faculty layoffs. SUNY Buffalo, for instance, announced an increase in student fees thanks to receiving $3.2 million less than the legislation agreed to by the governor and the legislature.[140] The very existence of SUNY technical colleges, already under-enrolled and recently mandated to offer four-year degrees, was threatened by RAM since their technical course offerings were generally more costly than traditional academic offerings. In fact, it appeared that RAM was designed, in part, to force the closing of these technical colleges. Third, RAM ripped the SUNY system apart. SUNY was no longer a single university system which, like the human body, required each campus to have a specific mission that made the function of the organic whole greater than the sum of its parts. Instead of working in unison, SUNY campuses would now compete against each other in a Darwinian struggle for survival. It was, as Scheuerman ironically noted, "Darwinism gone ape."[141] Fourth, RAM threatened to lower academic standards. By basing fiscal remuneration on enrollments and program costs, it became rational for campus managers to offer low-cost programs that would draw masses of students with little regard for traditional educational values and standards. Poorly enrolled foreign language, science, and math courses, however essential to a solid college education, had now become a fiscal liability. Indeed, RAM gave life to the old student joke about taking courses in basket-weaving, only it was becoming more of an intellectual reality than a joke.

Protecting academic standards is the province of the Faculty Senate. The union's role is to protect the workforce. Making the case that the trustees' financial plan distorted the legislature's intent to finance the costs of negotiations adequately, UUP again turned to the state's political arena for support. Almost immediately, UUP convinced both the Senate and Assembly chairs of the Higher Education Committees to sponsor RAM-busting bills. Unfortunately, the threat of a gubernatorial veto basically killed the bills in committee. Consequently, at UUP's request, the chair of the Assembly Higher Education Committee, Ed Sullivan, held a legislative roundtable in which student representatives and members of the union testified. The president of the student association agreed with UUP's assertion that the RAM process was devised secretly without input from the public or students, even though they would suffer the consequences.[142] The union focused on the impact of RAM on the nineteen campuses receiving less than the budget intended. UUP was not opposed to RAM per se, but it was concerned about its impact on individual campuses. The forum involved much give-and-take between Scheuerman and SUNY provost Peter Salins, a senior fellow at the Manhattan Institute, a right-wing think tank. Salins insisted that all campuses would receive sufficient funds, but when the NYSUT assistant director of legislation, Peter Martineau, produced data proving Salins's assertions wrong, the provost did not dispute Martineau's numbers.

With the eventual passage of the 2000–2001 state budget, the legislature responded to UUP's objections to RAM, now renamed the Budget Allocation Program. Martineau and others believed SUNY changed the name in response to UUP's public statements concerning the program's "RAMing" the public.[143] Assembly Higher Education chair Sullivan had previously made it clear that the legislature would not micromanage SUNY by substituting their version of a financial plan for RAM. Instead, both the Assembly and Senate approved legislation providing more oversight of the trustees. Once the governor signed the bill into law, SUNY was faced with new reporting requirements. The new law shed "sunshine" on the trustees' activities by directing the university to give legislators and other interested parties five days' notice prior to making RAM allocations to the campuses. SUNY was also required to notify the legislature, state comptroller, and budget director of every mission review allocation.[144] The new law did not kill RAM, but it made the trustees' fiscal plan subject to more public scrutiny in advance of their taking any action. This in itself was an important restraint on the options open to SUNY's trustees. The trustees played an active role in attempting to shift education policy to competitive market forces that infringed on SUNY's ability to offer a quality education, but they were even more active in assaulting academic freedom and the principle of shared governance.

The trustees' opening volley on academic freedom took place in early November 1997, at SUNY New Paltz. After faculty sponsored a conference, "Revolting Behavior: The Challenges of Women's Sexual Freedom," featuring, among other things, sex toys and photographs of genitalia. Governor Pataki and SUNY's trustees, led by de Russy, called for the firing of campus president Roger Bowen and demanded the cancelling of a similar conference scheduled for later in the month.[145] Faculty responded by complaining about these threats to academic freedom, and President Bowen called a press meeting, telling students that the conference had "everything to do with free speech."[146] UUP's president told delegates to the Winter 1999 Delegate Assembly that some people found the conference tasteful, others thought it distasteful. But that was all beside the point. The real issue, he continued, was that the trustees' threats had a chilling effect on other campus presidents, who were now likely to place restrictions on academic freedom.[147] Subsequently, UUP invited Bowen to speak at the Spring 2001 Delegate Assembly, but more importantly, the union and the Faculty Senate, its traditional rival, now entered into an informal partnership with UUP as the senior partner. UUP's Scheuerman and president of the Faculty Senate, Vincent Aceto, began working together to shape a response to the attack.

In the past, UUP and the Faculty Senate were often involved in turf battles over university issues. But the trustees' actions continued to bring the two organizations closer together. They again took action together after the trustees unilaterally attempted to impose a SUNY-wide core curriculum, even though individual campuses already had their own core requirements. The trustees devised their plan in closed executive session and secured a vote of approval by the entire board before allowing Faculty Senate chair, Vince Aceto, to speak. By then, of course, it was too late.[148] The Senate defined the issue as an attack on shared governance and academic freedom.[149] UUP agreed, but the union also believed the trustees' curriculum reform was more than an attack on faculty governance and academic freedom. UUP viewed it as part of a larger plan to restructure programs and lay off faculty, particularly those who taught in identity studies, such as African American and women's studies. Under this scenario of restructuring programs, the legislated Green Book protections against budgetary layoffs would not come into play. The trustees' proposal was an attack, as Aceto agreed, on multicultural studies.[150] Campus presidents, many of whom supported the faculty's position on the core curriculum, complained that implementation of the reform would cost large sums of money. They too recognized the possibility of layoffs, given the dismal track record of the trustees as fiscal advocates for SUNY. The union immediately offered to assist the Senate morally, politically, and financially, if necessary. The Senate's funding, after all, was controlled by the trustees. A grateful Senate accepted UUP's offer. UUP and the Senate created a joint committee to review the trustees' actions and recommend steps to stop the trustees. The joint committee drafted a resolution of no confidence in the trustees and called for their resignations, which each UUP and senate chapter passed, often unanimously.[151] The resolution listed seven ways in which the trustees failed to meet their responsibilities, including their perpetual failure to advocate for strong fiscal support for SUNY. New York's budget process was rather straightforward. In the fall of each year, state agencies submitted a budget proposal to the governor, who used this information to prepare a budget proposal for the legislature. For several years running, SUNY's trustees submitted flat, nongrowth or lower budget requests they presented to the governor. Consequently, the University Senate and UUP jointly criticized the trustees for their latent lack of advocacy for the university. SUNY's chancellor Ryan responded to the joint action by accusing the faculty leadership of being co-opted by UUP.[152] UUP forwarded the resolutions to legislators, the governor, and the media.

In an attempt to negotiate a settlement with the trustees, Aceto and Scheuerman arranged a meeting with trustee chair Tom Egan in New York City. At the opening of the meeting, Scheuerman informed Egan that he attended the meeting as a show of support and solidarity between the union and the Senate. Faculty governance, he said, was a Senate issue, not a union matter. Scheuerman offered to facilitate the meeting in the hope of reaching a settlement. Egan responded by saying he liked that idea, but then launched into a personal attack at Aceto, even threatening to cut off funding for the Senate. Scheuerman assured Aceto the union would assist in the Senate's funding if needed, but Egan continued his personal attacks on Aceto.[153] Needless to say, the meeting ended with no settlement. Scheuerman followed up the New York City meeting by informing the governor's office, legislators, and SUNY negotiators of Egan's uncooperative behavior. Several days later, the union and the Senate held a well-attended and well-publicized press conference at the Legislative Office Building in Albany, stating their joint vote of no-confidence charges against the trustees and publicly reiterating the charges in the resolution. This unprecedented action marked the first time in American higher-education history that a faculty union and its Senate counterpart jointly participated in a no-confidence vote of their university's trustees.

UUP's increasing political clout, including a tenfold increase in VOTE-COPE collections in a six-year period,[154] contributed to the emergence of several bills in the legislature restricting the future appointments of trustees. Ed Sullivan, as chair of the Assembly's Higher Education Committee, sponsored a bill (A-2560) prohibiting trustees from being under the supervision of the appointing authority, that is, the governor. Assemblyman Marty Luster introduced legislation subjecting prospective trustees to the same process as appointments to the judiciary.[155] State comptroller Carl McCall, who later became chair of the Public Higher Education Conference Board, at a Conference Board press conference called for the creation of a nominating board to screen and recruit trustees at CUNY and SUNY before they are appointed.[156] Again, the threat of a gubernatorial veto killed the bills, but the trustees and the governor did not operate in a political vacuum. Taking note of the internal turmoil at SUNY and the negative public and political reaction to their plan, the trustees gradually backed off, shifting control back to the faculty where it belonged.

The core curriculum ran into other problems that UUP brought to light. During the summer of 1999, UUP's president met with the new chair of the SUNY community college Senate to discuss and analyze the impact of the core curriculum on transfer students. The meeting was important because the community colleges had not joined in the action against the trustees. Community college leaders now showed interest in joining the fight against the core, further weakening the trustees' position. Consequently, the trustees, operating under a public microscope, began to back off by giving more autonomy to local campuses.[157] The unstated decision to gradually back off their core curriculum plan was a victory for both UUP and the two SUNY Senates. Of equal importance was the fact that by now it had become clear that the Senate and the union had replaced conflict with collaboration. Beginning in the mid 1990s, Faculty Senate leaders had regularly attended UUP Delegate Assemblies and the UUP president frequently spoke at Senate meetings. The two organizations cosponsored conferences, including an important one on academic freedom, and thanks to the trustees, both organizations assisted each other in significant struggles. As Scheuerman observed, the Senate and the union were sure to have some disagreements in the future, but a new era of cooperation had begun.[158]

The union's issues with the trustees continued throughout most of the Pataki administration. As reported all too frequently in these pages, the trustees failed to advocate for the university and at times even seemed to hold public institutions in contempt. Basically, most trustees were reactionaries educated at private colleges and universities and did not support public higher education. But their frequent extreme statements and retrograde positions tended to isolate them and make UUP, their primary adversary, look responsible and reasonable to elected officials and SUNY's top leaders alike. Trustee de Russy's public statements on identity politics at SUNY and the union's response clearly illustrate this tendency.

Trustee Candace de Russy, the most vociferous of the trustees, constantly complained about what she perceived as declining academic standards at the university, and even suggested SUNY should not be involved in graduate education. She attacked teacher-education programs at SUNY, and when informed that the passing rate of SUNY students was extraordinarily high, usually somewhere in the mid-90percent range, she responded by attacking the certification tests. They must be too easy, she claimed.[159] De Russy and other trustees wanted to return to the so-called "good old days" of the Little Red School House prior to mass public education, when the local elite went to private colleges while other men were laborers or farmers and women prepared for a life as homemakers.[160] By the late twentieth century the "good old days" were no longer the America we lived in or wanted to live in. The United States had become a very diverse society, most factories were closed, small family farms were mostly a thing of the past, and ordinary people now had opportunities that apparently ran against the grain of the trustees' vision of education and culture in the United States.

De Russy caused a huge stir among UUPers and the public when she was quoted in a local newspaper as saying that identity programs such as African American studies are academically weak and even anti-American. In her comments to Long Island's *Newsday*, de Russy singled out two campuses—Stony Brook and Old Westbury—for having such inferior programs. UUP responded at the winter 2002 Delegate Assembly by passing a resolution condemning de Russy's comments.[161] President Scheuerman also issued a public statement pointing out that Old Westbury did not even have an African American studies program. After Scheuerman's comments were picked up by the media, de Russy appeared on the Fox News show hosted by since-disgraced Bill O'Reilly. O'Reilly defended her by making misleading statements about UUP's position and the facts of identity politics at SUNY. Calvin Butts, the African American president of SUNY Old Westbury, a community activist and pastor of the Abyssinian Baptist Church in New York City, issued a statement denouncing de Russy's comments, as did chancellor King, who publicly supported Butts and made a statement of his own in opposition to de Russy's remarks. The de Russy brouhaha took place just as Governor Pataki was preparing to run for reelection against a respected African American, Carl McCall. Pataki, who had appointed both King as chancellor and de Russy to the SUNY Board of Trustees, certainly did not need any of his appointees making the kind of inflammatory statements de Russy had made. Pataki, in fact, was courting minority voters. The political context of de Russy's comments was not lost on the chancellor or other members of the board. At the next Board meeting de Russy was not received well by her colleagues. In fact, she felt somewhat ostracized. The union's response to the trustee's comments helped isolate her, but also moved the chancellor, President Butts, and the governor closer to the union's position.[162]

UUP's success in neutralizing the university's activist trustees was the culmination of the first eight years of the Scheuerman administration. During these years not only did UUP successfully weather unprecedented attacks on the university and the union's members, it also won a number of major victories at the bargaining table as well as in the political arena. At this juncture in its history, UUP had become a mature organization. Its political operation gave its president direct access to the state's top political leaders. As UUP's political clout grew, the university gradually turned to the union for political assistance. In return, UUP continued to garner extra contractual benefits for its members from SUNY. The following chapter describes the growing importance of UUP's political influence, how that influence helped preserve the university, and how the union used it to reap rewards for its members. It also chronicles UUP's continued success at the bargaining table and its emergence as the voice of higher-education unionism in the United States.

Chapter 7

UUP Matures: Part II, 2001–2007

As UUP Matures: More Victories

The United University Professions was created as a collective bargaining agent charged with negotiating terms and conditions of employment for bargaining-unit members. But the union's political activities and influence continued to play an increasingly important role in delivering benefits to members. In fact, UUP's efforts in the political arena had by now equaled collective bargaining in importance as a means of serving the needs of its membership. Collective bargaining and politics work in tandem, and nowhere is this approach more obvious than in UUP's response to the crucial issues facing the SUNY colleges of technology.

As previously noted, SUNY's colleges of technology were chronically underfunded and their faculty generally underpaid. RAM, of course, exacerbated these issues, placing the colleges in perpetual financial crisis. The situation worsened in 2001 when the trustees announced that these two-year institutions would have to offer four-year degrees without a boost is their budgets. As Scheuerman observed, when faculty members suddenly discovered that they were now responsible for four-year programs, they asked, how do we do this? Failing to provide additional resources to pay for the new mandate, the university essentially told the University Colleges of Technology (UCTs), you're on your own.[1] In fact, shortly after the program was initially announced, UUP successfully lobbied the legislature for additional funding for the technical colleges. But when SUNY received a call from the Senate Finance Committee asking how much the UCTs needed to meet their new obligations, the university administration said, shockingly, that they needed nothing.[2] Once SUNY said it did not want the money, UUP increased its determination to use its political influence to get the necessary funding to pay for additional faculty, raise faculty salaries, and provide new educational opportunities for existing faculty.[3]

The union began its campaign for adequate funding for the UCTs by arranging a meeting with UCT campus presidents to gain their active support. Given the trustees' general failure to seek sufficient budgets for SUNY, the support of the college presidents was a given. Initially SUNY advised campus presidents not to cooperate with the union. But after the union sent letters to rank-and-file members at the UCTs directing them to pressure campus presidents to cooperate with the union, the chancellor's top aid, Richard Miller, finally said, "I give up."[4] By now the union had become the university's primary advocate, and in so doing had gained the backing of budget-starved campus presidents across the university. Indeed, in many respects campus presidents viewed UUP as the lone advocate of their campuses as well as their faculty and staff. With the cooperation and overt backing of UCT presidents and the chancellor, the union arranged editorial board meetings with the local newspapers in each of the towns and small cities where SUNY had a college of technology. Participants in the meeting included the UUP president, who served as the primary spokesperson; the local chapter president, whose task was to give a local spin to the discussions; and UUP's communication and research directors. The purpose of the meetings was to raise the awareness of local politicians and taxpayers to the important role played by the colleges in their local communities. The meetings also sought to highlight salary inequities and to demonstrate the negative impact of underfunding on the colleges' potential as institutions of economic development.

These meetings succeeded in getting UUP's message out. Scheuerman reported to delegates in the winter of 2002 that the editorials and newspaper articles overwhelmingly supported the union's position. An article in the *Oneida Daily Gazette*, for instance, printed UUP statistics showing a $9,000 average salary disparity between UCT faculty and faculty at the colleges of arts and science, even though both institutions now had similar four-year missions.[5] In fact, some editorials were so helpful and flattering that UUP's president confessed "we would have been too embarrassed to write them ourselves."[6]

The newspaper articles had an immediate impact. After the stories appeared, Scheuerman received a call from SUNY chancellor Robert King, with whom he was gradually developing a good working relationship. King said he wanted to discuss the UCT issues and suggested that the two meet at his office. When Scheuerman arrived at the office, he noticed a pile of editorials and letters from campus presidents on King's desk. Clearly, UUP's message had gotten through. SUNY reversed its position from a year earlier. Consequently, the two agreed to work together to resolve the budget and salary issues at the colleges of technology.[7] After several additional meetings Scheuerman was able to report that the two had reached an agreement. The question, he said, was no longer whether a problem exists at the UCTs, but rather how much was needed to resolve it. The two developed a multiyear plan to make UCT salary levels comparable with salaries at the comprehensive colleges of arts and science and to update equipment at the colleges. UUP would lead the political offensive in the legislature with support from SUNY. Just as importantly, the two agreed and received the backing of campus presidents, that any money received from the legislature to address the issues would be distributed through a campus-based joint labor-management process. Management would not have the unilateral power to distribute the funds.[8] It was now up to UUP to get the dollars needed to finish the job.

Despite the fact that New York State faced an $8 billion deficit thanks to the terrorist attack of 2001, UUP's political efforts for the 2001-02 budget brought a gain of $2.42 million for the colleges of technology. The legislated money was designated to hire new faculty. But legislators told Scheuerman that UUP and SUNY could use the money for hiring or salary increases or both. Legislators said the line in the budget had to read that it was for new faculty because a few months earlier the state had talked about laying off thousands of state employees. Giving faculty extracontractual legislated raises under these conditions was not, in the eyes of legislators, good political optics. UUP's chapter leaders, with the assistance of state leadership, worked with their presidents to distribute the funds. Some faculty received raises on base of more than $2,000 in addition to negotiated across-the-board salary increases and discretionary moneys.[9]

The process was not uniformly smooth and free of problems. At Alfred, for example, the college president claimed he spent all the extra money for new faculty lines and there was none left for faculty on-base salary raises. Following a practice they characterized as "constructive tension," UUP's president and NYSUT lobbyist Martineau met with the chancellor's top aide and feigned righteous indignation. Concerned that the actions of Alfred's president threatened to undercut SUNY's working relationship with UUP, the chancellor intervened and the president of Alfred suddenly found dollars from other sources to finance the raises. UUP did not care where the money came from.[10] The $4.2 million UUP garnered from the legislature for the UCTs represented a very good first step in addressing their salary inequities. As Scheuerman noted, the political victory "captured the attention of UCT presidents."[11] In this super-tight budget year there were no other legislated add-ons in the budget. The UCTs were alone in receiving an extra monetary boost from the legislature.

The new budget also financed the New York State Theatre Institute, whose existence depended on annual funding from the legislature. Additionally, UUP managed to get what had now become the usual no-layoff language in the legislative Green Book. The union also secured a verbal commitment from Governor Pataki that SUNY would not lay off for budgetary purposes any bargaining-unit member, full- or part-time. When some SUNY campuses announced a spate of layoffs after passage of the tight state budget, the union held the governor to his word, and he kept it. More than a dozen faculty at the College of Old Westbury faced layoffs, but Pataki came up with $3.3 million to save their jobs. After forty-one part-timers had been nonrenewed at SUNY Albany, forty were given their jobs back. (The forty-first left the area.) SUNY Buffalo also rescinded firing notices.[12] What began as a rocky, hostile relationship between a fiscally conservative governor and an activist union had now morphed into a productive working relationship based on mutual trust and respect.

As in previous years, alongside the state budget process, the union also worked with the governor's education director to iron out a separate early retirement bill that initially excluded SUNY and CUNY. According to Scheuerman, it took several late-night meetings at the governor's office to convince the governor to include SUNY and CUNY in the incentive package. The union also made sure that faculty who retired prior to the passage of the final bill would receive the incentives it included.[13]

Faculty at the technology colleges received another boost when the Labor-Management Employment Committee modified its mission. The no-layoff agreement had left the Employment Committee with unspent state funding. Since SUNY had not laid off or retrenched bargaining-unit members, the committee did not have to use funds for retraining and professional career counseling. Rather than allow the funds to sit unused and eventually go back to the state, UUP and GOER agreed to modify the direction and goals of the committee. Many faculty at the technology colleges taught professional subjects such as carpentry and other specialized areas that did not require a doctoral degree. But to receive accreditation for the new four-year programs, the UCTs had to increase the percentage of faculty with doctoral degrees. Rather than restructure programs and replace existing faculty, the Employment Committee provided funds for faculty to earn the degrees they needed. Campuses worked with the union to identify the individual faculty members who needed the degrees and then financed their education. Frederick Kowal of Cobleskill, a future UUP president, was one recipient of these funds.

The union's work to prevent layoffs was hugely successful, but years of tight budgets led campuses to find a plethora of ways to save money, especially the practice of replacing departing full-time faculty with part-timers. This trend saved money, but also undercut the tenure system. At this juncture, SUNY had lost about 1,600 full-time faculty, replacing them mostly with poorly paid part-timers. Thanks to UUP, the bulk of the part-time faculty received full health coverage that the state paid for from moneys that did not come out of SUNY's budget, making this hiring practice even more attractive to the campuses. The UUP bargaining unit by now had risen to more than 27,000 members,[14] but the number of part-timers at SUNY had also increased drastically, now approaching about 38 percent of all classes taught. When UUP won a case that brought 1,000 adjuncts into the bargaining unit,[15] it became clear that part-time colleagues would play an increasing role at SUNY and in UUP. The union responded by overwhelmingly passing a constitutional amendment at the Winter 2002 Delegate Assembly providing for a part-time officer at each chapter.[16] As SUNY changed, UUP adapted to the changes.

The chief executive officers at SUNY's teaching hospitals also turned to UUP for political assistance. Hospital revenues had dropped precipitously, and some teaching hospitals might even have had to close. After failing to get a meeting with legislative leaders and the governor to address their financial plight, the CEOs of Downstate, Upstate, and Stony Brook traveled to Albany to meet with the UUP office to work out the details of a meeting they asked UUP to set up with the governor's people. The meeting took place following the 9/11 terrorist attack. Jeff Lovell, the governor's top education aide, represented the governor. The three hospital CEOs attended, as did the chapter presidents from each institution. It became immediately clear that the terrorist attack made new funding very unlikely. Finally, participants reached a consensus on a short-term solution for the hospitals' cash-flow problems. Discussions had revealed that the hospitals were spending millions in operational funds to purchase equipment. The short-term solution was to determine how much they had spent on equipment, which was really capital spending, and then capitalize the money by issuing long-term bonds. The bond money, all agreed, with the approval of auditors, could then be used for operational expenses. This prevented layoffs and hospital closings. Additionally, the governor committed to seeking a long-term solution once the fiscal squeeze passed. UUP, the governor, and the hospital CEOs worked jointly with the Division of Budget to iron out the details.[17]

Shortly after the 2002 gubernatorial election, an election in which the state's dire fiscal condition had not become a campaign issue, it became clear that New York faced a record-breaking fiscal crisis in 2003. This crisis not only put future salary equity gains at the UCTs on hold, it threatened the very future of SUNY. The state faced a budget deficit of $10 billion to $11 billion. In an interview with the *New York Times*, Abe Lackman, former secretary of the powerful Senate Finance Committee, now serving as head of the Commission on Independent Colleges and Universities (CICU), characterized New York's financial condition as the fiscal version of the movie *The Perfect Storm*.[18] Claiming that the state's budget shortfall could "be worse than the city's fiscal crisis of the mid-1970s,"[19] Lackman attributed the economic crisis to the terrorist attack of September 11 and the concomitant stock market decline. He noted that this was the first time in about sixty years that state revenues had declined for two years running. Back-loaded tax cuts further worsened the crunch. To make matters worse, Lackman said, the state's "rainy day" fund was exhausted in 2002, and about half of state spending was committed to debt services or mandates. This all suggested to Lackman that moderate across-the-board cuts were unlikely, which, as Scheuerman observed, is another way of saying the budget cuts would be severe.[20]

SUNY's trustees exacerbated the university's precarious situation by not making their annual budget request in the early fall, as other state agencies did. Submitting their request in mid-January meant there was no time for any public discussion of their proposal. Worse yet, the governor had insufficient time to review it, which in effect allowed the tight-fisted, budget-slashing Division of the Budget to decide how much SUNY should receive for 2003–04. The numbers in the governor's proposed budget were a worst-case scenario.

The governor's budget proposed to cut $183 million in state support from SUNY's general fund. That, according to UUP's president, translated into the loss of about 4,000 faculty positions.[21] The budget also dealt with the perpetual hospital shortfalls by recommending an appropriation of $92.6 million, a $500,000 increase, but it also proposed privatizing SUNY's teaching hospitals. Additionally, the budget proposal sought major cuts for the Educational Opportunity Programs (EOPs), the Educational Opportunity Centers (EOCs), and the New York State Theatre Institute. Further, there was no new money for the UCTs. The budget addressed the cuts to SUNY by proposing a tuition increase of $1,200 annually.

The union's battle for budget restorations for SUNY, as usual, would not take place in a vacuum. UUP would compete with the privates for budget restorations. The governor's proposed budget also cut Bundy Aid to private colleges and universities and planned to end Bundy funding for graduate education. Additionally, it proposed to withhold one-third of funds in the Tuition Assistance Aid Program (TAAP) until the student graduated.[22] This prompted Lackman, in his new role as head lobbyist for the privates, to claim the cuts close "the door to higher education for thousands of New Yorkers enrolled at independent colleges and universities."[23] SUNY would once again compete with the privates for limited public dollars.

The governor's proposed cuts illuminated the consequences of what Lackman had characterized as a perfect storm. But for UUP the storm had still another dimension. The union's agreement with the state was scheduled to expire at the end of June 2003. Consequently, much like in 1995, UUP would enter contract negotiations at a time when the state faced a massive fiscal shortfall. Only this time the situation was somewhat different. On the one hand, the deficit was now much higher, in fact about twice as high as the 1995 shortfall. That was the bad news. On the other hand, by now UUP had an effective political operation in place; the union was financially secure with a solid reserve fund; and over time its leadership had developed good working relationships with SUNY's leaders, top-level legislators, and the governor. The union had also created a research arm to provide data on the needs of public-higher education in New York State.

In preparation for upcoming budget battles, under the aegis of UUP's director of research, Thomas Kriger, UUP formed a new research institute called the Fund for Higher Education Research. Led by Ned Schneier, professor emeritus of CCNY, the new institute was designed to provide an independent voice, backed by research and data, to speak for public higher education. The institute would help coordinate research activities in higher-education institutions across the state, giving them a stronger voice in the fight for sufficient funding.[24] A number of prestigious individuals agreed to serve on the new institute's board, including former SUNY chancellor Clifton Wharton; Barbara Bartoletti, legislative director of the League of Women Voters of New York; Frank Mauro, executive director of the Fiscal Policy Institute; and Clyde Barrow, director of the Center for Policy Analysis at the University of Massachusetts at Dartmouth. The institute intermittently released to the legislature data-backed statements regarding the plight of public higher education.

UUP's half-million-member affiliate, NYSUT, apparently was paying more attention to higher-education issues than in the past. Its newspaper carried more college- and university-level stories, frequently featuring leaders of UUP. NYSUT also created a division of higher education, and with it, a NYSUT Higher Education Council that focused on higher-education budgets, organizing, and other issues pertinent to higher learning. UUP's president served as chair. The creation of the NYSUT council reveals how much UUP had matured. NYSUT and AFT saw UUP as a close and dependable ally. In fact, UUP played a major role in both organizations. Scheuerman chaired AFT's Program and Policy Council, an organization representing over 100,000 higher-education unionists nationwide, and a vice president on AFT's executive council. Later he would become the first and only higher-education person officially to serve on the AFT executive committee, the group of AFT officers who formulated policy proposals they then brought before the larger council. Scheuerman also served as assistant chair to Carl McCall on the Public Higher Education Conference Board. UUP, which had already become an important player in state politics, was fast becoming a major player on the national higher-education scene

A maturing UUP was ready for battle. In an attempt to build public support for SUNY, Scheuerman and UUP's research director, Tom Kriger, met with the Washington, DC–based consulting firm, Strothers, Duffy and Strothers, that UUP had previously hired to run its media campaign. After consulting with the firm's leaders, the union for the second year running decided to base its public relations campaign on polling of registered voters. This was an innovation for UUP, which in the past had made educated guesses about various public perceptions. Now in partnership with NYSUT first vice president Alan Lubin, UUP used the NYSUT polling center to ascertain how registered voters felt about SUNY, tax cuts, and alternate revenue sources for the state. The media blitz focused on SUNY's positive contributions to the state, especially to the upstate New York economy, and the need to maintain and build on these contributions.[25]

The ads also successfully pressured SUNY's chancellor to advocate more strongly for the university and to collaborate more with UUP. He and UUP's leaders met monthly, mostly at the UUP office. At these gatherings Scheuerman often urged King to advocate more strongly for SUNY. Otherwise, UUP's ads might have to go negative by highlighting some terrible fact such as, for instance, without sufficient funding, graduation from a SUNY institution in four years would become almost impossible. During one of these meetings Bob King's top aide, Dick Miller, gave the union a list of 20,000 venders with whom SUNY did business. This was significant. King had gradually become a strong advocate for the university, even bucking the governor's proposed cuts. UUP put the vendors list to work by contacting the vendors, again expressing the importance to their businesses of a well-funded SUNY. In March 2003, the union brought out "SUNY bucks" again as rank-and-file members flooded the Main Streets in upstate cities with SUNY campuses, reminding local merchants how cuts would hurt the local economy. Hundreds of merchants placed signs reading, "This Business Supports SUNY" in their store windows.[26] Chancellor King responded to UUP's efforts by making it clear that he was opposed to layoffs. But he suggested that a midyear budget cut by the governor on top of the proposed cuts could make layoffs inevitable.

Nevertheless, once again UUP managed to protect SUNY's workforce. Intensive UUP lobbying, consisting of dozens of UUP members swarming the legislative office building every week, was complemented by similar activity in legislators' district offices, including a "Rally in the Home District Day"[27] and an intensive upstate ad campaign, as well as a NYSUT-led massive public-education rally in Albany. Legislators responded to the pressure by passing a two-house bill at the end of April restoring the $183.5 million proposed cut to SUNY. The bill also addressed the need for new revenue sources by imposing a temporary increase in the state's sales tax and a temporary tax hike on the incomes of high earners. Initially the governor vetoed the bill, but the legislature in a very rare action overrode the gubernatorial veto.[28] The restoration for SUNY came in the form of a tuition increase, rather than additional state funds as UUP preferred.[29] Both houses included UUP's no-budgetary-layoffs language in the legislative Green Book. In short, UUP saved jobs during the state's worst fiscal crunch. Legislators also rejected the governor's plan to privatize the hospitals. In opposing privatization, UUP asked legislators the simple question of how a change in governance would save money. It would not! The union also reminded legislators that public hospitals provide a public service to care for the indigent, a function that private care centers could not match.[30] The hospitals received some $92.15 million more thanks to the Health Care Reform Act that subsidized teaching hospitals.

The trustees' implementation of Performance-Based Budgeting (PBB), formerly called RAM and then called BAP (Budget Allocation Process), created problems for several SUNY colleges. Since there was no new or additional money in the state budget, the campuses most dependent on state dollars rather than tuition money faced significant budget shortfalls. University centers and medical schools, institutions that needed to grant tuition waivers to remain competitive, fell into this category. The trustees' PBB program addressed this issue by shifting money from the comprehensive and technical colleges to the medical schools and university centers. To exacerbate matters, the trustees moved $22 million originally targeted for the state-operated campuses of SUNY into the statutory colleges at Cornell.[31] The trustees made this move even though state dollars at the private Ivy's statutory colleges covered over 90 percent of costs, while public funding for SUNY state-operated campuses hovered slightly below 40 percent.[32] The union raised the Cornell issue with the legislature and eventually received some extra funding, but the problem was not merely the trustees' failure to follow their own PBB guidelines. The real issue, Scheuerman remarked, was the lack of funds stemming, in part, from the trustees' failure to seek an adequate budget for SUNY in the first place. "If we focus on shifting monies and ignore the fact that there are not enough dollars to begin with, we'll end up pointing fingers at the different categories of campuses,"[33] Scheuerman concluded.

It cannot be emphasized enough that in a near-repeat of the 1995 negotiations scenario, UUP's contract with the state expired during a major fiscal crisis. The fiscal shortfall of $11.5 billion of 2002–03 was far worse than the $6 billion squeeze of 1995–96. Led by UUP's new chief negotiator, vice president for academics Phillip Smith, the union and the state traded proposals in February 2003. The state's demands were fairly reasonable. The state did not seek major givebacks and made no attempt to change the restrictive language of the outsourcing provision. In his report to delegates, Scheuerman characterized the bargaining talks as positive and amiable.[34] The real problem, he said, was the budget shortfall. Since there was no state money for salary, the union's salary demands fell on deaf ears. UUP's strategy, then, was to proceed slowly at the bargaining table while working with the legislature to secure new sources of revenue for the state.

With no reason for UUP to rush into an agreement, negotiations dragged on well past the contract's June 30 expiration date. This time, however, the state made no threats to stop funding the BTF, thanks to language changes in the 1995–99 contract making clear that such funding did not sunset. Union leaders also believed the membership would back the "go slow" approach because UUP's contract process was probably the most democratic in the labor movement, which meant, in Scheuerman's words, "our members own the proposal."[35] As the clock continued to tick without a new agreement, the union kept the support of rank-and-file members by once again creating a crisis committee to help organize support at the chapters. It also ordered minimicrophones in preparation for a series of demonstrations, but, Scheuerman cautioned, UUP's practice of what he called "rational militancy" was not about making people feel good, it was about results. Demonstrations should be part of a larger plan to get results. Scheuerman and Smith visited all the chapters to answer questions and keep the members informed. As in past hold-outs, the union also established regular negotiations bulletins to give members updated information.

Thanks to the legislature's willingness to impose temporary tax increases, along with some assistance from the federal government,[36] the state was in much better fiscal shape in 2004. A year earlier, budget analysts had talked about a two-year state deficit as high as $20 billion. That number was now projected to be around $6 billion or less. The $6 billion was a high number but much more manageable than a $20 billion shortfall. The union's plan to wait-and-see remained, and the membership held. On March 16, the state and UUP reached a tentative agreement. "We told our members that patience would pay off, and they believed us,"[37] chief negotiator Smith observed. There were no givebacks, and despite the state's large budget deficit, wage increases for average salary, including discretionary dollars, amounted to 15.6 percent during the life of the contract.[38] The salary increases were as follows: an $800 lump-sum payment, prorated for part-timers on contract ratification; across-the-board, on-base salary increases of 2.5 percent (plus 1 percent in discretionary money), 2.75 percent, and 3 percent over the next three years; an $800 on-base salary increase, prorated for part-timers, effective July 1, 2007; and, in an attempt to move toward a step salary system, a $500 achievement award effective April 1, 2007, for those with continuing or permanent appointments and reappointed to a five-year term appointment.[39] There were hikes in the location stipend, and a new location stipend was added for those who worked in Dutchess, Putnam, or Orange Counties.

All the labor-management committees were renewed with enhanced funding. Members who lived in New York City also received a tax break when using city mass transit. The Benefit Trust Fund received a 40 percent boost in funding, allowing UUP to continue its college scholarship program for bargaining-unit members and to improve existing benefits in the dental and vision plans. The Health Care Spending Account would now include some over-the-counter medications, while domestic-partnership coverage was also improved by shortening the waiting period for eligibility. Additionally, certain professional staff titles would move from Appendix A long-term appointments to make them eligible for continuing appointment.[40]

The contract became even better when UUP convinced SUNY, with GOER's approval, to include the first year of discretionary money with the on-base pay of 2.5 percent. SUNY's managers treasure the distribution of discretionary money, and many did not approve of this side agreement. But SUNY needed UUP's legislative assistance and turned to the union for help. UUP agreed to help, since, as Scheuerman said, "what they needed was exactly what we wanted to do anyway."[41] In return for its help, UUP reached an agreement that SUNY would distribute 1 percent in discretionary funds as an across-the-board salary increase.[42] Even though some UUP chapter leaders, led by Brooklyn Health Science Center's Rowena Blackman-Stroud, had worked in recent years with campus presidents to distribute discretionary dollars across the board, a university-wide dictum on the issue was entirely new. With the backing of GOER and SUNY, everyone eligible for the raise received a 3.5 percent increase rather than the 2.5

percent as originally negotiated. This constituted still another breakthrough for the union, yet another sign of its growing maturity and influence.[43]

Since the state removes most part-time faculty from the payroll once the semester ends, part-time faculty would lose their eligibility to participate in the ratification process if the vote were held during the summer months. To ensure the participation of as many union members as possible, UUP worked with the American Arbitration Association (AAA) to hold the ratification vote prior to the end of the spring semester while part-time members were still on the payroll and eligible to vote. To ensure maximum participation, UUPers had twenty-one days to vote and return their ballot, six days more than the AAA's recommended fifteen-day voting period. After completing the usual prevote information process, a process that included campus visits by the negotiations team and massive informational mailings to the membership that included a copy of the contract language, the vote was taken in late April. Once again, rank-and-file members overwhelmingly approved the new agreement. The ratification vote reached new highs for UUP. With 10,357 union members voting, the final tally was 10,023 in favor of ratification, 334 opposed. In other words, with more UUPers participating in the ratification process than ever before, a record 96.6 percent cast their ballots in favor of the new agreement.[44] Prior to the 1995–99 agreement, no contract had even come close to a 90 percent approval rate. The 2003–04 contract ratification vote marked the third consecutive time UUP reached this previously unprecedented level. Clearly, rank-and-file members approved of the union's work.

The union achieved another major victory in 2004. At the bargaining table SUNY agreed with UUP that it would limit the hiring of geographical full-time faculty (GFTer), a category of clinicians who received some or all of their salaries from clinical practice moneys. These GFTs worked primarily at the Buffalo Health Science Center, which generated clinical practice moneys at affiliated hospitals. But some GFTers received moneys from the state well below the negotiated minimum salary. Consequently, UUP filed a grievance claiming that GFTers who received any state salary were SUNY employees and therefore entitled to contractually negotiated minimal salaries. An arbitrator ruled in the union's favor. SUNY threatened to appeal, but in the end accepted the arbitrator's decision at a cost of $8 million to $10 million annually to SUNY.[45]

UUP did not spend much time celebrating its contract victory. Given New York's projected budget shortfall of about $6 billion, the union had geared up for another tough budget battle. The fight for a decent budget became a lot tougher when the trustees submitted still another budget proposal they characterized as a flat or no-growth proposal. But it was not even that. It was less. The trustees' requested the same amount of money they had asked for the year before, when the chancellor and others claimed their request was $39 million short.[46] By now

UUP had plenty of experience working with hostile trustees in a tough political
and fiscal setting. Starting in the previous autumn, Glenn McNitt, the new chair
of the UUP legislation committee, spent much of the fall visiting the chapters
and training rank-and-file members in the art of lobbying. McNitt's training sessions aimed at involving new members in the state and local political process.
Consequently, many new faces were added to UUP's growing cadre of member
lobbyists who worked with state legislators in their district offices or traveled to
Albany to present the union's case to legislators. In fact, the number had grown
so substantially that during the budget battle of the previous year the union
switched to specially focused advocacy days from general lobbying where all
interested members were invited.

While UUP continued hosting an occasional general lobbying day, such as its
annual legislative luncheon, the union's week-to-week lobbying days now focused
on issues special to core constituencies. The union held a UCT Day, a Four-Year
College Day, a University Center Day, a New York State Theatre Institute (NYSTI)
Day, a Health Science Center (HSC) Advocacy Day, an Opportunity Program
Day, a Librarian's Day, and a Retirees Day. Toward the end of the legislative session another mass general lobbying day followed all these focused days.[47] In the
meantime, UUP's president and his NYSUT lobbyists met frequently with the
Assembly speaker, the majority leader of the Senate, and the chairs of the Senate
and Assembly higher-education committees, as well as many other legislators.
Scheuerman also continued to meet regularly with the chancellor and the governor's top education aide. These advocacy activities were accompanied by a TV
ad campaign, a massive letter-writing and phone-call campaign to politicians of
both parties, and a well-attended rally in support of SUNY. In cooperation with
the UUP's Legislation Committee, UUP's Political Action Committee, headed by
Tom Tucker, signed up more than 400 new VOTE-COPE contributors.[48]

Budget prospects looked a bit better for UUP when the chancellor, who
had strategized with UUP over the budget, requested an extra $50 million in
his testimony before the legislature.[49] Chancellor King now supported the UUP's
call for more full-time faculty. But the April 1 deadline once again came and
went without a state budget. As media prodding and public grousing increased,
the legislature in early August finally passed a budget bill. Unfortunately, once
again the two-house budget deal did not include the governor's participation
and lacked his approval. The two-house budget proved to be quite responsive
to UUP's demands. It included the chancellor's request for an additional $50
million, $9 million of which was earmarked for new faculty lines, a major pri-
ority of UUP's, as well as $13 million of the $22 million the trustees previously
shifted from SUNY to Cornell. Legislative leaders also promised UUP to restore
the other $9 million in the next budget.[50] The budget also included another $2.4
million for the UCTs and continued the $92.6 million for the hospitals along
with an additional $13 million for hospital debt. The legislature again killed the

plan to privatize SUNY's teaching hospitals and rejected a proposed special tax on hospital revenues. UUP opposed the hospital tax, which would have severely hurt SUNY's medical schools and teaching hospitals. The legislative budget also restored cuts to the EOP and provided additional capital spending for SUNY, including desperately needed funds for the facilities of the EOCs at Buffalo and Rochester. UUP had worked with EOC managers and appropriate legislators to get necessary funds to rehabilitate the deteriorating EOC buildings in these two locations. The budget, at UUP's urging, also required SUNY to explain to the legislature its method of distributing funds to the campuses.[51] It looked like a very good year for UUP and SUNY.

On August 21 Governor Pataki once again wielded his line-item veto.[52] In trimming $235 million from the legislative budget, the governor cut all the legislative fiscal add-ons, including $2.4 million for the UCTs, money for the EOPs, and all money for capital improvements for the EOCs at Rochester and Buffalo. But the additional $92.6 million carried over for SUNY's hospitals was very good news. The $50 million in new dollars for SUNY's operating budget was untouched, but the governor placed a spending freeze that would spread spending of the $50 million over a three-year period.[53] Scheuerman warned that the veto "could have a particularly devastating effect on the technology colleges,"[54] and suggested that with growing enrollments and the loss of 1,000 full-time faculty from attrition over the past several years, SUNY might not have sufficient faculty to teach the courses necessary for graduation. UUP worked with its NYSUT affiliate and other interested organizations to get a repeat of the previous year's override of Pataki's veto. On October 15, an override vote was taken and lost by a single vote.[55] UUP and SUNY would have to carry on for the rest of the fiscal year without the anticipated and much-needed legislative add-ons.

Events outside the state budget process also brought potentially bad news for UUP members. Changes to the Fair Labor Standards Act (FLSA) by President Bush weakened overtime protections. This administrative fiat threatened to hurt UUPers at the health science centers, who often worked long hours. But the union's improving relationship with SUNY counterbalanced Bush's actions. UUP and the university agreed to go beyond the federal guidelines and adhere to the protections inherent in the recently negotiated agreement between the union and the state. In other words, UUPers did not lose their previous protections even though the federal law changed. During this time, UUPers had one more piece of good news. Despite a record two-year state budget deficit of about $17 billion, no bargaining-unit member had lost a job for budgetary purposes. This, indeed, was a major accomplishment.

Once the possibility of an override of the veto died, UUP had to prepare for another tough fiscal year and an equally challenging political situation. For the 2005–06 fiscal year the state faced a deficit of between $5 billion and $6 billion. But the budget deficit was just one piece of a larger fiscal problem. Court actions regarding the Campaign for Fiscal Equity (CFE) mandated additional state spending of $14 billion on New York City public schools over the next several years. The $14 billion for New York City didn't take into account the needs of upstate school districts requiring extra funding.[56] The final cost of the mandate would be considerably higher.

As usual, the union took a proactive position. During the previous fall Scheuerman and NYSUT lobbyist Christopher Black had worked closely with SUNY's chancellor and the university's new chief fiscal officer, David Richter, to get an executive budget proposal for fiscal 2005–06 that met the union's and SUNY's needs. With the backing of King, UUP helped persuade the trustees to make a moderately aggressive budget request. The trustees' proposal, astonishingly, included a boost of $87.1 million for SUNY's state-operated campuses. The request covered money for salary increases and another $8 million to pay for the costs of the important arbitration win at the Buffalo Health Science Center. It also restored funding for the EOCs and EOPs, and for the first time the trustees requested an additional $2.4 million for the UCTs. This action was very important. In the past, when UUP garnered money from the legislature for the UCTs, it was always as a member item, a legislative add-on. As such, it would not be carried through as part of the budget the following year. The trustees also sought to renew the $50 million for the state-operated campuses, as well as a hospital subsidy of $129 million, up from the previous subsidy of $92.6 million.

The governor's budget, released in January, had some good news for UUP and SUNY. It raised the amount SUNY could spend to meet negotiated salary increases by $73 million, but did not provide the revenue to pay for it. The governor's proposal increased hospital aid for the first time to cover the cost of salary increases, which in the past were paid out of hospital revenues, and the budget actually included money for NYSTI for 2005–06. Since NYSTI funding for the previous year was vetoed, the institution would run out of money on February 9, long before the start of the next fiscal year. This was prevented when Senate majority leader Joseph Bruno, following a series of meetings with Scheuerman and Black, found $250,000 as a member item for NYSTI.

In January, UUP's leaders held a meeting for chapter presidents to develop a legislative campaign. UUP conducted its usual upstate ad campaign, and its members sent thousands of letters and faxes to the governor and legislators. In addition to district lobbying, the union launched its annual lobbying program at the statehouse. Changes in the state's lobbying regulations prohibited the union from spending more than $2,000 per person to come to Albany and lobby for the union. Given the cost of transportation, housing, and food, the annual $2,000 ceiling limited the number of trips each UUP member-advocate could make.[57] Nevertheless, the union recruited additional rank-and-file volunteers. For once the legislature and the governor met the April 1 deadline, and by the time the session ended, President Scheuerman reported that some 400 different UUP members had lobbied for their union in Albany.[58]

On January 13, Chancellor King announced he was taking a six-month sabbatical leave. The announcement came on the heels of some disagreements he had with the trustees over his growing advocacy for SUNY and negative news reports concerning King's friendship with someone involved in a Canal Corporation scandal.[59] King eventually resigned and was replaced by another John Ryan, a former naval pilot and president of SUNY Maritime. Ryan served as interim chancellor until December 2005, when he was formally appointed to the position. Significantly, Ryan became SUNY's fifth chancellor since Scheuerman's election as UUP president in 1993. Clearly, the stability of the union's leadership within the context of SUNY's constant changes contributed to UUP's growing political influence. More and more, state legislators turned to the stable and predictable UUP for advice on SUNY.

As the saying goes, the governor proposes and the legislature disposes. The union's attempt to help the legislature "dispose" in a favorable way was as intensive as ever. In addition to the 400 lobbyists just mentioned, as well as the usual district lobbying, letter-writing, and fax campaigns, UUP strengthened its media outreach program. Its advertising campaign included statewide television ads, as well as chapter-specific newspaper, radio, and billboard advertisements. The TV advertisements featured UUP members and SUNY students urging the public to remind their legislators to "keep the promise, invest in SUNY." The outreach program also placed more emphasis on influencing legislators and opinion-makers through a barrage of letters to the editor, news releases, and press conferences. These efforts, Scheuerman reported to delegates in the fall of 2005, resulted in positive coverage in dozens of state, national, and higher-education newspapers and radio and internet outlets, including *Newsday*, the Associated Press, Ottaway News Services, the *Chronicle of Higher Education*, *Inside Higher Education*, Fox News, WAMC, the *Albany Times Union*, and New York News Connection. UUP's voice was being heard by more politicians, opinion-makers, and others than ever before.[60] The initial results were encouraging. Prior to the end of fiscal 2004–05, the governor released $28 million of the $34 million he had previously frozen. UUP agreed not to make a public announcement on the release of the funds so as not to embarrass the governor during these tough fiscal times.[61]

The legislative session ended with good results. The state's budget for fiscal year 2005–06 included an $84.5 million add-on to SUNY, despite the trustees' lack of advocacy; the state subsidy to SUNY's hospitals was increased by $36.8 million to $129.4 million; EOP funding, now fully restored, received an additional $820,000 to make up for the previous years' gubernatorial veto; EOC operations received an increase of $2.7 million, and another $24 million was earmarked for capital improvements at the EOCs; aid to the Theatre Institute increased to $455,000; the attempt to privatize the teaching hospitals was killed again; and the proposed 0.7 percent sick tax on gross hospital revenues was reduced to 0.35 percent in lieu of cuts to Medicaid funding to SUNY's hospitals.

UUP's role in the political arena allowed the union to use its political leverage on SUNY to negotiate additional fiscal benefits for its members. Since the $84.5 million was added to base, it would remain part of SUNY's budget, which meant that UUP could negotiate additional salary increases for UCT members and underpaid part-timers at the chapter level, with the UUP president and chancellor overseeing the enterprise. Ryan and Scheuerman had regular early-morning breakfast meetings, resulting in the chancellor's endorsement of UUP's political agenda and his willingness to work with UUP to address issues at the UCTs and with part-time faculty.[62] UUP, Scheuerman observed, was developing a partnership with SUNY based on SUNY's dependence on UUP's help in the political arena. Indeed, interim chancellor Ryan noted that SUNY needed UUP's political assistance, conceding that SUNY was not effective with the legislature, particularly the Assembly.[63] UUP agreed to help, provided that SUNY addressed salary issues at the UCTs and for the growing number of part-time members. Since UUP had successfully helped SUNY during the previous budget process, chapter negotiations between UUP's chapter leadership and SUNY's campus leaders began almost immediately. Within weeks the chapters at New Paltz, Cortland, Canton, and Delhi reported extracontractual negotiated raises for part-timers.[64] James Fort, chapter president at Cobleskill, negotiated extracontractual raises of $750 on base for full professors for three years running, and $500 on base for associate professors for three consecutive years.[65] Chapter negotiations for salary increases at other UCTs continued.

With chapter negotiations underway, SUNY and UUP jointly prepared for next year's SUNY budget. The union and the university were cooperating as never before. SUNY provost Peter Salins, a one-time adversary, gave UUP information on SUNY's role as an engine of economic development that UUP planned to use in its next advertising campaign.[66] The meetings between Scheuerman and Ryan proved productive. Ryan, a lifelong military man, believed in starting work early in the morning and getting to meetings on time. Scheuerman also held those beliefs. At their first breakfast meeting, scheduled for 7:30 a.m., Scheuerman arrived at 7:10 only to have Ryan, who was already there, ask him, "Where the hell were you?"[67] The two hit it off immediately. They agreed to speak honestly and bluntly with each other and to work for the betterment of the university and its professional and teaching faculty. Subsequent discussions focused on the chancellor's question of how he could improve SUNY's approach to the budget. Long discussions about the squeeze on SUNY's hospitals, particularly upstate, ensued.[68] With Ryan's blessings, the UUP president and NYSUT staff director Martineau held regular sessions with Betty Capaldi, the university's new vice chancellor and chief of staff, to discuss how to grow the university by as many as 2,500 new faculty positions.[69] The new administration agreed with the union: it was time to grow SUNY!

For the first time ever, UUP and SUNY worked together to prepare SUNY's budget request and move their mutual demands through the legislative process. Prior to testifying on the SUNY budget, both Ryan and Scheuerman met with Jeff Lovell at the governor's office to make the case for SUNY. They also met with representatives from the Division of Budget to correct what they believed to be a long-standing practice that hurt the university. At this meeting they focused on the cost of energy increases and how SUNY was the only state agency to pay for them out of operating costs. The university would save millions if the state assumed these costs. The union and the chancellor knew what SUNY and the faculty needed and put together a proposal to increase SUNY's funding by $221 million.[70] The problem was getting the trustees to submit the budget that met these needs. Ryan addressed that issue by putting pressure on the trustees.

At a well-attended open trustees meeting to discuss and accept the budget, UUP leaders were on edge because the budget Ryan originally presented to the trustees as having a 3 percent increase actually call for an increase of 12 percent. UUP's new director of communications, Denise Duncan Lacy, a former TV anchor person, arranged for plenty of media coverage and TV cameras. When publicly asked why he had not yet sought the permanent appointment as chancellor, Ryan responded by saying he did not know if he could work at a place that did not back his program. In other words, if the trustees refused to support his proposal, he might resign and certainly would not seek the permanent position. Ryan's stance pressured the trustees to support the budget request of $221 million and to make adjustments to their RAM/BAP formula. Trustee de Russy, apparently upset at the partnership between SUNY and UUP, accused the chancellor of being in the back pocket of the big union.[71]

The governor's proposed budget was a mixed bag for the university. The trustees had requested a $221 million hike in state support, but the governor cut that down to a mere $3.6 million. The executive budget did authorize a spending increase of $104 million and called for the hiring of 200 new faculty, but, again, only $3.6 million of the total amount derived from tax dollars. SUNY would have to fund the rest. The governor did deliver on the energy issue, providing an energy allocation of $45 million. The budget proposal also added another $10 million to the hospitals, but there was still another attempt to privatize the teaching hospitals. NYSTI funding was increased by $81,000, EOCs received a $28,000 increase, and the EOPs budget was upped by some $646,000.[72] The governor's budget also called for a cut in TAP funding of $190 million, which made UUP's task even more difficult. As Scheuerman pointed out in his report to delegates, when the legislative session ended and there was a pool of money for higher education, hundreds of thousands of SUNY, CUNY, and private-school students would scream for TAP restorations. And the first piece out of that pool of dollars would go to TAP. This meant, Scheuerman continued, "we better be screaming for what we want."[73] UUP was prepared to scream.

UUP was in great shape as it began its annual political campaign. In the early and mid-nineties, the UUP annual legislative luncheon was well attended by legislative staff and a handful of legislators, usually the chairs of the higher education committees. By now, however, the state's legislative leaders called the union to make sure they could speak at the gathering. Senate majority leader Joseph Bruno had become a regular speaker at the luncheons, as did his Assembly counterpart, Sheldon Silver. UUP's VOTE COPE contributions now exceeded $200,000 annually,[74] and the union's reserve fund topped $5 million.[75] UUP also hired SUNY's recently retired chief fiscal officer, David Richter, who had previously played a major role in the Division of Budget for over thirty-five years. Richter provided analyses that supported UUP lobbying efforts, particularly regarding the hospitals.[76] UUP's political action campaign mirrored that of previous years, with one notable addition. UUP decided to work more closely than ever with the student body. SUNY Albany student Jerome Garrett, working with research director Kriger, contacted student leaders across the university and brought them on board to support UUP's campaign for more new faculty positions. Garrett and Kriger gave student leaders copies of the TV ad to show to students in the dorms so they would email the legislature in support of UUP's program. The students were also asked to have their parents participate in the email campaign, as well as anyone else they could enlist. The goal was to hit the legislature with 100,000 to 150,000 emails.[77]

The legislature came through. It once again killed the proposal to privatize SUNY's teaching hospitals. In addition to maintaining the executive's proposed increase in the state's subsidy to SUNY hospitals of $10 million, for a total subsidy of $139.5 million, the legislative budget added $151 million to SUNY's operating budget and another $49 million for energy costs, plus an additional $29 million for energy for the 2005–06 fiscal year. The add-ons were enough to hire as many as 500 new faculty. Additionally, the budget also increased NYSTI funding by $81,000, and the EOP and EOC programs received a boost of $42.4 million and $2.7 million, respectively.[78] UUP again played a major role in the legislative increase in SUNY's operational budget.

As Scheuerman reported to delegates in the spring, a big breakthrough for the union came in February, when the state Assembly budget plan put $104 million in the budget for SUNY. The SUNY lobbyists, finally free of tight restraints from the trustees, complained that the $104 million was insufficient. The university, they claimed, needed $120 million to break even. More, they complained, the Assembly always set the ceiling on aid to SUNY but the Senate usually reduced the amount. UUP now intervened. Scheuerman contacted Chancellor Ryan, who was in China, and suggested a way to increase funding for SUNY. The chancellor initially hesitated, saying the legislative process was over, but he agreed to go along with the plan once he heard the details.[79] UUP had Dave Richter produce numbers indicating that CUNY was receiving a disproportionately larger share of higher-education dollars than SUNY. Scheuerman and NYSUT lobbyist Chris Black then met with Senate majority leader Joe Bruno and showed him the numbers. Bruno and the union leaders had a conversation about the prospect of holding onto a two-seat Republican majority in the Senate when downstate interests in higher education received disproportionately more assistance than cash-strapped SUNY. To hold onto upstate votes, Bruno agreed to add $25 million to the proposed budget. Scheuerman and Black then went down the hall and convinced Sheldon Silver to address SUNY's needs more aggressively. He did. The Assembly added $4 million more.[80] Later that autumn the New York State Lobbying Commission required the UUP president to register as a lobbyist.

Unfortunately, the governor once again exercised his line-veto option, killing $58.7 million of the legislature's add-ons for SUNY. UUP joined other unions and organizations opposed to the governor's vetoes. When legislative leaders urged UUP to do something publicly to justify another override of gubernatorial vetoes, UUP ran more TV ads in the Albany region describing the "crisis" in SUNY.[81] UUPers faxed thousands of letters to legislators and held a mass rally in which Senate majority leader Bruno spoke in favor of a veto override. Later that night, Assembly higher-education chair Ronald Canestrari also spoke in support of an override. In late April both houses overrode the bulk of the governor's vetoes.[82] The override restored all the moneys targeted by the legislature for SUNY.

The legislature delivered more for UUP later in the session when it finally passed the UUP-driven pension equity bill. Even though John Faso, the Republican candidate in the upcoming gubernatorial election, opposed any increase in public employee pensions and state legislatures across the nation were aggressively cutting public workers' pensions, both houses in New York's state legislature supported UUP's pension equity bill. UUP also gained the passage of legislation suggested by the SUNY Faculty Senate that put the chair of the Senate on the Board of Trustees. This step was in response to the paternalistic practice of the chair of the trustees not allowing any faculty representatives to speak at meetings without his permission.[83] Unfortunately for UUP, in mid-August Governor Pataki vetoed the pension equity bill. Given a pending state budget deficit and growing national political sentiment to reduce or terminate public employee pensions, there was no chance of a legislative override. The union planned to drive the bill through the legislature the next year and onto the desk of a new governor.[84]

Prior to the finalization of the budget, Kim Cline had replaced Betty Capaldi as vice chancellor and second in command of the university.[85] Cline advised campus presidents to continue negotiations for chapter extracontractual raises through the summer, because she recognized that UUP's role in securing a good SUNY budget justified making funds available for UUP projects on all campuses. By September, sixteen chapters had successfully negotiated raises for part-time colleagues, effective in the fall semester of 2006. At SUNY Albany, where the starting salary for part-time faculty was extremely low, the raise amounted to an 87 percent increase.[86] David Butler, Canton's chapter president, negotiated additional salary increases for tenured faculty at his college of technology. Canton's tenured faculty would receive an on-base salary increase of $2,500 in addition to all contractually negotiated raises.

UUP also settled two arbitration cases involving part-time faculty. Settlement terms gave $26,000 in back pay to one part-timer and $28,000 in back pay to another.[87] The union also saved the job of a member who was not renewed even though there were no contractual violations in the nonrenewal decision, by turning to state law instead of relying solely on contract language. Article 78 of New York State law requires a state agency to follow its own procedures. When former NYSUT lobbyist Peter Martineau, now staff director for UUP, looked at the nonrenewal case, it was clear to him that the contract was not violated, but it appeared that SUNY did not adhere to its own procedures. In an unprecedented action, NYSUT counsel took legal action and the nonrenewal was overturned. In addition to protecting members through its contract with the state and by use of it political influence, UUP had now found still another way to protect members outside standard contractual guidelines.

The union also came through with other new benefits for its members. Retirees were now eligible for dental and vision benefits[88] and bargaining-unit members could purchase new eyeglasses every twelve months rather than every twenty-four.[89] Dental coverage was also increased, as were hearing benefits. With prodding from UUP and other public-sector unions, the state decided to provide coverage for Gardasil, a cervical cancer vaccine new to the market. UUP received national prominence when AFT's president, Edward McElroy, appointed Scheuerman to AFT's executive committee, making the UUP president the first and, to this day, the only higher-education person to have a seat on the national affiliate's executive committee.[90] The committee, consisting of AFT's full-time elected officers and seven vice presidents, functions as the cabinet for the million-member-plus AFT. Scheuerman was also appointed coeditor of a new higher education journal, the *Journal of Collective Bargaining*. UUP was now in a position to play an even larger role in higher-education unionism.[91]

Demonstrating that social activism and bread-and-butter unionism are not mutually exclusive, UUP's activities ranged far beyond a narrow focus on the usual terms and conditions of employment that most unions view as their sole purpose. For instance, the union viewed the issue of gender equity seriously. As previously discussed, attorneys had advised UUP against taking legal action to attain gender pay equality. By 2006, with the worst of the state budgetary crises behind it, UUP decided to move ahead by conducting an updated study of gender inequality to bring to the bargaining table. The union even purchased a year's leave from SUNY Cortland for a member, Jamie Dangler, to research the issue. Another example of its social activism is the role UUP played in bringing more diversity to SUNY. After the university, with prodding from trustee de Russy, abolished its Office of Latino Affairs, Scheuerman, Kriger, and a UUP activist Raul Huerta traveled to the South Bronx to discuss a possible restoration of the office with Assemblyman Peter Rivera. As a result of the discussions, Huerta, Kriger, Assembly chair of higher education Ron Canestrari, and Chancellor Ryan visited the University of New Mexico to examine its recruitment and retention of Latino students and faculty. On their return they created a group to develop and implement a plan to improve diversity at SUNY. The group produced a document, *Ensuring SUNY's Ongoing Success: A Plan for Improving Latino Student Retention, Educational Performance and Academic Attainment*, that outlined a new diversity plan for the university. The plan was drafted by Huerta with the assistance of several UUP colleagues. SUNY purchased release time for Huerta to work on the document.[92] An immediate result of these activities was a promise from Rivera to provide $12 million to fund a new office of diversity at SUNY.[93] Within months SUNY created the office and hired Pedro Caban at the vice-provost level.

The fiscal outlook for SUNY was good, but more trouble surfaced in November 2006 when the Berger Commission, a commission appointed by the governor and state legislature to make recommendations regarding excess bed capacity at the state's hospitals, issued its final report. The report called for the merger or closing of fifty-nine of the state's hospitals, including the merger of SUNY's Upstate Medical center (UMU) with nearby Crouse Memorial under a unified governance structure other than SUNY.[94] Governor Pataki and most legislators supported the commission's recommendations because the state would receive an addition $1.5 billion a year from the federal government if it implemented the report's recommendations. The federal assistance was in addition to projected cost savings over ten years of about $8 billion.[95] Given these financial incentives within the context of a projected state budget deficit of $2 billion for the upcoming fiscal year, the commission's recommendations gained bipartisan political support.

While the Berger report was still being considered, Governor Pataki chose not to run for reelection. In November 2006, New York's voters elected Elliot Spitzer, a liberal Democrat, as their new governor. Spitzer's election meant a change in SUNY's Board of Trustees. Shortly after taking office Spitzer appointed UUP's friend, Carl McCall, to the SUNY Board along with Carl Hayden, who replaced Tom Egan as chair.[96] These appointments signaled a new cooperative relationship between the union and SUNY's trustees. UUP took immediate advantage of the new governor's positive overtures by presenting him and his transition team with a white paper on the university's budgetary needs. The paper, written with SUNY's backing, called for more new faculty positions.

Scheuerman subsequently met with the governor and members of his transition team to discuss the needs of the state's university system.[97] During the course of their conversation, the UUP president learned that Spitzer strongly supported the Berger Commissions' proposals. The new governor's intense political support of the commission's recommendations increased the already strong possibility that SUNY might now lose UMU.[98]

November 2006 also brought some good news for SUNY's labor force. UUP had previously joined CSEA; PEF; the American Federation of State, County and Municipal Employees (AFSCME); the Correctional Officers (NYSCOBA); and the Police Benevolent Association (PBA) in litigation aimed at reversing the state's decision to require all employees to pay a Medicare part B enrollee reimbursement. The Appellate Division of the New York State Supreme Court called the state's actions "arbitrary, capricious and contrary to law" and ordered the state to return moneys it had already collected. UUP and GOER worked out the details of the refund in the labor/management Committee on Health and Safety.[99]

By the time Spitzer took the oath of office in January 2007, UUP had already launched another aggressive political campaign to save UMU. Scheuerman and UMU president David Smith held a series of meetings with upstate legislators to discuss the impact of removing UMU from SUNY. UUP sponsored a TV commercial in the Syracuse and Buffalo areas that focused on the implications of privatizing the only public hospital in most of upstate New York. In fact, UMU was the only public hospital from Rochester east to the Vermont border and from the Canadian border south to Westchester County. Implementation of the Berger Commission's recommendations would almost certainly lead to the closing of the hospital's costly tertiary-care units, including its important burn center. The union continued its advocacy for UMU by introducing a YouTube commercial that emphasized the important role UMU played in providing healthcare in upstate New York. UUP also initiated letter-writing and email campaigns to state legislators, while participating with CSEA, PEF, and private-sector unions in demonstrations and marches aimed at keeping UMU in the SUNY system.[100]

The dramatic struggle over the Berger Commission's report was accompanied by two other major events. First, UUP once again was about to enter contract negotiations with SUNY and the state. Scheuerman appointed his vice president for academics, Fred Floss, to head the team. The change of gubernatorial administrations had slowed the negotiations process down because the new governor did not rush to appoint a new director of GOER. Finally, after Spitzer appointed Gary Johnson[101] as the new director of GOER, on April 19 the negotiations teams exchanged packages. Johnson was well known to UUP since he had worked as an associate counsel at NYSUT from 2004 until the time of his appointment. SUNY and the state did not ask for any significant givebacks.

The second major issue was, of course, the annual budget battle. In consultation with UUP, SUNY submitted a good budget proposal to the governor.

The university requested an additional $131 million to its operating budget, plus another $29 million for the hospitals. The university also asked for $751 million in capital funds for the state-operated campuses. The governor, who in his inaugural address promised to make the state's public higher-education institutions the best in the country,[102] submitted a very robust budget for SUNY. In addition to covering all mandatory costs, including energy expenses, the proposed budget added $143.2 million to SUNY and an additional $6.8 million to the hospitals. The NYSTI budget was increased by $48,000, allowing NYSTI members to return to a twelve-month employment schedule. The governor did not seek cuts to TAP, so UUP would not have political conflicts with students or the privates. Unfortunately, the budget failed to provide funds for additional faculty lines or enrollment growth.[103] UUP turned to the legislature to address those two issues, as well as the recommendations of the Berger Commission.

Once again UUP members lobbied in their home districts and in Albany. UUP activists sent thousands of letters and emails to legislators and the governor. In fact, the union had created and advertised in *The Voice* a link on the union website that allowed members to send emails from their home computers. This technology is common today but was a novelty in 2007. The union's TV campaign focused on SUNY's importance to the state's economy, particularly the depressed upstate areas. The annual legislative luncheon again witnessed top legislative leaders scrambling to speak to the capacity crowd of union members, legislators, and media personnel assembled in the well of the Legislative Office Building. Senate majority leader Joe Bruno echoed the union's TV campaign when he said, "There's no better investment we can make in our budget than to support higher education in this state."[104]

When the legislative session ended, most UUPers had reasons to smile. First, according to Scheuerman, the SUNY budget was the best in a generation. The legislature added an additional $17.5 million to the governor's proposed SUNY budget for a total increase of $160.7 million. The university was in the process of rebuilding and there were sufficient funds for more fruitful local negotiations. The legislative Green Book, in addition to containing the usual language prohibiting layoffs for budgetary purposes, once again had language circumventing the contract's zipper clause by justifying campus-level negotiations.[105]

Campus-based negotiations initially began with Chancellor King, who advised SUNY presidents that UUP would help funnel money into SUNY, but that the university must address the needs of the union, too.[106] Once the state budget crisis ended, these local negotiations continued. Now in 2007, Michael Smiles, president of the Farmingdale chapter, announced an agreement to address salary inequities at his college of technology. SUNY Farmingdale would use $100,000 from its current operating budget to address salary disparities. For the following year the college would direct another $100,000 from discretionary dollars to adjust salary disparities. The Farmingdale chapter also became the fourteenth chapter to negotiate extracontractual raises for part-time colleagues when the campus administration agreed to raise part-time salaries by 7 percent.[107]

The UUP claimed still another legislative victory when it helped kill a CSEA-backed bill that attempted to permanently resolve an ongoing representation issue between UUP and CSEA in CSEA's favor. Over the years, administrative assistants to department chairs were frequently CSEA members. This placed them under the CSEA contract in terms of pay grade and flexibility at work. Many of these assistants viewed UUP as a union for professional employees, as did their supervisors, and they often successfully petitioned the chancellor to move out of CSEA and into the UUP bargaining unit. At times, this created some tension between the two unions. UUP was growing at the expense of CSEA. In an attempt to circumvent the process it found unfavorable, CSEA found a sponsor for legislation restricting the chancellor's ability to make such moves.[108] The attempt failed and the status quo remained until a future UUP president, Phil Smith, signed an agreement giving up the bulk of UUP's rights to represent these workers.[109]

Much to UUP's chagrin, in March 2007 Chancellor Ryan suddenly announced his resignation.[110] Ryan was temporarily replaced by John Clark. The union had an excellent relationship with Clark, who had previously served as interim president at four SUNY colleges—Plattsburgh, Brockport, Alfred, and Optometry. Once again, the leadership instability at SUNY contrasted unfavorably with UUP's stability. Clark was SUNY's sixth chancellor or interim chancellor since Scheuerman's election as UUP president in 1993. Governor Spitzer, who had several personal meetings with UUP's president, recognized UUP's increasing relevance and political effectiveness by appointing President Scheuerman to his newly established Higher Education Commission. The commission was charged with making recommendations to improve higher education in the state. Scheuerman was the sole representative of higher-education unions on the board.[111]

UUP also beat back attempts to privatize UMU through the Berger Commission's recommendations. As noted, the union ran an aggressive political campaign, but it also took legal action. The legislative process to make the commission's recommendations become law was a passive one. That is, if the legislature failed to vote on the commission's recommendations by January 1, 2007, they would become law. UUP viewed this passive procedure as an opportunity to keep UMU within SUNY. Since the legislature had not voted on the recommendation by December 2006, NYSUT attorneys filed a lawsuit claiming that privatization of any SUNY unit, in this instance UMU, required legislative action. In the meantime, UUP and NYSUT now used their political clout to keep the legislature from taking a vote. The union's message to the public and legislators was twofold. First, UUP reminded legislators of the accountability issue. As part of SUNY, UMU was accountable to both SUNY and the legislature. Privatization, the union argued, would undercut this accountability and reduce the legislature's oversight of the institution. Second, UUP's television ads focused on the need for a public hospital capable of providing expensive tertiary care to the state's residents. The ad was effective; elected officials from both parties thanked UUP for giving them "wiggle room" to save UMU.[112] The lawsuit helped by galvanizing talks between the governor, Dave Smith, and the appropriate Crouse hospital officials. Finally Crouse and UMU came to an agreement that met all the requirements of the commission's recommendations without the privatization of UMU. UUP withdrew its legal objection and, significantly, UMU emerged as the only hospital of the fifty-nine targeted for mergers or closings by the commission's report to remain structurally intact.

The legislature again passed the pension equity bill that UUP had sought for many years and the new governor signed it into law. Passage of the pension equity bill for employees in the optional retirement program meant that all individuals with ten years or more of service who currently paid 3 percent of their salary to the ORP system would eventually not make that payment. As of April 1, 2008, the state would begin paying 1 percent a year for three years until the entire 3 percent was covered. The state would also pay the 3 percent cost to bargaining-unit members lacking ten years' employment once they met that standard. Given that this pension reform had a high price tag, costing the state $20 to 25 million annually, critics complained that it was unnecessary because ORP employees had already reaped the financial rewards of a bullish stock market. The union was judicious in making public statements about this major victory. After all, UUPers did benefit from a rising stock market, and now the state was increasing its subsidy to their pension investments. This did constitute what critics characterized as two bites of the apple. But the two-bites-of-the-apple observation is accurate only as long as the stock market continues to climb. Two years after the pension bill became law, reckless banking practices brought a recession and the stock market plummeted.[113]

Free Speech and Intellectual Leadership: UUP Assumes a National and International Role

Over the years, UUP had gradually developed its reputation as the intellectual leader of the American higher-education union movement. Once its president assumed the chair of AFT's Program and Policy Council (PPC), an organization representing over 100,000 higher-education unionists, UUP was thrust into the national and international spotlight. As chair, Scheuerman opened each year's AFT national higher-education meeting with an address, which was usually followed by a number of radio and TV interviews on issues relevant to institutions of higher learning. AFT also arranged a number of debates between Scheuerman and well-known advocates of antiunion or other controversial positions. One excellent debate occurred in Albuquerque, New Mexico, with Richard Chait, a Harvard professor who was in the news for his antitenure positions. As chair of the PPC, the UUP president also made several trips to Europe to make presentations about higher-education unionism in the United States.

By 2006, UUP had become the voice of free speech in the academy when it emerged as the leading opponent of the Academic Bill of Rights (ABoR). AFT, UUP, and most in higher education viewed the ABoR as an attack on free speech. ABoR was the brainchild of former-communist-turned-conservative David Horowitz and his Center for the Study of Popular Culture. The Academic Bill of Rights posited that left-wing preaching had replaced openness and teaching in the classroom. Horowitz wanted to solve this alleged problem by creating what he called balance, meaning every so-called left-wing statement should be countered by a rebuttal from the political right. Scheuerman and most other critics viewed ABoR as a quota system to give right-wing ideologues a voice on campuses. Horowitz and his followers issued a series of publications attacking left-wing faculty. A national blacklist of 101 "dangerous" American intellectuals was released, as well as a list of "the Dirty Thirty," a blacklist of thirty UCLA faculty. Horowitz released his book on the subject, *The Professors: The 101 Most Dangerous Academics in America.* The accusations and publication of the names of the accused potentially had a chilling effect on free speech throughout the higher learning community.

The accusations were taken seriously in the U.S. Congress,[114] and by many state legislatures. In New York, SUNY trustees Egan and de Russy tried to impose the ABoR on SUNY. To justify the imposition of ABoR, the trustees wanted to show just how widespread ideological suppression of ideas was at SUNY, so they conducted polls of all sixty-four of the university's campuses to prove their point. Much to their disappointment, they discovered that not a single one of SUNY's 480,000 students had complained about indoctrination in the classroom. Rather than admit that ideological indoctrination was not a problem at SUNY, Eagan concluded that students were just too afraid to raise the issue. Shortly after the trustees' failed attempt, a state senator from Syracuse introduced legislation in support of ABoR, but thanks to the efforts of UUP and NYSUT, he withdrew the bill within twenty-four hours.[115]

New York may have escaped the ideological onslaught on institutions of higher learning, but twenty-five other states introduced pro-ABoR legislation. As chair of AFT's PPC, Scheuerman was called on to testify at legislative hearings across the country on proposed AboR legislation. It soon became clear that proponents of ABoR could not document their claims. In Pennsylvania, Horowitz even had to admit that a particular act of intellectual suppression never took place. Weeks later, the Pennsylvania House committee issued its report. The bipartisan report of Democrats and Republicans unanimously found no need for the Academic Bill of Rights legislation, since Pennsylvania's colleges and universities had procedures in place that protected students.[116] At the same hearing, Horowitz approached Scheuerman, who gave the lead testimony against ABoR, and suggested that if UUP and its president believed in free speech, the union should invite him to speak at one of its meetings. In return, he invited the UUP president to participate in a conference he was holding in Washington, DC. Scheuerman agreed to speak in Washington but cautioned Horowitz that he needed to get approval from delegates for him to speak at a Delegate Assembly. When Scheuerman raised the issue of Horowitz speaking at a UUP Delegate Assembly, delegates began shouting their disapproval, actions that disappointed the UUP president because he believed in the marketplace of ideas.[117] Scheuerman did attend Horowitz's conference in Washington, DC, where he was received with cordial silence. SUNY trustee de Russy also attended the meeting.

The UUP president continued to speak, write, and testify against the ABoR. He was also involved in the AFT's role in forming the Free Exchange on Campus Coalition, a free-speech coalition of education, student, and advocacy groups. The coalition's support of academic freedom received recognition and financial support from George Soros's Open Society Institute. The Soros organization gave AFT a substantial grant to assist in coordinating the newly formed coalition.[118] Horowitz responded to these activities by attacking Scheuerman, UUP members, and the AFT in his book *Indoctrination U: The Left's War against Academic Freedom*. The written assaults complained about an AFT editorial attributed to the UUP president entitled the "Academic Bull of Rights," which was distributed to attendees at campus meetings where Horowitz spoke. He also vented against an editorial written by Scheuerman for UUP's *The Voice* entitled, "Have You No Decency, Sir?" Clearly, UUP's activities did not please Mr. Horowitz.[119] But that's no surprise. The architect of ABoR had not had a single significant legislative success. He had to blame someone.

Much of this chapter examined the many tough bread-and-butter issues the Scheuerman administration navigated. But during this period the union engaged in a great deal of social activism, too. In addition to leading the higher-education union movement's fight against political intrusion and for free speech, UUP advocated for gender and racial equality in a number of forums, running the gamut from financing gender-equity studies to forcing SUNY's trustees to reestablish an office of diversity. But that's not all. UUP was among a handful of unions to associate with the newly formed Labor Party in 1996, a workers' political movement led by Anthony Mazzochi, president of the Oil, Chemical and Atomic Workers International.[120] The Mazzochi movement failed almost before it got off the ground, but UUP never gave up its commitment to social activism. Later on, UUP became an early supporter of the Working Families Party. The union also played a major role in the New York State Labor/Religion Coalition, sending dozens of members to work with sister and brother union organizers in the *maquiladoras*, American-owned factories in Mexico just over the Texas border. In response to the outcries of fraud and accusations that the 2000 presidential election was stolen, UUP became a driving force in Rock the Vote, a national movement aimed at registering college students. UUP helped register thousands of students at SUNY campuses. UUP was almost always at the forefront in social-activist events, so much so, in fact, that President Scheuerman was even arrested and briefly jailed for participating in a demonstration in Manhattan in support of the right of graduate students at New York University to form a union.[121]

Scheuerman Leaves for the AFL-CIO: Future Prospects for UUP

In August 2007, Scheuerman announced he would resign from the UUP presidency at the end of November to assume the presidency of the National Labor College, a job he believed would play a significant role in rebuilding the labor movement.[122] In 2005 he added an annual State of the Union report in *The Voice* providing details to the entire membership of the past year's activities and the overall condition of the union. Still, he gave a final state of the union address to delegates at the Fall 2007 Delegate Assembly in Buffalo. Almost fifteen years after taking the presidency of a fiscally stressed organization, Scheuerman assured delegates that their union was in great financial condition, with a reserve fund approaching $6 million. UUP now had nearly 30,000 members, and member activism was at an all-time high. President Scheuerman summarized the union's political and contractual accomplishments[123] and noted that the constant changes in SUNY's leadership—a new chancellor almost every other year—created a political vacuum that UUP successfully filled. The departing president closed by repeating his familiar old mantra: the primary responsibility of UUP officers is to serve the interests of the union's members.[124]

The Scheuerman administration continued the practice started by President Nuala Drescher and expanded by Tim Reilly of making UUP committee appointments without regard to caucus affiliation. This tactic proved so successful that the oppositional Reform Caucus soon became more of a discussion group than a political organization. Nominations by the United Caucus essentially guaranteed election to UUP office. The disappearance of the Reform Caucus was not brought about simply by a policy of inclusiveness in committee appointments. The Scheuerman administration's social and cultural policies clearly demonstrated that the old divide between bread-and-butter unionism and a social-movement mentality were not mutually exclusive.

The Scheuerman administration did what all past UUP administrations had done: each previous administration had made UUP a stronger, more effective advocate for its members. Internal changes to UUP's governance structure helped pave the way for the Scheuerman administration to meet this obligation. Indeed, the 2001 constitutional amendment removing term limits proved to be a watershed in UUP's history. It allowed the union's leaders to develop productive relationships of trust and continuity with elected officials and bureaucrats alike.

After the removal of term limits the union reached new heights in the political arena, at the bargaining table, and at the chapter level, where local negotiations benefited the members. By the time Scheuerman resigned, UUP was at the apex of its power. The union had fulfilled its potential and was recognized throughout the higher-education community as the leading higher-education union in the United States. It's worth repeating what Bill Rock, a longtime UUP activist who attended the union's first Delegate Assembly, said during the 2001 debate over the removal of term limits. The union had matured, Rock observed, from its weak and tentative origins into "a marvelously strong organization fighting for everything that we believe in in higher education."[125] It was now up to future union leaders to build on the successes of the past to continue strengthening the union's ability to protect and serve its members.

Chapter 8

New Challenges and Future Prospects

The story of UUP is inextricably connected to the history of SUNY. Thanks in large part to the resistance of the state's private institutions of higher learning, New York was the last among the states to create a public university. When it finally did create SUNY in 1948, policymakers confirmed their commitment to the privates by making sure the new university would only supplement rather than compete with the privates. The establishment of SUNY and the state's treatment of its university ran against the trends of the time. Higher education in the post–WWII United States was undergoing a radical transformation. The GI Bill, the growth of the middle class, public reaction against institutionalized antisemitism, and the rise of a complex new economy demanding a more educated workforce all contributed to the expansion of higher-education institutions across the country. Spurred by growing enrollments, many evolved into mega-universities with multiple campuses. Faculty governance, long a feature of elite institutions, took on an expanding role in state schools as the practice of shared governance between faculty and campus managers matured.[1] SUNY was a notable exception to these growing trends.

On its creation and for more than a decade, SUNY was a second-rate institution. Most of its faculty lacked doctoral degrees, they generally had heavy teaching loads, and they had little interest in conducting serious research or time or institutional support for it. Faculty governance was virtually nonexistent, and the dean was second only to the omnipotent campus president in implementing a top-down management style that the vast majority of the faculty accepted. This all began to change after the election of Nelson Rockefeller, who poured hundreds of millions of dollars into SUNY to make it a first-rate university. Under Rockefeller's guidance, the university grew at warp speed. As a diverse population of postwar baby boomers approached college age, new buildings and campuses were constructed to meet their demand for higher education. The university recruited a more diverse, highly educated faculty, many holding doctoral degrees they had earned through the GI Bill. The prosperity of the Rockefeller years allowed campuses to offer faculty decent salaries, reasonable teaching loads, research opportunities, and the promise of promotions and job security. Rather than accept the heavy-handed management style of the past, the new faculty tended to value a university culture characterized by collegial relationships among scholars. The burgeoning new community of scholars questioned the authority of the university managers who gave the orders.

In 1967 state lawmakers responded to a series of public worker disputes by enacting the Taylor Law, legislation that gave public workers in New York the right to form a union. SUNY faculty and professional staff were ripe for unionizing. Many found the top-down management style unacceptable, but an abundance of state dollars papered over the faculties' frustration. When the flood of public dollars slowed down and almost dried up, most faculty members supported the formation of a collective bargaining agent. As described in chapter 2, after a series of iterations, conflicts, and false starts, SUNY faculty and professional staff formed the United University Professions. In 1973 the state certified what became UUP as the bargaining agent for all faculty and professional staff at the university's state-operated campuses. SUNY's faculty now had their own self-funded, independent organization with legal standing to protect and promote the interests of the faculty and professional staff.

Not surprisingly, the early years of the tenuous new organization were rife with conflict. UUP faced the prospect of bargaining for a single contract for a professionally diverse membership that ran the gamut from shepherd to brain surgeon and included everything in between.

Negotiating one contract to represent the interests of such diverse professional groups provoked conflict both internally and externally. CSEA, for example, challenged the new union's right to represent professional staff; doctors at the health science centers, unfavorably disposed toward the union and the role of clinical practice plans, sought a separate bargaining unit; supporters of the former SUFT and SPA factions of UUP remained at loggerheads. Staff resignations and massive retrenchments at the university, what one UUP activist characterized as a bloodbath, placed additional strains on the new union and its leaders. Lawrence DeLucia, UUP's first president, barely survived a vote of no confidence from the union's executive board and only avoided an impeachment vote by the union's delegates by announcing he would not seek reelection. Despite these conflicts and the general chaos that characterized the union's initial years, UUP negotiated a two-year settlement with the state that significantly improved the terms and conditions of members of the bargaining unit. In addition to negotiating across-the-board salary increases of 6.5 and 6.0 percent, UUP realized an important goal when it established a process for permanent appointment for nonteaching professionals.

The Wakshull administration continued to build on the foundation laid by DeLucia. Members benefited during Sam Wakshull's presidency through the contracts UUP negotiated with the state, contracts that provided members with significant raises annually. The contracts also established minimum salaries and added an additional new rank for librarians. On the political front, Wakshull expanded UUP's lobbying efforts, allowing a still-nascent union to take its first significant steps in the state's annual struggle for decent SUNY budgets. In fact, Wakshull arranged an historic "Save SUNY" day in which some 2,500–3,000 bargaining-unit members flooded Albany in a successful quest to save jobs and protect the university. Internally, the union grew stronger during Wakshull's tenure. After Governor Hugh Carey signed agency fee legislation into law in 1977, the union conducted a membership drive that tripled the number of members from about 2,000 to over 6,000. UUP also cemented its position as *the* union for SUNY by soundly beating back a representation challenge by the rival NEA. Nevertheless, internal unity and harmony were still in the distant future. The Wakshull years witnessed the rise of competing political caucuses within the union. Competition between the United Caucus and a breakaway group, the new Reform Caucus, led to internal struggles that sometimes diverted the leadership's energy and attention from the union's basic mission.

The union took major steps forward during the Nuala Drescher administration. UUP's political activities increased substantially. Weekly lobbying days were introduced, as was the "Friend of SUNY" award. The Morrisville decision resolved the issue of workload, and when the state tried to force UUP to reject the terms of the decision, the union successfully resisted. Yes, SUNY retrenched faculty, but cooperation between UUP and SUNY minimized the damage when the university terminated a number of unoccupied faculty lines. Labor-management committees assumed a major role in proving false the lie that unions bring mediocrity to higher-education institutions. These committees played an increasingly important role in sponsoring faculty research, travel, and participation in professional conferences. It was during the Drescher years that librarians became eligible to compete for labor-management research and travel grants. Through an astute use of the union's committee system, Drescher promoted the values of affirmative action and diversity. UUP took a leading role among unions in promoting these values. With issues of health and safety at the campuses becoming a concern, UUP took the then-radical step of hiring a health-and-safety officer to protect SUNY faculty from exposure to hazardous material on the campuses. In the waning years of the Dresher administration, the vice presidents' positions became full-time, allowing both the vice president for academics and the vice president for professionals to better serve the members. Thanks to the recent round of negotiations, the vice president for professionals faced a formidable task. That office would now focus on a new program that rationalized salaries and professional work obligations. These many actions signified the union's growing maturity and its increasing ability to serve its members effectively. Consequently, UUP gained a much broader base of support among bargaining-unit members.

Internally, during the Drescher years caucus competition grew more intense. Drescher responded to these political conflicts by appointing Reform Caucus delegates to key committee positions, thereby reducing the level of hostilities between the union's two political parties. She also brought fiscal stability to the union. A union cannot protect or effectively represent its members without sufficient financial resources. The cost of maintaining staff, waging legal battles, conducting elections, and keeping members informed via direct mailings and in-house publications are just a few of the many functions of a union requiring significant financial expenditures. On taking office Drescher learned that the union was, to put it bluntly, a financial mess. UUP's fiscal state was so bad that merchants would not accept its credit card. A series of fiscally responsible actions by the Drescher administration soon brought the union back to sound financial footing so it could meet its moral and legal obligations to its members.

By the time Tim Reilly took the leadership reins of UUP, the union was on solid financial and political ground. UUP's increasing effectiveness since its inception had created a strong base of support among its ever-growing membership. Reilly immediately built on this foundation when UUP and the state settled their contract negotiations in 1988 and its successor agreement in 1991. The new three-year agreement reached in 1988 contained a number of innovations. These trail-blazing changes circumvented the limitations imposed by the state's informal practice of pattern bargaining, a system in which all state unions generally receive the same wage and salary packages. The 1988–91 contract "buried" extra moneys inside the contract. In addition to decent across-the-board raises, there were location stipends to address the higher cost of living in downstate New York, and Excellence Awards as well as on-base awards for those with tenure or continuing appointment. The Excellence Awards also reinforced the union's long-term efforts to enrich the professional lives of faculty and professional staff, enhance the quality of education offered at the university, and make SUNY a first-rate institution of higher learning. Reilly's second contract (1991–95) was fiscally weak in that it failed to provide salary increases for two of the four years and terminated the Excellence Awards and the payments for those with tenure, but it cleverly pushed any plans SUNY had to negotiate additional parking fees down to the campus and chapter levels. While other state unions paid new parking fees, UUP's local negotiations blocked imposition of new fees, eventually forcing SUNY to give up its quest to use parking as a source of revenue.

The Reilly administration was also innovative in the political sphere, setting up a system of core lobbyists who traveled to Albany weekly. In an effort to reach the hearts and minds of legislators, Reilly also channeled many of UUP's resources to political advertisements. Unfortunately, the results were mixed at best. During the Reilly years, retrenchments were significant, and there was even talk of closing several campuses. The New York State Theatre Institute was retrenched at SUNY

Albany only to emerge as an independent entity and UUP's smallest chapter. But more than any of his predecessors, Reilly worked to promote union solidarity and bring UUP into the forefront of the higher-education labor movement. He increased the size of UUP's committees, allowing more members to participate in their deliberations. Building on Drescher's commitment to appoint Reform Caucus members to UUP's committees, Reilly's committee appointments cut across caucus lines as never before. Delegate assemblies became, in part, forums to discuss and pass resolutions on important social-justice and solidarity issues, often leading UUP to commit large sums of money in support of a myriad of different causes. Under Reilly's guidance, UUP published its vision for SUNY in the form of an impressively bound report entitled *SUNY's Future*. With the fiscal backing of UUP, President Reilly hosted a higher-education-oriented radio broadcast on public radio in nine states. Indeed, under Reilly UUP developed a public face. Unfortunately, the union's expenditures outstripped its revenues, and when Reilly left office, UUP was once again in a precarious fiscal position.

UUP reached a new level of maturity in 1993 when delegates elected Bill Scheuerman president with the backing of both caucuses. This scenario repeated itself seven more times. During the more than fourteen years of Scheuerman's administration, the union continued to serve its membership ever more effectively. But the new administration's first years were not easy. In a near–mirror image of the fiscal crunch President Drescher faced on taking office in 1981, Scheuerman took the reins of a fiscally unstable union and immediately began addressing the union's financial problems. Later, Brooklyn's Rowena Blackman-Stroud was elected treasurer in 1994, and the two formed a team that took the necessary steps to again restore UUP's fiscal solvency, including a healthy reserve fund. The administration also had to address potentially serious internal ethics issues. By bringing the ethical issues—officers' housing allowance, the use of chartered flights—to the executive board, the new administration signaled its commitment to openness and transparency. Consequently, the ethical concerns were resolved, and the administration gained the trust and support of members who had often complained of the appearance of impropriety.

Significantly, the Scheuerman administration took office just prior to the election of a fiscally conservative governor, who sought to cut SUNY's budget as never before. The term "crisis" is often overused and abused, much like the local store that has a perpetual going-out-of-business sale but never closes. But the early and mid nineties were days of real crisis for SUNY and the union. Not only did SUNY face massive layoffs from budget reductions, but on expiration of the 1991–95 contract, state negotiators sought an end to permanent appointments at the university. To further worsen matters, CSEA quickly accepted the terms of the agreement, and all the other statewide unions soon agreed to the state's outsourcing provisions. UUP stood alone in opposing outsourcing.

Now politically isolated from sibling unions and pressured by the state, UUP's new leaders viewed the crisis as an opportunity to strengthen the union and increase its ability to better serve the membership. The crisis worsened when the state refused to fund the union's Benefit Trust Fund. But UUP refused to yield, and its members stayed firmly behind the union, continuing to back its newly elected leaders. More rank-and-file members than ever before actively participated in the battle for a decent contract, a good state budget, and the restoration of the BTF. Finally, after years of constant struggle, UUP prevailed, becoming the only statewide union to escape outsourcing. This victory was not only a major coup for members of the bargaining unit, it sent a message to key political players in Albany that UUP had the strong backing of its membership. Support for the union during these difficult times is illustrated by the record turnout in the contract ratification vote on the 1995–99 agreement and the fact that about 95 percent of the voters supported the new agreement, still another record. As discussed in chapter 6 in great detail, the 1995 agreement included a number of innovations, which union leaders complemented by slyly slipping the union's life-insurance liabilities into the BTF without informing the newly elected governor. Over the years this has saved UUP millions of dollars. The three subsequent contracts with the state negotiated by the Scheuerman administration, including the 2007 agreement that was settled less than three weeks after Scheuerman's departure, all had annual salary hikes, as well as numerous other gains for both full- and part-time members. One such improvement came when chief negotiator Frederick Floss convinced state negotiators to assume the cost of UUP's college scholarships, a program earlier established by the Scheuerman team and financed through the BTF. UUP's members again set new records in the ratification vote, with 97.5 percent voting in favor of the new agreement.[2]

The union's delegates were apparently more than satisfied with the work of their elected officers. In 2001, after twice extending the number of terms an officer could serve, delegates removed the constitutional officers' term limits entirely. With continuity in office, UUP's president developed relationships of trust with the governor, legislators, and SUNY's leaders. The union prospered. In fact, during the Scheuerman years the union's political activities became almost as important as collective bargaining in enhancing members' interests. Taking a pragmatic approach to political action, UUP worked effectively with the governor, legislators of both political parties, campus presidents, and SUNY's chancellor. These cooperative efforts in the political sphere brought untold benefits to members of UUP's bargaining unit. Thanks to the union's political work, members had new job security protections and received extra contractual raises and a spate of other benefits described in chapter 6. As more members participated in union activities, VOTE-COPE contributions ballooned, increasing from $13,000 annually in 1993 to over $200,000 when Scheuerman left UUP in late 2007. The number of UUPers involved in core lobbying grew so much that the union organized lobbying days by campuses and constituent type. The union decided to hone its own political demands with precision and clarity and leave questions of tuition to student advocacy, thereby countering legislators' claims that they couldn't respond to the union's needs because they did not know what the union really wanted. UUP also improved its relationship with NYSUT and AFT, with its president eventually playing leading roles in both organizations. During the Scheuerman years UUP joined or created a number of new political entities, all designed to increase the union's political clout. UUP even worked more closely than ever before with colleagues in SUNY's Senate and entered a formal partnership with its former rival AAUP.

As UUP's political operation grew stronger, the union continued to successfully resist efforts to downsize SUNY and privatize its teaching hospitals. Important innovations suggested by NYSUT lobbyist Peter Martineau, including the no-layoff language in the Green Book, made retrenchments and layoffs a thing of the past, despite record-breaking cuts to the university. The use of the land-lease approach as a way to allow the university to use private moneys without infringing on the right of union representation, another Martineau idea, represented still another major breakthrough for UUP. The union's decision to focus on goals rather than getting bogged down in debates over budget numbers controlled by SUNY put UUP on the offensive and cleared the way for future political gains. And these gains came hard and fast, culminating in pension reform that gave UUPers what legislators characterized as two bites of the apple. The constant change of chancellors at SUNY, combined with the growing strength and political acumen of the union, catapulted UUP into the forefront of political struggles affecting the university. Indeed, the failure of SUNY's trustees to advocate for the university made it clear to legislators, the governor, and the public alike that UUP had become SUNY's leading and most effective advocate. The union, not SUNY's trustees, convinced legislators to provide funds for additional full-time faculty. UUP's political successes and close work with the legislature led a stream of SUNY's chancellors to ask the union for political assistance with the legislature. In return for the union's help, the university, under UUP's guidance, provided extra-contractual dollars to address a series of important issues, including salary inequities. SUNY's reliance on UUP's political might brought other benefits to UUP's members as well. For instance, after an arbitration decision on a Brockport workload case reversed the important Morrisville decision, SUNY gladly signed a Memorandum of Understanding (MOU) with UUP to maintain the status quo.

Following the removal of term limits it became clear that UUP had become the nation's leading higher-education union. Unions nationally and internationally looked to UUP for direction. UUP appeared to be everywhere. The union's research department, headed by Tom Kriger, prepared "best practice" documents for national distribution by AFT on such issues as online instruction and treatment of part-timers. Scheuerman regularly spoke at rallies and to the media throughout the United States and Europe. When the Academic Bill of Rights threatened to undercut free speech on campuses across the nation, UUP's president emerged as the higher-education labor movement's leading defender of free speech. UUP's ascension as the leading higher-education labor union did not happen overnight. It was the result of years of slow but steady progress by each union administration. From its unsteady origins in 1973 through the Scheuerman years to 2007, every UUP administration built on the previous one to improve the professional lives of its members. At this point UUP had become the intellectual reservoir of the American labor movement.

UUP's record of achievement shows just how effective a higher-education union can be in protecting and enhancing the professional lives of its members and in promoting the well-being of a public university. Is it realistic to expect this kind of success to continue? After all, times are changing, and the labor movement is under attack as never before since unions created the middle class in America.[3] After years of hemorrhaging members, unions today represent only 6.4 percent of workers in the private sector, down from about 33 percent in the 1950s.[4] The public sector is doing much better, with some 34.4 percent of public workers in unions.[5] But the public sector is facing a major squeeze now, too. In an era of tax cuts and tight state budgets, Tea Party governors such as Wisconsin's Scott Walker and his like-minded colleagues across the country promote the idea that public workers are overpaid and enjoy costly Cadillac healthcare plans, and pensions that taxpayers can no longer afford. More, their argument goes, when public workers do not get what they want at the bargaining table, they get it from state legislators they control through enormous campaign contributions. These anti-union governors claim to protect taxpayers by breaking public-sector unions. To worsen matters, the recent Supreme Court decision in the Janus case raises the possibility that UUP could lose a significant number of members and experience a sharp decline in dues revenue. If UUP's members believe that the 1 percent of their salary they pay in union dues is a good investment, the impact of the court's decision might be minimal. But that raises the question: what has the union done for me lately? Unfortunately, UUP's long history of progress and success ended in the years following Scheuerman's departure.

In a special election held in February 2008, UUP delegates elected UMU's Phillip Smith, a former UUP vice president of academics, to the presidency. Up to this juncture in its history, UUP always played a proactive role at the bargaining table and in the political arena. Smith changed that. The financial collapse of 2008 hit New York hard, creating a state budget deficit estimated at $1.7 billion for fiscal year 2009, $3.2 billion for 2010, and between $7 billion and $8 billion the following year.[6] Rather than resist massive budget cuts to SUNY and build public support for maintaining the university's workforce and educational mission, Smith decided, to use his words, to "hide in the grass."[7] In other words, UUP's president hoped that state budget cutters would not notice SUNY's several-hundred-million-dollar annual cost to taxpayers.

Hiding in the grass basically meant cutting back the union's political program and public persona. During Smith's term of office, UUP dissolved most of its political coalitions, terminated its partnership with AAUP, and watched the chair of AFT's PPC go to the head of the CUNY union. A community-college member became chair of the NYSUT Higher Education Committee. The New York State Higher Education Board was dissolved, along with the other coalitions and political organizations that UUP created or worked with to promote SUNY's interests. Smith also deemphasized the need for VOTE-COPE, downplayed core lobbying, and made no attempt to restore the important no-layoff language in the legislature's annual Green Book. With the decline in the union's political efforts, many UUPers were retrenched or nonrenewed for budgetary reasons; an entire UUP chapter, the Theatre Institute, was lost, and the closing of Stony Brook's Southampton campus was announced.[8] The latter was saved when a student group litigated against the closing, but UUP played no role in the litigation. Smith did not contest management's decision to close the campus; he merely had UUP staff inform faculty of their contractual rights and protections. SUNY also retrenched the twenty-four UUPers employed at the New York Network, and SUNY Downstate issued a three-phase plan to nonrenew temporary or probationary appointments at that campus.[9] Other SUNY campuses also announced retrenchments and nonrenewals. In short, Smith's strategy was not unlike that of the squid in Dreiser's *The Financier*: Every day a little boy passes a tank containing a lobster and a squid. The squid responds to the lobster's attacks by hiding in a cloud of ink. But every day the boy notices that different parts of the squid are missing until one day the squid isn't there at all. Hiding in the grass, hiding in the ink. Same strategy, similar results.

Despite Smith's efforts to minimize UUP's public persona, his administration received unprecedented negative publicity during the height of the faculty layoffs. A front-page story of the *Albany Times Union* blasted Smith and several other UUP officers for attending an annual benefits conference in Hawaii rather than participate in a faculty meeting at SUNY Albany to discuss retrenchments at that campus. Attendance at the conference was paid for by the union's Benefit Trust Fund,[10] but members viewed this junket as UUP officers using union dues to vacation in Hawaii while colleagues were losing their jobs.

The Smith team negotiated a contract during tough fiscal times. The new five-year agreement commencing in July, 2011, gave no raises for the first two years, a $500 on-base payment for the third year plus a 0.5 percent discretionary award not paid on base salary. Each of the last two years had a 2 percent on-base raise plus $250 on base in 2014, $500 on base in 2015, and 0.5 percent discretionary, again not on base. For 2016 the contract provided a 1 percent discretionary bonus that again did not go on base.[11] In the past, negotiated discretionary raises were usually added to the recipient's base salary. But Smith and his negotiations team, headed by Jamie Dangler of Cortland College, now opposed SUNY's practice of discretionary pay increases because they viewed discretionary pay as arbitrary and opposed it on principle. Once it became clear that a new agreement would have to contain discretionary moneys, union negotiators made an ideological point of demonstrating their opposition by insisting that discretionary moneys be paid as bonuses rather than on base salary. This decision to favor bonuses over on-base pay increases cost many UUPers thousands of dollars over the years. The new contract also reduced payments into the joint labor management committees, terminated the college scholarship program for UUP dependents, and raised the cost of health insurance premiums by 6 percent. Additionally, the state's Deficit Reduction Program initially held back nine days' pay from all bargaining unit members, eventually reimbursing them for seven of the nine.[12] After working without a new contract for almost two years, UUP members reluctantly approved the new agreement. Some 77 percent of voters supported the new contract, a drop of 20 percent from the approval rate of the previous (2007–2011) agreement.[13] At a meeting of the negotiations committee, Smith publicly commented that this was probably the worst contract in UUP history.[14]

Contract enforcement did not fare any better. After UUP won an important arbitration that would finally allow the union to contest SUNY's practice of suspending employees without pay in some disciplinary cases, Smith signed an MOU with SUNY that forfeited that right. Smith had initially directed NYSUT's director of staff Peter Martineau to sign the document, but after consulting with NYSUT counsel, Martineau refused.[15] Smith subsequently removed Martineau and replaced him with the assistant staff director Martin Coffey. NYSUT apparently disapproved of Smith's treatment of Martineau and decided to leave the assistant director's position vacant. This meant that UUP had lost a much-needed field-staff position that was essential to protect the contractual rights of its members. After Coffey retired several months later, Smith appointed a friend and officer colleague, John Marino, to the director's position. In announcing the appointment, Smith made no mention of Marino's qualifications, focusing instead on their close personal friendship.[16] Although he had no previous training, Marino was now in charge of a large, complex department that handled contract enforcement issues across the state.

Marino's appointment as staff director also raised an important ethical question. According to UUP's procedures, full-time officers who serve a minimum of four years are entitled to a paid UUP sabbatical leave to prepare for their return to a university setting. With the full support of Smith, Marino received his sabbatical pay without taking a sabbatical or preparing in any way to return to a university. Instead of returning to the university as UUP policy dictates, he assumed his new NYSUT position as UUP director of staff and was immediately placed on the NYSUT payroll.[17] Many delegates reacted strongly to this apparent violation of the union's rules and basic ethical values. One outspoken activist publicly suggested that spending over $80,000 in dues on Marino's nonexistent sabbatical was a conflict of interest and openly criticized Smith for cutting off discussion of the issue by declaring his questions out of order.[18] The ethical issue raised by Marino's sabbatical pay aside, Marino was just not prepared for the job. A GOER staffer even suggested that UUP was not well represented while the final language for the 2011–2016 contract was being written. Ray Haines, SUNY's attorney, wrote the language while Marino stood by in passive agreement. Several years later, Fred Kowal, who succeeded Smith as president, recognized his staff director's limitations by hiring an attorney to do most of the director's traditional work.

In 2013 Smith decided not to run for reelection. He was replaced by Fred Kowal of Cobleskill. Kowal has taken steps to reverse the union's precipitous decline. On taking office, the new president noted that "UUP had ceded our voice of political responsibility and had no presence or voice in the legislature."[19] Kowal took immediate action by reviving the core lobbying program and reestablishing UUP's now-moribund legislative and research departments. UUP also began to reestablish its national leadership role when Kowal was appointed chair of AFT's PPC. As noted previously, Kowal also hired an attorney to perform most of the staff director's functions. But there is much more to do. Since the protective language in the Green Book has not been restored, SUNY faculty still face budgetary layoffs.

Stalemated contract negotiations also increased the pressure on UUP. When the union's 2011–16 contract with the state expired in July 2016, union members had worked for a year and a half without a successor agreement. Bargaining-unit members did not receive any salary increases during this period. When the across-the-board salary hikes of the expired contract are factored in, SUNY faculty had received a total of $750 on base and a 4.0 percent salary increase over the past seven years. however meager these below-inflation-level raises were, they were mostly erased by the loss of two days' pay through the state's Deficit Reduction Plan, as well as the higher cost of health insurance. Fortunately, shortly after the contract's expiration, the Kowal administration entered into a new agreement with the state. The six year contract contains a lump sum payment of $600, and a 2 percent raise for each year, retroactive to 2016. It also provides for a 1 percent discretionary bonus for 2018, and 1 percent each additional year on salary base to be divided equally for discretionary salary increases and to address salary compression. UUP members overwhelmingly supported the contract with a favorable ratification vote approaching 98 percent.

Strong membership support for the new contract is encouraging in light of the weak performance of the Smith administration and the Court's decision in the case of *Janus v. American Federation of State, County and Municipal*

Employees.[20] The Janus ruling enables bargaining unit members to reap the benefits of collective bargaining without paying any dues and could lead to a mass exodus of dues-paying UUP members from a union that has struggled over the past several years. But there is some hope. The new contract is a step in the right direction. In cooperation with AFT, President Kowal recently established an Organizing Department to conduct an aggressive educational program that includes face-to-face meetings with rank-and-file members to remind them of the union's long record of achievement and effective representation. At this point in time, the program is just getting underway and its effectiveness is uncertain. But one issue is crystal clear: UUP's reaction to a negative decision will now determine its future well-being and, more importantly, that of the almost 40,000 members of the SUNY family that UUP represents.

Note on Sources

The principal source for research for this book was the United University Professions Records, which are housed at the University at Albany Library's M. E. Grenander Department of Special Collections and Archives. The volume of that collection is more than 161 cubic feet, and there are six reels of microfilm. The bulk of the material covers the years from 1964 to 2000. In addition, the Grenander Department holds the United University Professions Oral History Project, which consists of thirty-seven interviews recorded on audio tape and transcribed. Especially for the years after 2000, but also to some extent for earlier years, we have accessed some materials held by the UUP Administrative Office in Albany, NY, and records in the Faculty Senate Office at that location. Also consulted are some materials currently in the possession of William E. Scheuerman. Currently, arrangements are being made to transfer those files to the Grenander Department. We have also made use of papers at the New York State Archives and Records Administration in Albany. While we have found a fair amount of useful information there, current government regulations have prevented us from examining some of the files we would like to have seen. The New York State United Teachers Field Services Department Files at the Cornell University Library's Kheel Center for Labor-Management Documentation and Archives in Ithaca, NY, also have been consulted. The American Federation of Teachers' papers at the Walter Reuther Archives, Wayne State University, proved useful in providing leads for addition research into UUP's relationship with the AFT. Unfortunately, we were not able to access any of the records of the State University of New York, since they have yet to be processed in any way and are presently stored in a warehouse. We understand that negotiations currently are underway to have those materials transferred to an archival repository, most likely the New York State Archives.

Notes

Introduction

1. Ruth Milkman and Stephanie Luce, "The State of the Unions 2017: A Profile of Organized Labor in New York City, New York State, and the United States," The Joseph F. Murray Institute for Worker Education and Labor Studies, September 2017.

2. The literature on the decline of unions is voluminous. Important works include Stanley Aronowitz, "On the Future of American Labor," *Working USA* (Spring 2005), 271–91; Phillip Dine, *State of the Unions: How Labor Can Strengthen the Middle Class, Improve Our Economy and Regain Political Influence* (New York: McGraw-Hill, 2008); Bill Fletcher, Jr., and Fernando Gaspin, *Solidarity Divided* (Berkeley: University of California Press, 2008); Richard Hurd, "Contesting the Dinosaur Image: The Labor Movement's Search for a Future," *European Review of Labour and Research* 7 (Autumn 2001), 451–65; Kim Moody, *U.S. Labor in Trouble and Transition: The Failure of Reform from Above, the Promise of Revival from Below* (London: Verso, 2007).

3. "Union Members," News Release, Bureau of Labor Statistics, U.S. Department of Labor, January 19, 2018.

4. See: Center for State and Local Government Excellence and the National Institute on Retirement Security (NIRS), *Out of Balance? Comparing Public and Private Sector Compensation Over 20 Years*, Commissioned Report, April 2010.

5. Sid Plotkin and Bill Scheuerman, "The Tea Party Creams Labor," mronline. org.2011/05/05/the-tea-party-creams-labor.

6. Michael Hoover, "Ransacking the Public Sector: The Assault on Government Employee Unions," mronline.org/2017/07/07/ransacking-the-public-sector.

7. Mary Bottari, "Behind Janus: Documents Reveal Decade-Long Plot to Kill Public Sector Unions," *In These Times* (March 2018), inthesetimes.com/features/janus-supreme-court-unions-investigations.html.

8. Ibid.

9. Mark Gruenberg "Trump Administration Files Anti-Union Brief in Janus Case," USW Blog, December 19, 2017, www.usw.org/blog/2017/trump-administration-fles-anti-union-brief-in-janus-case.

10. Joe Davidson, "Trump Administration Escalates Attack on Federal Unions with One-Sided Agreement at Education," *Washington Post*, Power Post Perspective, March 16,

2018, www.washingtonpost.com/news/;powerpost/wp/2018/03/16/trump-adminstration-excalates-attack-on-federal-unions-with-one-sided-agreement-at-education.

Chapter 1: The State University of New York
Prior to Unionization

1. New York State Commission on Higher Education, "Meeting the Increased demand for Education in New York State: A Report to the Governor and the Board of Regents" (Albany: New York State Education Department, 1960). Hereafter called the Heald Commission report.

2. The literature is voluminous on this subject. See, for instance, Jeffery Stonecash, "Politics and the Development of the SUNY System: The Persisting of the Privates," unpublished manuscript, March 1991; Richard Scher, "The State and Private Colleges and Universities: The Politics of Private Higher Education in New York" (PhD diss., Columbia University, 1972); Oliver Carmichael, *New York Establishes a State University* (Nashville, TN: Vanderbilt University Press, 1955); T. Norman Hurd and Gerald Benjamin, eds., *Rockefeller in Retrospect: The Governor's New York Legacy* (Albany: The Nelson Rockefeller Institute of New York, 1989), 115–33; Robert Connery and Gerald Benjamin, *Rockefeller of New York: Executive Power in the State House* (Ithaca, NY: Cornell University Press, 1979); Judith Glazer, *Nelson Rockefeller and the Politics of Higher Education in New York State* (Albany, NY: The Nelson Rockefeller Institute of Government, 1989).

3. Roger L. Geiger, *The History of Higher Education: Learning Our Culture from the Founding to World War II* (Princeton, NJ: Princeton University Press, 2015). For a brief discussion of the role played by the church in eighteenth-century American higher education, see Jurgen Herbst, "The Eighteenth Century Split between Private and Public Higher Education in the United States," *History of Education Quarterly* 15 (Autumn 1975), 273–80.

4. Martin Fausold, "A Draft History of the State University of New York," 2, unpublished manuscript, 1988, M. E. Grenander Department of Special Collections and Archives, University at Albany, State University of New York, Martin L. Fausold Papers, Box 1, Folder 53–54.

5. Carmichael, *New York Establishes a State University*, 4.

6. Paul J. Scudiere, "A Historical Survey of State Financial Support of Private Higher Education in New York," (Ed. D. diss., State University of New York at Albany, 1975), 34–41.

7. Ibid., 40.

8. Stonecash, "Politics and Development of the SUNY System," 2.

9. Ibid.

10. Scudiere, "State Financial Support of Private Higher Education," 52–58.

11. Ibid., 70.

12. Todd Ottman, "Forging SUNY in New York's Political Cauldron," in *SUNY at Sixty: The Promise of the State University of New York*, eds. John B. Clark, W. Bruce Leslie, and Kenneth P. O'Brien (Albany, NY: SUNY Press, 2010), 16.

13. Ibid., 16–17.

14. Scudiere, "State Financial Support of Private Higher Education," 74.

15. Ottman, "Forging SUNY," 17.

16. Oliver C. Carmichael, "The Background of the State of New York," in "Addresses Given at the Organizational Meeting of the State University of New York, Hotel ten Eyck, Albany, N.Y." (April 4, 1949), 5. Cited in Glazer, *Nelson Rockefeller,* 3.

17. Stonecash, "Politics and Development of the SUNY System," 3.

18. For a good summary of the issue see Harold S. Wechsler, "The Temporary Commission Surveys Bias in Admissions," in *SUNY at Sixty,* 29–38.

19. Fausold, "History of the State University of New York," 16.

20. *United States President's Commission on Higher Education, Higher Education for American Democracy: A Report* (Washington, DC: US Government Printing Office, 1947).

21. Richard Norton Smith, *Thomas E. Dewey and His Times* (New York: Simon and Schuster, 1982), 47.

22. New York State. *Report of the Temporary Commission on the Need to Create a State University: February 16, 1948* (Albany: Williams Press, 1948).

23. Stonecash, "Politics and Development of the SUNY System," 5.

24. Connery and Benjamin, *Rockefeller of New York,* 298.

25. *Report of the Temporary Commission on the Need to Create a State University,* 18.

26. Glazer, *Nelson Rockefeller,* 3.

27. State University of New York. *Functions of a Modern University, Proceedings of the First Symposium Sponsored by the State University of New York, January 27–28, 1950,* 315.

28. State University of New York, Report Number 11. *Trends in Enrollments and Degrees Granted 1948–1970* (Albany: Central Staff Office of Institutional Research, January 1971), 68–70.

29. Glazer, *Nelson Rockefeller,* 3–4.

30. Freda R. H. Martins, "Concepts of State University of New York at Its Beginnings: 1947–1958," unpublished manuscript, September 1989.

31. Theodore C. Blegen, "The Harvest of Knowledge: A Report on the Research Problems and Potentials of the State University of New York" (Albany: Research Foundation of the State University of New York, 1957); also Nancy Diamond, "Documenting Research at SUNY University Centers: A Comparative Approach," in *SUNY at Sixty,* 159–70.

32. For a concise summary see Glazer, *Nelson Rockefeller.*

33. "Text of Inaugural Address," *New York Times,* January 2, 1959.

34. Benjamin and Hurd, eds., *Rockefeller in Retrospect,* 108.

35. Nelson A. Rockefeller, *Public Papers of Governor Nelson A. Rockefeller, Fifty-Third Governor of the State of New York* (Albany: State of New York, 1961), 475–78.

36. State University of New York Faculty Senate. "Faculty Senate Minutes," State University of New York, University Faculty Senate Collection, M. E. Grenander Department of Special Collections and Archives, University at Albany, State University of New York, October 24, 1960, box 1, folder 22, October 31. 1961, box 1, folder 24.

37. Gould Obituary by Wolfgang Sayon, *New York Times,* July 16, 1997.

38. Rockefeller's commitment to building the Albany mall and the expansion of physical facilities at the State University of New York led to comparison with the pharaohs building the pyramids. These comparisons were not always favorable and led

observers to comment on what they characterized as the governor's "edifice complex." A recent use of this term appears in Gerald Benjamin's review of Richard Norton Smith, *On His Own Terms: A Life of Nelson Rockefeller* in *Political Science Quarterly* 30 (Winter 2015–16), 777–78.

39. "1965–66 AAUP Grades and Percentages of Faculty with Doctorates in Units of State University of New York, Table 2," in "Final Report of the Subcommittee on Economic Growth of the Faculty Senate, June 15, 1966." Transcript, SUNY Faculty Senate.

40. Transcript, SUNY Faculty Senate Meeting, May 14–15, Bound Transcripts, Faculty Senate Office, SUNY Systems Administration, Albany, NY. (These transcripts are erroneously labeled "Minutes.")

41. Minutes, Special Meeting of SUNY Faculty Senate, February 20, 1965, University Faculty Senate Collection, series 1, box 1, folder 32.

42. Minutes, SUNY Faculty Senate Meeting, May 1955, ibid., box 1, folder 10.

43. Minutes, SUNY Faculty Senate Meeting, October 22–23, 1956, ibid., series 1, box 1, folder 12.

44. Minutes, SUNY Faculty Senate Meeting, 11–12 May 1959, ibid., box 1, folder 19.

45. *SUNY Faculty Senate Bulletin* 1 (April 1967), 1, Faculty Senate Office.

46. Fred Burelbach interview by Angelica Lewis, May 15, 1990, transcript of tape recording, 3–9, United University Professions Oral History Transcripts, Grenander Department of Special Collections and Archives, University at Albany, State University of New York. Note: All interviews in this collection were conducted by Angelica Lewis.

47. Robert DuBois interview, June 4, 1990, 2–3, UUP Oral History.

48. Henry Steck interview, March 2, 1990, 9, UUP Oral History.

49. Joseph Lamendola interview, October 13, 1990, 18, UUP Oral History.

50. Eugene Link interview, April 6, 1990, 12, UUP Oral History.

51. Dorothy Gutenkauf interview, July 20, 1990, 6, UUP Oral History.

52. Transcript, SUNY Faculty Senate Meeting, December 9, 1963, 5–7, Faculty Senate Office.

53. Ibid.

54. Transcript, SUNY Faculty Senate Meeting. June 15, 1966, 1–2, ibid.

55. Policies of the Board of Trustees, State University of New York, 1966, 1.

56. Donald E. Leon, "Is There Merit in the Merit System?" *SUNY Faculty Senate Bulletin* 1 (February 1967), 4–5, Faculty Senate Office.

57. In 1967, for instance, discretionary increase made up 60 percent of the total salary package.

58. *SUNY Faculty Senate Bulletin*, 1 (February 1967), 1, Faculty Senate Office.

59. Ibid., 5.

60. Transcript, SUNY Faculty Senate Meeting, November 3–4, 1967, 34, ibid.

61. Fred Burelbach interview, May 15, 1990, 9, UUP Oral History.

62. Donald E. Leon, "Is There Merit in the Merit System?" *SUNY Faculty Senate Bulletin* 1 (February 1967), 1–2, 8, Faculty Senate Office.

63. Steck interview, 7; Bruce Atkins interview, March 23, 1990, 13, UUP Oral History.

64. Robert Davidson interview, May 4, 1990, 2, UUP Oral History.

65. Transcript, SUNY Faculty Senate Meeting, February 6–7, 1970, 69–70, Faculty Senate Office.

66. Ibid., 193.

67. Minutes, SUNY Faculty Senate Meeting, October 22–23, 1956, ibid.

68. Minutes, Special Meeting of SUNY Faculty Senate, January 29, 1957, 1, ibid.

69. Ibid.

70. Transcript, SUNY Faculty Senate Meeting, November 23, 1959, 10, ibid.

71. Ibid.

72. Transcript, SUNY Faculty Senate Meeting, May 15–16, 1961, 12, ibid.

73. Ibid., 11–12.

74. Transcript, SUNY Faculty Senate, "Grievance Procedures for Professional Service Employees of State University," April 20, 1967, ibid.

75. Transcript, SUNY Faculty Senate Meeting, February 6–7, 1970, 206–12, 303–5, ibid.

76. "College Special Joint Personnel Committee of SUNY Faculty Senate, Report on Oswego," September 1, 1970, University Faculty Senate Collection; Grievance Committee, Box 1, Folder 1, p. 5, ibid.

77. Sam Wakshull interview, April 19, 1990, 7–8, UUP Oral History.

78. Ibid.

79. Transcript, SUNY Faculty Senate Meeting, February 6–7, 1970, 208, Faculty Senate Office.

80. Transcript, SUNY Faculty Senate Meeting, October 23, 1970, 28, ibid.

81. Transcript, SUNY Faculty Senate Meeting, December 10, 1963, 5, ibid.

82. Transcript, Faculty Senate Meeting, May 8–9, 1970, 87–81, 182–188, ibid.

83. Robert Hall interview, April 5, 1990, 2, UUP Oral History.

84. Josephine Weiss interview, March 22, 1990, 12; Thomas Matthews interview, May 3, 1990, 14; Robert Potter interview, March 15, 1990, 15, UUP Oral History.

85. Henry Geerken interview, May 4. 1990, 13, UUP Oral History.

86. Transcript, SUNY Faculty Senate Meeting, May 8–9, 1970, 230, Faculty Senate Office.

87. Minutes, SUNY Faculty Senate Meeting, November 8, 1954, Box 1, Folder 8, 4, University Faculty Senate Collection.

88. Transcript, SUNY Faculty Senate, October 24, 1960, 315, Faculty Senate Office.

89. Minutes, SUNY Faculty Senate, October 1955, Box 1, File 11, 3, University Faculty Senate Collection.

90. Morris Budin interview, October 12,1990, 15, UUP Oral History; see also Harvey Inventasch interview, March 1, 1990, 16, UUP Oral History.

91. Transcript, SUNY Faculty Senate Meeting, October 23, 1970, 40, Faculty Senate Office.

92. Transcript, SUNY Faculty Senate Meeting, February 5, 1971, 26, ibid.

93. Transcript, SUNY Faculty Senate Meeting, May 15–16, 1961, 17, ibid.

94. Judith Wishnia interview by William Scheuerman, January 31, 2013.

95. D. Jo Schaffer interview by William Scheuerman, May 4, 2013.

96. Akira Sonbonmatsu interview, October 12, 1990, 36, UUP Oral History.

97. Susan Puretz interview, March 23, 1990, 1, UUP Oral History.

98. Frank Ray interview, May 3, 1990, 27–28, UUP Oral History.

99. Paul Lauter interview, August 13, 1990, 7, UUP Oral History; Weiss interview, 3.

Chapter 2: The Right to Bargain Collectively 1967–73

1. A good summary of these events is to be found in chapter 9 of Jewel Bellush and Bernard Bellush, *Union Power and New York: Victor Gotbaum and District Council 37* (New York: Praeger, 1984).

2. The official title of the Taylor Law is "The Public Employees' Fair Employment Act and Article 4 of the New York State Civil Service Law."

3. Herman Doh, "Collective Bargaining in SUNY: The Story of the Senate Professional Association," *Journal of the College and University Personnel Association* 25 (January 1974), 23.

4. Joseph W. Garbarino, *Faculty Bargaining: Change and Conflict* (New York: McGraw-Hill, 1975), 17.

5. Kenneth P. Mortimer, "A Decade of Campus Bargaining: An Overview," in *Campus Bargaining at the Crossroads*, ed. Joel M. Douglas (New York: National Center for the Study of Collective Bargaining in Higher Education and the Professions, Baruch College, City University of New York, 1982), 97–102.

6. David J. King, *Collective Bargaining in Higher Education: Up the Creek or Down the Slippery Slope* (Washington, DC: Fund for the Improvement of Post Secondary Education, 1979).

7. Nuala McGann Drescher and Irwin H. Polishook, "Perspectives on the Development of Faculty Unions in the United States," *Journal of Tertiary Educational Administration* 7 (May 1986), 8.

8. Garbarino, *Faculty Bargaining*, 52–56.

9. Beverly T. Watkins, "Bargaining Rights Denied Professors at Boston University," *Chronicle of Higher Education* (July 11, 1984), 1; Mortimer, "Decade of Campus Bargaining," in *Campus Bargaining at the Crossroads*, 98–99.

10. Robert K. Carr and David K. Van Eyck, *Collective Bargaining Comes to the Campus* (Washington, DC: American Council on Education, 1973).

11. Robert E. Carnahan, "Faculty Attitudes of Alienation Related to Specific Professional and Environmental Characteristics in Higher Education: Collective Bargaining as a Consequence of These Attitudes and Characteristics," ERIC Document 225452 (1982).

12. Barbara A. Lee, "Governance at Unionized Four-Year Colleges: Effect on Decision-Making Structures," *Journal of Higher Education* 50 (1979), 565–85; Polishook, "Unions and Governance: The CUNY Experience," *Academe* 68 (January–February 1982), 15–17; Jack L. Nelson, "Collective Bargaining's Myths and Realities," ibid., 9–12.

13. Drescher and Polishook, "Perspectives on the Development of Faculty Unions," 13.

14. Philip G. Altbach, "Stark Realities: The Academic Profession in the 1980s," in *Higher Education in American Society*, eds. Philip G. Altbach and Robert O. Berdahl (Buffalo: Prometheus, 1981), 23–32; Garbarino, *Faculty Bargaining*, 157.

15. Garbarino, *Faculty Bargaining*, 17–18.

16. Clarence Taylor, *Reds at the Blackboard: Communism, Civil Rights and the New York City Teachers Union* (New York: Columbia University Press, 2011), 304–12.

17. Drescher and Polishook, "Perspectives on the Development of Faculty Unions," 8.

18. Verne A. Stadtman, "Happenings on the Way to the 1980s," in *Higher Education*, eds. Altbach and Berdahl, 101–10; American Association of University Professors,

"The Annual Report of the Economic Status of the Profession, 1983–84," *Academe* 70 (July–August 1984), 4.

19. Stadtman, "Happenings," 101–10.

20. Altbach, "Stark Realities," 221–38.

21. Ibid.; M. G. Scully, "Colleges, States Weigh Rules to Make Tenure Harder to Get, Easier to Lose," *Chronicle of Higher Education* (December 8, 1982), 1; C. S. Farrell, "They Took My Chair Away: Effect of Layoffs on Tenured Professors," ibid., 23; Ralph S. Brown, "Report on the Conference: Faculty and Higher Education in Hard Times," *Academe* 69 (January–February, 1983), 4–8.

22. J. Victor Baldridge and F. R. Kemerer, "Images of Governance: Collective Bargaining Versus Traditional Models," in *Governing Academic Organizations: New Problems, New Perspectives*, eds. Gary L. Riley and J. Victor Baldridge (Berkeley, CA: McCutchan, 1977), 257–68; Garbarino, *Faculty Bargaining*, 83–133; Beverly T. Watkins, "AAUP as a Union: The Tensions Endure," *Chronicle of Higher Education* (July 7, 1982), 1.

23. American Association of University Professors, "Statement on Collective Bargaining," *Academe* (September–October 1983), 142.

24. Robert Granger to Samuel Gould, January 9, 1970, United University Professions Records, subgroup III, series 3.1, box 5, folder 28, Grenander Department of Special Collections and Archives, University at Albany, State University of New York.

25. State University Professional Association, "Memorandum to All Members of the Non-Academic Professional Staff," n.d., UUP Oral History, series 3, box 2, file 47.

26. Neil Brown to Samuel Gould, January 8, 1979, ibid., subgroup III, series 3.1, box 5, folder 29.

27. Joel True testimony, "Transcript of Hearings," November 20, 1973, PERB, C-0091, box 57, 1394–96, New York State Archives.

28. Documents submitted by Richard Glasheen, spring 1990, UUP Oral History, series 3, box 2, file 47.

29. Terence N. Tice and Grace W. Holmes, eds., *Faculty Bargaining in the Seventies* (Ann Arbor, MI: Institute of Continuing Legal Education, 1973), 55; Carnegie Council on Policy Studies in Higher Education, *Faculty Bargaining in Public Higher Education: A Report and Two Essays* (San Francisco: Jossey-Bass, 1977), 82.

30. Robert Helsby interview by Ivan D. Steen, transcript of tape recording, December 11,1982, Ivan D. Steen Papers, box 4, folder 7, Grenander Department of Special Collections and Archives, University at Albany, State University of New York.

31. Henry L. Mason, "Faculty Unionism and University Governance," in *Encountering the Unionized University*, issue ed. Jack N. Schuster (San Francisco: Jossey-Bass, 1974), 1.

32. Wakshull interview, 5, UUP Oral History.

33. See Martin Fausold Papers, State University of New York at Geneseo Library and Archives for an overview of the FASUNY activities. Fausold was a long-term activist in the organization.

34. "Faculty Senate Brief," 34, Unit Determination Hearings, box 59, New York State Archives.

35. Doh, "Collective Bargaining," 23; "Faculty Senate Brief," 36.

36. "Faculty Senate Brief," 24–25.

37. Ibid., 25–29.

38. Ibid., 30.

39. Ibid.

40. Morgan D. Dowd to Gerald Hackman, October 11, 1968, UUP Records, subgroup II, series 2, box 5, folder 7.

41. Neil Brown to Samuel Gould, January 8, 1970, ibid., subgroup III, series 3.1, box 5, folder 2.

42. Jon K. LeGro, "Memorandum to All Faculty," December 19, 1968, ibid., subgroup II, series 2, box 5, file 7.

43. Ibid.

44. Eugene Link interview, April 6, 1990, 21, UUP Oral History.

45. "Employers Brief," 82, Unit Determination Hearings, box 59, New York State Archives.

46. PERB, C-0253, July 16, 1968, Stenographic Record, 40, PERB, New York State Archives, 17492–17.

47. Ibid.

48. Mason, "Faculty Unionism," 1.

49. Ibid., 44.

50. Ibid., 45.

51. PERB, C-0253, September 11, 1968, Stenographic Record, 880, New York State Archives, 17492–08.

52. Ibid., 875–993.

53. State University Federation of Teachers Brief, 12, New York State Archives, 17492-08, box 59.

54. Public Employment Relations Board of the State of New York, *Official Decisions, Opinions, and Related Matters* 2 (1969) 3492, Board Decisions, 2-3070.

55. PERB, C-0253, September 11, 1968, Stenographic Transcript, 874.

56. PERB, *Official Decisions* 2 (1969) 3492.

57. Ibid., 3494.

58. Jerome Lefkowitz, Brief, August 25, 1970, 19–21, New York State Archives, 17492-08, box 30, folder 3.

59. Samuel J. Wakshull, as *President, State University Federation of Teachers, v. Helsby, et al.*, ibid., box 30, folder 3.

60. Unit Determination Hearing, Stenographic Transcript, PERB, C-0253, 151819, New York State Archives.

61. G. A. Cahill to Board of Directors of FASUNY, December 19, 1968, UUP Records, subgroup II, series 2, box 5, folder 7.

62. "Letter to All Members of the Non-Academic Professional Staff" on State University Professional Association letterhead, n.d., UUP Oral History, series 3, box 2, folder 47.

63. State University Professional Association, Memorandum, February 28, 1970, ibid., subgroup III, series 3.1, box 5, folder 29.

64. Brown to Gould, January 8, 1970, ibid., subgroup III, series 3.1, box 5, folder 25.

65. Granger to Gould, January 9, 1970, ibid., subgroup III, series 3.1, box 5, folder 29.

66. Brown to Gould, January 8, 1970, ibid., subgroup III, series 3.1, box 5, folder 25.

67. Memorandum to Cortland Campus SUPA Members, February 21, 1970, ibid., subgroup III, series 3.1, box 5, folder 29.

68. "To All Members of the Non-Academic Professional Staff," on SUPA letterhead, n.d., research materials from John Valter, UUP Oral History, series 3, box 2, folder 47.

69. Granger to Non-Teaching Professionals, ibid.

70. Granger to Paul T. Burch, October 7, 1969, ibid., subgroup IV, series 6, box 2, folder 20.

71. Martin W. Finkin, AAUP Brief, March 7, 1969, 19, Unit Determination Hearings Transcript, New York State Archives, 1742-08, box 59.

72. Granger to Non-Teaching Professionals, January 19, 1970, UUP Records, subgroup III, series 3.1, box 5, folder 29.

73. Doh, "Collective Bargaining," 24.

74. Ibid.

75. Granger Memo, "Role of the NTP."

76. James Reidel to Robert Granger, November 21, 1968, ibid., subgroup III, series 3.1, box 5, folder 29; Reidel to Members of the University Faculty Senate, December 15, 1968.

77. Reidel to Members to the University Faculty Senate, December 25, 1968, ibid.

78. Ibid.

79. Senate Brief, Unit Determination Hearings, box 59, New York State Archives.

80. John M. Sherwig to Samuel B. Gould, May 4, 1967, Faculty Senate Office, SUNY Systems Administration.

81. "Governor's Committee Addressed," *Faculty Senate Bulletin* 3 (April 1969), 4, ibid.

82. Paul T. Burch to Shirley E. Wurz, October 1, 1960, UUP Records, subgroup IV, series 6, box 2, folder 20.

83. Sherwig to Members of the University Faculty Senate, August 12, 1969, Faculty Senate Office, SUNY Systems Administration.

84. Unit Determination Hearings Transcript, box 59, New York State Archives.

85. Report of Theodore Wenzl, CSEA Board of Directors Meeting Transcript, March 12, 1970, CSEA Records, series 1, reel 5, Grenander Department of Special Collections and Archives, University at Albany, State University of New York.

86. Ibid.

87. Ibid.

88. Robert Granger to SUPA Executive Committee, January 19, 1979, transmitting letter of Frank C. Erk to Neil Brown, January 16, 1970, UUP Records, subgroup III, series 3.1, box 8, folder 29.

89. Ibid.

90. SUPA Memorandum, February 28, 1970, UUP Records, subgroup III, series 3.1, box 5, folder 29.

91. Erk to Granger, March 27, 1970, Faculty Senate Office, SUNY Systems Administration.

92. Ibid.

93. Ibid.

94. Ibid.

95. Ralph J. Flynn to Dean Streiff, February 10, 1970, UUP Records, subgroup II, series 2, box 5, folder 8.

96. Ibid.

97. Doh, "Collective Bargaining," 24.

98. *SUPA Newsletter* 1 (September 1970), 4, research materials from John Valter, UUP Oral History, series 3, box 2, folder 49.

99. Granger to Non-Teaching Professionals, September 4, 1970, UUP Records, subgroup II, series 2, box 5, folder 8.

100. John Valter to SUPA Members, October 29, 1970, ibid.

101. Charles Santelli interview, April 4, 1990, UUP Oral History.

102. Granger to Non-Teaching Professionals, September 4, 1970, UUP Records, subgroup II, series 2, box 5, folder 8.

103. SPA Representative Council Meeting Minutes, October 10, 1970, UUP Records, subgroup II, series 2, box 5, folder 14.

104. Ibid.

105. SPA Offices Meeting Minutes, October 30, 1970, UUP Records, subgroup II, series 2, box 5, folder 14.

106. James H. Williams to Corbin Gwaltney, January 7, 1971, ibid., folder 11.

107. Philip Encinio to Charles Bob Simpson, January 25, 1972, UUP Records, subseries III, series 3, box 1, folder 4.

108. Doh, "Collective Bargaining," 25.

109. Santelli interview, 6, UUP Oral History.

110. Davidson interview, 11, ibid.

111. Atkins interview, 9, ibid.

112. James Stewart interview, February 26, 1990, 6, ibid.

113. Doh, "Collective Bargaining," 25.

114. SPA Representative Council Meeting Minutes, October 10, 1970, UUP Records, subgroup II, series 2 box 5, folder 14.

115. Board of Incorporators Meeting Minutes, July 10, 1970, ibid., folder 8.

116. SPA Officers Meeting Minutes, October 20, 1970, ibid., folder 14.

117. Ronald W. Bush to NYSTA Members, November 8, 1970, ibid., folder 8.

118. Conversation with Fred Miller, October 6, 2014. At the time of SPA's organization, Miller was the president of the SUNY-wide organization bringing together directors of university theater programs.

119. Robert Hart to Director of PERB, September 11, 1970, UUP Records, subgroup II, series 2, box 5, folder 11.

120. Robert Granger speech, Eastern Washington College, Spokane, Washington, November 5, 1971, ibid., folder 9.

121. Atkins interview, 7, UUP Oral History.

122. Doh, "Collective Bargaining," 25.

123. Granger to Ron Bush, Phil Encinio, and Robert Hart, December 8, 1970, UUP Records, subgroup II, series 2, box 5, folder 11.

124. Doh, "Collective Bargaining," 25.

125. Santelli interview, 6–7; Sanbonmatsu interview, 18, UUP Oral History.

126. Doh, "Collective Bargaining," 26.

127. SPA to SUNY Professional Staff, January 7, 1970. The votes were: SUFT, 3,287; SPA, 2,974; AAUP, 704; No Agent, 546; Ballots challenged or declared void, 600.

128. Drew, Report on Election Results, UUP Records, subgroup IV, series 6, box 2, folder 20.

129. Doh, "Collective Bargaining," 26.

130. PERB Certification of Senate Professional Association, January 28, 1971, UUP Records, subgroup IV, series 6, box 2, folder 20.

131. SPA to SUNY Professional Staff, December 30, 1970.

132. Santelli interview, 6–8, UUP Oral History.

133. Atkins interview, 11–13, ibid.

134. Robert Hart to "Colleague," September 4, 1970, UUP Records, subgroup II, series 2, box 5, folder 8.

135. Doh, "Collective Bargaining," 27.

136. Santelli interview, 32, 35, UUP Oral History.

137. Granger Speech at Eastern Washington College, November 5, 1971, 3, UUP Records, subgroup II, series 2, box 5, folder 9.

138. SPA Representative Council Meeting Minutes, May 22, 1971, ibid., folder 14.

139. Ibid.

140. Santelli interview, 32, UUP Oral History; Testimony of Robert Granger, Transcript of Hearing on Petition to Split the Unit, November 20, 1973, 368–69, PERB, C-0991, New York State Archives.

141. Santelli interview, 16–17.

142. Doh, "Collective Bargaining," 29.

143. Ibid., 31.

144. Robert Potter interview, 25, UUP Oral History.

145. Ibid., 29.

146. Santelli interview, 10, UUP Oral History.

147. Ibid., 10–11.

148. Testimony of Robert Granger, November 20, 1973, 04.

149. Ibid., 408–9.

150. Ibid., 423.

151. Doh, "Collective Bargaining," 31; Negotiations Committee Meeting Minutes, February 29, 1971, UUP Records, subgroup VI, series 1, box 1, folder 5.

152. Granger Speech at Eastern Washington College, November 5, 1971, 3, UUP Records, subgroup II, series 2, box 5, folder 9.

153. SPA Representative Council Meeting Minutes, May 22, 1971, ibid., folder 14.

154. "Outline of History of Negotiations with the Senate Professional Association," 1, SPA Exhibits, Legislative Hearing, July 6, 1973, New York State Archives, 17879-00, box 2.

155. SPA Newsletter (May 5, 1971), UUP Records, subgroup II, series 2, box 5, folder 12.

156. "Outline History of Negotiations with SPA," 1–2.

157. Ibid., 2.

158. "State University of New York Contract Leads the Way," Today's Education (reprint), UUP Records, subgroup II, series 2, box 5, folder 11.

159. Alfonsin interview, 186, UUP Oral History.

160. Josephine Wise interview, March 22, 1990, ibid.

161. Caesar J. Naples to Philip A. Encinio, December 28, 1971, UUP Records, subgroup VI, series 1, box 1, folder 5.

162. Doh, "Collective Bargaining," 33.

163. Cross-Examination of Robert Granger, Transcript of PERB Hearing C-0991, 899–900, New York State Archives, box 57.

164. Alfonsin interview, 186, UUP Oral History.

165. Burelbach interview, 26, ibid.

166. Drew interview, ibid.

167. Davidson interview, ibid.

168. Burelbach interview, 30–31, ibid.

169. Ibid., 32.

170. Doh, "Collective Bargaining," 33.

171. "Outline of History of Negotiations with SPA," 2–3.

172. Ibid., 3.

173. Santelli interview, 8, UUP Oral History.

174. "Outline of History of Negotiations with SPA," 4.

175. Doh, "Collective Bargaining," 38.

176. "Outline of History of Negotiations with SPA," 4.

177. Ibid.

178. Doh, "Collective Bargaining," 38.

179. "Outline of History of Negotiations with SPA," 5.

180. Medical and Dental Faculty Compensation Plans, State University of New York, Health Sciences Centers, Audit Report (AL-ST-54-81; NY-ST-13-8), working draft, August 20, 1982, 1 [Hereafter referred to as Draft Audit, 1982]. UUP Records, subgroup VI, series 2, box 1, folder 22; Letter transmitting the Draft Audit to Chancellor Clifton Wharton, ibid., folder 5.

181. Ibid.

182. A good insight into these years is to found in Connery and Benjamin, *Rockefeller of New York*.

183. "Resolutions of the Board of Trustees Pertinent to Medical Service Groups and Excerpts from the State Education Law," June 18, 1959, 3, UUP Records, subgroup III, series 3.1, box 5, folder 24.

184. Ibid., 2.

185. Ibid., 3.

186. Draft Audit, 1982, 9.

187. Chapter 246 of the Laws of 1972, subsection 2 of the Public Health Law.

188. Draft Audit, 1982, 3–5.

189. L. N. Young to Members of the Professional Staff at Cortland, January 30, 1971, UUP Records, subgroup II, series 1, box 1, folder 5.

190. Michael Horowitz to Drs. Beutner, Feldman, Glaseer, Levy, King, McNally, Sandler, and Tainter, January 27, 1971, ibid., series 2, box 5, folder 11.

191. SPA Negotiations Committee Meeting Minutes, February 5–7, 1971, ibid., subgroup VI, series 1, box 1, folder 5.

192. Doh, "Collective Bargaining," 32.

193. Valter, "Unit Determination in Higher Education," 22–23, 30, UUP Oral History, series 3, box 2, folder 49.

194. Encinio to Chapter Presidents, Executive Board, Representative Council, April 13, 1973, UUP Records, subgroup VI, series 1, box 1, folder 7.

195. SPA-GOER Agreement re: Clinical Practice, 1973–74, Appendix I, 3 January 1974, ibid., series 2, box 1, folder 17.

196. Draft Audit, 1982, 2.

197. SPA-GOER Agreement, appendix I.

198. Ibid., appendix III.

199. O. M. Lilien to "Colleagues," June 18, 1973, UUP Records, subgroup III, series 3.3, box 5, folder 24.

200. Lilien and Zebulon Taintor to Leonard Kershaw, December 5, 1973, ibid.

201. Letter transmitting Audit Report to Chancellor Wharton, 5, UUP Records, subgroup VI, series 2, box 1, folder 5.

202. Agreement on UUP Policy for Health Sciences Centers, May 16, 1975, ibid., folder 24.

203. Draft Audit, 1982, 3–4.

204. Ibid., 4–5.

205. Murray A. Gordon to Samuel Wakshull and Eli A. Friedman, December 4, 1975, UUP Records, subgroup VI, series 2, box 1, folder 18.

206. Draft Audit, 1982, 2.

207. Dennis Gaffney, *Teachers United: The Rise of New York State United Teachers* (Albany: SUNY Press, 2007), 50.

208. Ibid., 69–70.

209. Ibid., ch. 6;

210. Edward Wesnofske to SUFT Executive Board, February 14, 1973, UUP Records, subgroup IV, series 6, box 3, folder 12.

211. Doh, "Collective Bargaining," 35.

212. Atkins interview, 11, UUP Oral History.

213. Doh, "Collective Bargaining," 35.

214. Alfonsin interview, 27–28, UUP Oral History.

215. SUFT, "Membership Newsletter," n.d., UUP Records, subgroup IV, series 6, box 2, folder 20.

216. Atkins interview, 19, UUP Oral History.

217. Santelli interview, 37–38, ibid.

218. Wesnofske to SUFT Executive Board, February 14, 1973, UUP Records, subgroup IV, series 6, box 3, folder 12.

219. Doh, "Collective Bargaining," 35.

220. Alfonsin interview, 27, UUP Oral History.

221. Doh, "Collective Bargaining," 35–36.

222. Joseph Drew, Letter to Editor of the *Reporter*, March 1973, UUP Records, subgroup II, series 1, box 1, folder 12.

223. SPA Executive Board Meeting Minutes, January 1, 1973, ibid., series 2, box 5, folder 14; Doh, "Collective Bargaining," 36.

224. SUFT Executive Board Meeting Minutes, March 11, 1972, UUP Records, subgroup IV, series 6, box 2, folder 20.

225. Ibid.

226. Wesnofske to Granger, May 17, 1972, ibid., subgroup II, series 2, folder 10.

227. SUFT Executive Board Meeting Minutes, November 18, 1972, ibid., subgroup IV, series 6, box 2, folder 20.

228. SUFT, "Membership Newsletter," December 1972, ibid., subgroup II, series 2, box 5, folder 10.

229. Doh, "Collective Bargaining," 36. Doh suggests that the division was SUFT: 26, SPA: 58.

230. Alfonsin interview, 71–72, UUP Oral History.

231. Burelbach interview, 21, ibid.

232. Ibid., 20.

233. Ibid., 22.

234. Doh, "Collective Bargaining," 36–37.

235. Ibid., 37.

Chapter 3: The Emergence of United University Professions, 1973–81

1. Melvin H. Osterman to Robert B. Granger, May 15, 1973, UUP Records, subgroup II, series 2, box 4, folder 17; Edward Alfonsin interview, August 15, 1990, 230–31, UUP Oral History; Executive Board Meeting Minutes, July 13–14, 1973, February 8, 1974, UUP Records; Delegate Assembly Meeting Minutes, October 12, 197; PERB Decisions, Case Nos. C-40253/0260/0262/0263/0264/0351, February 21, 1974.

2. Lawrence DeLucia to Osterman, May 31, 1974, UUP Records, subgroup II, series 2, box 4, folder 17.

3. Osterman to Arthur Levitt, June 4, 1974, ibid.

4. Frederick J. Lambert to Leonard Kershaw, June 4, 1974, ibid.

5. Dorothy Gutenkauf to Chapter Presidents, June 13, 1974, ibid.

6. DeLucia and Patricia Buchalter to Members of the Bargaining Unit, July 27, 1973, ibid., subgroup II, series 2, box 6, folder 25.

7. Executive Board Meeting Minutes, August 11, 1973, UUP Records.

8. CSEA "Petition for Certification and Decertification," August 11, 1973, UUP Records, subgroup II, series 2, box 5, folder 27.

9. Paul E. Klein to James Roemer, October 1, 1973, ibid.

10. Klein to Roemer, Noel D. Cohen, and John Dean, October 10, 1973, ibid., subgroup II, series 2, box 4, folder 9.

11. Executive Board Meeting Minutes, October 12–13, 1973, UUP Records.

12. Martin Lapidus to AAUP Chapter Presidents in SUNY, December 20, 1973, UUP Records, subgroup II, series 2, box 5, folder 24.

13. Theodore C. Wenzl to SUNY Professionals, January 18, 1974, ibid., subgroup II, series 2, box 6, folder 25.

14. PERB Decision, Case No. C-0991, January 21, 1974.

15. Bargaining Proposal, March 17, 1976, UUP Records, subgroup II, series 2, box 5, folder 5.

16. SUNY-UNITED *Voice* (July 1973), ibid., subgroup II, series 2, box 8, folder 7.

17. Resolution from Stanley Goldstein, M.D., June 4, 1973, ibid., subgroup II, series 2, box 5, folder 5.

18. Executive Board Meeting Minutes, July 14, 1973, UUP Records.

19. Executive Board Meeting Minutes, August 10, 1973, UUP Records.

20. Charles S. Lipani to DeLucia, July 25, 1973, ibid., subgroup II, series 2, box 8, folder 7.

21. Executive Board Meeting Minutes, September 14, 1973, UUP Records.

22. Doris Knudsen to O. M. Lilie, S. Goldstein, S. Jonas, Z. Tainter, C. Lipani, September 28, 1973, UUP Records, subgroup II, series 2, box 8, folder 7; Knudsen to DeLucia, Medical Caucus Negotiators, Chapter Presidents of Health Sciences Center, December 3, 1973, ibid.

23. John J. Valter to Janet Axelrod, November 1, 1973, ibid., subgroup II series 2, box 5, folder 5.

24. Valter to DeLucia, November 1, 1973, ibid.

25. Executive Board Meeting Minutes, November 10, 1973, UUP Records.

26. Executive Board Meeting Minutes, January 19, 1974, ibid.

27. Executive Board Meeting Minutes, May 10, 1974, ibid.

28. Delegate Assembly Meeting Minutes, May 9, 1975, ibid.

29. Executive Board Meeting Minutes, October 25, 1974, ibid.

30. Eli A. Friedman to DeLucia, November 12, 1974, UUP Records, subgroup II, series 2, box 5, folder 5.

31. Leland Marsh to DeLucia, November 18, 1974, ibid.

32. DeLucia to Friedman, November 21, 1974, ibid.

33. Gutenkauf to Friedman, November 27, 1974, ibid.

34. Gutenkauf to Marsh, November 30, 1974, ibid.

35. Negotiations Committee Minutes, December 12, 1974, ibid., subgroup VI, series 1, box 1, folder 15.

36. Executive Board Meeting Minutes, December 13, 1974, UUP Records.

37. Gutenkauf to Health Sciences Centers Chapter Presidents, May 11, 1975, ibid., subgroup II, series 2, box 5, folder 5.

38. Report and Recommendation of Fact-Finding Panel of Public Employment Relations Board, May 18, 1973, ibid., subgroup VI, series 1.1, box 1, folder 7.

39. Message from Gov. Nelson A. Rockefeller to the New York State Legislature, May 22, 1973, ibid.

40. DeLucia to Harold Newman, May 24, 1973, ibid.

41. John E. Kingston to Malcolm Wilson, Labor Relations Subject Files, U50/2, Office of Employee Relations Papers, 17879-00, New York State Archives.

42. Kenneth M. MacKenzie to Presidents, State University of New York, March 21, 1974, ibid.

43. President's Report, Delegate Assembly Meeting Minutes, May 10–11, 1974, UUP Records.

44. DeLucia to Marsh, June 5, 1973, ibid., subgroup VI, series 1.1, box 1, folder 7.

45. Marsh to Negotiation Committee Members, July 31, 1973, ibid., folder 14.

46. Gutenkauf to Chapter Presidents, August 28, 1973, ibid.

47. DeLucia to Marsh, August 16, 1973, ibid.

48. DeLucia to Osterman, October 11, 1973, ibid.

49. Osterman to DeLucia, October 24, 1973, ibid.

50. DeLucia to Osterman, November 8, 1973, ibid.

51. DeLucia to Fred Lambert, November 13, 1973, ibid.

52. DeLucia to Negotiating Team, January 26, 1974, ibid., folder 15.

53. Alfonson interview, 103–4,186–87, UUP Oral History.

54. Caesar J. Naples to Presidents, State University of New York, Presidents, Community Colleges, May 8, 1974, UUP Records, subgroup II, series 2, box 2, folder 8.

55. Lapidus to Paul Smith, January 27, 1975, ibid., box 1, folder 40.

56. Executive Board Meeting Minutes, June 21, 1974, UUP Records.

57. President's Report, Delegate Assembly Meeting Minutes, October 12–13, 1973, ibid.

58. Gutenkauf interview, 93–94, UUP Oral History.

59. Doris Knudsen interview, May 25, 1990, ibid.

60. See, for example, interviews with: Alfonsin, 83; Inventasch, 24; Robert Potter, 26–27; Burelbach, 24; Lauter, 55, ibid.

61. DeLucia to Joseph Drew, September 16, 1973, UUP Records, subgroup II, series 2, box 3, folder 17.

62. Richard Hyse to Budget Committee, September 19, 1973, ibid.

63. Drew to All Budget Committee Members, September 25, 1973, ibid.

64. DeLucia to Drew, September 26, 1973, ibid.

65. Executive Board Meeting Minutes, October 12, 1973, UUP Records.

66. See, for example, interviews with Joseph Drew, June 4, 1990, 24; Burelbach, 33; Knudsen, 50–52, UUP Oral History.

67. Executive Board Meeting Minutes, January 31, 1975, UUP Records.

68. Delegate Assembly Meeting Minutes, May 10, 1975, ibid.

69. See, for example, interviews with Burelbach, 24; Lauter, 56; Sanbonmatsu, 30–31; Wakshull, 31–32, UUP Oral History.

70. *New York Times*, July 14, 1975.

71. DeLucia to Dear Colleague, March 31, 1975, subgroup II, series 2, box 3, folder 22, UUP Records.

72. *New York Times*, July 14, 1975.

73. "New York State Assembly Standing Committee on Higher Education Retrenchment Report," subgroup IV, series 7, box 6, folder 40, UUP Records.

74. 1974–1976 Agreement between the State of New York and United University Professions, Inc., 37.

75. "Assembly Retrenchment Report."

76. Ibid.

77. Alfonsin interview, 102, UUP Oral History.

78. "Assembly Retrenchment Report."

79. Wakshull interview, 35, UUP Oral History.

80. Interviews with: Nuala Drescher, September 13, 1990, 59; Matthews, 12; Drew, 32, 34–35; Robert Potter, 30–31; Wakshull, 44, UUP Oral History.

81. Wakshull interview, 35, ibid.

82. Jim Conti to Field Representatives that Service UUP Chapters, May 5, 1977, Field Services Department Files, New York State United Teachers Records, Martin P. Catherwood Library, Kheel Center for Labor-Management Documentation and Archives, Cornell University.

83. Tony Ficcio to Jim Conti, May 5, 1977, ibid.

84. Coordinator's Meeting, July 19, 1977, ibid.

85. Executive Board Meeting Minutes, September 16, 1977, UUP Records.

86. Coordinator's Meeting, November 29, 1977, Field Services Department Files, NYSUT Records.

87. Wakshull interview, 41, UUP Oral History.

88. Knudsen interview, 77–78, ibid.

89. Coordinators Meeting, April 5, 1975, Field Services Department Files, NYSUT Records.

90. Gaffney, *Teachers United*, 135–42; "Report to the Membership of UUP from Ed Alfonsin, Secretary," March 22, 1976, subgroup III, series 3, box 1, folder 23, UUP Records.

91. President's Report, Delegate Assembly Meeting Minutes, October 8, 1976, UUP Records.

92. Fred Lambert to UUP-Assigned Field Representatives, January 14, 1977, Field Services Department Files, NYSUT Records.

93. Executive Board Meetings Minutes, January 14, 1977, UUP Records.

94. Wakshull to Donald Wollett, March 8, 1977, subgroup VII, series 1, box 1, folder 18, UUP Records.

95. Wakshull to Wollett, March 10, 11, 16, 1977, ibid.

96. Wakshull to Wollett, March 16, March 30, 1977, ibid.

97. SUNY AAUP Representation Committee to Dear Colleague, April 4, 1977, ibid., subgroup III, series 3, box 1, folder 1.

98. Hartmann to Kershaw, April 13, 1977, ibid., subgroup VII, series 1, box 1, folder 11.

99. Hartmann to Kershaw, April 18, 1977, ibid.

100. See, for example: Wakshull to Kershaw, May 24, 1977, ibid; Hartmann to Kershaw, ibid., folder 12.

101. Kershaw to Jerome B. Komisar, September 21, 1977, ibid.

102. Ibid., subgroup III, series 3, box 1, folders 1 and 2.

103. Executive Board Meeting Minutes, March 10, 1978, UUP Records.

104. Morton S. Baratz to Wakshull, April 18, 1978, UUP Records, subgroup III, series 3, box 1, folder 1.

105. Executive Board Meeting Minutes, May 5, 1978, UUP Records.

106. Executive Board Meeting Minutes, June 3, 1978, ibid.

107. Louis Harris and Associates, "A Study of the Attitudes of the SUNY Staff toward Collective Bargaining and UUP Representation," June 1978, Field Services Department Files, NYSUT Records.

108. NYEA Petition, August 8, 1978, UUP Records, subgroup III, series 3, box 1, folder 25.

109. Charles Baker and Associates to Strategy Team, August 11, 1978, Field Services Department Files, NYSUT Records.

110. NYEA Steering Committee to Wakshull, September 14, 1978, ibid.

111. NYEA to SUNY Staff, September 15, 1978, UUP Records, subgroup III, series 3, box 1, folder 23.

112. Charles Baker to "Inner Circle," September 21, 1978, Field Services Department Files, NYSUT Records.

113. UUP Press Release, September 21, 1978, UUP Records, subgroup III, series 3, box 1, folder 25.

114. Baker to "Inner Circle," September 21, 1978, Field services Department Files, NYSUT Records.

115. Wakshull to Harvey Milowe, October 31, 1978, ibid.

116. Jeffrey M. Selchick to John M. Crotty, November 2, 1978, ibid.

117. Albert Shanker, "Where We Stand," *New York Times*, November 19, 1978.

118. Damon Stetson, "Vote at State U. Shortly to Test 2 Rival Unions," *New York Times*, November 24, 1978.

119. Shanker, "Where We Stand," *New York Times*, December 3, 1978.

120. *New York Times*, December 23,1978.

121. See, for example, interviews with Knudsen, Alfonsin, and Drew, UUP Oral History.

122. Lauter interview, 86, ibid.

123. Inventasch interview, 35–36, ibid.

124. Ibid., 36–38; Alfonsin interview, 202–3, UUP Oral History.

125. Inventasch to Chapter Presidents, October 17, 1975, UUP Records, subgroup VI, series 1, box 1, folder 27.

126. Agenda for October 7, 1975, Meeting of SUNY Negotiations Advisory Committee, OER Papers, 16223-91A, box 8, New York State Archives.

127. Agenda for November 3 Meeting of SUNY Negotiations Committee, ibid.

128. Kershaw to SUNY Negotiations Committee, December 2, 1975, ibid.; UUP "Negotiations Bulletin," No. 1 UUP Records, subgroup III, series 3.1, box 4, folder 24.

129. UUP Conceptual Proposals, OER Papers, 16223-91A, box 8.

130. UUP Direct Compensation Demand, UUP Records, subgroup VI, series 1, box 3, folder 14.

131. Employee Insurance Section to OER, March 29, 1976; Thomas J. Peterson, Jr., to Kershaw, March 25, 1976; Peterson to Kershaw, April 2, 1976; Kershaw to Wollett, April 6, 1976, OER Papers, 16223-91A, Box 8, New York State Archives.

132. UUP Records, subgroup VI, box 2, folders 2, 3, 4.

133. Conti to Coordinators, Field Services Department files, NYSUT Records.

134. Wakshull interview, 38, UUP Oral History.

135. Ernest Boyer, Memorandum to Presidents, June 29, 1976, UUP Records, subgroup VI, series 1, box 1, folder 33.

136. "State Walks Out of Negotiations Meeting," ibid., box 2, folder 4.

137. UUP "Negotiations Update," November 8, 1976, ibid.

138. *The Voice* 5 (December 20, 1976), 3, 6, UUP Records, subgroup VII, series 2, box 5, folder 5.

139. Ibid., 5 (March 1977).

140. 1977–1979 Agreement between the State of New York and United University Professions, Inc.

141. Ibid.

142. Inventasch interview, 44–46, UUP Oral History.

143. Drescher interview, 62, ibid.

144. State's Negotiation Notes, November 1, 1977, OER Papers, 16223-91A, box 8, New York State Archives.

145. Ibid., December 7, 1977.

146. Ibid., December 14, 1977.

147. Ibid., January 11, January 25, 1977; Wakshull to All members of the UUP bargaining unit, January 25, 1977, UUP Records, subgroup VI, series 1, box 3, folder 24A.

148. Delegate Assembly Meeting Minutes, February 4, 1978, UUP Records.

149. UUP "Negotiations Bulletin," March 18, 1978, UUP Records, subgroup VI, series 1, box 3 folder 24A.

150. State's Negotiations Notes, February 22, 8, 15, March 29, 4, 20, April 27, 1978, OER Papers, 16223-91A, box 8, New York State Archives.

151. Delegate Assembly Meeting Minutes, May 6, 1978, UUP Records.

152. UUP "Negotiations Bulletin," May 18, 1978, UUP Records, subgroup VI, series 1, box 3, folder 24A.

153. State's Negotiations Notes, June 7, 8, 1978, OER Papers, 16223-91A, box 8, New York State Archives.

154. UUP "Negotiations Bulletin," June 9, 1978, UUP Records, subgroup VI, series 1, box 3, folder 24A.

155. UUP News Release, July 15, 1978, ibid., subgroup VIII, series 2A, box 1, folder 1.

156. Wakshull to Meyer S. Frucher, January 19, 1979, UUP Records, subgroup VII, series 1, box 1, folder 5; Frucher to Wakshull, January 23, 1979, ibid.

157. Executive Board Meeting Minutes, April 6, 1979, UUP Records.

158. UUP "Leadership Bulletin," May 10, 1979, UUP Records, subgroup IV, series 6.1, box 2, folder 9.

159. UUP "Negotiations Bulletin," May 31, 1979, ibid., subgroup VI, series 1, box 3, folder 24A.

160. UUP "Negotiations Bulletin," June 1, 1979, ibid.; State of New York, Governor's Office of Employee Relations, Press Release, June 1, 1979, UUP Records, subgroup VI, series 1, box 3, folder 22.

161. Executive Board Special Meeting Minutes, June 7, 1979, UUP Records.

162. Sharon Villines to Dear Colleague, July 3, 1979, UUP Records, subgroup IV, series 6.1, box 2, folder 21.

163. UUP "Leadership Bulletin," July 10, 1979, ibid., subgroup VIII, series 2A, box 1, folder 1.

164. Executive Board Meeting Minutes, July 13, 1973, UUP Records.

165. Delegate Assembly Meeting Minutes, September 21, 1974, ibid.

166. Wakshull to Chapter Presidents, Executive Board and Legislative Committee, January 24, 1977, UUP Records, subgroup III, series 3.1, box 7, folder 1.

167. Delegate Assembly Meeting Minutes, February 5, 1977, UUP Records.

168. Legislation Committee Report, Delegate Assembly Meeting Minutes, May 6–7, 1977; Wakshull to "All UUP Representatives," March 7, 1977, UUP Records, subgroup II, series 2, box 5 folder 21.

169. Executive Board Meeting Minutes, February 1, 1979, UUP Records.

170. Report of the Legislation Committee, Fall Delegate Assembly, October 5–6, 1979, UUP Records, subgroup IV, series 6.1, box 1, folder 8.

171. Michael Finnerty to Clifton R. Wharton, Jr., November 27, 1979, UUP Records, subgroup III, series 3.1, box 5, folder 23.

172. Wharton to Finnerty, November 29, 1979, ibid.

173. Wharton to Hugh Carey, December 16, 1979, ibid., box 6, folder 1.

174. Wakshull to Dear Colleague, December 19, 1979, ibid.

175. UUP and SASU Joint Press Release, January 11, 1980, ibid., box 5, folder 23.

176. Executive Board Meeting Minutes, January 31, 1980, UUP Records.

177. UUP News Release, February 25, 1980, UUP Records, subgroup VIII, series 2A, box 1, folder 1.

178. Executive Board Meeting Minutes, April 11, 1980, UUP Records.

179. *New York Times*, April 29, 1980.

180. Delegate Assembly Meeting Minutes, May 9, 1980, UUP Records.

181. Stanley Fink to Wakshull, May 12, 1980, UUP Records, subgroup III, series 3.1, box 5, folder 22.

182. Alan Shank interview, March 2, 1990, 8, UUP Oral History.

183. Malcolm A. Nelson interview, March 23, 1990, 20, ibid.

184. Delegate Assembly Meeting Minutes, May 7, 1977, UUP Records.

185. Delegate Assembly Meeting Minutes, May 6, 1979, ibid., Diane Cimineli interview, May 4, 1990, 14–15, UUP Oral History

186. Nelson interview, 27; Puretz interview, 23–24; Elizabeth Tiger interview, March 22, 1990, 5–6; William Cozort interview, May 4, 1990, 3, UUP Oral History.

187. Nelson interview, 26; Cozort interview, 5; Alfonsin interview, 142–43; John Crary interview, October 13, 1990, 10, ibid.

188. Nelson interview, 26, ibid.

189. Delegate Assembly Meeting Minutes, May 10, 1980, UUP Records.

190. Cozort interview, 42–43, UUP Oral History.

191. Delegate Assembly Meeting Minutes, May 9, 1981, UUP Records.

Chapter 4: Organizational Structure, Internal Disagreement, Innovation, and Growth, 1981–87

1. *The Voice*, April 1983, 1.

2. Nuala McGann Drescher to Herbert Magidson, May 13, 1983, UUP Records, subgroup III, series 4, box 3, folder 2.

3. *The Voice*, October 1981, 1.

4. Drescher to Louis Stollar, May 26, 1985, UUP Records, subgroup III, series 4, box 5, folder 8.

5. Larry Flood to Drescher, n.d., ibid., series 7, box 5, folder 13.

6. *The Voice*, June 1985, 2; Drescher to John Pohlmann, March 11, 1986, UUP Records, subgroup IV, series 7, box 1, folder 10; Joseph G. Flynn to Drescher, March 18, 1985, ibid., box 2, folder 2.

7. Winter 1982 Delegate Assembly Meeting Transcript, 32, UUP Records.

8. *The Voice*, March 1982, 6.

9. Drescher to Patricia Koenig, July 1, 1981, UUP Records, subgroup III, series 4, box 2, folder 14; Drescher to Jerome B. Komisar, November 5, 1984, ibid., folder 8.

10. Bernard F. Ashe to Drescher, October 9, 1986, ibid., series 7, box 5, folder 16.

11. Ibid., series 4, box 5, folders 12–13; Drescher to Jeff Osinski, May 28, 1985, ibid., series 7, box 5, folder 16.

12. Drescher to Clifton R. Wharton, November 10, 1983, ibid., series 4, box 5, folder 16; *The Voice*, April 1985, 3.

13. Drescher to Edward Koch, December 9, 1981, UUP Records, subgroup III, series 4, box 2, folder 22. Similar letters were sent to all members of the state legislature.

14. Drescher, Testimony re: Day Care, ibid., box 1, folder 9.

15. *The Voice*, May 1985, 8.

16. Sanbonmatsu interview, 36, UUP Oral History.

17. Fall 1986 Delegate Assembly Meeting Transcript, 29–44, UUP Records; Drescher to Pohlmann, March 13, 1986, ibid., subgroup IV, series 7, box 1, folder 10.

18. Fall 1983 Delegate Assembly Meeting Transcript, 12, UUP Records.

19. *The Voice*, May 1985, 5.

20. "Campaign Statement of Paul Lauter," *The Voice*, March 1981, 1.

21. Lauter interview, 63–65, UUP Oral History.

22. Jill Marie Andia, "GSEU Contends UUP Is Bidding for GAs and TAs," *University at Buffalo Reporter*, December 5, 1985, 1; Winter 1985 Delegate Assembly Meeting Transcript, 78, UUP Records.

23. Winter 1982 Delegate Assembly Meeting Transcript, 5, ibid.

24. Spring 1981 Delegate Assembly Meeting Transcript, 64, ibid.; *The Voice*, March 1982, 6.

25. Winter 1982 Delegate Assembly Meeting Transcript, 18–20, 46, 61, UUP Records.

26. Jerome Lefkowitz to Ashe, UUP Records, subgroup III, series 4, box 3, folder 18; Drescher to "Dear Colleague," June 25, 1982, ibid., subgroup IV, series 7, box 1, folder 20; "Faculty Union Faces Insurance Refunds," *Albany Times Union*, June 24, 1982 (copy), ibid.

27. Winter 1983 Delegate Assembly Meeting Transcript, 111, UUP Records.

28. Fall 1982 Delegate Assembly Meeting Transcript, 5, ibid.

29. *The Voice*, March 1982, 6; Treasurer's Report, Spring 1983 Delegate Assembly Meeting Transcript, 2, UUP Records; *Albany Knickerbocker News*, April 2, 1982.

30. Spring 1985 Delegate Assembly Meeting Transcript, 29, UUP Records; *The Voice*, March 1985, 8.

31. Drescher to Chapter Presidents, Executive Board, March 24, 1987, UUP Records, subgroup IIIA, series 1, box 1, folder 2.

32. *The Voice*, October 1981, 3; ibid., December 1981, 19; Joyce Y. Villa to Evelyn Hartmann, January 1983, UUP Records, subgroup IV, series 6, box 2, folder 7.

33. Drescher, Testimony at Board of Trustees Hearing, October 9, 1982, Canton, NY, ibid., subgroup III, series 4, box 2, folder 25.

34. Richard Benedetto, "Political Hardball over SUNY Budget," *Empire State Report* 15 March 1982, 12.

35. Winter Delegate Assembly Meeting Transcript, 2, UUP Records.

36. *The Voice*, January 1982, 1; ibid., April 1982, 2; Winter 1982 Delegate Assembly Meeting Transcript, 17, UUP Records.

37. *The Voice*, March 1982, 3; ibid., April 1982, 10–11.

38. Winter 1982 Delegate Assembly Meeting Transcript, 20, UUP Records.

39. Willis H. Stephens, "SUNY: 1975–1982: A Budgetary Battle of Access versus Quality," UUP Records, subgroup III, series 4, box 4, folder 2; Winter 1982 Delegate Assembly Meeting Transcript, 21, UUP Records.

40. Drescher to Charles Hansen, October 20, 1982, ibid., subgroup III, series 4, box 2, folder 7. Similar letters were sent to Paul Lauter, David Nielsen, AFT's senior member of the higher education department, Bernard Ashe, a labor attorney from NYSUT and others from the affiliates with special expertise in negotiation of higher education contracts.

41. Winter 1982 Delegate Assembly Meeting Transcript, 14–30, UUP Records; Report of the Negotiations Committee, 30–32, ibid.; *The Voice*, December 1981, 1.

42. Fall 1981 Delegate Assembly Meeting Transcript, 8–9, UUP Records.

43. Drescher, conversation with the authors, August 15, 2016.

44. Spring 1982 delegate Assembly Meeting Transcript, 30–31, UUP Records. In the "Report of the President," Drescher quoted Hodes at the conference both had participated in as panelists addressing the use and abuse of part-time faculty.

45. *The Voice*, December 1981, 1.

46. Ibid., April 1982, 2.

47. Memorandum of New York State Department of Civil Service, transmitted in letter of Bradley J. Overton to Drescher, January 3, 1983, UUP Records, subgroup III, series 4, box 3, folder 7.

48. UUP Press Release, August 25, 1982, ibid., subgroup IV, series 7, box 5, folder 19.

49. *The Voice*, August 1982, 1; *New York Times*, September 18, 1982.

50. Meyer Frucher to Drescher, telegram, September 3, 1982, UUP Records, subgroup VI, series 2, box 1, folder 22.

51. *The Voice*, August 1982, 1.

52. Fall 1983 Delegate Assembly Meeting Transcript, 44–48, UUP Records.

53. Medical and Dental Faculty Compensation Plans, Draft Audit Report, 1982, subgroup VI, series 2, box 1, folder 22.

54. Ibid., 43–55.

55. "State University and Staff Doctors Agree on a Pact," *New York Times*, September 12, 1982.

56. Drescher to Norman J. Klopmeyer, November 11, 1982, UUP Records, subgroup III, series 7, box 1, folder 31.

57. Howard L. Sauder to Herbert N. Wright, July 29, 1982, ibid., series 2, box 1, folder 21.

58. Ronald Sullivan, "New York and Union Reach Pact on Medical Faculty Income Limit," *New York Times*, October 4, 1983.

59. *The Voice*, October 1983, 1.

60. Objectives of the Joint Labor Management Cooperation Committees, UUP Records, subgroup IV, series 7, box 5, folder 17; NYS/UUP Joint Labor-Management Committee, Overview, ibid., box 4, folder 13;

61. *The Voice*, October 1983, 1.

62. Ibid., September 1984, 8.

63. Overview; *The Voice*, May 1984, 8.

64. *The Voice*, May 1984, 3.

65. Wharton to Drescher, June 1, 1985, UUP Records, subgroup III, series 4, box 5, folder 5.

66. *The Voice*, February 1983, 7; ibid., August 1983, 3; Drescher to Chapter Presidents, June 26, 1983, UUP Records, subgroup III, series 4, box 2, folder 25.

67. State University of New York Press Release, February 1, 1983, ibid., box 4, folder 1.

68. Wharton to SUNY Board of Trustees, February 22, 1983, ibid., box 3, folder 32.

69. Sam Livingston to Ray Skuse, February 10, 1983, ibid., box 4, folder 1.

70. Drescher, Testimony before Senate Committee on Higher Education, January 6, 1983, quoted in *The Voice*, February 1983, 8; Winter 1983 Delegate Assembly Meeting, Transcript, 6–7, UUP Records; Drescher to Chapter Presidents, Executive Board and Staff, February 3, 1983, mailgram, UUP Records, subgroup III, series 4, box 5, folder 12; Drescher, Testimony, February 2, 1983, ibid., box 4, folder 13.

71. Winter 1983 Delegate Assembly Meeting Transcript, 8, UUP Records.

72. Livingston to Skuse, February 10, 1983, ibid., subgroup III, series 4, box 4, folder 1; *The Voice*, June 1983, 2.

73. Paul T. Veillette, "New York State's Fiscal Condition and Budget and Their Implications for Higher Education," *City Almanac*, October 1983, 17–21.

74. Fall 1983 Delegate Assembly Meeting Transcript, 9–10, UUP Records.

75. Doris Knudsen to Livingston, February 3 and 4, 1983, Morris Budin to Livingston, February 2, 1983, UUP Records, subgroup III, series 4, box 4, folder 2.

76. Sylvan Nagler to Drescher, February 9, 1983, ibid.

77. Drescher to "Dear Colleague," February 2, 1983, ibid.; UUP Budget Bulletin #3, 2 February 1983, ibid., box 3, folder 30.

78. Winter 1983 Delegate Assembly Meeting Transcript, 75–78, UUP Records; Meyer S. Frucher to the Editor, *New York Times*, November 26, 1983.

79. Albany University Senate Executive Committee, Resolution on Differential Tuition Proposal, UUP Records, subgroup III, series 4, box 4, folder 2; Winter 1983 Delegate Assembly Meeting Transcript, 58–72, UUP Records.

80. Ibid., 58, 63, 42.

81. UUP Budget Bulletin #3, February 2, 1983, UUP Records, subgroup III, series 4, box 3, folder 2; Proposed Legislative Action Program to Stop Retrenchments, ibid., box 4, folder 2; Winter Delegate Assembly Meeting Transcript, 69, UUP Records.

82. Spring 1983 Delegate Assembly Transcript, 8, ibid.

83. UUP Budget Bulletin, March 3, 1983, ibid., subgroup III, series 4, box 4, folder 2; Steven Cox Testimony, February 10, 1983, ibid., folder 3.

84. Drescher to Elizabeth Hoke, December 17, 1982, ibid., subgroup IV, series 7, box 5, folder 28.

85. Drescher to James Tierney, April 5, 1983, and to David A. Gallatley, and to 16 others, March 10, 1983, ibid., folder 29.

86. Winter 1984 Delegate Assembly Meeting Transcript, 23, UUP Records.

87. Drescher to Mario Cuomo, March 4, 1983, ibid., subgroup III, series 4, box 2, folder 24.

88. Joseph L. Bruno to Drescher, March 10, 1983, ibid.

89. Robert Perrin, to Presidents of State Operated Campuses and SUNY Press Release, February 1, 1983, ibid., box 4, folder 1.

90. Anthony M. Masiello to Drescher, April 12, 1983, ibid., folder 24.

91. Drescher to Chapter Presidents, Executive Board, April 8, 1984, ibid., folder 4.

92. Wharton to Drescher, May 8, 1984, ibid., box 5, folder 6.

93. *The Voice*, March 1984, 1, 3; Drescher to Stanley Fink, April 23, 1984, UUP Records, III, series 4, box 2, folder 25.

94. Wharton, Testimony to Joint Hearings of Assembly Ways and Means Committee and Senate Finance Committee, February 15, 1984, 1–2, ibid., folder 5.

95. *New York Times*, February 3, 1984.

96. Drescher to Albert Shanker, April 4, 1994, UUP Records, subgroup III, series 4, box 1, folder 3.

97. Gene I. Maeroff, "Commission Will Study State University Future," *New York Times*, February 3, 1984; Tom Buckham, "Wharton Denies UB Showcasing at Expense of Others," *Buffalo News*, February 14, 1984 (copy), UUP Records, subgroup III, series 4, box 3, folder 23.

98. Drescher, Testimony before the Independent Commission, June 19, 1984, 2, ibid., subgroup IV, series 7, box 4, folder 7.

99. Drescher to Eight Chapter Presidents, February 2, 1984, ibid., subgroup III, series 4, box 3, folder 22.

100. Independent Commission on the Future of the State University Press Release, January 16, 1985, 3, ibid., folder 23.

101. Ibid., 7.

102. Drescher, Testimony before the Assembly and Senate Higher Education Committees, Joint Hearing, February 12, 1985, UUP Records, subgroup III, series 4, box 2, folder 18.

103. Winter 1985 Delegate Assembly Meeting Transcript, 13, UUP Records.

104. Spring 1985 Delegate Assembly Meeting Transcript, 57–61, ibid.

105. Sharon Gazin, "Accord Reached on SUNY Bill," *Albany Knickerbocker News*, June 25, 1985 (copy), ibid., subgroup III, series 4, box 2, folder 19; Drescher to Patricia Koenig Ballard, June 17, 1985,

106. *The Voice*, April 1985, 2.

107. Ibid., 2, 6.

108. Spring 1985 Delegate Assembly Meeting Transcript, 52–54, UUP Records; Fall 1986 Delegate Assembly Meeting Transcript, 14, ibid.

109. UUP Legislation Program for 1985, ibid., subgroup III, series 4, box 2, folder 18.

110. *The Voice*, June 1983, 8.

111. Ibid., March 1985, 8.

112. "UUP Unveils Its Multi-Faceted Education Program," ibid., April 1985, 4–5.

113. David E. Truax to Drescher, September 4, 1985, UUP Records, subgroup III, series 4, box 3, folder 24.

114. *The Voice*, April 1985, 3, June 1985, 7; Fall 1983 Delegate Assembly Meeting Transcript, 10–13, UUP Records.

115. Drescher to Willard A. Genrich, June 17, 1982, ibid., subgroup IV, series 7, box 2, folder 6.

116. *The Voice*, March 1983, 12.

117. "Committee Releases Report on Part-timers," ibid., November 1983, 3.

118. Ibid., March 1984, 3.

119. Ibid., June 1985, 6.

120. Donald Nolan, "For Information, Medical Malpractice Insurance," April 12, 1985, enclosed with Drescher to Legislation Committee, April 15, 1985, UUP Records, subgroup III, series 4, box 4, folder 28; Spring 1985 Delegate Assembly Meeting Transcript, 54–57, UUP Records.

121. Peter Kane, letter to Drescher, October 25, 2017.

122. Abraham Helland to Charles Hansen, December 3, 1981, UUP Records, subgroup 3, series 4, box 2, folder 28. This is typical of the expressions of discontent experienced by many professionals in the unit.

123. Fall 1982 Delegate Assembly Meeting Transcript, 90–93, UUP Records.

124. Employee Relations Report, July 6, 1982, ibid., subgroup III, series 4, box 1, folder 15.

125. Drescher to Chapter Presidents, September 15, 1981, ibid., series 7, box 5, folder 22.

126. Fall 1982 Delegate Assembly Meeting Transcript, 98, UUP Records.

127. *The Voice*, August 1982, 5.

128. Ibid., 8; Fall 1982 Delegate Assembly Meeting Transcript, 103–4, UUP Records.

129. Winter 1984 Delegate Assembly Meeting Transcript, 57–61, ibid.

130. Ibid., 60.

131. Ibid., 55.

132. Maria Rita Rudden to Samuel Livingston, May 16, 1985, ibid., subgroup IIIA, series 1, box 1, folder 6.

133. *The Voice*, July 1984, 3.

134. Ibid., November 1984, 1, 3.

135. Jeffrey Schmaltz, "Contract Negotiations Start between State and Workers," *New York Times*, February 11, 1985.

136. Sidney Braverman to Drescher and Livingston, February 14, 1985, UUP Records, subgroup IV, series 7, box 5, folder 24; Drescher to Braverman, March 21, 1985, ibid.

137. Ibid., box 3, folder 17 contains a series of letters dealing with the Empire Plan and its potential operation sent to the office in response to the UUP request for an evaluation.

138. Drescher to NYSUT Executive Board, November 13, 1985, ibid., subgroup III, series 4, box 3, folder 2.

139. *Albany Knickerbocker News*, June 27, 1985 (copy), ibid., box 2, folder 20; Bennett Roth, "Two Mediators Appointed for SUNY Talks," *Albany Times Union*, June 28, 1985 (copy), ibid., box 5, folder 8.

140. John M. Reilly, "Why Won't the State Move Yet?" *The Voice*, November 1985, 1.

141. Executive Board Meeting Minutes, December 6, 1985, UUP Records; *The Voice*, December 1985, 1; Winter 1986 Delegate Assembly Meeting Minutes Transcript, 17, UUP Records.

142. Mary Wessling, "SUNY/UUP Contract Negotiation at Standstill," Ottaway News Service, n.d. (copy), ibid., subgroup IV, series 7, box 5, folder 8; Drescher to Ashe, October 25, 1985, ibid., subgroup III, series 4, box 3, folder 6.

143. *The Voice*, December 1985, 1, 2; *New York Times*, November 17, 1985; UUP Records, subgroup IV, series 7, box 4, folder 24 contains copies of these ads.

144. See *The Voice*, November 1985, 1–5.

145. Winter 1986 Delegate Assembly Meeting Transcript, 7, 10, 45, 52, UUP Records.

146. Drescher to Chapter Presidents and Executive Board, October 8, 1985, ibid., subgroup III, series 4, box 3, folder 33.

147. Jeff Leibowitz, "State U. Employees Assail Stalled Talks," *New York Times*, December 8, 1985.

148. Drescher to Ashe, October 25, 1985, UUP Records, subgroup III, series 4, box 3, folder 6.

149. Livingston to Thomas Hartnett, July 7, 1985, ibid., subgroup IV, series 7, box 5, folder 26.

150. Reports on Negotiations Demonstration, February 19, 1986, ibid., box 4, folders 25 and 26; box 5, folder 8.

151. "College Union Talks of Strike or Other Job Action," *Oneonta Daily Star*, February 29, 1986 (copy), ibid., box 5, folder 8.

152. Fall 1985 Delegate Assembly Meeting Transcript, 5, UUP Records.

153. "Open Letter to Governor Cuomo," *Albany Times Union*, February 25, 1986.

154. Drescher to Irwin Polishook, December 3, 1984, UUP Records, subgroup IV, series 7, box 5, folder 23.

155. Winter 1986 Delegate Assembly Meeting Transcript, 115, UUP Records.

156. Drescher, conversation with the authors, August 15, 2015.

157. "Union Leaders Decry SUNY Workers' Pact," *Newsday*, March 7, 1986 (copy), UUP Records, subgroup IV, series 7, box 5, folder 8.

158. Winter 1986 Delegate Assembly Meeting Transcript, 176, UUP Records.

159. David Kreh to Librarian Members of UUP, April 25, 1986, ibid., subgroup IV, series 7, box 4, folder 22.

160. *The Voice*, June 1986, 3.

161. Drescher Statement, "The New Agreement and Health Benefits," UUP Records, subgroup IV, series 7, box 7, folder 17.

162. *The Voice*, June 1986, 1.

163. "As We Move Forward with the New Agreement," ibid., May 1986, 2; ibid., March 1986, 2.

164. Drescher to Mitch Vogel, July 18, 1986, UUP Records, subgroup IV, series 7, box 3, folder 33.

165. Spring 1986 Delegate Assembly Meeting Transcript, 58–70, UUP Records.

166. Ibid., 37–38.

167. Ibid., 107.

168. *The Voice*, July 1986, 8.

169. Ibid., September–October 1986, 5.

170. Ibid.; ibid., November–December 1986, 2, 3, January–February 1987, 1, 2.

171. Fall 1986 Delegate Assembly Meeting Transcript, 14–16, UUP Records.

172. Ibid., 3, Part II, 5.

173. Ibid., 6–7.

Chapter 5: Expanding the Role of UUP, 1987–93

1. Delegate Assembly Minutes, May 2, 1987, UUP Records.

2. *The Voice*, May–June 1987.

3. William Scheuerman to "Dear Colleague," September 8, 1987, UUP Records, subgroup 4, series 2, box 1, folder 25.

4. *The Voice*, February 1988.

5. John M. Reilly to Elizabeth D. Moore, November 2, 1987, UUP Records, subgroup III, series 5, box 7, folder 29.

6. Scheuerman to Christopher F. Eatz, December 9, 1987, New York State Archives, 16223-00A, box 2.

7. State Notes of December 9, 1987, Meeting, ibid., box 3; UUP "Negotiations Update," December 23, 1987, UUP Records, subgroup IV, series 1, box 7, folder 26A.

8. Scheuerman to Chapter Presidents, December 10, 1987, ibid., subgroup III, series 5, box 7, folder 21.

9. UUP Minutes of the Exchange Session, January 21, 1988, ibid.; State Proposals for the Professional Services Negotiating Unit, ibid., subgroup VI, series 1, box 7, folder 34.

10. UUP "Negotiations Update," February 23, 1988, ibid., folder 16.

11. *The Voice*, February 1988.

12. UUP "Negotiations Update," March 28, 1988, UUP Records, subgroup VI, box 7, folder 31A.

13. State Notes of April 1988 Meeting, New York State Archives, 16223-00A, box 3.

14. Reilly and Scheuerman to UUP Members, June 14, 1988, UUP Records, subgroup VI, series 1, box 7, folder 20; State of New York Governor's Office of Employee Relations, 1988 UUP Negotiations News Release, NYS Archives, 16223-00A, box 2.

15. *Albany Times Union*, June 20, 1988.

16. Transcript of June 21, 1988 Negotiations Session, Tony Wildman Files, UUP Administrative Office, Albany, NY.

17. *The Voice*, July 1988.

18. Negotiations Committee Report, Fall 1988 UUP Delegate Assembly Meeting, UUP Records, subgroup III, series 5, box 7, folder 26.

19. Thomas A. Corigliano to "Dear Colleague," September 14, 1990, ibid., subgroup VI, series 4.2, box 1, folder 25.

20. *The Voice*, February 1991.

21. UUP "Negotiations Bulletin," June 21, 1991, UUP Records, subgroup VI, series 4.2, box 1, folder 6.

22. Transcript of the Joint Committee on Health Benefits Meeting, July 2, 1991, Tony Wildman Files.

23. Reilly to Chapters, Executive Board and All Bargaining Unit Members, July 2, 1991, ibid.

24. UUP "Negotiations Bulletin," July 16, 1991, ibid., subgroup VI, series 4.2, box 1, folder 6.

25. UUP "Negotiations Bulletin," June 5, 1992, ibid., folder 9.

26. UUP and Governor's Office of Employee Relations Joint Press Release, June 26, 1992, ibid., folder 7.

27. UUP "Negotiations Bulletin," July 1, 1992, ibid., series 1, box 8, folder 4.

28. Executive Board Special Meeting Minutes, July 7, 1992, UUP Records.

29. Report of the Negotiations Committee, 1992 Fall Delegate Assembly, ibid., subgroup VI, series 4.2, box 1, folder 11.

30. Harry K. Spindler to Presidents, State Operated Campuses, July 14, 1989, ibid., subgroup III, series 5, box 9, folder 15.

31. Agreement between the State of New York and United University Professions, 1988–1991, ibid., subgroup VI, series 1, box 7, folder 15A.

32. Joyce Yapple Villa to Reilly, August 14, 1989, ibid., subgroup III, series 5, box 9, folder 15.

33. Anthony Wildman to Corigliano and Fred Wooley, September 7, 1989, ibid.

34. Delegate Assembly Meeting Minutes, September 22, 1989, UUP Records.

35. Wildman, Corigliano, and Wooley to Reilly and Livingston, September 28, 1989, ibid., subgroup III, series 5, box 9, folder 15.

36. Wildman, Corigliano, and Wooley to Reilly and Livingston, October 6 and 19, 1989, ibid.

37. Jerome B. Komisar to Presidents, State-operated Campuses, January 30, 1990, ibid., subgroup IV, series 1, box 3, folder 4; Raymond J. Haines, Jr., to Wildman, January 31, 1990, ibid., subgroup III, series 5, box 9, folder 16.

38. Corigliano to Chapter Presidents, February 28, 1990, ibid., subgroup IV, series 1, box 3, folder 4.

39. Regional Meetings, March 1990 Checklist of Parking Activities, ibid., subgroup III, series 5, box 9, folder 16.

40. Resolution Passed by City Council of Oneonta, NY, on March 20, 1990 (copy), ibid., folder 17.

41. Editorial, *Oneonta Daily Star*, April 28, 1990 (copy), ibid.

42. Lawrence Govendo, to George Marcus, March 21, 1990 (copy), ibid.

43. Joseph T. Pillitere to Ross B. Kenzie, April 10, 1990 (copy), ibid.

44. *Albany Times Union*, June 7, 1990, ibid.

45. *Schenectady Gazette*, April 26, 1990, ibid.

46. Reilly and Corigliano to Chapter Presidents, Executive Board, Labor Relations Specialists, March 30, 1990, ibid.

47. Reilly to Moore, May 3, 1990, ibid.

48. Decision-Step 2, "In the Matter of a Grievance Involving United University Professions, All Campuses," SUNY file #90-23, SUNY Decision #90-23, June 12, 1990, ibid.

49. *The Chronicle of Higher Education*, June 30, 1990, ibid., subgroup IV, series 1, box 3, folder 8.

50. Agreement between the State of New York and United University Professions, 1988–1991, ibid., subgroup VI, series 1, box 7, folder 15A.

51. Delegate Assembly Meeting Minutes, February 4, 1989, UUP Records.

52. *Cortland Standard*, September 1, 1990, ibid., subgroup III, series 5, box 12, folder 10.

53. *At Canton*, 17, Extra #1, September 4, 1990, ibid.

54. Reilly to Chapter Presidents and Executive Board, September 11, 1990, ibid.

55. Executive Board Meeting Minutes, October 11, 1990, UUP Records.

56. Retrenchment and Layoff Counts as of 8/30/91, ibid., subgroup III, series 5, box 12, folder 10.

57. *The Voice*, April 1989.

58. Special Labor-Management Meeting at the Invitation of President Swygert, Minutes, July 5, 1991, UUP Albany Chapter Files (uncataloged).

59. President's Report, UUP Albany Chapter Executive Committee Meeting, August 19, 1991, ibid.

60. Delegate Assembly Meeting Minutes, September 27, 1991, UUP Records.

61. *The Voice*, October 1991.

62. Ibid., May 1992; UUP Albany Labor Management Meeting Minutes, August 19, 1991, UUP Albany Chapter Files (uncataloged).

63. Executive Board Meeting Minutes, December 18, 1992; Ivan D. Steen, conversation with the authors, November 27, 2017.

64. Executive Board Meeting Minutes, December 18, 1992, UUP Records.

65. Delegate Assembly Meeting Minutes, January 29, 1993, ibid.

66. Report of the President, Fall 1987 Delegate Assembly Meeting, September 18–19, 1987, ibid., subgroup III, series 1, box 3, folder 20.

67. Reilly to Chapter Presidents, January 13, 1988, ibid., folder 27.

68. UUP News Release, January 25, 1988, ibid.

69. UUP "Legislative Alert," January 29, 1988, ibid., series 5, box 6, folder 19.

70. Report of the President, Spring 1988 Delegate Assembly Meeting, May 6, 1988, ibid., series 1, box 4, folder 2.

71. *New York Times*, April 24 and May 24, 1988.

72. *The Voice*, July 1988.

73. Janet Potter to Chapter Presidents, November 10, 1988, UUP Records, subgroup III, series 5, box 14, folder 6.

74. Executive Board Meeting Minutes, December 2, 1988, UUP Records.

75. Student Association of the State University of New York and United University Professions News Release, December 12, 1988, ibid., subgroup III, series 5, box 13, folder 24.

76. Samuel Weiss, "Shutdown of Campuses Considered," *New York Times*, December 15, 1988.

77. Reilly to Chapter Presidents and Executive Board, December 15, 1988, UUP Records, subgroup III, series 1, box 4, folder 17.

78. *New York Times*, December 20, 1988.

79. Ibid.

80. Executive Board Meeting Minutes, January 13, 1989, UUP Records.

81. Talking Points for UUP Lobby Day, March 15, 1989, ibid., subgroup III, series 5, box 7, folder 3.

82. UUP "Legislative Alert," March 24, 1989, ibid., subgroup IV, series 4, box 6, folder 17.

83. Albert Shanker, "Where We Stand," *New York Times*, March 26, 1989.

84. D. Bruce Johnstone to Shanker, March 29, 1989, UUP Records, subgroup III, series 5, box 13, folder 25.

85. *New York Times*, April 19, 1989.

86. UUP "Legislative Alert," April 20, 1989, UUP Records, subgroup III, series 5, box 13, folder 24.

87. *New York Times*, May 3, 1989.

88. UUP "Legislative Alert," May 18, 1989, subgroup III, series 5 box 13, folder 24.

89. Ibid., August 8, 1989, box 6, folder 22.

90. Ibid., January 9, 1990, folder 23.

91. Executive Board Meeting Minutes, January 12, 1990, UUP Records.

92. *New York Times*, May 19, 1990.

93. Ibid., August 26, 1990.

94. UUP "Legislative Alert," February 16, 1990, UUP Records, subgroup III, series 5, box 6, folder 23.

95. Janet Potter to Chapter Presidents, July 6, 1990, ibid.

96. Ibid.

97. President's Report, Winter 1991 Delegate Assembly Meeting, January 21, 1991, box 1, folder 2.

98. Executive Board Meeting Minutes, January 31, 1991, UUP Records.

99. Delegate Assembly Meeting Minutes, February 1, 1991, ibid.

100. UUP "Legislative Alert," April 12, 1991, ibid., subgroup III, series 5, box 1, folder 2.

101. Reilly to Shanker, April 16, 1991, ibid., box 7, folder 31.

102. "Notice of Events to Be Held on Tuesday, April 30, 1991, to Protest State Budget Cuts," ibid., series 1, box 5, folder 23; Report of the Legislation Committee, Spring 1991 Delegate Assembly Meeting, May 3–4, 1991, ibid., subgroup IV, series 4, box 6, folder 19.

103. Elizabeth Kolbert, "New York State Budget: The Legislature's Version," *New York Times*, June 2, 1991.

104. *New York Times*, June 11, 1991; *The Connection*, June 12, 1991, UUP Records, subgroup IV, series 1, box 3, folder 16.

105. *New York Times*, June 30, 1991.

106. *Albany Times Union*, June 29, 1991, UUP Records, subgroup III, series 5, box 1, folder 1.

107. UUP "Legislative Alert," December 14, 1991, ibid., box 7, folder 31.

108. UUP and NYPIRG Leadership to UUP Chapter Presidents, Legislation Committee, and Legislative Liaisons, January 28, 1992, ibid., folder 1.

109. 1992–93 Executive Budget Highlights, State University of New York, State Operated Campuses, Prepared for NYSUT's Committee of 100, February 25–26, 1992, ibid., box 8, folder 16.

110. UUP News Release, March 31, 1992, ibid., box, folder 29.

111. *New York Times*, April 2, 1992.

112. Samuel Weiss, "CUNY and SUNY See 1,000 Dismissals," ibid., April 9, 1992.

113. Editorial, ibid., April 22, 1992.

114. UUP News Release, April 12, 1992, UUP Records, subgroup III, series 5, box 7, folder 7.

115. Janet Potter to Chapter Presidents and Executive Board, June 4, 1992, ibid., subgroup IV, series 4, box 6, folder 21.

116. UUP "Legislative Alert," July 13, 1992, ibid., subgroup III, series 5, box 6, folder 30.

117. UUP News Release, January 15, 1992, ibid., series 1, box 5, folder 27.

118. Report of the Legislation Committee, Fall 1992 Delegate Assembly Meeting, September 25–26, 1992, ibid., subgroup IV, series 4, box 6, folder 21.

119. Ibid.

120. "John M. Reilly, Statement in Opposition to Differential Tuition, Distributed to Members of NYS Senate and Members of NYS Assembly," December 16, 1991, ibid., subgroup III, series 5, box 14, folder 15.

121. Report of the Legislation Committee, Fall 1992 Delegate Assembly Meeting, September 25–26, 1992, ibid., subgroup IV, series 4, box 6, folder 21.

122. UUP "Legislative Alert," October 28, 1992, ibid., subgroup III, series 5, box 6, folder 30.

123. UUP "Legislative Alert," December 16, 1992, ibid., subgroup IV, series 1, box 3, folder 25.

124. United University Professions Summary of the 1993–94 Executive budget, ibid., subgroup III, series 5, box 2, folder 14.

125. "SUNY News," January 19, 1993, ibid.

126. Report of the Legislation Committee, Spring 1993 Delegate Assembly Meeting, May 7–8, 1993, ibid., subgroup IV, series 4, box 6, folder 21; *New York Times*, April 6, 1993.

127. UUP News Release, June 18, 1987, UUP Records, subgroup III, series 1, box 3, folder 9.

128. Reilly to Chapter Presidents, March 5, 1990, ibid., box 5, folder 9.

129. Reilly to Ivan D. Steen, November 23, 1990, UUP Records (uncataloged).

130. Reilly, Testimony at Public Hearing of the SUNY Board of Trustees Committee on University Revenue and Tuition Policy, December 7, 1990, UUP Records, subgroup III, series 1, box 5, folder 19.

131. Reilly to Members of NYS Senate and NYS Assembly, December 16, 1991, ibid., box 14, folder 15.

132. Executive Board Meeting Minutes, January 30, 1992, UUP Papers.

133. United University Professions 1990 Legislative Program, ibid., subgroup III, series 5, box 6, folder 22.

134. United University Professions 1991 Legislative Program, ibid., subgroup IV, series 4, box 6, folder 19.

135. United University Professions 1993 Legislative Program, ibid., series 1, box 3, folder 28.

136. Delegate Assembly Meeting Minutes, May 5–6, 1988, UUP Records.

137. Delegate Assembly Meeting Minutes, May 5–6, 1989, ibid.

138. Delegate Assembly Meeting Minutes, September 22–23, 1989, ibid.

139. *The Voice*, May 1989.

140. Delegate Assembly Meeting Minutes, 1990–93, UUP Records.

141. United University Professions, *SUNY's Future: Expanding the Mission, Fulfilling the Promise* (Albany, NY: United University Professions, March 1990), ibid., subgroup VIII, series 3.3, box 1, folder 41.

142. *New York Times,* June 10, 1990.

143. Reilly to Mario M. Cuomo, June 21, 1990, UUP Records, subgroup III, series 1, box 5, folder 13.

144. Johnstone to Presidents, State University of New York, June 5, 1990, ibid.

145. Peter B. Kahn to Reilly, n.d., ibid., series 5, box 14, folder 23.

146. M. T. Flemming, Comment, n.d., ibid.

147. Selma Kaplan to Reilly, January 17, 1990, ibid., box 16, folder 35.

148. Reilly to Robert Porter, February 6, 1990, ibid., series 1 box 5, folder 8.

149. Executive Board Meeting Minutes, August 10, 1990, UUP Records.

150. Executive Board Meeting Minutes, March 2, 1990, ibid.

151. *The Connection,* June 12, 1991, ibid., subgroup VI, series 1, box 3, folder 16.

152. Reilly to Edward McElroy, April 8, 1993, ibid., subgroup III, series 5, box 16, folder 25.

153. Report of the President, Delegate Assembly Meeting, February 5–6, 1988, ibid., series 1, box 3, folder 27.

154. Cozort interview, 55, UUP Oral History.

155. Supplemental Report of the Treasurer, Delegate Assembly Meeting, May 7–8, 1993, UUP Records, subgroup IV, series 1, box 3, folder 29.

156. Delegate Assembly Meeting Minutes, May 5, 1989, UUP Records.

157. Finance Committee Meeting Minutes, March 30, 1990, ibid., subgroup IV, series 4, box 4, folder 10.

158. Joint Meeting of Finance and Constitution Study Committees Minutes, June 28, 1990, ibid.

159. Delegate Assembly Meeting Minutes, October 13, 1990, UUP Records.

160. Delegate Assembly Meeting Minutes, February 1–2, 1991, ibid.

161. Executive Board Meeting Minutes, October 11, 1990, ibid.

162. Delegate Assembly Meeting Minutes, October 12, 1990, ibid.; *The Voice,* November 1990.

163. Reilly to Chapter Presidents and Newsletter Editors, April 23, 1993, UUP Records, subgroup IV, series 4, box 4, folder 11.

164. *The Voice,* September 1991.

165. Delegate Assembly Meeting Minutes, May 7, 1988, UUP Records.

166. Delegate Assembly Meeting Minutes, May 6, 1989, ibid.

167. Delegate Assembly Meeting Minutes, May 5, 1990, ibid.

168. Delegate Assembly Meeting Minutes, May 4, 1991, ibid.

169. Delegate Assembly Meeting Minutes, May 2, 1992, ibid.

170. Frank Ray to Executive Board, November 19, 1990, ibid., subgroup IV, series 1, box 3, folder 3.

171. Delegate Assembly Meeting Minutes, February 1, 1992, UUP Records.

172. Atkins interview, 47, UUP Oral History.

173. Nelson interview, 29, 42, ibid.; Puretz interview, 20, ibid.; Tiger interview, 7, ibid.

174. Shank interview, 32–33, ibid.; Cozort interview, 55, ibid.

175. Puretz interview, 35, ibid.

Chapter 6: UUP Matures: Part I: 1993–2001

1. Scheuerman, a political theorist by training, had previously been president of the Oswego Chapter of UUP, a member of UUP's executive board, and chief negotiator of the 1988–91 contract. He was serving as vice president for academics at the time of his election to the UUP presidency.

2. Spring 1993 Delegate Assembly Meeting Transcript, 1:14, UUP Records.

3. The "Era of Good Feelings" was how the period of unity and political cooperation was characterized following the War of 1812.

4. "New Chief Says He Wants a More Activist Education Union," *Albany Times Union*, May 31, 1993.

5. Report of the Legislation Committee, 1992, UUP Records, subgroup IV, series 2, box 2, folder 2.

6. A pass-through provision automatically passes any increases in affiliate dues (NYSUT and AFT) onto the membership. Without a pass-through, the union must pay the hikes with existing moneys.

7. Fall 1990 Delegate Assembly Meeting Transcript, 2:110, UUP Records.

8. Ibid., 118.

9. Ibid., 140.

10. Ibid., 155.

11. William E. Scheuerman, Preliminary Report of the President, Winter 1995 Delegate Assembly, UUP Archives Box 11443, UUP Administrative Office, Albany, NY.

12. Ibid.

13. Ibid.

14. Winter 1996 Delegate Assembly Meeting Transcript, 33, UUP Records.

15. Ibid.

16. Spring 1989 Delegate Assembly Meeting Transcript, 1:104.

17. Scheuerman, Preliminary Report of the President, Fall 1994 Delegate Assembly, Scheuerman's personal collection.

18. Scheuerman, Preliminary Report of the President, Winter 1996 Delegate Assembly, ibid.

19. Executive Board Meeting Minutes, August 13 and December 10, 1993, UUP Records.

20. Scheuerman, Preliminary Report of the President, Fall 1994 Delegate Assembly.

21. New York State's Regents Commission on Higher Education, *Higher Education, New York's Opportunity Industry: Sharing the Challenge* (New York, 1993). See also *The Voice*, December 1993, 4.

22. Fall 1993 Delegate Assembly Meeting Transcript, 1:33, UUP Records.

23. Ibid., 39–40.

24. Ibid.

25. Peter Martineau, conversation with William Scheuerman, September 12, 2017. Martineau, former Senate Finance Committee staff member, later served as NYSUT lobbyist assigned to UUP (1993–2002, and NYSUT director of staff assigned to UUP (2002–2008).

26. Fall 1993 Delegate Assembly Meeting Transcript, 1:23, UUP Records.

27. Ibid., 34.

28. Winter 1994 Delegate Assembly Meeting Transcript, 1:24–26, ibid.

29. Sidney Plotkin and William E. Scheuerman, *Private Interests, Public Spending: Balanced Budget Conservatism and the Fiscal Crisis* (Boston: South End Press, 1994), 83.

30. "Pataki Warns of Painful Cuts to Close Deficit, *New York Times*, December 2, 1994, nytimes/1994/12/02/nyregional/Pataki-warns-of-painful-cuts-to-close-deficit.html.

31. Nicole Kaeding, "Pataki's Fiscal Record," *Cato at Liberty*," May 27, 2015.

32. Ibid.

33. Winter 1997 Delegate Assembly Meeting Transcript, 16, UUP Records.

34. James Dao, "Pataki Asks CUNY and SUNY to Cut Costs," *New York Times*, January 28, 1995, nytimes.com/1995/01/28/nyregional/Pataki-asks-cuny-and-suny-to-cut-costs.html.

35. UUP "Crisis Bulletin," February 1, 1995, UUP Records, subgroup VI, series 1, 9, box 10, folder 48.

36. *Buffalo News*, March 13, 1995, buffalonews.com/1995/03/13/suny-vows-drastic-cuts-in-budget-fray-would-close-eight-sites-increase-tuition-1600; Ian Fisher, "SUNY Trustees Plan Cuts Under Pataki Budget Plan," March 15, 1995, nytimes.com/1995/03/15/nyregional/suny-trustees-plan-cuts-under-pataki-budget-plan.html.

37. Scheuerman, Preliminary Report of the President, Spring 1995 Delegate Assembly, Scheuerman's personal collection.

38. UUP "Crisis Bulletin," February 24, 1995, UUP Records, subgroup VI, series 4.3, box 10, folder 4B.

39. The Pataki "activist" trustees closely emulated the ideas of far-right conservatives James Buchanan and Nicos Devletoglou, who called for cuts in funding for public institutions of higher learning, higher tuition rates, and a reduction in faculty governance. As will be seen, SUNY's new trustees followed these recommendations. James M. Buchanan and Nicos E. Devletoglou, *Academia in Anarchy: An Economic Diagnosis* (New York: Basic Books, 1970).

40. James Barron, "SUNY Chancellor Resigns Post After Battling Pataki's Trustees," *New York Times*, May 1, 1995, nytimes.com/1996/05/01/nyregion/suny-chancellor-resigns-post-after-battling-pataki-s-grustees.html; Rick Karlin, "SUNY's Chancellor Quits," *Albany Times Union*, May 1, 1996.

41. Ibid.

42. Ibid.

43. See *The Voice*, October 1995, 7.

44. See Barbara Silverstone, Report of the Legislation Committee, Spring 1996 Delegate Assembly, Scheuerman's personal collection.

45. Scheuerman, Preliminary Report of the President, Spring 1995 Delegate Assembly, ibid.

46. A good example of media coverage includes: "Faculty Union Says SUNY Is Losing Profs," *Syracuse Post Standard*, March 31, 1997.

47. Scheuerman, Preliminary Report of the President, Spring 1995 Delegate Assembly, Scheuerman's personal collection.

48. Winter 1995 Delegate Assembly Meeting Minutes, 8, UUP Records.

49. The new Pataki administration promised to take a tough stance against the state's union, and initially it did just that. In fact, during the Pataki administration's first

eighteen months in office, New York State had more charges of Taylor Law violations filed against it than it did during all of 1992, 1993, and 1994. See "State Charged With Record Number of Taylor Law Violations," UUP "News Release," October 10, 1996, UUP Records, subgroup VI, series 1.9, box 10, folder 38.

50. State of New York, Governor's Office of Employee Relations, State Proposals for Negotiation with United University Professions, February 23, 1995, ibid., folder 25.

51. David Bauder, "Raise Standards, A New Trustee Says," *Albany Times Union,* March 15, 1995.

52. UUP "Negotiations Bulletin," April 1995.

53. For a clear description of the Taylor Law and workload obligations at SUNY, see Tony Wildman to Ray Skuse, July 21, 1995, subgroup VI, series 4.3, folder 8.

54. Minutes of the Negotiations Committee Meeting, April 13, 1996, ibid.

55. "CSEA-NYS Contract Ratified," *The Public Sector,* 18 (June 1995), Library.albany.edu/special/findaids/resources/csea/The-Public-Sector_1995-06.pdf.

56. Memorandum of Understanding (M.O.U.) New York State Governor's Office of Employee Relations and United University Professions on Clinical Practice Matters at the State University at Buffalo, August 31, 1992, 1, Scheuerman collection.

57. State of New York, Local Mediation Procedures in the Matter of Mediation between New York/Governor's Office of Employee Relations and United University Professions, April 9, 1996, ibid.

58. State of New York Professional Services Bargaining Unit, Stipulation of Settlement, OER File Number 94-08-829, 94-08-0087, 95-08-86, 90-08-473, 91-08-698, 93-08-897, 88-08-1285, 91-08-1349, 91-08-888, 89-08-1020, 91-08-699, 89-08-1020, 89-08-404, 89-08-46, 88-08-1311, March 29, 1996, ibid.

59. See Article 29, Agreement between the State of New York and United University Professions, July 1, 1999–June 30, 2003. This article incorporates the Policies of the Board of Trustees, Article XVI, into the contractual agreement.

60. "Memorandum of Agreement between the State of New York and United University Professions Re: Clinical Practice Firewall," February 1, 2001, Scheuerman collection.

61. Scheuerman, Preliminary Report of the President, Spring 1995 Delegate Assembly, ibid.

62. Ibid.

63. Ibid.

64. Ibid.

65. UUP News Release, "State Charged with Record Number of Labor Law Violations," October 10, 1996, UUP Records, subgroup VIU, series 1.9, box 10, folder 37.

66. Negotiations Committee Meeting Minutes, April 13, 1996, 2, ibid.

67. Memorandum of Understanding between the New York State Governor's Office of Employee Relations and United University Professions, September 11, 1995, Scheuerman collection.

68. Scheuerman, Preliminary Report of the President, Winter 2004 Delegate Assembly, ibid.

69. UUP News Release, May 8, 1996, ibid.

70. Scheuerman to Patrick Lyons, February 2, 1997, UUP Records, subgroup III, series 1, box 10, folder 4.

71. Scheuerman to Chapter Presidents and Crisis Mobilization Committee, February 6, 1997, subgroup VI, series 1.9, box 10, folder 34.

72. "UUP Urges Members to Keep Momentum in Action Plan," UUP "Crisis Bulletin," February 14, 1997, ibid., folder 38.

73. Tom Matthews to Chapter Presidents, Crisis Committee and Executive Board, January 29, 1997 (email), ibid., series 4.3, box 1, folder 38.

74. Fall 1996 Delegate Assembly Meeting Transcript, 46–47, UUP Records.

75. "Faculty Union Says SUNY Is Losing Profs," *Syracuse Post Standard*, March 31, 1997.

76. Dennis L. Hefner to Scheuerman and Chancellor John Ryan, February 14, 1997, UUP Records, subgroup III, series 1, box 9, folder 4.

77. Thomas E. Matthews, Testimony on the Status of Negotiations between the United University Professions and New York State Presented to the SUNY Board of Trustees, May 28, 1997, ibid., folder 30.1.

78. Agreement between the State of New York and United University Professions, July 1, 1995–July 1, 1999, Article 39.

79. Ibid., Appendix 27.

80. "Tentative Agreement Awaits Ratification," *The Voice*, September 1997, 3.

81. "Questions and Answers about the Tentative Agreement," August 12, 1997, UUP Records, subgroup III, series 1, box 9, folder 30.

82. Fall 1997 Delegate Assembly Meeting Transcript, 47, UUP Records.

83. "Questions and Answers about the Tentative Agreement," ibid., subgroup III, series 1, box 9, folder 30.

84. "Tentative Agreement Awaits Ratification," *The Voice*, September 1997, 3.

85. UUP News Release, "SUNY Academics and Professional Faculty Ratify Contract," September 19, 1997, UUP Records, subgroup VI, series 4.3, box 1, folder 30.

86. This number includes a $71.8 million lump sum cut, inflationary costs of $16.6 million, revenue shortfall from fiscal 1995–96 of $16.1 million, and a midyear cut of $15 million.

87. "On the Chopping Block," *The Voice*, March 1996, 3.

88. See Barbara Silverstone, Report of the Legislation Committee, Spring 1996 Delegate Assembly, Scheuerman collection.

89. Scheuerman, Preliminary Report of the President, Spring 1996 Delegate Assembly, ibid.

90. Winter Delegate Assembly Meeting Transcript, 5, UUP Records.

91. Henry Steck, "Three Historical Moments: Contested Visions of the State University of New York," in *SUNY at Sixty*, eds. Clark, Leslie, and O'Brien, 210.

92. "SUNY's Spin Doesn't Add Up," *The Voice*, March 1996.

93. "Lawmakers Restore SUNY Funding," ibid., September 1997, 2.

94. Ibid.

95. "On the Chopping Block," ibid., March 1996, 3.

96. Fall 1996 Delegate Assembly Meeting Transcript, 26–27, UUP Records.

97. Winter 2001 Delegate Assembly Meeting Transcript, 12, ibid.

98. Fall 1998 Delegate Assembly Meeting Transcript, 33, ibid.; "Hospital Flex, RAM Keeps Heat on Albany," *The Voice*, September 1998, 4.

99. Ibid.

100. Winter 1998 Delegate Assembly Meeting Transcript, 41, ibid.

101. Fall 1998 Delegate Assembly Meeting Transcript, 54, ibid.

102. Winter 1999 Delegate Assembly Meeting Transcript, 1:31, ibid.

103. Ibid., 2:13.

104. "To the Point," *The Voice*, March 2000, 2.

105. Lisa Feldman Reich, "State Spending Plan in Place, Finally," ibid., May/June 2000, 3.

106. Fall 2000 Delegate Assembly Meeting Transcript, 22, ibid.

107. "To the Point," *The Voice*, March 1999, 2.

108. State of New York, Governor's Office of Employee Relations, State Proposals for Negotiations with United University Professions, February 11, 1999, Scheuerman collection.

109. "CSEA Members Reject Pact; Size of Raise Blamed," *Buffalo News*, March 25, 1995.

110. Spring 1999 Delegate Assembly Meeting Transcript, 19, UUP Records.

111. Ibid., 18.

112. Ibid., 20.

113. "UUP, State Reach Tentative Contract Agreement," UUP Press Release, July 16, 1999, Scheuerman collection.

114. Fall 1999 Delegate Assembly Meeting Transcript, 14–15, UUP Records.

115. Agreement between the State of New York and United University Professions, 1999–2003.

116. Spring 1999 Delegate Assembly Meeting Transcript, 40–42, UUP Records.

117. Winter 2001 Delegate Assembly Meeting Transcript, 25–27, ibid.

118. State of New York Voluntary Labor Tribunal, In the Matter of the Interest Arbitration Between: The State of New York: State University at Binghamton (SUNY) and United University Professions (AFL-CIO), RE: Parking Fees, Case #97-IP, December 20, 1999, Scheuerman collection.

119. Karin L. Mattison, "UUP, State Agee on Contract Enhancements," *The Voice* May/June 2000, 3.

120. Spring 2000 Delegate Assembly Meeting Transcript, 20, UUP Records.

121. Fall 2001 Delegate Assembly Meeting Transcript, 54–57, ibid.

122. Winter 2000 Delegate Assembly Meeting Transcript, 17–18, ibid.

123. Ibid., 38.

124. UUP got off to a good start with Chancellor King. The former director of DOB was publicly criticized for heading the largest public university in the United States even though he had no academic experience. Scheuerman publicly rejected that criticism by saying the new chancellor should be given a chance to succeed. The criteria Scheuerman suggested were: Will he advocate for SUNY? Will he respect shared governance? And does he support academic freedom? See Scheuerman, "Next Chancellor Must Advocate on SUNY's Behalf," *Albany Times Union*, December 18, 1999.

125. Lisa Feldman Reich, "UUP Assembles Support for Agenda," *The Voice*, February 2003, 11.

126. Elmer E. Schattschneider, *The Semi-Sovereign People: A Realist's View of Democracy in America* (New York: Holt, Rinehart and Winston, 1960).

127. Spring 2000 Delegate Assembly Meeting Transcript, 35, UUP Records.

128. Ibid., 33.

129. Frank Maurizio, "UUP Mourns Loss of Higher Education Advocate," *The Voice*, February 2003, 11.

130. Fall 2001 Delegate Assembly Meeting Transcript, 2:39, UUP Records.

131. Ibid., 12.

132. Ibid., 15.

133. Ibid., 63.

134. Ibid., 29.

135. Ibid., 27.

136. Ibid., 56–61.

137. Ibid., 66.

138. Scheuerman, "To the Point," *The Voice*, October 1998, 2.

139. Ibid.

140. Ibid.

141. Frank Maurizio, "Union Criticizes RAM at Legislative Forum," ibid., November 1998, 4.

142. Ibid.

143. Martineau conversation with Scheuerman, September 12, 2017.

144. Mattison, "State Spending Plan in Place," *The Voice*, May/June 1000, 3:l See also Fall 2000 Delegate Assembly Meeting Transcript, 20–21, UUP Records.

145. Kimberly Schaye, Jon R. Sorenson, Larry Sutton, "College Prez Won't Resign," *New York Daily News*, November 8, 1997, Dailynews.com/archives/news/college-prez-wont-resign-article-1.778961.

146. Ibid.

147. Winter 2000 Delegate Assembly Meeting Transcript, 21–23, UUP Records.

148. Spring 1999 Delegate Assembly Meeting Transcript, 21–22, UUP Records.

149. Vincent Aceto, "SUNY Faculty Wants a Say in Curriculum," *Albany Times Union*, April 22, 1999.

150. Maurizio, "UUP, Senate Publicly Chastise Trustees," *The Voice*, May/June 1999, 5.

151. "To the Point," ibid., 2.

152. Karen W. Arenson, "SUNY Faculty Leaders Say Faith in Trustees Is Gone," *New York Times*, April 9, 1999.

153. Spring 1999 Delegate Assembly Meeting Transcript, 24, UUP Records.

154. VOTE-COPE contributions jumped from about $13,000 in 1993 to over $130,000 by October 1999, Fall 1999 Delegate Assembly Meeting Transcript, 72, ibid.

155. Liza Frenette, "Academic Freedom Under Attack," *The Voice*, May/June 2000, 11.

156. Frenette, "McCall Seeks Better Trustee Selection Process," ibid., March 2000, 10.

157. Fall 1999 Delegate Assembly Meeting Transcript, 41–42, UUP Records.

158. "To the Point," *The Voice*, May/June 1999, 2.

159. Scheuerman, "Activist Trustees Need Rigorous Public Oversight," Letters to the Editor, *Chronicle of Higher Education*, October 31, 1996, UUP Records, subgroup III, series 1, box 8, folder 5.

160. "To the Point," *The Voice*, March 1995, 4.

161. Winter 2002 Delegate Assembly Meeting Transcript, 9–13. UUP Records.

162. Spring 2002 Delegate Assembly Meeting Transcript, 58–62, ibid.

Chapter 7: UUP Matures: Part II, 2001–2007

1. Winter 2001 Delegate Assembly Meeting Transcript, 20–21, UUP Records.

2. Fall 2002 Delegate Assembly Meeting Transcript, 26, ibid.

3. Ibid., 21.

4. Fall 2001 Delegate Assembly Meeting Transcript, 40, ibid.

5. For a good example see Cliff Dought, "SUNY Morrisville Faculty Wants Even Pay," *Oneida Daily Dispatch*, June 14, 2001.

6. Ibid., 35.

7. Winter 2002 Delegate Assembly Meeting Transcript, 36, UUP Records.

8. Ibid., 37.

9. Fall 2002 Delegate Assembly Meeting Transcript, 28–30, ibid.

10. Martineau, conversation with Scheuerman.

11. Feldman, "UUP Makes More Headway as 2002 Session Concludes," *The Voice*, September 2001, 4.

12. Fall 2002 Delegate Assembly Meeting Transcript, 41–42, UUP Records.

13. Ibid., 32.

14. Spring 2002 Delegate Assembly Meeting Transcript, 77, ibid.

15. Winter 2001 Delegate Assembly Meeting Transcript, 44, ibid.

16. Winter 2002 Delegate Assembly Meeting Transcript, 18, ibid. The official vote was 185 in favor to 22 opposed.

17. Fall 2001 Delegate Assembly Meeting Transcript, 31–36, ibid.

18. Joyce Purnick, "Metro Matters, Perfect Storm, Seen Heading for the Budget," *New York Times*, November 11, 2002, nytimes.com/2002/11/11/nyregion/metro-matters-perfect-storm-seen-heading-for-the-budget.html.

19. Ibid.

20. Scheuerman, Preliminary Report of the President, Winter 2993 Delegate Assembly, Scheuerman collection.

21. Spring 2003 Delegate Assembly Meeting Transcript, 15, UUP Records.

22. Budget.nygov/pubs/archive/fy0304/fy0304littlebook/overview004.pdf., 14.

23. Buffalonews.com/2003/01/29/Pataki-budget-bombshell-sending-shock-waves-record-deficit-to-affect-all-new-yorkers.

24. Darryl McGrath, "Crunching Numbers and Quelling Critics," *The Voice*, November 2003, 6–7.

25. Scheuerman, Preliminary Report of the President, Winter 2003 Delegate Assembly, Scheuerman collection.

26. "UUP Members Out to 'Buck' Cuts to the State University," *The Voice*, April 2003, 5.

27. Scheuerman, Preliminary Report of the President, Spring 2003 Delegate Assembly, Scheuerman collection.

28. Fiscal Policy Institute, "Balancing New York State's 2004–05 Budget in a Sensible Manner," January 2004, 16, www.fiscalpolicy.org.

29. Lisa Feldman Reich, "Legislature Restores Proposed SUNY Cuts," *The Voice*, May/June 2003.

30. Ibid.

31. Scheuerman, Preliminary Report of the President, Winter 2004 Delegate Assembly, Scheuerman collection.

32. Scheuerman, Preliminary Report of the President, Fall 2004 Delegate Assembly, ibid.

33. Ibid.

34. Ibid.

35. Scheuerman, Preliminary Report of the President, Spring 2003 Delegate Assembly, ibid.

36. Fiscal Policy Institute, "Balancing," 16.

37. McGrath, "UUP Ratifies New Contract," *The Voice*, May/June 2004, 6.

38. Scheuerman, Preliminary Report of the President, Spring 2004 Delegate Assembly, Scheuerman collection.

39. UUP News Release, March 16, 2004, ibid.

40. "Questions and Answers, 2003–07 Tentative Contract Agreement," UUP mailing to membership., ibid.

41. Spring 2004 Delegate Assembly Meeting Transcript, 32, UUP Records.

42. Ibid.

43. Ibid., 31.

44. McGrath, "UUP Ratifies New Contract," *The Voice*, May/June 2004, 6.

45. Scheuerman, Preliminary Report of the President, 2005 Winter Delegate Assembly, Scheuerman collection.

46. Scheuerman, Preliminary Report of the President, 2004 Winter Delegate Assembly, ibid.

47. Ibid.

48. Scheuerman, Preliminary Report of the President, 2004 Spring Delegate Assembly, ibid.

49. Fall 2004 Delegate Assembly Meeting Transcript, 33, UUP Records.

50. Ibid., 48.

51. Ibid., 28.

52. Michael Cooper, "Pataki Vetoes $235 Million From Legislature's Budget," *New York Times*, August 21, 2004, nytimes.com/2004/08/21/nyregion/Pataki-vetoes-235-million-from-legislature-s-budget.html.

53. "To the Point," *The Voice*, October 2004, 19.

54. Ibid.

55. Norm Oder, "NY Legislators Don't Override Veto," libraryjournal.com/2004/10/ljarchives/ny-legislators-don't-override-veto/#.

56. Scheuerman, Preliminary Report of the President, Winter 2005 Delegate Assembly, Scheuerman collection.

57. Winter 2005 Delegate Assembly Meeting Transcript, 31–33, UUP Records.

58. Spring 2005 Delegate Assembly Meeting Transcript, 41, ibid.

59. "SUNY Chancellor to Take Leave," *Free Republic*, January 12, 2005, freerepublic.com/focus/f-news/1319539/posts.

60. Scheuerman, Preliminary Report of the President, Fall 205 Delegate Assembly, Scheuerman collection.

61. Fall 2005 Delegate Assembly Meeting Transcript, 54, 63, UUP Records.

62. Executive Board Meeting Minutes, June 24, 2005, Scheuerman collection.

63. Winter 2006 Delegate Assembly Meeting Transcript, 19, UUP Records.

64. Executive Board Meeting Minutes, August 11, 2005, Scheuerman collection.

65. Fall 2005 Delegate Assembly Meeting Transcript, 49, UUP Records.

66. Executive Board Meeting Minutes, August 11, 2005, Scheuerman collection.

67. Fall 2005 Delegate Assembly Meeting Transcript, 72, UUP Records.

68. Ibid., 72–74.

69. Executive Board Meeting Minutes, June 24, 2005, Scheuerman collection.

70. Winter 2006 Delegate Assembly Meeting Transcript, 19, UUP Records.

71. Ibid., 22.

72. Executive Board Meeting Minutes, January 19, 2006, Scheuerman collection.

73. Winter 2006 Delegate Assembly Meeting Transcript, 36, UUP Records.

74. Ibid., 70.

75. As of August 31, 2005, the UUP fund balance reached $5,376,272. Rowena Blackman-Stroud, Supplemental Report of the Treasurer, Winter 2006 Delegate Assembly, Scheuerman collection.

76. Winter 2006 Delegate Assembly Meeting Transcript, 31–32, UUP Records.

77. Ibid., 45–47.

78. Scheuerman, Preliminary Report of the President, Spring 2006 Delegate Assembly, Scheuerman collection.

79. Spring 2006 Delegate Assembly Meeting Transcript, 45–49, UUP Records.

80. Ibid., 47–48.

81. Ibid., 57.

82. Danny Hakim, "Legislature Overrides Most Budget Vetoes, But Pataki Says He Will Block Some Items," *New York Times*, April 27, 2006, nytimes.com/2006/04/27/nyregion/legislature-overrides-most-budget-vetoes-but-pataki-says-he-will.html?mcubz1.

83. Fall 2006 Delegate Assembly Meeting Transcript, 39, UUP Records.

84. Ibid., 37–38.

85. Executive Board Meeting Minutes, August 18, 2006, Scheuerman collection.

86. Scheuerman, Preliminary Report of the President, Fall 2006 Delegate Assembly, Scheuerman collection.

87. Ibid., 65–66.

88. Spring 2006 Delegate Assembly Meeting Transcript, 88, UUP Records.

89. Fall 2006 Delegate Assembly Meeting Transcript, 51, UUP Records.

90. Ibid., 53.

91. Scheuerman, Preliminary Report of the President, Fall 2006 Delegate Assembly, Scheuerman collection.

92. Ibid.

93. Fall 2006 Delegate Assembly Meeting Transcript, 68, UUP Records.

94. Berger Commission, Summary of Major Recommendations, Final Report, 28 November 2006, bcnys.org/what'snew/2006/1129bergersummary.pdf.

95. Ibid.

96. Governor Andrew Cuomo appointed McCall as chair of the Board of Trustees in 2011.

97. Winter 2007 Delegate Assembly Meeting Transcript, 31, UUP Records.

98. Ibid.

99. "Unions Score Medicare Part B Victory in Court," *The Voice*, January 2007, 12.

100. Executive Board Meeting Minutes, January 12, 2007, Scheuerman collection; Scheuerman, Preliminary Report of the President, Spring 2007 Delegate Assembly, ibid.

101. Ibid.

102. "Gov. Elliot Spitzer's Inaugural Address," *New York Times*, January 1, 2007, nytimes.com/2007/01/01/nyregion/01cnd-stext.html.

103. Executive Board Meeting Minutes, February 8, 2007, Scheuerman collection.

104. "Addressing UUP Advocates," *The Voice*, March 2007, 7.

105. Scheuerman, Preliminary Report of the President, Fall 2007 Delegate Assembly, Scheuerman collection.

106. Fall 2007 Delegate Assembly Meeting Transcript, 25, UUP Records.

107. Scheuerman, Preliminary Report of the President, Fall 2997 Delegate Assembly, Scheuerman collection.

108. Ibid.

109. Ray Haines, Jr., to James Hennerty, March 27, 2009, ibid.

110. "SUNY Chancellor Will Announce Resignation, Report Says," *Chronicle of Higher Education*, March 7, 2007, chronicle.com/article/suny-chancellor-will-announce/38317.

111. Eliot Spitzer, Governor of the State of New York, Executive Order No. 14: Establishing the New York State Commission on Higher Education, Official Compilation of Codes, Rules and Regulations of the State of New York, Title 9, Executive Department, Subtitle A, Governor's Office, Chapter 1, Executive Orders, Part 6.

112. For a complete summary of the struggle and issues, see Fall 2007 Delegate Assembly Meeting Transcript, 46–52, UUP Records.

113. Andrew Ross Sorkin, *Too Big to Fail: The Inside Story of How Wall Street and Washington Fought to Save the Financial System and Themselves* (New York: Viking, 2009); Robert B. Reich, *Aftershock: The Next Economy and America's Future* (New York: Alfred A. Knopf, 2010).

114. June Kronholz, "Republicans Wade into Campus Politics," *Wall Street Journal*, October 4, 2005.

115. Winter 2006 Delegate Assembly Meeting Transcript, 24, UUP Records.

116. Scheuerman, Preliminary Report of the President, Spring 2006 Delegate Assembly, Scheuerman collection.

117. Ibid., 64–67.

118. Scheuerman, Preliminary Report of the President, Spring 2007 Delegate Assembly, Scheuerman collection.

119. David Horowitz, *Indoctrination U: The Left's War Against Academic Freedom* (New York: Encounter Books, 2007), ch. 6.

120. "What Happened to the Labor Party?" An interview with Mark Dudzic, jacobinmag.com/2015/10/tony-mazzochi-mark-dudzic-us-labor-party-wto-nafta-globalization-democrats-union.

121. Scheuerman, Preliminary Report of the President, Fall 2005 Delegate Assembly, Scheuerman collection.

122. Scheuerman, Preliminary Report of the President, Fall 2007 Delegate Assembly, ibid.

123. Fall 2007 Delegate Assembly Meeting Transcript, 17–44, UUP Records.

124. Scheuerman, Preliminary Report of the President, Fall 2007 Delegate Assembly, Scheuerman collection.

125. Fall 2001 Delegate Assembly Meeting Transcript, 2:29, UUP Records.

Chapter 8: New Challenges and Future Prospects

1. Edwin D. Duryea, "The University and the State: An Historical Overview," in *Higher Education,* eds. Altbach and Berdahl, 13–33.

2. "United University Professions Ratifies New Four-Year Contract," UUP News Release, December 19, 2007, Scheuerman collection.

3. The literature on the role of labor unions in creating the middle class after World War II is voluminous. Good examples include Stanley Aronowitz, "On the Future of American Labor," *Working USA,* Spring 2006, 271–91; Phillip Dine, *State of the Unions: How Labor Can Strengthen the Middle Class, Improve Our Economy and Regain Political Influence* (New York: McGraw Hill, 2008); Reich, *Aftershock.*

4. Bureau of Labor Statistics, *Economic News Release,* January 26, 2017.

5. Ibid.

6. New York State Budget, 2008–2009 and 2009–2010, ballotqedia.org/new-york-state-budget-(2008–09) (2009–2010).

7. Fred Floss, conversation with Scheuerman, December 9, 2017. Floss is a former UUP vice president for academics and the chief negotiator of the 2007–11 contract.

8. Lisa W. Foderaro, "Facing Cuts, Stony Brook Will Close Programs," *New York Times,* April 7, 2010, nytimes.com2010/04/08/nyregional08stonybrook.html.

9. Executive Board Meeting Minutes, June 14, 2012, Scheuerman collection.

10. Scott Waldman, "Hawaii Show Called a Must See for Union," *Albany Times Union,* November 18, 2010.

11. Article 20, Agreement between the State of New York and United University Professions, July 2, 2011–July 1, 2016.

12. "2011–2016, New Contract Provisions," UUP mailing to members, n.d., Scheuerman collection.

13. "UUP Members Approve New Five-year Pact with State," UUP News Release, June 4, 2013, Scheuerman collection.

14. Edward Quinn, conversation with Scheuerman, August 20, 2017. Quinn is a former UUP membership development officer, who attended the negotiations committee meeting when Smith made the statement.

15. Martineau conversation with Scheuerman.

16. Philip Smith to UUP chapter leaders, June 22, 2011 (email), Scheuerman collection.

17. Fall 1980 Delegate Assembly Meeting Transcript, 7–8, UUP Records.

18. Paul Zaaremka to UUP officers, past officers and members of the Executive Board, April 21, 2013 (email), Scheuerman collection.

19. Frederick Kowal conversation with Scheuerman, April 16, 2018.

20. Adam Liptak, "Supreme Court Will Hear Case on Mandatory Fees to Union," *New York Times*, September 28, 2017, nytimes.com/2017/09/28/us/politics/supreme-court-will-hear-case-on-mandatory-fees-to-unions.html.

Index

www.ingramcontent.com/pod-product-compliance
Lightning Source LLC
Chambersburg PA
CBHW021220270326
41929CB00010B/1205